Edward Judson Hill

The probate jurisdiction and practice in the courts of the state of Illinois : containing the law of wills, of administration and of guardian and ward and rules of court

Being a guide for executors, administrators, guardians and conservators

Edward Judson Hill

The probate jurisdiction and practice in the courts of the state of Illinois : containing the law of wills, of administration and of guardian and ward and rules of court
Being a guide for executors, administrators, guardians and conservators

ISBN/EAN: 9783337157234

Printed in Europe, USA, Canada, Australia, Japan

Cover: Foto ©Suzi / pixelio.de

More available books at **www.hansebooks.com**

THE
PROBATE
JURISDICTION AND PRACTICE

IN THE

COURTS

OF THE

STATE OF ILLINOIS,

CONTAINING THE

LAW OF WILLS, OF ADMINISTRATION AND OF GUARDIAN AND WARD
AND RULES OF COURT:

BEING A

GUIDE FOR EXECUTORS, ADMINISTRATORS,
GUARDIANS AND CONSERVATORS, IN THE MANAGEMENT
AND SETTLEMENT OF ESTATES.

By EDWARD J. HILL,

AUTHOR OF "THE COMMON LAW" AND "CHANCERY PRACTICE," ETC.

FOURTH EDITION.

By HENRY BINMORE,

ATTORNEY, ETC.

CHICAGO:
E. B. MYERS, LAW PUBLISHER,
121 AND 123 MONROE STREET.
1880.

PREFACE.

As a system, the Jurisdiction and Practice in Probate, Guardianship and Conservation in Illinois are remarkably simple and uniform. The statutes have undergone very little change for many years, recent revisions and changes apparently, having proved but little more than a re-arrangement. They are well drawn, and have been quite fully defined and clearly expounded. Aiming almost exclusively at the useful and practical, it devolved upon the author to present these statutes and decisions in such a way as to render them easily understood, and of ready reference not only by the lawyer, but by the non-professional reader, the executor, the administrator, the guardian, the conservator, the business man, — those who have occasion to do business in and through the probate court. This is a more difficult task than it might at first appear.

To the undertaking, on a careful survey of the whole field of inquiry, I determined to bring a methodical arrangement which should furnish at the outset a key to the entire subject. This arrangement will appear by a glance at the SUMMARY OF CONTENTS. The subject-matter of the jurisdiction and of this treatise, therefore, I have attempted to display hand in hand together, so as to evolve the practice. The high character of the decisions of the supreme court, and the thorough and systematic statutes of Illinois, when applied to such an arrangement, at once gave assurance of the propriety of the plan proposed. They fit, with peculiar force, into their allotted places. If I have measurably succeeded in making them more manifest and useful, the success of my present undertaking, owing to the merit of such statutes and decisions alone, seems to me a foregone conclusion. The performance is now submitted to a critical, though charitable profession and a generous public.

Acknowledgments are due and hereby made to Hon. James B. Bradwell, to F. H. Kales, Hiram Barber, Jr., D. J. Avery, Julius Rosenthal and A. M. Pence, Esqs., of the Chicago bar, and to Hon. B. D. Meek, County Judge of Woodford county, and many others for valuable suggestions. I am greatly indebted to Hon. P. H. Walker, of the supreme court, and Hon. M. R. M. Wallace, County Judge of Cook county, for their considerate counsel in planning and perfecting the work. To all these gentlemen, the thanks of the author and publisher are hereby tendered.

CHICAGO, *August* 15, 1873.

EDWARD J. HILL.

FOURTH EDITION.

That three editions of this work have been completely exhausted, demonstrates its utility to the classes of persons to whose use it was originally dedicated. Since the last edition appeared, there have been numerous changes in the laws treated upon, and many decisions of the supreme court have tended to their elucidation. Probate courts have also been authorized in counties having a population of one hundred thousand persons. These matters I have attempted to produce in these pages. I have not thought it necessary, on all occasions, to amend the title of the court as contained in the original acts; where the county court is mentioned, it is used as well to include probate courts, where they may be established. This can lead to no error.

The Revised Statutes of 1874 are out of print, but I have retained the references to that volume. This for the reason that the possessors of the volume may refer to it, if so it shall please them. These references, however, are equally applicable to COTHRAN'S ANNOTATED STATUTES, recently issued from the press. In that volume the paging of the statutes of 1874 is preserved.

The labor of revising this work was originally assigned to WILLIAM MILLER, Esq. His engagements were such that a considerable delay seemed inevitable, while there has been a constant demand for the work. Thus the task was transferred to the subscriber, who trusts the additional matter will increase the value of the treatise.

HENRY BINMORE.

CHICAGO, *May* 15, 1880.

SUMMARY OF CONTENTS.

	PAGE.
Chapter I.— Jurisdiction	1–9
SEC. I. Introduction	1–3
SEC. II. County Courts, xiii–xxi — In Probate	3–9
Chapter II.— Testate Estates	10–60
SEC. I. Wills	10–27
SEC. II. Probate of Wills..	27–53
SEC. III. Executors	53–60
1. Appointment	53–54
2. Powers and Duties...	54–57
3. Renunciation, Resignation and Removal	57–60
Chapter III.— Intestate Estates	61–101
SEC. I. Introduction	61–64
SEC. II. Appointment of Administrators	64–82
SEC. III. Powers and Duties	82–96
SEC. IV. Resignation and Removal	96–101
Chapter IV.— Persons and Estates of Infants or Minors,	102–135
SEC. I. Infants...	102–107
SEC. II. Appointment of Guardians.....................................	107–117
SEC. III. Powers and Duties; Guardian and Ward	118–122
SEC. IV. Resignation and Removal.....................................	122–135
Chapter V.— Incapacitated Persons and their Estates...	135–156
SEC. I. Idiots, Lunatics, Drunkards, etc.............................	135–138
SEC. II. Appointment of Conservators................................	138–147
SEC. III. Commitment and Detention; Forms	147–156
Chapter VI.— Personal Estate in Administration........	157–185
SEC. I. Kinds of Personal Property; collection and disposition of, by the executor or administrator...	157–183
SEC. II. In the hands of Guardians and Conservators	183–185

SUMMARY OF CONTENTS.

	PAGE.
Chapter VII. — Real Estate in Administration	186–214
SEC. I. Through the Executor	186–192
SEC. II. Through the Administrator	192–207
SEC. III. Through the Guardian	207–214
SEC. IV. Through the Conservator	138, 213

Chapter VIII. — Expenses, Allowances, Claims and Legacies 215–237

SEC. I. Demands classified; the widow's award; funeral expenses, and expenses of last illness 215–222
SEC. II. Claims against Estates 222–232
SEC. III. Legacies 232–237

Chapter IX. — Accounts 238–250
SEC. I. By the Executor or Administrator 238–242
SEC. II. By the Guardian and Conservator 243–250

Chapter X. — Descent 251–271
The Law of 251–271

Chapter XI. — Appeals 272–274
From the County Court 272–274

Chapter XII. — Miscellaneous Matters 275–293
Miscellaneous Matters 275–297
Miscellaneous Provisions of the Act of April 1, 1872 278–283
Miscellaneous Statutes 283–289
Miscellaneous Decisions 289–291
Proclamation by Sheriff 291
Oaths and Affirmations; Forms 291–293

Chapter XIII. — Costs and Fees 294–300
Costs in Court and Officer's Fees 294–300

Chapter XIV. — The Probate Record 295–337
Practice, Pleadings, Suggestions and Forms ... 295–337

Logical Summary of the Act of April 1, 1872 339–343
Logical Summary of Act of March 20, 1872 .... 343, 344
Addenda 344–346
Rules of the Probate Court of Cook County 347–352

JURISDICTION

OF

COUNTY AND PROBATE COURTS.*

SECTION 1. There shall be in each of the counties of this State, now created and organized, or which may hereafter be created or organized, a court of record, to be styled "The County Court of ———— County." Said court shall have a seal.

§ 2. Said courts shall sit in the court-houses or usual places of holding courts in the several counties of this State, or in suitable rooms provided therefor at the county seat.

§ 3. The county judge in each county shall be elected on the Tuesday after the first Monday in November, in the year 1877, and on the Tuesday after the first Monday in November every fourth year thereafter, and shall enter upon the duties of his office on the first Monday of December after his election, and shall hold his office for four years and until his successor is elected and qualified.

§ 4. The county judge shall, before entering upon the duties of his office, take and subscribe, and file with the secretary of state, the following oath:

"I do solemnly swear (*or* affirm, *as the case may be*), that I will support the constitution of the United States, and the constitution of the State of Illinois, and that I will faithfully discharge the duties of the office of county judge according to the best of my ability."

§ 5. County courts shall have jurisdiction in all matters of probate, settlements of estates of deceased persons, appointment of guardians and conservators, and settlements of their accounts; all matters relating to apprentices; proceedings for the collection of taxes and assessments; and in proceedings by executors, administrators, guardians and conservators for the sale of real estate for the purposes authorized by law, and such other jurisdiction as is or may be provided by law. All of which, except as hereinafter pro-

---

*An act to extend the jurisdiction of county courts, and to provide for the practice thereof, to fix the time for holding the same, and to repeal an act therein named. Approved March 26, 1874. In force July 1, 1874, as since amended. Cothran's Ann'd Stats., 416-24.

Act of 1874, as amended.

vided, shall be considered as probate matters, and be cognizable at the probate terms hereinafter mentioned.

§ 6. The terms of the county court for probate matters shall commence on the third Monday of each month during the year, except the months prescribed in this act for the holding of law terms, and shall be always open for the granting of letters testamentary and guardianship, and for the transaction of probate business, and hearing applications by insolvent debtors for discharge from arrest or imprisonment, and all matters cognizable at the probate terms shall also be cognizable at the law terms.

§ 7. The county courts shall have concurrent jurisdiction with the circuit courts in all that class of cases wherein justices of the peace now have, or may hereafter have, jurisdiction where the amount claimed or the value of property in controversy shall not exceed one thousand dollars ($1,000), concurrent jurisdiction in all cases of appeals from justices of the peace and police magistrates: *Provided*, appeals from the county judge, when sitting as justice of the peace, shall be taken to the circuit court as now, and in all criminal offenses and misdemeanors where the punishment is not imprisonment in the penitentiary or death, all of which shall be cognizable at the law terms hereinafter mentioned.

§ 8. The law terms of the county court, except as otherwise hereinafter provided, shall commence on the second Monday of the months as follows, to wit: in the counties of—

§ 9. Adams, on the first Mondays of February, June and October.
§ 10. Alexander, in March, July and November.
§ 11. Bond, in January, June and November.
§ 12. Boone, in March, June and December.
§ 13. Brown, in January and June.
§ 14. Bureau, in January, June and October.
§ 15. Calhoun, in January and June.
§ 16. Carroll, in February, June and November.
§ 17. Cass, in April and October.
§ 18. Champaign, in January, May, August and November.
§ 19. Christian, in April, June, October and December.
§ 20. Clark, in January, June and September.
§ 21. Clay, on the third Monday in January and June.
§ 22. Clinton, in February and August.
§ 23. Coles, in March and July.
§ 24. Cook, in January, February, March, April, May, June, July, August, September, October, November and December.
§ 25. Crawford, in January and June.
§ 26. Cumberland, in October.

Act of 1874, as amended.

§ 27. DeKalb, in April, July and December.
§ 28. DeWitt, in January and June.
§ 29. Douglas, in January and July.
§ 30. Du Page, in January and June.
§ 31. Edgar, in June and December.
§ 32. Edwards, in January and July.
§ 33. Effingham, in June and November.
§ 34. Fayette, in June and December.
§ 35. Ford, in February and June.
§ 36. Franklin, on the third Monday of February and August.
§ 37. Fulton, in February and October.
§ 38. Gallatin, on the third Monday of April and November.
§ 39. Greene, in December and June.
§ 40. Grundy, in January, June and September.
§ 41. Hamilton, in June and December.
§ 42. Hancock, in April, July and December.
§ 43. Hardin, in February and August.
§ 44. Henderson, in April and October.
§ 45. Henry, in April, August and December.
§ 46. Iroquois, in January, May and October.
§ 47. Jackson, in January, May and November.
§ 48. Jasper, in February and August.
§ 49. Jefferson, on the third Monday of March and September.
§ 50. Jersey, in January and June.
§ 51. Jo Daviess, in April, December, and on the third Monday of September.
§ 52. Johnson, in February and August.
§ 53. Kane, in June, September and December.
§ 54. Kankakee, in February, July and November.
§ 55. Kendall, in March, September and December.
§ 56. Knox, in April, August and December.
§ 57. Lake, in January and June.
§ 58. LaSalle, in March, September and December.
§ 59. Lawrence, in April and October.
§ 60. Lee, in December and June.
§ 61. Livingston, in March, June, September and December.
§ 62. Logan, in March, August and November.
§ 63. McDonough, in June and December.
§ 64. McHenry, in March and November.
§ 65. McLean, in April, August and December.
§ 66. Macon, in February, July and October.

Act of 1874, as amended.

§ 67. Macoupin, in June.
§ 68. Madison, in February and August.
§ 69. Marion, in April and November.
§ 70. Marshall, on the fourth Mondays of April, August and November.
§ 71. Mason, in January, June and October.
§ 72. Massac, in February and July.
§ 73. Menard, in January, May and September.
§ 74. Mercer, in January, April, July and October.
§ 75. Monroe, in January and June.
§ 76. Montgomery, in January, May and September.
§ 77. Morgan, on the second Monday in January, and on the third Mondays in April and September.
§ 78. Moultrie, in January and June.
§ 79. Ogle, in February, June and November.
§ 80. Peoria, in January, April and September.
§ 81. Perry, in February and September.
§ 82. Piatt, in June and November.
§ 83. Pike, in January and August.
§ 84. Pope, on the third Monday of July of each year.
§ 85. Pulaski, in January, June and September.
§ 86. Putnam, in October.
§ 87. Randolph, in January and June.
§ 88. Richland, in January and July.
§ 89. Rock Island, in March, July and November.
§ 90. St. Clair, in March, July and November.
§ 91. The law terms of the county court of Saline county shall commence on the second Mondays in the months of February and August.
§ 91½. Sangamon, in April, July and December.
§ 92. Schuyler, in February and August.
§ 93. Shelby, in January and July.
§ 94. Scott, in February and August.
§ 95. Stark, in June and December.
§ 96. Stephenson, in February, May and October.
§ 97. Tazewell, in January, April and October.
§ 98. Union, in May and November.
§ 99. Vermilion, in January, April and October.
§ 100. Wabash, in October.
§ 101. Warren, in February, April, July and October.
§ 102. Washington, in January and July.
§ 103. Wayne, in January and July.
§ 104. White, in February and August.

Act of 1874, as amended.

§ 105. Whiteside, in January, May and October.
§ 106. Will, in March, July, September and November.
§ 107. Williamson, in March, August and December.
§ 108. Winnebago, in March and November.
§ 109. Woodford, in August.

§ 109½. The court shall continue open from day to day until all business before it is disposed of.

§ 110. Unless the court shall otherwise order, the jury for the law terms of the county court shall be drawn and summoned in the same manner as is provided for the drawing and summoning juries for the terms of the circuit court. When a jury is not summoned as above provided, it shall be the duty of said court, on the first day of each term thereof, to call all the cases for trial on the docket, to ascertain whether a jury will be required. If a jury shall be demanded by either party to any suit pending, or by any defendant or the State's attorney in any criminal suit, the court shall thereupon set such case or cases for trial, and direct the clerk of said court to issue a *venire* for twelve competent jurors, unless the parties to such suit or criminal proceeding shall elect to have the same tried by six jurors, and deliver the same to the sheriff or coroner, who shall summon such jurors from the body of the county, to be and appear before said court at the term set for the return of said *venire;* and if, by reason of non-attendance, challenge or otherwise, said jury shall not be full, the panel may be filled by talesmen. Said court shall have the same power to compel the attendance of jurors and witnesses as the circuit court has, and shall be governed by the same rules in impaneling the jury. Said court may retain such jury for all the jury trials of said term. The per diem and mileage of said jurors shall be the same as they are for similar services in the circuit court, to be paid out of the county treasury upon the certificate of the county clerk: *Provided,* that in case the sheriff, coroner or bailiff be interested in any jury case pending, or in case any party interested, or any attorney, may object to any sheriff, coroner or bailiff selecting the jury, if the court shall think such objection reasonable, the court shall appoint an impartial bailiff to summon such jury.

§ 111. The court shall have the power to impanel a jury in any case cognizable at the probate terms as well as at the law terms, whenever it shall be necessary for the trial of any matter pending before the court.

Act of 1874.

§ 112. The process, practice and pleadings in said court in common-law cases shall be the same as in the circuit court in similar cases, and the process, orders and judgments of said court shall have the same forms, force, lien and effect as in like cases in the circuit court; and the clerk of said county court shall charge and collect like fees as the clerk of the circuit court for similar services. Process in cases cognizable at the law terms of the county court shall be made returnable at the law terms.

§ 113. The sheriff, in person or by his deputy, shall attend the sittings of the county court of his county, preserve order in the same, and execute the legal commands and process thereof: *Provided*, that the sheriff shall receive pay for attending upon the sittings of said court only when requested so to do by the court.

§ 114. Whenever the county judge of any county is interested in the estate of any diseased person, and the letters testamentary or of administration shall be grantable in the county of such judge, such facts shall be entered upon the records of such court and certified to the circuit court of such county: *Provided*, that in case the judge is interested only as a creditor, no change need be made except in relation to his claim.

§ 115. Upon the filing of a copy of such certificate with the clerk of the circuit court, such court shall have full and complete jurisdiction in all matters pertaining to such estate, and may make all orders and take all proceedings therein which might have been made or taken in the county court if the judge thereof had not been interested.

§ 116. In all cases transferred to the circuit court under the two preceding sections, the clerk of such court shall have the same authority to grant citations and letters testamentary and of administration in vacation as is given to clerks of the county courts.

§ 117. All offenses cognizable in county courts shall be prosecuted by information of the State's attorney, attorney-general or some other person, and when an information is presented by any person other than the State's attorney or attorney-general, it shall be verified by affidavit of such person that the same is true, or that the same is true as he is informed and believes. Before an information is filed by any person other than the State's attorney or attorney-general, the judge of the court shall examine the information, and may examine the person presenting the same, and require other evidence and satisfy himself that there is probable cause for

Act of 1874, as amended.

filing the same and so indorse the same. Every information shall set forth the offense with reasonable certainty, substantially as required in an indictment, and may be filed either in term time or in vacation, and the proceedings thereon shall be the same, as near as may be, as upon indictment in the circuit court, except as herein otherwise provided. Nothing in this act shall be construed to affect the jurisdiction of justices of the peace.*

§ 118. The court in term time, or the judge in vacation, shall fix the amount of bail to be required of the accused, and the clerk shall indorse the same upon the capias, except that when the capias is issued in term time the same may be made returnable forthwith when it shall not be necessary to fix the amount of bail until the accused is brought into court.

§ 119. The court may receive the plea of guilty and pass judgment, or if the accused will waive a jury and be tried by the court without a jury, the court may, upon notice being first given to the State's attorney, try the cause and pass judgment as well at a probate as a law term of said court.

§ 120. When the grand jury of the circuit court shall indict for offenses cognizable in the county court, such indictments may, in the discretion of said circuit court, be certified under the seal thereof to the county court for process and trial, which process shall be the same as like process in the circuit court.

§ 121. In certifying indictments from the circuit court to the county court, the clerk of the circuit court may use the following form, substantially:

STATE OF ILLINOIS,)
County of , } *ss.:*

"I, , clerk of the circuit court, in and for the county of , aforesaid, do certify that the within bill of indictment was on the day of , duly presented in open court by the grand jury of said county, and being duly examined by the said circuit court, it was ordered by the court that the same be certified by the clerk of the circuit court to the county court for process and trial, which is done accordingly."

Which certificate, when indorsed on the back of any indictment, shall be sufficient to warrant a trial and conviction of any party charged in any indictment so certified, and shall be deemed a sufficient record to authorize the county court to try the party so

---

* Judge McAllister holds this section to be unconstitutional, as in conflict with § 5, Art. II, and § 29, Art. VI, Const. 1870. See *The People ex rel. Smith v. Brown*, 67 Ill. 435; *Myers v. The People*, 67 Ill. 503.

Act of 1874, as amended.

indicted: *Provided*, either party may ask for and obtain a rule on the clerk of the circuit court for a complete record, duly and properly certified, of any cause pending in the county court having been certified as aforesaid; and it shall be the duty of the clerk of the circuit court to obey any rule of the county court for the purpose aforesaid, and when a complete record shall be so certified to the county court, said court shall be governed thereby in all respects in all its proceedings.

§ 122. Appeals may be taken from the final orders, judgments and decrees of the county courts to the circuit courts of their respective counties in all matters except as provided in the following section, upon the appellant giving bond and security in such amount and upon such conditions as the court shall approve, except as otherwise provided by law. Upon such appeal, the case shall be tried *de novo*.

§ 123. Appeals and writs of error may be taken and prosecuted from the final orders, judgments and decrees of the county court to the supreme court or appellate court, should such a court be established by law, in proceedings for the sale of lands for taxes and special assessments, and in all common law and attachment cases, and cases of forcible detainer and forcible entry and detainer. Such appeals and writs of error shall, when not otherwise provided, be taken and prosecuted in the same manner as appeals from and writs of error to circuit courts.

In all appeals in criminal cases, the court shall fix the amount of the recognizance, and when the same is executed, the defendant shall be discharged from imprisonment until otherwise ordered by the appellate court, on the dismissal or trial of the appeal; and the securities may deliver their principal, and be subject to liabilities, to be enforced as in other cases of recognizance.

§ 124. The several county courts shall have the power to hear and determine all causes pending in such courts at the time this act shall take effect, and to enforce all judgments, orders and decrees entered therein, or in any cause of which they may have had jurisdiction previous to the taking effect of this act. Appeals and writs of error may be prosecuted from such judgments, orders and decrees.

§ 125. An act entitled "An act to increase the jurisdiction of county courts," in force July 1, 1872, is hereby repealed: *Provided*, that nothing herein contained shall be construed to affect any rights or remedies that may have accrued under said act hereby repealed.

Act of 1877.

Nor shall any suit or proceeding pending in the county court, under the act hereby repealed, be abated by such repeal, and all such suits or proceedings pending, when this act takes effect, shall stand continued to the first term of court to be held under the provisions of this act.

SECTION 1. That the county judges of the several counties of this State, with like privileges as the judges of the circuit courts of this State, may interchange with each other, hold court for each other, and perform each other's duties when they find it necessary or convenient.*

PROBATE COURTS.†

SECTION 1. *Be it enacted by the People of the State of Illinois, represented in the General Assembly:* That there shall be established in each county of this State, now created and organized, or which may be hereafter created and organized, and which has a population of one hundred thousand, or more, a court of record to be styled, "The Probate Court of (name of) county." Such court shall have a seal and may from time to time, as may be necessary, renew or alter the same. The expense of such seal, and of renewing and altering the same, shall be paid by the county.

§ 2. Said courts shall be held in the court-houses of the respective counties in which they shall be established, or in the usual places of holding courts, or in suitable rooms provided therefor at the county seat.

§ 3. The judge of said court in each county, in which such court shall be established, shall be elected on the Tuesday next after the first Monday in November, at the same election at which the county judge is elected, and every fourth year thereafter, and shall enter upon the duties of his office on the first Monday of December after his election, and shall hold his office for a term of four years and until his successor is elected and qualified, and shall be known as the probate judge of (name of) county.

§ 4. The probate judge of each county in which a probate court shall be established shall, before entering upon the duties of his

---

*An act to authorize county judges to interchange, hold court for each other and perform each other's duties. Approved May 21, 1879; in force July 1, 1879.

†An act to establish probate courts in all counties having a population of one hundred thousand, or more, to define the jurisdiction thereof, and regulate the practice therein, and to fix the time for holding the same. Approved April 27, and in force July 1, 1877. Laws 1877, p. 79. Cothran's Ann'd Rev Stats., 424 *et seq.*

Act of 1877.

office, take and subscribe and file with the secretary of State the oath required by the constitution.

§ 5. Probate courts shall have original jurisdiction in all matters of probate, the settlement of estates of deceased persons, the appointment of guardians and conservators and settlement of their accounts, and in all matters relating to apprentices, and in cases of the sales of real estate of deceased persons for the payment of debts. And as soon as such court is organized in any county, the county court of such county shall turn over to the probate court all of its probate records, and all files, books and papers of every kind relating to probate matters in such county court, and all records, files and papers in matters of guardianship and conservators, and the clerk of the probate court shall be authorized to demand and receive from the county clerk all such records, files, books and documents, and upon the receipt thereof, the probate court shall proceed to finish and complete all unfinished business relating to probate, guardianship and conservatory matters in the manner provided by law.

§ 6. The terms of the probate court shall commence on the third Monday of each month during the year, and shall be always open for the granting of letters testamentary, letters of administration and guardianship, and for the transaction of probate business and all other matters of which it has jurisdiction, and shall continue open, from day to day, until all business before it is disposed of.

§ 7. The probate court shall have the power to impanel a jury, for the trial of issues or matters of fact, in any matter or matters pending before the court, and for such purpose the court may at any time, when it becomes necessary to have a jury, direct the clerk of said court to issue a venire for either six or twelve competent jurors and deliver the same to the sheriff or coroner or any bailiff of the court, who shall summon such jurors from the body of the county to be and appear before said court at any term or day named in such venire, and if by reason of non-attendance, challenge or otherwise, said jury shall not be full, the panel may be filled by talesmen. Said court shall have the same power to compel the attendance of jurors and witnesses as the circuit court has, or may hereafter have, and jurors to act as such in said court shall possess the same qualifications and be entitled to the same privileges of exemption and subject to the same rules of challenge, for cause or peremptorily, as jurors in the circuit courts of the State. When such jury shall be brought into said court the court may retain such jury during the

Act of 1877.

term, or any portion thereof, as may be necessary for the trial of any matter or matters of fact which in the discretion of the court requires a jury. The *per diem* and mileage of said jurors shall be the same as they are for jurors in the circuit court, to be paid out of the county treasury upon the presentation of a certificate of the clerk of said court, issued to each juror at the time of thei discharge, certifying to the number of days he may have attended court as a juror and the amount of juror fees and mileage due him.

§ 8. The process, practice and pleadings in said court shall be the same as those now provided, or which may hereafter be provided, for the probate practice in the county courts of the State, and all laws now in force, or which may hereafter be enacted concerning wills, or the administration of estates, shall govern and be applicable to the practice in the probate courts of the State.

§ 9. The sheriff, in person or by his deputy, shall attend the sittings of the probate court of his county, preserve order in the same and execute the legal commands and process thereof.

§ 10. Whenever the probate judge of any county is interested in the estate of any deceased person, and the letters testamentary or of administration shall be grantable in the county of such judge, such estate shall be probated in the county court of such county, unless the county judge be also interested, in which event the facts of such interest may be entered of record in the probate court of the county, and certified to the circuit court of the county, and upon the filing of such certificate with the clerk of the circuit court, such court shall have full and complete jurisdiction in all matters pertaining to such estate, under all laws of this State concerning the administration of estates or the probate of wills; and in all cases so transferred the clerk of said circuit court shall have the same power in all matters of such estate, in term time or vacation, that the clerk of the probate or county court has: *Provided*, that, if the probate judge is only interested as a creditor, no change may be made, except in relation to his claim.

§ 11. Appeals may be taken from the final orders, judgments and decrees of the probate courts to the circuit courts of their respective counties, in all matters except in proceedings on the application of executors, administrators, guardians and conservators for the sale of real estate, upon the appellant giving bond and security in such amount and upon such condition as the court shall approve, and upon such appeal the case shall be tried *de novo*.

Act of 1877.

§ 12. Appeals and writs of error may be taken and prosecuted from the final orders and decrees of the probate court to the supreme court in proceedings on the application of executors, administrators, guardians and conservators for the sale of real estate. Such appeals and writs of error, when not otherwise provided, shall be taken and prosecuted in the same manner as appeals from and writs of error to the circuit court.

§ 13. There shall be elected at the same time as the probate judge is elected, a clerk of the probate court, who shall hold his office for a term of four years and until his successor shall be elected and qualified. Before entering upon the duties of his office he shall take and subscribe the oath required by the constitution of the State.

§ 14. Every such clerk shall, before entering upon the duties of his office, give bond with two or more sureties, to be approved by the judge of the court of which he is clerk, which bond shall be in such penalty, not less than five thousand dollars ($5,000), as may be determined by such judge, payable to the People of the State of Illinois, and conditioned for the faithful performance of the duties of his office and to pay over all moneys that may come to his hands by virtue of his office to the parties entitled thereto, and to deliver up to his successor in office all moneys, papers, books, records and other things appertaining to his office whole, safe and undefaced, which bond shall be copied at large upon the records of the court and then filed in the office of the secretary of State, upon which such clerk shall be immediately commissioned by the governor and enter upon the duties of his office.

§ 15. Every such clerk shall attend in person to the duties of his office when it is practicable so to do, and perform all the duties thereof which can reasonably be performed by one person; *Provided, however*, he may, when necessary, appoint deputies, who shall take the same oath or affirmation as is required of the principal clerk, which shall be entered at large upon the records of the court, and the principal clerk shall, in all cases, be responsible for the acts or omissions of his deputies.

§ 16. Every such clerk shall attend the sessions of their respective courts, issue all process thereof, preserve all the files and papers thereof, make, keep and preserve complete records of all the proceedings and determinations thereof, and do and perform all other duties pertaining to their said offices as may be required by law or

Act of 1877.

the rules and orders of their courts respectively, and shall enter of record all judgments, decrees and orders of their respective courts before the final adjournment of the respective terms thereof, or as soon thereafter as practicable.

§ 17. It shall be the duty of the county board of every county in which there shall be established a probate court in pursuance of this act, to provide the clerk thereof with all necessary blanks, books, stationery, pens and ink for their respective offices, the same to be paid for out of the county treasury, and in case such supplies should not be so furnished, then the clerk of such court shall furnish the same, from time to time, as may be necessary, the cost thereof to be allowed by the county board and paid out of the county treasury.

§ 18. The necessary rooms, office and furniture, the proper vaults or other safe means of keeping the archives of their respective offices shall be provided for the clerks of the probate courts, in their respective counties, by the county, and the cost thereof paid out of the county treasury.

§ 19. It shall be the duty of the probate clerk to deliver over to his successor in office, and of his successor to demand and receive from him, all the books, papers, records, and other things appertaining to his office, or in his possession by virtue of his office, and should he refuse or neglect to do so, the court shall have power to use such compulsory process and take such measures as may be necessary to compel the delivery as aforesaid, according to the true intent and meaning hereof.

§ 20. In all matters concerning the probate of the estates of deceased persons, the granting of letters testamentary or of administration, letters of guardianship, the manner of keeping the records of said court, the form of docket entries, journals, fee books, memorandums, the form of process, the recording of papers and documents connected with any matter of which said court has jurisdiction, the clerk of said court shall be governed by and follow all laws now in force, or which may hereafter be enacted, concerning similar matters in the county courts of the State.

§ 21. The clerk of the probate court shall charge and collect for each official act the same fees as are allowed to clerks of the county courts of the State in probate matters,* which fees shall be charged

---

* This section is amended by act of May 29, 1879, in force July 1, 1879, by which act a complete schedule of fees was adopted. See Cothran's Ann'd Stats., 1880, p. 715, § 55a; also see *post*, chapter Fees.

D

Act of 1877.

in accordance with the laws now in force or which may hereafter be enacted concerning fees and salaries, and according to the class to which the county belongs. Such clerk shall keep full, true and correct accounts of all fees collected by him, and report the same in accordance with said laws, for the keeping of which accounts no fees shall be allowed such clerk, and the same shall be open for inspection by the county board, in accordance with said laws, and all fees in excess of the compensation allowed to such clerk, and necessary clerk hire and other expenses, shall be paid into the county treasury in accordance with said laws concerning fees and salaries.

§ 22. Clerks of the probate court shall receive such compensation, or salary, as shall be allowed them by the county board, together with the amount of their necessary clerk hire, stationery, fuel and other expenses, in accordance with the provisions of the constitution; *Provided*, that in the county of Cook the probate clerk shall receive, aside from clerk hire, necessary expenses for fuel and stationery, the sum of three thousand dollars ($3,000) per annum as his only compensation, to be paid out of the fees of his office.

§ 23. Probate judges shall be allowed such salary as shall be fixed by their respective county boards, to be paid out of the county treasury.

§ 24. When a vacancy shall occur in the office of judge of the probate court of any county, the clerk of the court in which the vacancy exists shall notify the governor of such vacancy. If the unexpired term of the office made vacant is less than one year, at the time the vacancy occurs, the governor shall fill such vacancy by appointment; but if the unexpired term exceeds one year, the governor shall issue a writ of election as in other cases of vacancy to be filled by election.

PROBATE JURISDICTION AND PRACTICE.

CHAPTER I.

OF THE JURISDICTION AND PRACTICE GENERALLY.

SECTION I. Introduction.
    II. County courts — in probate.

SECTION I. — INTRODUCTION.

1. Testate and intestate estates.
2. The probate of wills and execution of trusts thereby created, administration of intestate estates, guardians, conservators, etc.
3. Subdivision and scope of the subject.
4. The high character of the trusts involved.
5. Care requisite in the development of the subject.

1. TESTATE AND INTESTATE ESTATES. The probate jurisdiction pertains to testate or intestate estates. The person who makes a will is a testator; one who has died is termed a decedent. If a decedent leave a will, he dies testate; his is a testate estate. The decedent who leaves no will dies intestate and his is an intestate estate.

2. THE PROBATE OF WILLS, and the due execution of the trusts thereby created, and the administration of the estates of intestates, embrace the entire jurisdiction proper, in probate. But the care of estates of the insane, the inebriate or drunkard, the infant and those otherwise incapacitated, and the care and custody of their persons, are closely allied and akin to the conservation of the estates of deceased persons and, too, is here confined to the county or probate judge.

3. Hence, in the DEVELOPMENT OF OUR SUBJECT, we propose to treat of:

    I. The jurisdiction and practice generally.
    II. The probate of wills and the execution of the trusts thereby created, or the proper administration of testate estates.
    III. The proper administration of intestate estates.
    IV. The proper care and custody of the persons and the conservation of the estates of the incapacitated.

Introduction.

    V. The relation of guardian and ward.
   VI. The disposition of personal property:
      I. By executors.
     II. By administrators.
    III. By conservators.
    IV. By guardians.
  VII. The disposition of real property.
      I. By executors.
     II. By administrators.
    III. By conservators.
    IV. By guardians.
 VIII. The payment of expenses, allowances, debts and legacies.
   IX. The settlement of accounts.
    X. The law of descent or inheritance.
   XI. Costs and fees.
  XII. Appeals.
 XIII. Miscellaneous matters.

Naturally, divided thus into general subdivisions, it is our purpose to display the subject-matter of this treatise, through the several chapters, subdividing each into a convenient number of sections, interspersing throughout the work the approved forms and precedents, supporting the whole by notes and references to the statutes and adjudications of the courts.

4. THE HIGH CHARACTER OF THE TRUSTS INVOLVED. We shall endeavor to adapt our work to the intelligence of those who are called upon to discharge the high trusts involved, and, at the same time, furnish the practitioner as well as the courts, in as concise form as possible, an exposition of the entire course of procedure in the several branches of our subject, which we have above suggested.

The trust relations here created are of the highest character known to the law, and demand the unceasing vigilance of the courts in order to preserve the property of those whom the law through this jurisdiction seeks to protect.

Recent statutes, carefully drawn and systematically arranged, aid materially in the work before us, and furnish, almost without comment, plain and concise rules of procedure. But the decisions of the courts showing the development of these statutes are necessary to a clear and full exposition of the law. To know what the law is we must know its history. Therefore, hand in hand with the statutes, we shall endeavor to give these decisions in substance as they are to be found in the Illinois Reports.

Introduction.

5. CARE REQUISITE IN DEVELOPING SUCH A SUBJECT. Great care is necessary in developing such a subject. The elaborate discussions to be found, however, in these reports, bearing directly upon the questions involved, when properly applied, will furnish the best guide in matters where good counsel is so often needed.

SECTION II.— COUNTY AND PROBATE COURTS.*

1. They are courts of record.
2. They have general jurisdiction in probate.
3. Their judgments, final and conclusive, unless reversed.
4. Constitutional and statutory provisions.
5. Constitution of 1818.
    (1) Courts of probate created in 1821.
    (2) Probate court in 1845.
6. Constitution of 1848; county courts from 1849.
7. Constitution of 1870; original jurisdiction given to the county and probate courts.
8. This jurisdiction involves sacred trusts.
9. R. S. 1874, *p.* 339.
10. Terms for probate business.
11. County clerk.
12. The judgments, orders and decrees in probate, not to be collaterally attacked; the rule in the United States supreme court.
13. Decisions in Illinois.
    (1) Incidental powers; no discretion in prescribed cases; exclusive jurisdiction over personalty; none over realty; but see R. S. 1874, *p.* 121.
    (2) Rules of practice.
14. Equitable jurisdiction over claims against intestate estates.
15. Statutory provisions.
16. Scope of the subject.
17. Deceased persons, either testates or intestates; testate estates; intestate estates.
18. Incapacitated persons — persons not *sui juris*, etc.
19. Executors, administrators, guardians, conservators, all officers of the court.
20. The law of descent.
21. Appeals.
22. Method characteristic of the subject.

---

* The act of March 26, 1874, in force July 1, 1874, "to extend the jurisdiction of county courts," etc., and "An act to establish probate courts in all counties having a population of 100,000 or more," etc., passed April 27, in force July 1, 1877, with some subsequent amendments, contain a revision of all laws in relation to jurisdiction of these courts. These are re-printed (amendments to July 1, 1879), *ante, pp.* xiii *et seq.* See Cothran's Ann'd Stats., 1880, *pp.* 416 *et seq.*

County Courts.

1. COUNTY AND PROBATE COURTS ARE COURTS OF RECORD.(*a*)

2. They have GENERAL JURISDICTION over a particular class of cases. It is a limited but not an inferior jurisdiction.(*b*) When these courts adjudicate upon the matters over which they have general jurisdiction, as the administration of estates, as liberal intendments will be indulged in their favor as to proceedings of circuit courts.(*c*)

3. THEIR JUDGMENTS are final and conclusive as to all matters within their jurisdiction and their decrees, within the sphere of probate jurisdiction cannot be collaterally attacked, except for want of jurisdiction.(*d*) Among these are included all the judicial powers which, prior to the act of February 12, 1849(*e*), in this State had been vested in probate courts and probate justices of the peace, the judicial officers of such courts, as they were for a time styled.(*f*)

4. CONSTITUTIONAL AND STATUTORY PROVISIONS. To arrive at a clear understanding of the subject, it will be necessary to examine the constitutional and statutory provisions, relating to this jurisdiction, which have, heretofore, existed in Illinois, and which, to a great extent, yet remain in force under the constitution of 1870.

5. CONSTITUTION OF 1818. This constitution ordained that, "the judicial power of this State shall be vested in one supreme court, and such inferior courts as the general assembly shall, from time to time, ordain and establish."(*g*)

(1) COURTS OF PROBATE. Under this limitation of power (*h*) the act of February 10, 1821, was passed to establish courts of probate and the manner of proceeding therein.(*i*)

(2) PROBATE COURT. To this act several amendments of no present practical importance were made(*j*), from time to time, until the general revision of 1845(*k*), in which the PROBATE COURT was provided for.(*l*)

6. CONSTITUTION OF 1848. The experience of thirty years,

(*a*) *Ante, pp.* xiii *et seq.*
(*b*) *Propst* v. *Meadows*, 13 Ill. 157.
(*c*) *Moffitt* v. *Moffitt*, 69 Ill. 641; *Bostwick* v. *Skinner*, 80 id. 147.
(*d*) *Moffitt* v. *Moffitt*, 69 Ill. 641.
(*e*) Laws 1849, p. 62.
(*f*) R. S. 1845, ch. 85; *Hanna* v. *Yocum*, 17 Ill. 387; *Doe* v. *Hileman*, 1 Scam. 323.
(*g*) Const., 1818, Art. iv, § 1.
(*h*) *The People* v. *Wilson*, 15 Ill. 388.
(*i*) Laws 1821, *p.* 119; 2 Gilm. 657.

(*j*) Act, February 12, 1823, Laws 1823, *p.* 132; Act, January 12, 1825, Laws 1825, *p.* 87; see Laws 1829, *p.* 37; R. S. 1833, 145; 1 Laws 1837. 176; 2 Laws 1837, 46; Laws 1839, *p.* 39; Act, February 1, 1843, Laws 1843, *p.* 185.
(*k*) See Gross' Index to Laws *p.* 27, c. lxxxv, R. S. 1845.
(*l*) R. S. 1845, *pp.* 426–429, appendix Nos. 21, 22.

In probate.

undoubtedly, taught the sovereign people of Illinois the necessity of a more systematic organization in which to center such a jurisdiction. Hence(*m*), the COUNTY COURT was provided for with one judge to be elected for a term of four years in each county, and clothed *inter alia* " with all probate and such other jurisdiction as the general assembly may confer in civil cases."

But " the county commissioner's courts and the probate justices of the several counties were continued " until the general assembly acted.(*n*) According to the early decisions of the supreme court (*o*) it seems that the first three sections of ch. 85 (*p*) were superseded by the act of February 12, 1849, the county judges taking the jurisdiction and place of probate justices of the peace, under the then new constitution.(*q*)

7. CONSTITUTIONAL PROVISIONS. The constitution of 1870 (*r*) confers upon county courts, for which it provides "original jurisdiction in all matters of probate, settlement of estates of deceased persons, appointment of guardians and conservators, and settlements of their accounts, in all matters relating to apprentices," etc. The same instrument provides as to probate courts, as follows: " The general assembly may provide for the establishment of a probate court in each county having a population of over 50,000, and for the election of a judge thereof, whose term of office shall be the same as that of the county judge, and who shall be elected at the same time and in the same manner. Said courts, when established, shall have original jurisdiction of all probate matters, the settlement of estates of deceased persons, the appointment of guardians and conservators and settlement of their accounts, in all matters relating to apprentices; and, in cases of the sales of real estate of deceased persons for the payment of debts.(*s*)

8. THIS JURISDICTION and the practice pertaining to it involve the sacred trusts over which the court of chancery exercises its protecting power(*t*), and which are of paramount importance in the administration of justice and the regulation of private affairs. These trusts are reposed in the county or probate courts, as the

---

(*m*) In Art. v, § 16–19.
(*n*) See § 6, Schedule, Const. 1848; Laws 1849, *p*. 62 ; 1 Gross' Comp. 526.
(*o*) *Hanna* v. *Yocum*, 17 Ill. 387.
(*p*) P. 426, R. S. 1845.
(*q*) Const. 1848, Art. v, §§ 16–20 ; schedule, § 6 ; R. S. 1845, *p*. 426, §§ 4–21, appendix, Nos. 21, 22 ; R. Laws 1833, Scates' Comp., *p*. 656, § 1.
(*r*) Art. vi, § 18.
(*s*) Const. 1870, Art. 6, § 20.
(*t*) See HILL's CH. PR., *Trusts*, 431, 432 ; *Freeland* v. *Dazey*, 25 Ill. 294.

County Courts.

case may be, in this State as to courts not of inferior but of special and original jurisdiction, superior within their appropriate sphere of action. They have no modes of procedure of practice, however, excepting such as are derived from the statutes of their creation.(*u*)

9. The revision of the statutes of 1874, with some few amendments, contains the existing law as respects the jurisdiction in probate matters conferred upon county courts. The act of April 25, 1877, contains the same in regard to probate courts; both acts considered together prescribe the process, practice and pleadings in these courts. To these we shall refer in dealing with our subject.(*v*)

10. TERMS for probate business are held on the third Monday of every month, except as changed by statute.(*w*)

11. CLERKS. Being courts of record, both county and probate courts have clerks. The county clerk acts in the former. In the latter the position is filled by an officer thereto elected.(*x*)

12. DECREES, ETC., IN COLLATERAL ACTION OR SUIT. It has, in some of the States, been held that the orders and decrees of judges of probate and of county judges in probate proceedings, are not like judgments of the common-law courts, conclusive until reversed; but they may be attacked in collateral suits or proceedings. This, however, has been greatly limited as a general doctrine, either by statute or adjudication. The leading case on this subject, and the firm ground taken by the supreme judicial tribunal of the nation in upholding the proceedings of such courts, and recognizing them as having original jurisdiction of all matters confided to them, may be taken as perhaps the best exposition of their power and jurisdiction, and the extent to which their orders, judgments or decrees may be collaterally questioned. The rule of the U. S. supreme court is:

Upon a proceeding *in personam*, where there are adverse parties, the jurisdiction of the court depends upon its power over the subject-matter and the parties; where the proceeding is *in rem*,* the

---

(*u*) *Piggott* v. *Ramey*, 1 Scam. 145; *Marston* v. *Wilcox*, id. 60; *Ferguson* v. *Hunter*, 2 Gilm. 657; *Moody* v. *Moody*, 11 Me. 247; *Fairfield* v. *Gulliver*, 49 id. 360; *School Insp.* v. *People*, 20 Ill. 525; *Chicago* v. *Colby*, id. 614.

(*v*) See p. xiii, *supra*.
(*w*) Id.
(*x*) Act April 27, 1877, § 13, *ante, p.* xxiv; Cothran's Ann. R. Stat., p. 426.

* No case has received severer criticism than that of *Grignon* v. *Astor*, but the U. S. supreme court adheres tenaciously to it. *Comstock* v. *Crawford*, 3 Wall. 396; 2 Hill's C. L. 645. The cases in Illinois do not seem to conflict, for the reason that, as says Mr. Justice SCOTT, "The proceedings under our statute to sell the real estate of an intestate to pay debts is not purely a proceeding *in rem*. Parties in interest are necessary thereto by the positive provisions of the law." *Botsford* v. *O'Conner*, 57 Ill. 72. See chapter vii, *infra*.

In probate.

jurisdiction of the court depends upon its power over the thing, the subject-matter before them, without regard to the persons who may have an interest in it; all the world are parties. Of this nature is a proceeding before a competent court to sell the real estate of an indebted intestate; the administrator represents the land, all persons claiming under the intestate are parties, the action of the court operates on the estate, not on the heirs of the intestate, and the purchaser obtains not their title but one paramount.(y)

13. THE RULE IN ILLINOIS. It was early decided in Illinois:

(1) That courts exercising probate jurisdiction, generally, may exercise all powers necessary to the enforcement of their judgments within the scope of that jurisdiction, and may exercise, as an incident of the power granted, such other powers as are necessary to the execution of that which is specifically granted. Thus, these courts have power to revoke letters of administration obtained through fraud; the right to inquire of the fraud is necessarily incidental to the power given by statute, to hear and determine the right of administration;(z) but the legislature having directed these courts as to the mode of their procedure, they must proceed conformably to the mode prescribed. Such a court could render no judgment in favor of heirs or devisees against an executor or administrator, for failing or refusing to pay over to such heirs or devisees their distributive shares of the estate of the deceased. The remedy would be by attachment for contempt.(a) As courts of general and original jurisdiction in probate matters, they are not inferior courts in the language of the common law, but they are courts of limited or special jurisdiction, having cognizance only of matters specially circumstanced. Their record setting forth the facts or circumstances which give jurisdiction, and in that regard leaving nothing to be inferred and containing nothing to raise a doubt upon that subject, then they are not to be regarded as inferior courts. The character of the court and its right to proceed to act, the subject-matter of the record being exemplified, its decrees, in a collateral proceeding, cannot be attacked. The jurisdiction only is subject to attack collaterally; mere errors can only be urged in a direct proceeding to reverse.

(y) *Grignon* v. *Astor*, 2 How. 319; *Hanna* v. *Yocum*, 17 Ill. 387; see 1 Hill's C. L. 42–56; *The Tug Montauk* v. *Walker*, 47 Ill. 336; *Hurd* v. *Slaten*, 43 id. 348; *Botsford* v. *O'Conner*, 57 id. 72.
(z) *Marston* v. *Wilcox*, 1 Scam. 60.
(a) *Piggott* v. *Ramey*, 1 Scam. 145.

County Courts.

These courts have exclusive jurisdiction over the personalty.(b) As to the realty their jurisdiction is limited, in the case of county courts by the statute of March 26, 1874, to "proceedings by executors, administrators, guardians and conservators for the sale of real estate for the purposes authorized by law," and, in the case of probate courts, by the constitution of 1870, to "cases of the sales of real estate of deceased persons for the payment of debts."

(2) They may establish RULES OF PRACTICE (c) which should, when made, be placed upon their records; such rules cannot rest in parol, they should have reasonable publicity and not operate retrospectively.(d)

14. They have a sort of EQUITABLE JURISDICTION over claims presented for allowance.(e)

The constitution of 1870, giving original jurisdiction to the county and probate courts, where authorized to be established, in probate and other matters, they may be considered in Illinois as standing, so far as relates to the force and effect of their adjudications in such matters on an equal footing with circuit courts, to the full extent of their special jurisdiction, as shown above.(f)

15. THE STATUTORY PROVISIONS. The statutes concerning administration of estates; adoption of children; apprentices; descent; dower; lunatics, idiots, drunkards and spendthrifts; guardian and ward and wills, provide the mode of practice and procedure which will be considered in order.

16. SCOPE OF THE SUBJECT. As the end and scope of the jurisdiction, now in review before us, is the proper administration not only of the estates of the deceased, but also of the estates of the incapacitated, it seems necessary, in order to an easy and natural arrangement of our subject, that we should consider the procedure and practice of the county courts, the means to this end, and classify them, with reference to the persons whose estates thus become the subject-matter for judicial action.

17. DECEASED PERSONS in probate are divided into two classes:

(1) Those who make wills and, therefore, die testate, and leave, for probate jurisdiction, testate estates.

(b) But see act of February 12, 1849, Gross, 526, 527; *Ferguson* v. *Hunter*, 2 Gilm. 657.
(c) *Holloway* v. *Freeman*, 22 Ill. 197.
(d) *Owens* v. *Ranstead*, 22 Ill. 161.
(e) *Hurd* v. *Slaten*, 43 Ill. 348.

(f) *Botsford* v. *O'Conner*, 57 Ill. 72; *Hanna* v. *Yocum*, 17 id. 387; *Clark* v. *Thompson*, 47 id. 25; *Willoughby* v. *Dewey*, 54 id. 26; see 1 Hill's Com. Law, 40–56; 2 id. 645.

In probate.

(2) Those who make no wills and, therefore, die intestate, and leave, for such jurisdiction, intestate estates.

18. INCAPACITATED PERSONS, whose property is subjected to the jurisdiction, may also be divided into two classes:

(1) Infants.

(2) Other incapacitated persons.

Hence, the subject-matter of this jurisdiction divides naturally into 1. Testate estates; 2. Intestate estates; 3. Estates of infants; 4. Estates of the insane and other incapacitated persons.

19. EXECUTORS, ETC., OFFICERS OF THE COURT. All these estates are made up of the two classes of property known to the law as personal and real, to which appertain as distinguishing characteristics different rules of enjoyment and disposition. Testate estates are managed by and through executors, the appointees of their testators; intestate estates through administrators; estates of infants through guardians and the estates of the incapacitated persons through conservators, all appointees and officers of the court, subject to its process, orders and decrees, and liable to account when required not only to the court but to those interested as *cestuis que trust* in these estates. The funds in hand are to be disposed of in the payment of expenses, allowances, debts, legacies, etc.

20. THE LAW OF DESCENT. In the distribution of these estates finally, the law of descent furnishes well-defined rules. Costs and fees accrue in the proceedings.

21. APPEALS are provided for. There are other matters pertaining to the jurisdiction which it will be necessary to incidentally consider. We shall close the volume with the inevitable appendix containing, among other things, the concise and excellent rules of the probate court of Cook county, with forms, etc.

22. METHOD. By thus subjecting the matters before us to methodical arrangement under the rules of analysis, we are prepared to discuss with greater satisfaction the important details and admire the system and harmony which pervade the procedure and practice in such matters. The highest trusts known to the law pertain to testate estates, therefore, we purpose to consider them first, which brings us to another chapter.

CHAPTER II.

TESTATE ESTATES.

WILLS, THEIR PROBATE AND THEIR EXECUTION.

  Section I. Wills.
    II. Probate of wills.
    III. Executors.

SECTION I.—WILLS.

1. Definition.
2. Who may make a will.
3. Requisites of a will.
4. Nuncupative will.
5. Codicils.
6. Forms.
 (1) Of a will.
 (2) Of a codicil.
 (3) Of a nuncupative will.
7. Revocation.
8. Production of the will.
9. Construction of wills.

1. DEFINITION. A WILL is the legal declaration of a man's intention respecting the manner in which he would have his property, or estate, disposed of after his death. The terms *will* and *testament* are synonymous. When the will operates upon personal property, it is called a *testament;* when upon real estate, a *devise.*(a) The more general and popular denomination of the instrument, embracing equally real and personal estate, is that of last will and testament.

2. ALL NATURAL PERSONS, unless restricted or incapacitated may transmit their property to posterity by will. There are two causes which prevent a person from the valid execution of such an instrument.

1. Want of mind; 2. Inability by reason of want of age.

In this State the power of a testator of sound mind to dispose of his estate is unlimited, both as to person and object, unless, indeed, there be excepted the person of a witness to the instrument and its execution. Any person subscribing as a witness and all claiming under him are debarred from taking under the provisions of the will he has so subscribed. As to him, all devises, legacies and

---

(a) 4 Kent's Com. 500; Bouv. L. D., *Will.*

Wills.

interests are void unless there be joined with him at least two other credible and competent witnesses. Nevertheless, if such witness would have been entitled to any share of testator's estate, were the will not existing or established, he will be entitled to that proportion of the estate he would have received from an intestate estate, to the extent it does not exceed the special devise or bequest made to him by the will; (*b*) he may pass by his own children, and he may prescribe the time and mode in which the bounty shall be enjoyed, provided he therein contravenes no principle of public policy or rule of right. (*c*) Every person aged twenty-one years, if a male, or eighteen, if a female, being of sound mind and memory, shall have power to devise real estate, or any interest they may have in the same, and to dispose of personal estate of every description by will. (*d*)

The law in force at the time of the death of the testator or intestate controls his estate, but the will, though legally executed by a competent person, is wholly inoperative to convey title and for most other purposes till it has been probated. (*e*)

3. THE INDISPENSABLE REQUISITES OF A WILL are, that it must be signed by the testator or by some one for him and in his name, in his presence and by his direction, and be attested in his presence by two or more witnesses. (*f*)

4. NUNCUPATIVE WILL. This is a will or testament orally made or declared before witnesses and afterward reduced to writing. Nuncupative wills have been abolished in England by statute 1 Vict. ch. 26, § 9, with an exception in the case of soldiers in actual military service, and mariners and seamen at sea. This is so, too, in several of the States of the Union. The statute of wills of the State of Illinois recognizes such wills, declaring they shall be good and available in law for the conveyance of personal property, if committed to writing within twenty days after the making thereof, and proven before the court of probate by two or more credible, disinterested witnesses, who were present at the speaking and publishing thereof. They must testify that they were present,

---

(*b*) Coth. Ann'd. Rev. Stats., 1880, 1537, § 8.
(*c*) *Rhoads* v. *Rhoads*, 43 Ill. 230; *Heuser* v. *Harris*, 42 id. 425.
(*d*) 4 Kent's Com. 502; R. S. 1874, ch. 148, § 1, *p.* 1104; Laws 1872, Myers' ed., *p.* 131; Act of 1861, relating to married women; Hill's Chan. Pr. 433, 610; *Trish* v. *Newell*, 62 Ill. 106.
(*e*) *Paschall* v. *Hailmam*, 4 Gilm. 285, Hill's Chan. Pr. 56–70.
(*f*) *Rigg* v. *Wilton*, 13 Ill. 15; R. S. 1874, *p.* 1101; *Flin* v. *Owen*, 58 Ill. 111; Coth. Ann'd. Stats., 1534.

heard the testator pronounce the words, believed him to be of sound mind and memory, that testator desired those present to bear witness such was his will, and that at the time testator was in his last sickness. Other two witnesses, equally disinterested, must prove such will was committed to writing within ten days of the death of testator. The court must also be satisfied there existed no fraud, compulsion or other improper conduct operating on testator.

The supreme court of Illinois has seemed somewhat to change its opinion in relation to these statutory requirements of a nuncupative will. In the case of *Weir v. Chidester*, 63 Ill. 453, it held that a substantial but not a literal compliance with the statute is required. That it was only necessary words should be used expressing a clear intention to give the estate to a certain person; that any form of expression which would indicate to those present that testator desired them, or some of them, to bear witness to his disposition of his property, would be sufficient. In *Morgan v. Stevens*, 78 Ill. 287, the same court required the strictest compliance with the statute. In this case, however, it appeared that the alleged testator lived during some six days, being all the time in condition to make a written will. It did, however, state, as a general proposition, that the provisions of the statute must have a rigid and strict construction and must be strictly enforced by the courts. Later, in *Herrington v. Stees*, 82 Ill. 50, this was so far modified as to hold that if a person in a sickness from which he afterward died, being impressed with the probability of approaching death, deliberately made his will according to the statute, it was not to be rejected, because, as a fact, he may have had time to reduce it to writing, as well as that no formal request of the testator to the attesting witnesses is required; that it is sufficient if his desire was clearly manifested that they bear witness to the same.

5. A CODICIL is an addition or supplement to a will, and is a part of it, the two making but one instrument; it must be executed with the same solemnities as a will. Its office is to explain the dispositions made by the will, to add to or alter it.

There may be more than one codicil to a will.

A NUNCUPATIVE WILL, REDUCED TO WRITING.

The following is the will of A B, mariner, soldier (*as the case may be*), of   , who being sick, and nigh unto death, which occurred the day following at 6 o'clock, A. M., the same was made by

Wills.

the said A B, in the presence of the persons whose names are hereto subscribed, and who were specially requested by the said testator to take notice of the same as witnesses, and was in these words :

I give my watch to A B, my silver spoons to C D (*detailing each particular*). All the rest I give to my wife, and she will carry this out. She shall be the executrix.

Done in the sick chamber of said A B, on   18   , at 9 o'clock, P. M.

$$\left.\begin{array}{c} \text{A B,} \\ \text{C D,} \\ \text{E F,} \end{array}\right\} \text{Witnesses.}$$

7. REVOCATION OF A WILL. No will, testament or codicil shall be revoked otherwise than by burning, canceling, tearing or obliterating the same by the testator himself, or in his presence, by his direction and consent, or by some other will, testament or codicil, in writing, declaring the same, signed by the testator in the presence of two witnesses, and by them attested in his presence. No words spoken will avail to revoke or annul any will, testament, devise or codicil in writing, executed in accordance with law. By statute of April 9, 1872, in force July 1, 1872, (*g*) it is expressly enacted that a marriage shall be deemed a revocation of a prior will; that is to say, this statute applies to marriages which have taken or shall take place after the date of the act, and not to such as have been had prior to its passage.(*h*)

Unless a will or codicil be revoked in some one of these modes, it continues operative. The *intention* to revoke must be made apparent, in the manner provided by the statute. If a will is burned, canceled, torn or obliterated by accident, it is not thereby revoked, for its contents in such case may be proved.(*i*) The revocation is the voluntary, intelligent act of the person making the will.

By the English law, if a child of the testator should be born after the execution of the will, and no provision be made for it in the will, and the whole estate has been disposed of to its exclusion, it amounts to a revocation of the will; but our statute (*j*) expressly provides that in such case the will shall not be revoked; but unless it shall appear by such will that it was the intention of the testator to disinherit such child, the devises and legacies granted by such will shall be abated in equal proportions, to raise a portion for such

---

(*g*) Coth. Annd. R. Stats. 1880, *p*. 543.
(*h*) *In re Tuller*, 79 Ill. 99.
(*i*) 4 Kent's Com. 521.

(*j*) § 10, R. S. 1874, 819. Cothran's Annotated Rev. Statutes, *p*. 543.

child equal to that which it would have been entitled to receive out of such testator's estate, if he had died without making a will.

The statute enabling a woman, married or sole, to deal with her separate estate, she may in either event execute and declare a will. This will be subject, of course, to the statute, heretofore mentioned as to the revocation of wills by marriage. The revocation of a will must, when intended to be effectual, be made in the form prescribed by statute.*

8. PRODUCTION OF THE WILL.

(1.) Venue.
(2.) Proceedings.
(3.) Petition for process to compel the same.
(4.) Order for process and the entry.
(5.) Attachment to compel the production of a will.
(6.) Jurisdiction, facts essential to, must appear.
(7.) The withholding the will.
(8.) Destruction or secretion, a felony.
(9.) Compulsory process.
(10.) Renunciation, how made and recorded.
(11.) Administrator with the will annexed.

(1.) VENUE. The proper county in which to proceed for the probate of a will, in case of a resident decedent, is the county of his domicile or home.(*l*) In case of a non-resident decedent, and lands be devised, in the county where the lands or some part of them lie.(*l*) If there be no lands, then in the county where the testator died or where the estate or the greater part of it is.

(2.) PROCEEDINGS. On the death of a testator or testatrix, it becomes the duty of the custodian to deliver up the will to the county court of the proper county.(*m*) In case of failure or refusal on the

---

(*k*) *In re Tuller*, 79 Ill. 99. Stat. of Wills, R. S. 1845, 540 ; Hill's
(*l*) § 11, R. S. 1874, *p.* 1103 ; 17 of Chan. Pr., Domicile, 50, 51.
(*m*) § 12, R. S. 1874, *p.* 1104.

* The act of 1861 enables married women to exercise dominion over their separate estate, and clothes them with the *jus disponendi* as if they were *sole*, or unmarried. Hill's Ch. Pr. 433, 610. See also act of March 30, 1874, in relation to husband and wife. R. S. 1874, ch. 86, p. 576. Cothran's Statutes, 1880, p. 1538.

Wills.

part of such custodian so to do, an attachment to compel the production of the will may be obtained at the instance of any person interested in the matter. Any party desiring the production of the will of a decedent, which he knows to be in the custody of any person within the jurisdiction, may file a petition(n) or representation, substantially in form as follows:

(3.) PETITION FOR PROCESS TO COMPEL THE PRODUCTION OF A WILL.

STATE OF ILLINOIS, } ss: *In the County Court of*   *County.*
County of   .

To the Hon.   , *judge of said court:*

The petition of A B respectfully showeth that he is a resident of said county; that on the   day of   , A. D. 18   , C D, who then resided in said county, died at   , leaving a last will and testament in the custody of E F, of said county; that E. F hath not as yet delivered up the said will to this honorable court, according to the statute in such case made and provided. Wherefore, your petitioner prays that the necessary process may be issued to compel the production of said will.   A B.

STATE OF ILLINOIS, } ss:
County of   .

A B, being duly sworn, says, that he is the person whose name is signed to the above and foregoing petition, and that all the facts therein stated are true of his own knowledge.

         A B.

Subscribed and sworn to before me,
this   day of   , A. D. 18   .
         Clerk (*N. P.* or *J. P.*)

(4.) ORDER AND ENTRY. Upon such a representation, the court will make the order, and the clerk an entry:

In the matter of the application
of A B for the production of
the will of C D, deceased.

It having been made to appear by the representation of A B that on the   day of   , A. D. 18   , C D, who then resided in said county, died at   , leaving a last will and testament in the custody of E F of said county, and that E F hath not as yet delivered up the said last will to this court, according to the statute in such case made and provided; now, therefore, ordered that an attachment be issued to compel the production of the said will to this court.

Then the clerk will issue the attachment in form as follows:

(*n*) The representation of nearly all facts, upon which the action of the court is based, in the several causes of procedure, is made by means of a petition. See PROBATE RECORD, *infra*.

Wills.

(5.) ATTACHMENT TO COMPEL THE PRODUCTION OF A WILL.

STATE OF ILLINOIS, } ss:
County of   .}

The People of the State of Illinois: To the sheriff of said county, greeting:

WHEREAS, It is represented to the county court of said county, that C D, deceased, caused his last will and testament to be placed in the possession of E F, for safe-keeping (or that the same has fallen into his possession, as the case may be), and that the said E F fails and refuses to deliver up the said last will to the county court of said county. We, therefore, command you to attach the body of the said E F, and bring him before this court at the court-house at   , on the   day of   , next, to show cause, if any he can, why he should not be fined and imprisoned for so failing and refusing to deliver up said last will and testament of the said C D. And hereof make return as the law directs.

Witness,   , clerk of our said court, and the seal thereof, at   , aforesaid, this   day of   , A. D. 18 .
[L. S.]   , Clerk.

(6.) JURISDICTION. It is essential that it should appear in the petition, that the court to which application is made is the proper one,* in order to give the court jurisdiction.

(7). THE WITHHOLDING THE WILL subjects the custodian to a penalty of $20 per month, in an action of debt.

(8.) THE DESTRUCTION OF A WILL, or its secretion for the space of six months, is made tantamount to larceny.(*o*)

(9.) COMPULSORY PROCESS. On the production of the will, if the court have jurisdiction, the court may, of its own motion, inaugurate proceedings against the executor or executors named therein to compel him or them to either accept or renounce the trust. (*p*)

In case of refusal to accept the trust, the renunciation should be made in writing and recorded.

(10.) RENUNCIATION BY EXECUTOR. In case an executor named wishes to renounce, he should not, in any way, intermeddle with the estate of the deceased, but, immediately on learning of his appointment, transmit or deliver to the county court of the proper county his formal renunciation:

RENUNCIATION.

To Hon.   *, Judge of the County Court of*   *county, in the State of Illinois:*

I, A B, do hereby renounce the appointment of executor, conferred on me by the will of   , deceased, late of   , county of

(*o*) § 12, Act of 1872.   (*p*) Act March 20, 1872, §§ 7, 18.

---
*See *Venue*, p. 14, *supra*.

Wills.

, State of   , and refuse to take any part in its probate, and pray that you will duly file and enter of record this, my renunciation; and I further state that I have not, in any manner, intermeddled with the estate of said deceased.   A B.
           , Ill., this   day of   , A. D. 18 .

(11.) ADMINISTRATOR WITH THE WILL ANNEXED. On entering the renunciation of a sole executor, the estate is to be administered according to the will. The court, on proper application or of its own motion, will then proceed to the appointment of an administrator, *cum testamento annexo*, who becomes to all intents and purposes the actual executor of the will.(*q*)

9. CONSTRUCTION OF WILLS.* Courts, in construing a will, are bound to give effect to every clause in a will, if possible, and at the same time, to the intention of the testator.(*r*) A husband died testate, leaving a widow, but no children or lineal descendants, and provided, in his will, that the income of one-half of his personal estate should be paid to his widow during her life, and at her death should be distributed among his collateral kindred, and bequeathed the other half to various persons. The widow renounced the will, and set up claim to the entire personal estate. *Held*, that in such case the widow was only entitled to one-third of the personal property remaining after the payment of debts, in addition to the award of specific property.(*s*) By the widow's renunciation of the will, the property of her husband is not thereby converted into an intestate estate. The will remains, notwithstanding she declines its provisions in her favor; and in such case, the forty-sixth section of the statute of wills, which applies only to intestate estates, has no application. The phrase, "her share in the personal estate of her husband," which occurs in the tenth section of the dower act, must be understood as intending to give to the widow, in such case, only such share of the personal estate as shall be equal to one-third part.(*t*) A testator, in his will, bequeaths to his wife an annuity, together with the use and occupation of the homestead during her natural

---

(*q*) See chapter iii, *infra*.
(*r*) *Jones* v. *Doe*, 1 Scam. 276.
(*s*) *McMurphy* v. *Boyles*, 49 Ill. 110.

(*t*) Id. But see § 78, act April 1, 1872;
p. 219 *infra*.

*As this is a work of practice and not elementary, without attempting any arrangement, we have, for convenient reference, added to this section most of the cases to be found in the Illinois reports involving the construction of wills. The professional reader would naturally consult these cases themselves, while the layman, of necessity, must rely upon the legal adviser for counsel in such intricate matters, as the cases will show. If, however, the reader desire to pursue this subject systematically and thoroughly, the work of Hon. I. F. REDFIELD, LL. D., on wills, will be a valuable assistant. See Hill's Chan. Pr. 56-70, for an intricate case and an able opinion as to a will. See also ch. x, *infra*, and *Markillie* v. *Ragland*, 77 Ill. 98.

Wills.

life, or, in lieu of the homestead, bequeaths to her $1,000, to be paid to her by his executors five years after testator's death, or sooner, if she shall prefer to use it in the erection of a dwelling-house, upon a lot given her for that purpose, if she so elects, together with certain other town lots, to further aid and assist in the erection of such dwelling-house. *Held*, that under such a will the widow could not be barred in her election, between these provisions contained in the will, prior to the expiration of the five years after the testator's death, or prior to a tender, by the executors of the will, of the alternative devise of $1,000.(*u*)

Where a testator devised land to his wife " to hold and dispose of the same as she may see proper during her widowhood," the devisee will not take an estate of inheritance which will pass to her heirs, the language of the devise clearly limiting the extent of her interest.(*v*) The construction to be given to the tenth and eleventh sections of our statute of dower, in determining the share of the widow in the personal estate of her deceased husband, where she has renounced his will, is, that she is entitled to one-third of the personal estate after the payment of debts. And the fact that there are children in this case in nowise affects the question.(*w*) Where a will empowered the executor to sell all of the testator's lands "outside of St. Clair county," for the payment of his debts, this was an express limitation upon the power of the executor, so far as it was derived under the will, to sell the lands of the testator lying outside of that county.(*x*) Where the power of the executor to sell lands for the payment of debts is limited by the will to lands situate in certain counties, and the proceeds of sales so permitted prove insufficient to pay the debts, the executor may apply to the proper court and procure an order to sell so much of the lands reserved from sale in the will as may be necessary to pay the residue of the debts. In no other way can the executor obtain the authority to sell the lands beyond that given by the will.(*y*) The rule is, if there be no words in any part of the will to control, the words or terms used must be interpreted according to their strict and technical import. So construing them, the persons appointed by law to succeed to an estate, as in case of intestacy, are the persons designated. An estate left in

(*u*) *Gale* v. *Gale*, 48 Ill. 471.
(*v*) *Mulberry* v. *Mulberry*, 50 Ill. 67.
(*w*) *Skinner* v. *Newberry*, 51 Ill. 203.
(*x*) *Kinney* v. *Knoebel*, 51 Ill. 113.
(*y*) Id.

Wills.

such a condition as to the disposition of it, is, to all intents and purposes, an intestate estate.(z)

A will containing no specific devises or bequests, but simply appointing the executors to administer the estate, and directing the payment of the debts of the testator, provided as follows: "And the remainder or balance of my interest, of every kind whatsoever, may be distributed to my heirs at law, according to the statute of Illinois, for such case made and provided." *Held*, that such a direction is equivalent to a devise or bequest to those who would take the estate under our statute of distributions if the estate were intestate.(z) The owner in fee of a tract of land in this State devised his property as follows: "I leave and bequeath all the property, movable and immovable, of which I may die possessed, to my said wife; this legacy is made in *usufruct*, and during the life-time of my said wife, and at her death the whole of which will revert to the children which I have, or may have, from such marriage." *Held*, that on the death of the testator, the widow took, under this devise, a life estate in the land, a freehold, and, under our statute, subject to execution.(a) A will provided as follows: "I give and bequeath all of the rents and profits of my farm, that I now own, in the town, county and State aforesaid, to my wife, Deliverance R. Lester, and also all my personal property, consisting of live stock, and also the interest on all moneys and credits due me at my death, so long as she remains my widow, except hereafter devised; and after her death or marriage, I wish the property and real estate to be equally divided between my children," etc. *Held*, this was not an absolute gift of the personalty to the widow, but was intended as a bequest to her, to be enjoyed during her life or widowhood, having reference as well to the live stock, moneys and credits, as to the use of the farm. They were not of that perishable character which forbade a life estate being created in them. It is a general principle, that where an interest, short of absolute ownership, is given in the general residue of personal estate, terms for years, and other perishable funds of property which may be consumed in the use are to be converted or invested, so as to produce a permanent capital, and the income thereof only is to go to the legatee for life. So in this case, the tenant for life should convert the live stock into money, and

---

(z) *Rawson* v. *Rawson*, 52 Ill. 62;   (a) *Newman* v. *Willetts*, 52 Ill. 99.
Hill's Chan. Pr. 62.

save the principal for those who were to come to its enjoyment on her death or marriage.(b)

Where a life estate is created in personal property, with a limitation over, a court of chancery may require the legatee for life to give security to the remainder-man that the fund shall not be wasted or misapplied. An exception to the rule that there may be a life estate in chattels which are not of a perishable nature, and a limitation over, is in case of a bequest of specific things, as corn, hay and fruit, of which the use consists in the consumption. The gift of such articles for life is, in most cases, of necessity, a gift of the absolute property, for the use and the property cannot exist separately.(b) The mere making of a bequest to a creditor of the testator, of a sum of money equal to or greater than the debt, and which might in the particular case be regarded as a satisfaction of the debt, would not operate to defeat an allowance of the claim against the estate, to be paid in due course of administration, with other debts in the same degree. Such a legacy must be paid before it can be set up as a discharge of the debt. When a creditor to whom his debtor has made a bequest, equal to or greater than his debt, obtains an allowance and payment of his claim, and afterward demands his legacy from the executor, the latter may then raise the question whether it was intended as a gift, independently of the payment of the debt, or merely as a satisfaction of the debt.(c) M. devised and bequeathed by will all his estate to his daughter R.; but if she died before she became of age, then to his friend G. S.; R. died before she became of age, and G. S. died before R. It was *held*, that the devise to G. S. was a good, executory devise, and that the estate passed to his heirs.(d) A testator, after devising all his estate, real and personal, to his wife, so long as she should remain his widow, proceeded: "Upon the marriage or death of my wife, it is my will and desire that all the property which I leave in her possession, or that may accrue from it, may be equally divided between all my brothers and sisters' children, giving each one an equal share, except J. J. R., my brother Leonard Ross' oldest son, who I do not intend shall have any share of my estate." This was held a devise of after-acquired real estate, and disherison of J. J. R.(e) If land be devised to a person for

(b) *Burnett* v. *Lester*, 53 Ill. 325.
(c) *Malony* v. *Scanlan*, 53 Ill. 122.
(d) *Ackless* v. *Seekright*, Breese, 46.
(e) *Willis* v. *Watson*, 4 Scam. 64.

Wills.

life, and "at her death she may dispose of it as she pleases," an estate for life only passes, and the devisee may dispose of the reversion or inheritance by deed or by will.(*f*) Where real estate is devised, and by the conditions of the will is to be sold, and the money distributed among the devisees, it must be treated as a devise of money, and not of land. Though a devisee may elect to take land instead of the money, yet the character of the devise cannot be changed from money to land without the concurrence of all the devisees. In such case, one devisee cannot convey a valid title to any part of the land, neither can the interest of one of the devisees be sold on execution. A purchaser at a sheriff's sale of the interest of one of the devisees, in such case, is not entitled to receive that portion of the money produced by the sale of the land to which the devisee was entitled under the will, the devisee having no interest in the land which could be levied upon under execution. A *femme couverte* is competent to elect to take the land instead of the money; but the same forms and solemnities are required for that election as are by law necessary to enable her to convey her fee.(*g*) Under the statute of wills, the real estate of the deceased is liable for his debts and funeral expenses, as a secondary fund; and it would not be otherwise under a will, charging all debts and legacies upon the realty, unless the intention to change the legal order of liability was very clear. Where it was directed by will that all debts and funeral expenses were to be paid out of the first moneys that should come into the executor's hands, from any portion of the estate, real or personal, and legacies were given in the same will, and the lands were not devised to the executors, but a power given them to sell generally, when they think proper, without expressing any object for the sale, or directing any application of the proceeds, and there is no proof that the personalty was not sufficient to pay debts, funeral expenses and legacies, the lands will descend to the heirs subject to be incumbered or sold at the executors' discretion. Such a power of sale is a naked power, and though courts will uphold rights derived from its proper exercise, equity will not compel its exercise.(*h*) If a testator disposes of property, in which he has a limited interest, *e. g.*, curtesy, it becomes a question of intention, to be decided from the terms of the instrument, how

(*f*) *Fairman* v. *Beal*, 14 Ill. 244.
(*g*) *Baker* v. *Copenbarger*, 15 Ill. 103.

(*h*) *Clinefelter* v. *Ayers*, 16 Ill. 329.

large an interest he meant to devise.(*i*) A clause in a will, bequeathing "all real and personal estate, except as hereinafter indicated," to certain devisees, necessarily includes lands out of the State in which the will was made, which could pass by it; and a subsequent direction to executors to sell such land "or otherwise as they shall deem proper," does not take the land out of the general clause, but only empowers the executors to change its form.(*j*) A testator devised real estate to his wife and two others, and to the survivor or survivors, to hold the same until his youngest child should, if a son, become twenty-one, and, if a daughter, eighteen years old, in trust for all his surviving children, their heirs and assigns, as tenants in common. *Held*, that all the testator's children living at his death were his devisees, all taking a vested fee simple estate (subject to the trust estate), which, so subject, could be sold by them or on execution.(*k*) If the devisees would also be heirs at law of the estate devised, they cannot be held to have forfeited the estate, until it be shown that they committed the breach of the condition with full knowledge both of the conditions and its consequences.(*l*) *Held*, that the following words of devise in a will gave the devisee an estate of inheritance: "I will and bequeath to my oldest daughter, Margaret Jane Elizabeth Holliday, eighty acres of land where my house and well stand, to her and heirs forever, never to be mortgaged nor sold forever."(*m*) Where a will directed that the debts of the testator be paid out of the avails of personal property, unless other arrangements could be made; that a house should be built; that certain legacies should be paid his children at their majority, and for that purpose his executors might dispose of real estate; that his wife should have the control of all his property, until the youngest child should become of lawful age, for the support, education and maintenance of the children, and directed how the property should be divided. It was *held*, that after the payment of the debts, and the reservation of sufficient estate to satisfy the specific legacies, the residuum should be under the control of the wife, until the event should occur, when, under the will, the remainder was to be distributed, and that the wife received not in fee but as trustee. That the wife had not even a

(*i*) *Wilbanks* v. *Wilbanks*, 18 Ill. 17.
(*j*) *Hurt* v. *McCartney*, 18 Ill. 129.
(*k*) *Hempstead* v. *Dickson*, 20 Ill. 193.
(*l*) *Shackelford* v. *Hall*, 19 Ill. 212.
(*m*) *Holliday* v. *Dixon*, 27 Ill. 33.

Wills.

life-estate in the remainder, but only the power to control in the interim, before distribution was required within the limit directed by the will. That, should the wife attempt to abuse the trust, a court of equity would restrain her, and compel a proper application of the estate.(*m*) Under such a will, the wife was not to account to the probate court, until the time fixed by the will for the distribution of the estate; also, that the money received on the sale of the land, after payment of the debts, and the specific legacies due, after reserving enough for the other legacies, should be paid to the widow.(*n*) Where A devised to his wife for life his homestead to use, as if fully her own, and on her death, part of the same over, and the land not included in the above bequest to his wife to dispose of at her death, and owned only the homestead, it was *held*, that a deed in fee by her took effect on her death, and that she could not dispose of her life interest.(*o*) A devise to a wife of all testator's property, except such portion of certain described lands as shall be necessary for the payment of debts, to hold during widowhood, vests a life estate in the widow.(*p*) A husband devised certain land to his wife, "to have and to hold during her natural life, to occupy and use said land in the same way as it would be lawful for her to do if the title were full and complete in her * * * to dispose of at her death to any person she may think best to live with her and take care of her." *Held*, that the wife had no power to alien during her life.(*q*) A devise was of all the residue of the testator's estate, there was no limitation over. *Held*, that, under the statute, the devisee took the fee of the realty.(*r*) Where the owner of land devises the same, there being a growing crop on the land at the time the title of the devisee vests, the crop being owned by the testator and another as tenants in common thereof, the portion of the crop which would have belonged to the testator, had he lived until it matured, would pass with the land under the devise, there being no reservation of the crop in the will.(*s*) A testator devised to M. "so much of lots renumbered 1 and 2 in block No. 15, in the southern addition of Miller and others to Bloomington, as is now inclosed by fence, including the house where the widow C now lives." These lots were inclosed by an

(*m*) *Holliday* v. *Dixon*, 27 Ill. 33.
(*n*) *Estate of Whitman*, 22 Ill. 511.
(*o*) *Pulliam* v. *Christy*, 19 Ill. 331.
(*p*) *Batterton* v. *Yoakum*, 17 Ill. 288.
(*q*) *Christy* v. *Ogle's Ex'rs*, 33 Ill. 295.
(*r*) *McConnel* v. *Smith*, 23 Ill. 611.
(*s*) *Creel* v. *Kirkham*, 47 Ill. 344; see, also, *Powell* v. *Rich*, 41 id. 466.

exterior fence, and there were also two interior fences running north and south, so as to form three distinct inclosures. The house occupied by the widow C was on the north-west corner of lot 2, and was inclosed in the separate division formed by a portion of the north and south exterior fences, and all of the outside western fence and the interior fence equally dividing lot 2. The dwelling-house of the testator was on lot 1. *Held*, that the western half of lot 2 alone passed by the devise.(*t*) A testator devised a portion of his estate to the "children of his brother," giving the brother uncontrolled management and disposal of the same till the youngest child should become of age. *Held*, that the brother took, thereby, a particular estate which prevented the devise from vesting in possession in the children till the youngest child became of age, and, therefore, a child born after the death of the testator was included in the devise.(*u*) A testator, by one clause in his will, gave his wife $1,200 in money, and his household furniture "to her and her heirs and assigns forever;" and by the next clause gave her the balance of all his personal property, of every description, etc., "to be at her own disposal and for her own proper use and benefit during her natural life." *Held*, that, under the last clause, she took only a life interest in the residuary estate.(*v*) A will contained this clause: "I give and bequeath to my beloved wife, Antonia, all my real and personal estate, wherever situated, in fee simple, absolute forever; that is to say, that my said wife shall have all of the benefits thereof until the expiration of her life, at which time my son Anton shall be the only heir of real or personal estate that may be left." *Held*, that the wife took only an estate for life in the real estate, and that there was a remainder in fee to the son.(*w*) A testator gave to his wife all his estate, to be disposed of in any way that would best support her for life, but if his sons, John and Thomas, should take care of their mother, they were to have certain lands, but if they failed to support her, then she could sell the land, or any part of it, to support herself; but if the sons complied with these conditions, they were to take immediate possession of the land; there were bequests to other children. *Held*, that the testator intended to charge his entire estate with the support of his widow; that the question of support was a condition subsequent,

---

(*t*) *Mason* v. *Ely*, 38 Ill. 188.
(*u*) *Handberry* v. *Doolittle*, 38 Ill. 202.
(*v*) *Boyd* v. *Strahan*, 36 Ill. 356.
(*w*) *Siegwald* v. *Siegwald*, 37 Ill. 430.

Wills.

the word "comply" being used in the sense of "assent," and when John and Thomas assented, the estate passed to them, burdened with the condition of the support of the mother; and that the widow of John being his heir, and proffering to support the widow, had a right to inherit and possess the estate, and could compel the grantee of the widow to reconvey to her.(*x*) *Held*, that the following clause of a will intends a distribution *per capita*, and not *per stirpes*: "The balance remaining of said fund, I hereby direct shall be equally divided between the children of my late brother P., and my brother-in-law B., of the city of Chicago, a large portion of my property having been received through his father, and the father of my late wife."(*y*) A testator directed that part of the proceeds of his estate should be invested, and that one of his devisees should be entitled to it when he "became of the age of twenty-one;" adding, "should he die before he arrives at the age of twenty-one, or die without heirs," then the estate shall go to another devisee. *Held*, that the word "or" was to be construed as "and," and that, on the devisee attaining his majority, although without issue, the legacy vested absolutely in him.(*z*) A testator directed his executor to sell all his real estate, and, after paying his debts, to divide the proceeds equally among his four children, and in case any of them died, "then to be divided among their children; the child or children of each one taking their deceased parent's portion among them." *Held*, that one of them, having died intestate before the conversion of the estate into money, leaving issue, his portion should be paid over to his administrator, to be held in trust for his children, his widow being entitled to no interest therein.(*a*) A testator directed, in his will, that his whole estate, except a discretionary reservation by his executrix and executor for the support of his widow and education of his youngest children, be invested and re-invested in United States bonds, and that, "at the end of fifteen years from and after his death, the trust thus created shall cease, and all his estate then be distributed among his wife and children in this manner, viz.: the sum of $10,000 to be paid to his wife, to be held by her as her absolute property; the remainder to be divided among his children according to the laws of this State, each one of the children to be charged with such sums as have been,

(*x*) *Jennings* v. *Jennings*, 27 Ill. 518.
(*y*) *Pitney* v. *Brown*, 44 Ill. 363.
(*z*) *Kindig* v. *Smith*, 39 Ill. 300.
(*a*) *People* v. *Jennings*, 44 Ill. 488.

or may be, charged against them as advancements." Five of the children were adults. *Held*, that the testator had power so to dispose of his estate, and the will was valid.(*b*) A husband devised to his wife one-third of all his real estate, " to be used and occupied by her, with the rents and profits thereof, for and during the term of her natural life," with a remainder in trust for his children, with a provision that, if they should permit any portion of the real estate to be sold for taxes, and it should not be redeemed, they should forfeit the unredeemed portion. *Held*, that the wife was not relieved from paying the taxes accruing upon her estate. A testator, by the terms of his will, required the division and payment of his property, not otherwise bequeathed, to his two children when the younger should attain twenty-one years, to be held by them during life, and, in the event of the death of either, before arriving at the age of twenty-one, without lawful heirs, his share to go to the survivor on arriving at majority. And a condition was annexed that they should not have the power to sell or incumber the fund, or subject it to sale on legal process for their debts, and if any effort was made to sell or incumber it, the party so attempting should forfeit his share, and it should pass to the next person in remainder; and, in the event of the death of the legatees, or a forfeiture of the property, if they have lawful issue or descendants of such issue, the property to vest in them, and if neither have issue, then the property to vest in certain collateral relatives designated in the will. *Held*, that the bequest was not void for perpetuity.(*c*)

AN ABSOLUTE PROHIBITION OF MARRIAGE, till twenty-one years of age, in a devise, is reasonable and lawful, and is a good condition subsequent, the violation of which may defeat a vested estate.(*d*) Words of inheritance are not necessary to pass an estate in fee simple, by will.(*e*) In this State, a testator may devise after-acquired real estate.(*f*) If there be in a will two devises of the same property to different persons, the first creating an estate of inheritance, the second, without words of perpetuity, will not destroy the first, and will create a life estate only, with reversion in the heirs of the first devisee.(*e*)

We have added the cases to be found in the Illinois reports on

(*b*) *Rhoads* v. *Rhoads*, 43 Ill. 239.
(*c*) *Waldo* v. *Cummings*, 45 Ill. 421.
(*d*) *Shackleford* v. *Hall*, 19 Ill. 212.
(*e*) *Jones* v. *Doe*, 1 Scam. 276.
(*f*) *Willis* v. *Watson*, 4 Scam. 64.

Probate of wills.

this subject as collated under the subject of trusts in our work for another jurisdiction. By consulting the text-books of Jarman, Wigram, Redfield and Willard, the reader, if he desire to pursue this subject further, will find ample room for investigation and research. We now pass to the probate of wills, through which they are put into execution.

SECTION II.—PROBATE OF WILLS.

1. Definition.
2. The probate record.
3. Duties of executor.
   1. Before probate.
   2. Before entering upon duty.
4. Practice.
5. Petition for letters.
6. Oath of executor.
7. His bond.
8. The hearing.
   1. Subpœna to witnesses.
   2. Attachment to compel attendance.
3. *Dedimus potestatem*.
4. Instructions.
5. Proof of wills.
   1. The decisions.
   2. The Statute.
9. Clerk's entries and forms of certificate of proof.
10. The letters testamentary.
11. Nuncupative will.
    1. Citation to persons interested.
    2. Notice to non-residents.
12. Foreign will.
13. Lost will.

1. THE PROBATE OF A WILL is the proof, made before an officer or court, designated by law for such purpose, that the instrument is the act of the person purporting to have executed it. The probate of a will is an absolute necessity of the law; the testator cannot evade it.(*j*)

All proceedings before the county court, the same being a court of record, produce, as at common law or in chancery, a record.

2. THE PROBATE RECORD is as essential as the chancery or the common-law record is, respectively, to such jurisdictions. And, because these courts are of special jurisdiction, even greater care is due to their preparation. It must never be forgotten that the record must affirmatively show the jurisdictional facts that collateral impeachment may be avoided.

A party seeking the probate of a will must file, in the office of the county or probate clerk of the proper county, a verified petition, and produce the will, if it be not lost or destroyed; upon this petition and the will the court immediately will act.

3. PRELIMINARY DUTIES OF EXECUTOR.

(1.) BEFORE PROBATE. The executor must see that the will is proved and recorded, within thirty days from the testator's death,

(*j*) *Harris* v. *Douglas*, 64 Ill. 466.

in the proper county, or he may present the will and declare his refusal to accept the executorship; either of these under penalty of a fine of twenty dollars per month after the expiration of the thirty days allowed him, which fine may be recovered by any person in any court of competent jurisdiction. Any person of the age of seventeen years, of sound mind and memory, may be an executor; but the court controls the estate, in all cases, where the executor is under twenty-one years of age, until he reaches his majority. (*k*) It is a statutory duty of the court, in the event of the appointment of a minor, one of unsound mind or one who is convicted of crime, unless there be another executor, who accepts the trust, to grant, to some competent person, administration with the will annexed, that he may act until the minor becomes of full age or the disability of the others be removed.

The power of the executor over the estate of the deceased, before probate of the will and obtaining letters testamentary, extends to the burial of the deceased, the payment of necessary funeral charges, and the taking care of the estate.(*l*)

(3.) BEFORE ENTERING UPON HIS DUTIES, he must apply to the court for letters testamentary, take the oath, and give a bond, with good and sufficient security, in a sum double the value of the estate.(*m*) Sureties may be waived, when the testator leaves visible estate more than sufficient to pay all his debts and shall so direct by his will, unless the court sitting in probate shall see cause, from its own knowledge or the suggestion of creditors or legatees, to suspect the executor of fraud, or that the personal estate will not be sufficient to satisfy all the debts.

4. PRACTICE; HOW TO BE APPOINTED EXECUTOR. Take the will to the county court of the proper county; obtain from the clerk a petition and a bond in blank; fill them out with care; write on the back of the petition the names of two persons to serve as appraisers; file them with the clerk; pay his costs and fees; have two of the subscribing witnesses to the will sworn, examined by the court and their testimony reduced to writing and filed in court. Present the bond signed and in a penalty of double the value of the estate to be administered; get the bond approved, file it and take the oath of office. These steps taken, the clerk will make the record, and issue letters testamentary. The record is made up of the petition, the bond, the oath, the orders, including the will and the testimony reduced to writing.

(*k*) §§ 2, 3, R. S. 1874, *p.* 104.
(*l*) § 4, id.

(*m*) §§ 6, 7, R. S. 1874, *p.* 105; Cothran's Statutes, 1880, *p.* 49.

Probate of wills.

The following form is used in the probate court of Cook county for the

5. Petition for Letters Testamentary.

State of Illinois, } ss: In the county court of   county.
    county.   Of the   Term, A. D. 18   .

To the Hon.   , judge of said court:

The petition of   respectfully shows that he is a resident of said county: that on the   day of   , A. D. 18   ,   of   , in said   county, departed this life at   , leaving a last will and testament, duly signed and attested as your petitioner believes, which he now presents to your honor for probate. That said testator in said will nominated your petitioner,   , executor thereof. That said deceased left property and effects as follows: (here state.)

That the value of the whole estate of said deceased does not exceed   dollars. That said deceased left him surviving   , his only heirs at law. That your petitioner resides at   , and   willing to accept and undertake the trust confided to   in said will, wherefore your petitioner prays that the said will may be admitted to probate, and letters testamentary thereon may be issued to   after proper hearing and proof, and that all other necessary orders may be made.

State of Illinois, } ss:
    County of   .

        , being duly sworn, says that the foregoing petition by   subscribed is true.

Sworn to and subscribed before me,   ,
clerk of the county court of   county,
this   day of   , A. D. 18   .
                                        , *Clerk.*

At the time of proving the will the executor will be required to take and subscribe the oath as follows:

6. Oath of Executor.

I do solemnly swear (or affirm), that this writing contains the true last will and testament of the within-named A B, deceased, so far as I know or believe; and that I will well and truly execute the same, by paying first the debts, and then the legacies mentioned therein, as far as his goods and chattels will thereunto extend, and the law charge me; and that I will make a true and perfect inventory of all such goods and chattels, rights and credits, as may come to my hands or knowledge, belonging to the estate of said deceased, and render a fair and just account of my executorship, when thereunto required by law, to the best of my knowledge and ability. So help me God.(*m*)

                    (Signed.)   A B.

This oath must be attached to and form a part of the probate.

(*m*) § 6, R. S. 1874, *p.* 105.

Probate of wills.

The bond is prescribed:

7. EXECUTOR'S BOND.

Know all men by these presents, that we,   , of the county of   , and State of Illinois, are held and firmly bound unto The People of the State of Illinois in the penal sum of   dollars, current money of the United States, which payment well and truly to be made and performed, we, and each of us, bind ourselves, our heirs, executors and administrators, jointly, severally and firmly by these presents.

Witness our hands and seals, this   day of   , A. D. 18   .*

The condition of the above obligation is such, that if the above bounden   , execut   of the last will and testament of   , deceased, do make or cause to be made a true and perfect inventory of all and singular the goods and chattels, rights and credits, lands, tenements and hereditaments, and the rents and profits issuing out of the same, of the said deceased, which have or shall come to the hands, possession or knowledge of the said   , or into the possession of any other person for   , and the same so made do exhibit in the county court for the said county of   , as required by law; and also make and render a fair and just account of   actings and doings, as such execut   , to said court, when thereunto lawfully required; and do well and truly fulfill the duties enjoined on   in and by the said will; and shall, moreover, pay and deliver to the persons entitled thereto all the legacies and bequests contained in said will, so far as the estate of the said testator will thereunto extend, according to the value thereof, and as the law shall charge   , and shall, in general, do all other acts which may, from time to time, be required of   by law, then this obligation to be void, otherwise to remain in full force and virtue.

[L. S.]
[L. S.]
[L. S.]

The bond must be approved, *i. e.,* the securities appear in person before the court, are examined by the court touching their responsibility, and, if approved, the approval is indorsed on the bond; it is then filed and recorded.(*n*)

8. THE HEARING OR EXAMINATION. Excepting in the case of a nuncupative will, it is not customary to give public notice of the hearing or examination. The practice prescribed for contesting the probate, is the bill in chancery, or an appeal.(*o*) The statute provides, first, that "when any will, testament or codicil shall be exhibited in the county court for probate thereof, as aforesaid, it

---

(*n*) § 7, R. S. 1874, *p.* 105.
(*o*) R. S. 1874, *p.* 1102. Parties in interest may contest in probate, as well as in chancery, or on appeal, hence the propriety, if not the necessity, of notice. *Duncan* v. *Duncan*, 23 Ill. 364.

Probate of wills.

shall be the duty of the court to receive probate of the same without delay, and to grant letters testamentary thereon to the person or persons entitled, and to do all other needful acts to enable the parties concerned to make settlement of the estate at as early a day as shall be consistent with the rights of the respective persons interested therein."

NOTICE. Although the statute prescribes no notice, yet notice should be given by citation (*p*) to all parties interested in the estate, of the time of the hearing; and before proceeding to allow or disallow the will, there should be ample opportunity for all to be heard. Within three years after the date of the probate, a bill in chancery may be filed to contest the validity of the will. An appeal may also be taken, and a hearing *de novo* had in the circuit court.(*p*) Where there is no contest, to satisfy the court and speed the proceedings, *waiver of notice* may and should be given by indorsing a request upon the application:

REQUEST AND WAIVER.

The undersigned, being all parties interested in the within petition, hereby request that said will be probated without further notice.

Dated at   , this   day of   , A. D. 18   .

                                                          A B.
                                                          C D.
                                                          E F.

In case the parties are numerous, non-resident or unknown, it might be well to publish a citation, as prescribed under a nuncupative will.(*q*)

(1.) SUBSCRIBING WITNESSES. It is the duty of the subscribing witnesses to appear under prescribed penalties, and testify concerning the execution and validity of the will. The ordinary process to bring in these witnesses is the

SUBPŒNA.

STATE OF ILLINOIS, } *ss*:
  County of   .

The People of the State of Illinois, to the sheriff of said county, greeting:

You are hereby commanded to summon O P, in your county, to appear before the county court of said county, at the court-house in said county, on the   day of   , then and there to testify the truth of, and concerning the execution and validity of, the last will and testament of A B, deceased, to

---

(*p*) See page 47, *infra*.   (*q*) See page 51, *infra*.

Probate of wills.

which his name appears as a subscribing witness. And have you then and there this writ.

Witness,   , clerk of our said court, and the seal thereof, at   ,
this   day of   , A. D. 18 .   , *Clerk.*

[SEAL.]

This may be served by any person *sui juris*, by reading it to the witness. One day's attendance and mileage should be paid to the witness.

If the witness fails or refuses to attend, on proof of the service by affidavit:

PROOF OF SERVICE.

STATE OF ILLINOIS, } *ss:*
Cook County.   }

L M, being duly sworn, says that he served the within subpœna upon O P therein named, by reading to him the same and paying (or tendering to) him in person, at   , in said county, on the   day of   , A. D. 18 the sum of $, for his attendance and mileage.   L M.

Subscribed and sworn to before me, this }
    day of   , A. D. 18 .   }
                     , *Clerk.*

The court would order an

(2.) ATTACHMENT.

(*Caption.*)

Whereas, the probate of a certain instrument, purporting to be the last will and testament of C D, late of O., in said county, deceased, is now pending in the county court of   county; and whereas, it has been made to appear that O P, of O., in said county, has been duly summoned to appear before our said court as a witness in said proceedings, and has been paid (or tendered) his legal fees therefor, and that the said O P has not so appeared, and has thereby committed a contempt of this court; now, therefore, you are hereby commanded to take the body of the said O P (if he may be found in your county) and bring him forthwith before our said court, to answer to the charge of contempt, and also to give evidence of what he knows in relation to the execution of said will. Hereof fail not, and make due return of this writ and the manner in which you have executed the same.

[L. S.]   (*Teste.*)

RETURN.

STATE OF ILLINOIS, } *ss:*
      County. }

I have this day arrested the within named O P, and now have him before the said court as within directed.   T. M. B., *Sheriff.*
                                                    By G. S., *Deputy.*

Probate of wills.

EXAMINATION OF THE WITNESSES. On the day appointed or set apart for the hearing, the witnesses being in attendance, the judge or counsel for the person seeking probate of the will propounds the usual interrogatories : What is your name ? Is this your signature ? Where do you live ? Did you see A B sign his name to this instrument ? Did you hear him acknowledge this name to be his signature ? Did he know at that time the contents of this instrument and declare it to be his last will and testament in your presence and in the presence of all the persons who signed this instrument ? Was he then of sound mind and memory ? Did you sign it in his presence ? Did you sign it at his request or by his consent ? About how old was A B when he signed or acknowledged said will?

It must satisfactorily appear, by the testimony of two or more credible witnesses, declaring on oath or affirmation, in open court (1) that they were present and saw the deceased sign the will or codicil in their presence, or acknowledged the same to be his free act and deed ; (2) that they believed the testator to be at that time of sound mind and memory. The witnesses are not required to be in the presence of each other when they sign their names ;(s) so, also, if the witnesses to a will are, while signing their names to it, where the testator can see them if he choose, they are practically in his presence within the meaning of the statute. (t)

The will itself must be in writing, and signed either by the testator or by some person in the testator's presence, by the testator's direction. It must be attested by two or more credible witnesses ; *i. e.,* two or more must subscribe it as witnesses.

These attesting witnesses are, if living, to be called to prove the will, if they reside in the county where the will is to be proved ; if they reside out of the county or State where the proceedings are pending, then the court will, on the suggestion of such fact, issue under its seal a

(3.) DEDIMUS.

STATE OF ILLINOIS,⎱ *ss :*
County of .⎰

The People of the State of Illinois, to
Whereas, it appears to us that , witness , attesting the will of , deceased, the probate of which will is now depending in our county court of county, in and for the county of , aforesaid, and that the said witness reside at , aforesaid, without the said State of Illinois, and that person attendance cannot be procured at the probate of said

---

(s) *Flinn* v. *Owen,* 58 Ill. 111.   (t) *Ambre* v. *Weiskaar,* 74 Ill. 109.

Probate of wills.

will: Now, know ye, that we, in confidence of your prudence and fidelity, have appointed you commissioner to examine the said witness   , and do therefore authorize and require you to cause the said witness   to come before you, at such time and place as you may therefor designate and appoint, and diligently to examine the said witness   , on the oath or affirmation of the said witness   by you first duly in that behalf administered, and faithfully to take and certify in due form of law the attestation of the said witness   to said will, which is herewith inclosed; and the same, when thus taken, together with this commission and the said will, to certify into our said county court of   county with the least possible delay.

Witness,   , clerk of our said court, and seal thereof at   , in said county, this   day of   , A. D. 18   .

, *Clerk.*

[SEAL.]

From the probate court of Cook county every dedimus is accompanied with specific instructions, as follows:

(4.) INSTRUCTIONS.

AS TO THE MODE OF TAKING, CERTIFYING AND RETURNING DEPOSITIONS ACCORDING TO THE STATUTE LAWS OF ILLINOIS.

[1. *Caption to the deposition.*]

The attestation of   , of the county of   and State (or "Territory") of   , a witness of lawful age, produced, sworn and examined, upon his corporal oath, on the   day of   , in the year of our Lord one thousand eight hundred and   , at the office (or "house") of   , in the town (or "city") of   , in the county of   , and State (or "Territory") aforesaid, by me,   , a commissioner (or "by us," if more than one commissioner, inserting all the names of the commissioners) duly appointed by a *dedimus potestatum* or commission issued out of the clerk's office of the county court of   county, in the State of Illinois, bearing *teste* in the name of   , Esq., clerk of the said county court, with the seal of the said court affixed thereto, and to me (or "us," if more than one) directed as such commissioner (or "commissioners") for the examination of the said   , a witness to the will of   , deceased, the probate of which will is now pending and undetermined in the said county court.

The said   , being first duly sworn by me (or "by   , one of the said commissioners, if more than one) as a witness in the matter of the probate of said will, previous to the commencement of his examination, to testify the truth in relation to said will, so far as he knew, testified and deposed as follows:

(Here insert the testimony of witness.)

After the deposition is taken, the testimony should be read over to the witness, and if he assents to the truth of the testimony as

Probate of wills.

written down, the witness will then sign his name at the bottom of the deposition, and swear to the truth of it before the commissioner (or "before one of the commissioners," if more than one). This oath is in addition to the preliminary oath which is administered previous to the commencement of his examination.

The commissioner should then certify as to the time, place and manner of taking the attestation, as follows:

I,   , of the county of   , and State (or Territory) of   , a commissioner duly appointed to take the attestation of the said   , a witness, whose name is subscribed to the foregoing attestation, do hereby certify that, previous to the commencement of the examination of the said   as a witness in the matter of the probate of the annexed will of   , deceased, he was duly sworn by me as such commissioner (or " by   , one of said commissioners," if more than one), to testify the truth in relation to the matter of said will, so far as he knew concerning the same; that the said attestation was taken at my office (or "at the house of   "), in the city (or "town") of   , in the county of   , and State (or " Territory ") of   , on the   day of   , A. D. 18   ; and that after said attestation was taken by me (or " us ") as aforesaid, the testimony of said witness, as written down, was read over to the said witness; and that thereupon the same was signed and sworn to by the said witness   , before me (or " us "), the oath being administered by   , one of the said commissioners (where there are more than one), as such commissioner, at the place and on the day and year last aforesaid.

(Signed)   , *Commissioner*.

The foregoing certificate of the commission should be at the foot or bottom of the attestation, immediately following the signature of the witness.

The commissioner should then fold up the attestation as thus taken and certified, together with the commission, and inclose the whole in a suitable wrapper or envelope, and then seal up the same securely with three seals, writing his name transversely across the middle seal; or, if two commissioners, they will each write their names, one on each of the outside seals; or, if three commissioners, then each one will write his name across one of the seals in manner aforesaid. The commissioner (or commissioners) will also indorse the proper title of the proceeding transversely across one end of the package thus sealed up, according to the proper title of the proceeding, thus: "In matter of the probate of the will of   , deceased," and direct the same to the proper address of the clerk, who may have issued the commission, and transmit the same by mail to the

Probate of wills.

proper post-office. No person, or the attorneys or agents of any person, at all interested in the event of the proceeding, are permitted by law to dictate, write or draw up any part of the attestation required to be taken as aforesaid. This commission issues in pursuance of section 4 of the act of March 20, 1872, of the general assembly of the State of Illinois, the directions and provisions of which are to be followed in the execution of said commission, and is in the words and figures following:

"When any will, testament or codicil shall be produced to the county court for probate of the same, and any witness attesting such will, testament or codicil shall reside without the limits of this State or the county in which such will, testament or codicil is produced for probate, or shall be unable to attend said court, it shall be lawful for the county court to issue a *dedimus potestatum* or commission, annexed to such will, testament or codicil, directed to some judge, justice of the peace, mayor or other chief magistrate of the city, town, corporation or county where such witness may be found, authorizing the taking and certifying of his or her attestation in due form of law. And if the person to whom any such commission shall be directed shall certify, in the manner that such acts are usually authenticated, that the witness personally appeared before him, and made oath or affirmation that the testator or testatrix signed and published the writing annexed to such commission, or acknowledge the execution thereof, as his or her last will and testament, or that some other person signed the testator's name by his or her direction; that he or she was of sound mind and memory, and that said witness subscribed his or her name as a witness thereto, in the presence of the testator or testatrix, and at his or her request, such oath or affirmation shall have the same operation, and the will shall be admitted to probate in like manner as if such oath or affirmation had been made in the court from whence such commission issued."

N. B. — It is important to the validity of the attestation that these requirements and instructions should be strictly attended to. One caption will answer for the attestations of several witnesses, where they are all taken at the same time and place, to be read as evidence in the same suit, by so modifying the form here given as to make it applicable to the number of witnesses to be examined; as, for instance, at the commencement, say: "The attestations of A B, C D and E F, of the county of   and State of   , witnesses of law-

Probate of wills.

ful age, produced, sworn and examined on their respective corporal oaths," etc., and then in the latter part of the caption say: "The said A B, C D, and E F, being first duly sworn by me as witnesses in the said matter," etc. Then at the commencement of each attestation say: "The said A B, a witness produced and sworn as aforesaid, in the matter of the probate of the will of   , deceased."

The attestation should then be read over to the witness, and signed and sworn to by him before the next witness is examined. Then proceed with the second and third witnesses in like manner to the end.

One certificate as to the time, place and manner of taking such attestation, and that each one was signed and sworn to by such witnesses respectively, will be sufficient, provided due care be taken to insert the names of ALL the witnesses, and the certificate in other respects be in conformity with the form given in the first instance.

Great care should always be taken to attach such attestation firmly together by means of tape or ribbon, and using wax or wafers when necessary.

TO WHOM THE *DEDIMUS* MAY ISSUE. This dedimus may issue to some judge, justice of the peace, mayor or other chief magistrate of the city, town or corporation or county where such witnesses may be found.

HOW OBTAINED. File an affidavit in form substantially as follows:

STATE OF ILLINOIS,} *ss:* *County court of   county. In probate.*
County of   .

In the matter of the probate of }
the last will and testament of }
A B, deceased.   }

STATE OF ILLINOIS,} *ss:*
County of   .

L M, being duly sworn, says that O P, one of the subscribing witnesses to the said will, now resides at the city of New York, in the State of New York.
(*Jurat.*)   L M.

Under the statute of 1872, the dedimus is to be annexed to the will, testament or codicil, directed as above to a judge or magistrate, authorizing the taking and certifying of the attestation in due form of law,(*t*)

(*t*) §§ 4, 7, R. S. 1874, *p.* 1102.

Mr. Jones gives a short form for the dedimus(*u*), with the prescribed certificates, as follows:

(Venue.)   DEDIMUS.

The People of the State of Illinois: To J. L., a Justice of the Peace in and for   county, State of   , greeting:

Whereas, the annexed last will and testament has been produced to the county court of said county for probate thereof; and it is suggested that O P, one of the subscribing witnesses to the same, is to be found in   county and State of   ; you are, therefore, hereby authorized to take and certify the attestation of the said O P, if to be found in your county, to the said last will and testament in due form of law, and to make return thereof to this court.

[L. S.]   (*Teste.*)

The proof required by the foregoing dedimus must be in one of the following forms, both of which should accompany the dedimus, as an instruction to the commissioner.

The certificate may be as follows:

No. 1.

STATE OF   } *ss:*
County of

In pursuance of the authority in me vested, by the annexed dedimus, I, this day, caused personally to come before me, a justice of the peace of said county, at   , in said county, the said O P, who, being duly sworn, on his oath, did say, that the said A B signed and published the writing annexed to said dedimus as his last will and testament; that the said testator, at the time of signing and publishing the same, was of sound mind and memory, and that the said O P subscribed his name as a witness thereto, in the presence of the said testator, and at his request.   J L.

Given under my hand and seal, this }
     day of   , 18 .   }
         A B.

Or as follows:

No. 2.

STATE OF   } *ss:*
County of

In pursuance of the authority in me vested, by the annexed dedimus, I, this day, caused personally to come before me, a justice of the peace of said county, the said O P, who, after being duly sworn, on his oath, did say that he was present at the time when the writing annexed to said dedimus was signed and published as the last will and testament of the said A B; that Mr.   signed the name of the said A B thereto by the direction of the said A B, and in the presence of the said O P; that the said A B, at the time the same

(*u*) Jones' Forms, pp. 343, 344.

was signed and published, was of sound mind and memory, and that the said O P subscribed his name as a witness thereto, in the presence of the said testator, and at his request. J L.

(*Jurat.*)

Where subscribing witnesses' depositions are wanted, the short forms of Mr. Jones are to the point and applicable. But in case such subscribing witnesses, or any of them, die or remove to parts unknown to the parties concerned, then it becomes necessary to use the general form(*v*) which has obtained under the general statute of evidence.(*w*)

5. PRACTICE. Before admitting the will to probate, it should affirmatively appear from the testimony and the record and files of the court, as follows:

(1.) That the court is the proper court to receive the will.

(2.) That the testator is dead.

(3.) That the application or petition is in form, good in substance, and properly verified.

(4.) That due notice of the hearing has been given, if notice has been ordered and citations issued; and proper proofs of service and publication must be filed. The returns to the dedimus, if any, must be in form, etc.

(5.) Then it must be proved beyond a doubt that the instrument presented and under consideration is the last will and testament of the decedent, according to the Statute of Wills.

The first two points are essential to jurisdiction, for if the court be not the court of the proper county, or if the testator be not yet dead, the court has no jurisdiction.(*x*) The third and fourth points relate to the practice, which we have endeavored to carefully detail and display. If the petition be defective, it may, then, be amended and cured; if sufficient notice has not been given, the hearing should be continued until proper notice has been given. If the depositions are objectionable or insufficient, they may be retaken. In matters of practice of this nature the court has, by the statute, a large discretion.(*y*) "To do all other needful acts" covers the broadest discretionary power. The constitution conferring, as we have seen,(*z*) original jurisdiction, and the statute power to do all other needful

(*v*) See pp. 33–37, *supra*.
(*w*) 2 Hill's C. L., Evidence, p. 294; § 6, R. S. 1874, *p.* 1102.
(*x*) See VENUE, page 14, *supra*.
(*y*) § 7, R. S. 1874, *p.* 1102.
(*z*) See page 7, *supra*.

Probate of wills.

acts, the scope of the jurisdiction is as broad as it could well be made. Hence, we have added the resume of the decisions of the supreme court, that from the highest stand-point known to our law, the subject before us may be carefully studied, and the probate business be continually held up to its proper place and dignity alongside of the venerated systems of chancery and common law. The fifth point is the all-important consideration. The issue is, whether or not the instrument submitted be the last will and testament of the decedent? If yea, the will should be received and probated. If nay, it should be promptly rejected.

To test the instrument, the requisites of a will, generally, have already been considered.(*a*) Now comes their application. The following questions must all be answered by the testimony in the affirmative, to prove the will:

(1.) Was the testator, at the time of making the alleged will, a person of lawful age?

(2.) Was the testator, at the time of making the alleged will, "a person of sound mind and memory?"

(3.) Is the will "reduced to writing?"

(4.) Was it signed either "by the testator or by some person in his or her presence, and by his or her direction?"

(5.) Was it attested in the presence of the testator by two or more credible witnesses.

(6.) Had the testator, at the time of his decease, a mansion-house or known place of residence in this county? If nay, does he devise lands? If yea, are they or any of them in this county? If nay, did he die in this county? If nay, is the estate, or a greater part thereof, in this county?

To solve these questions takes us through the whole range of the probate of the will on the merits, brings us back to the point of departure — the jurisdiction, and requires a careful study of the statute in the light of the decisions. We will now examine the adjudicated cases.

(1.) PROOF OF WILLS. On an appeal from an order of the court sitting in probate, admitting a will to record, a party seeking to establish a will must prove the testator was of disposing mind and memory at the time he made it, and this cannot be shown merely by proof that he was so at some anterior period. And in such case, the defendants having

---

(*a*) See page 17, *supra*.

Probate of wills.

put in evidence the testimony of the subscribing witnesses to the will, given when it was admitted to probate, it then devolved upon the plaintiff to show the incompetency of the testator, by proof sufficient to overcome the *prima facie* case made through the testimony of the subscribing witnesses. It is no objection that the attesting witnesses to a will were not present when it was signed by the testator; provided he acknowledged it as his will and requested them to sign as witnesses.(*c*) In this State a subscribing witness need not know that he has been attesting the execution of a will, the statute not requiring any declaration or publication.(*d*) A testator, after signing his will, called the subscribing witnesses into the room, and after causing the attestation clause to be read to them, handed them a pen with which they signed in his presence. *Held*, that the acknowledgment was sufficient, and the execution valid. Where one of the subscribing witnesses to a will testified that he does not know whether the testator was of sound mind or not, the proof of the will is defective.(*e*) In this State evidence is admissible in probate of a will, by one of the subscribing witnesses that the testator either signed the will in his presence or acknowledged his signature to him, he could not remember which.(*f*)

By the ordinance of 1817, but two of the subscribing witnesses to a will are required to prove it, and a will attested by three, one to whom is a devisee in the will, is valid.(*g*) As with deeds, so with wills, the parties making them cannot invalidate them by their own parol declarations made previously or subsequently, and evidence thereof is not admissible upon the issue of validity.(*h*) A will written on the same sheet as a codicil, or unmistakably referred to in it, is proved by proof of the codicil, so far as the latter does not revoke it. Under our statute, parties in interest may contest a will in the probate court as well as in chancery, and, therefore, should be allowed to cross-examine the attesting witnesses in the probate court.(*i*) After detailing the facts on which an opinion is based, a witness, not an expert, may express that opinion to the jury, as to the soundness of mind of a testator.(*j*)

(*c*) *Holloway* v. *Galloway*, 51 Ill. 159.
(*d*) *Dickie* v. *Carter*, 42 Ill. 376.
(*e*) *Allison* v. *Allison*, 46 Ill. 61.
(*f*) *Brownfield* v. *Brownfield*, 43 Ill. 147; *Flinn* v. *Owen*, 58 Ill. 111.
(*g*) *Ackless* v. *Seekright*, Breese, 46.

(*h*) *Dickie* v. *Carter*, 42 Ill. 376; *Rutherford* v. *Morris*, 77 Ill. 397.
(*i*) *Duncan* v. *Duncan*, 23 Ill. 364; *Wolf* v. *Bollinger*, 62 Ill. 368.
(*j*) *Roe* v. *Taylor*, 45 Ill. 485.

Probate of wills.

The acquisition of lands confers no fixed and permanent right for an individual to devise them, according to the law, at the time of the acquisition. (*l*) The statute of wills (Rev. Stats., 1845, p. 536, § 1) and conveyances (id., p. 102, § 1), enables a testator to convey by will after acquired lands without republication. The only question is of intention. (*m*) Where the certificate to the probate of a will in a foreign State shows that it was executed and proved according to the laws of that State, and such certificate is in the mode required by our statute, it is admissible in evidence. And it is no objection that the will was proved by only one of the subscribing witnesses, when, by the laws of the State where such will was made, but one witness was necessary to prove its execution. (*n*) A will not properly authenticated is not admissible as evidence for any purpose. (*o*) Where the certificate of the probate of a will, made in another State, shows that the will was duly executed and proved agreeably to the laws and usages of such State, and such certificate is conformable to the statute of this State (Rev. Stats., ch. 109, § 8), the will is sufficiently proved. A will executed and proved in another State need not be filed in the probate court of this State. (*p*) The act of taking proof of the execution of a will is a ministerial, and not a judicial act, and is not conclusive of the validity of the will; and a will cannot be read in evidence, in a suit of ejectment, which was admitted to probate upon insufficient proof. (*q*)

Where a testator bequeaths a debt due him to a legatee, the legatee cannot resort to a court of equity for its recovery. (*r*) Where a will directs that the testator's real estate may be disposed of by his executor, but omits to appoint any executor, an administrator with the will annexed has no authority to sell such real estate under the will. (*s*) Under the statute, on appeal from the decision of the probate court, in relation to the probate of a will, it is proper for the circuit court to direct the trial to be had before a jury, and on such trial it is not competent for either party to introduce any testimony in relation to the sanity of the testator, except that of the subscribing witnesses, who may be sworn and testify before a jury; and

(*l*) *Sturgis* v. *Ewing,* 18 Ill. 176.
(*m*) *Peters* v. *Spillman,* 18 Ill. 370.
(*n*) *Gardner* v. *Ladue,* 47 Ill. 211; see 2 Hill's C. L. 403.
(*o*) *Farrell* v. *Patterson,* 43 Ill. 52.

(*p*) *Shephard* v. *Carriel,* 19 Ill. 313; and see 2 Hill's C. L. 403.
(*q*) *Furguson* v. *Hunter,* 2 Gilm. 657.
(*r*) *Doyle* v. *Murphy,* 22 Ill. 502.
(*s*) *Hall* v. *Irwin,* 2 Gilm. 176.

Probate of wills.

unless two of said witnesses concur in the belief that the testator was of sound mind at the time of executing the will, it cannot be admitted to probate. The belief of the witnesses may be formed not only upon what transpired at the time of executing the will, but also upon events which happened before ; and the jury need not inquire into the foundation of the witnesses' belief, nor the circumstances under which, nor the time when, such belief was formed. The trial in the circuit court should be *de novo ;* and as to all the questions, except the sanity of the testator, the parties are not restricted to the testimony of the subscribing witnesses or the evidence adduced before the court of probate.(*t*) The rule, however, is different in the case of an appeal from an order denying the probate of a will. The party seeking its probate is not confined to the two attesting witnesses to establish either the execution of the will, or the sanity of the testator.(*u*) On the trial of an issue out of chancery, arising under the Revised Statutes, 1845, ch. 109, section 6, the burden of proof is on the party affirming the execution and validity of the will, and he has the right to open and conclude the argument of the cause. Under such an issue, the party holding the affirmative is bound to prove that the contested paper is the last will and testament of the testator.(*v*)

On trial of an issue of fact under a bill to impeach a will, unless objected to when offered, the original affidavit, required by the statute to be filed in the county court in proof of the execution of the will, may be read to the jury in evidence instead of a certified copy thereof.(*w*) Notwithstanding the probate, the issue is to be submitted to the jury as a new and original question, to be determined exclusively upon the evidence introduced before them. The trial is *de novo,* and without regard to the fact that the instrument has been admitted to probate.(*v*) The certificate of the oaths of the attesting witnesses, at the time of the probate, may be offered in evidence by either party ; but it is to receive such weight only as the jury may think it deserves, in connection with the other proof in the case. On the question of the sanity of the testator, no particular quantum of evidence is necessary in order to sustain the validity of the will, upon the trial of an issue out of chancery, under the statute ; but

(*t*) Gale's Stat. 718; *Walker* v. *Walker,* 2 Scam. 291 ; 80 Ill. 469.
(*u*) *Crowley* v. *Crowley,* 80 Ill. 469.
(*v*) *Rigg* v. *Wilton,* 13 Ill. 15.
(*w*) *Potter* v. *Potter,* 41 Ill. 80.

the jury should determine the facts upon the weight of evidence as in other cases. It is not essential that the subscribing witnesses should be called, or that, when called, they should concur in their testimony; other witnesses may be examined, even to contradict the subscribing witnesses.(*w*) The omission to name a child in a last will does not, of itself, prove that the testator was incapacitated, nor will such omission destroy its validity.(*x*) The fact that a testator had been insane some years prior to the execution of his last will, does not create a presumption that insanity was present at the time of the publication of it; especially where it is shown that, after a cure, no symptoms of a return of the malady were ever manifested.(*x*) A contestant of a will, on the ground of insanity, fraud or other cause, has the burden of proof.(*y*) To invalidate a will on the ground of fraud or compulsion, it must be of such a character as to destroy the testator's free agency.(*y*) Mere honest argument or persuasion, and such influence as one person may properly obtain over another, are insufficient to affect the validity of the will.(*z*) On a bill seeking to set aside a will on the ground of undue influence, evidence is inadmissible for the purpose of disproving the charge of a previous will which has been canceled, the testamentary disposition of which is totally variant from those made by the will in question. On a bill seeking to set aside a will on the ground of undue influence, where a witness has expressed a decided opinion as to the mental capacity of the testator, it is proper, on cross-examination, to inquire as to business transactions with the testator, occurring at about the time his opinion of the mental capacity of the testator had reference to, and as to how the testator, at that time, conducted himself. An understanding of the nature of the business about which a testator is engaged, of the kind and value of the property devised, and of the persons who are the natural objects of his bounty, and of the manner in which he wished to dispose of his property, is evidence of the possession of testamentary capacity, unless the testator is affected with some morbid or insane delusion as to some one of those natural objects of his bounty.(*z*) See NOTE, p. 51.

(2.) THE ACTS OF 1872. We are now prepared to understandingly recapitulate the statutory requirements.(*a*)

(*w*) *Rigg* v. *Wilton*, 13 Ill. 15.
(*x*) *Snow* v. *Benton*, 28 Ill. 306.
(*y*) *Dickie* v. *Carter*, 42 Ill. 376; *Roe* v. *Taylor*, 45 id. 485.

(*z*) *Roe* v. *Taylor*, 45 Ill. 485.
(*a*) §§ 1, 2, R. S. 1874, p. 1101.

Probate of wills.

OF LAWFUL AGE. A male, 21; female, 18.

OF SOUND MIND AND MEMORY. This must be shown by the fact that, when they saw the will made, they believed the testator to be of sound mind and memory. If there be any doubt on this point, the questions arising would require considerations involving much of medical jurisprudence, to which we have room only to refer.(*b*)

REDUCED TO WRITING. A will may be written or printed. If written, the writing may be in ink or by pencil.(*c*)

SIGNED BY THE TESTATOR or by some person in his or her presence, and by his or her direction. The signature may be by mark, and if so, it will be presumed that the testator could not write his name in full.(*d*)

If signed by some other person, it must have been in the name and presence of the testator, at the express request of the testator, in the presence of at least two of the subscribing witnesses; a silent assent of the testator is not sufficient.(*e*)

The court must, upon the whole, be satisfied that the testator was fully apprised of its contents; and knew and intended the instrument to be his will.(*e*)

ATTESTED IN THE PRESENCE OF THE TESTATOR.(*f*) Credible witnesses(*g*), *i. e.*, competent witnesses before a jury.

WHEN THE COUNTY JUDGE IS A WITNESS; HIS TESTIMONY, HOW TAKEN.

In all cases where a county judge, or such other person as may be authorized by law to grant probate of wills and testaments, may and shall have become a witness to any will or testament which is required by law to be proved before him as such county judge or person authorized to grant probate, as aforesaid, and the testimony of such witness is necessary to the proof of the same, then, and in such case, it shall be his duty to go before the circuit court of the county in which such will is to be admitted to record, and make proof of the execution of the same, in the same manner that probate of wills is required to be made in other cases. And it shall be the duty of the clerk of the circuit court aforesaid, forthwith to certify such will,

---

(*b*) 1 Redf. ch. 3, and cases and works cited.
(*c*) Id., p. 165.
(*d*) Id., p. 205.
(*e*) Id., 207; 42 Ill. 376; note (*n*), p. 47, *infra*.
(*f*) 4 Kent's Com. 514 (*b*).
(*g*) *Jones* v. *Larrabee*, 47 Me. 474.

Probate of wills.

proven as aforesaid, to the county court of the county; and said will shall thereupon have the same force and effect that it would have had if it had been proven by one credible witness before the county court; and, if there are other witnesses to said will, the county court shall take their evidence in support of said will, as in other cases.(*i*)

ATTESTING CREDITOR. If any lands, tenements or hereditaments shall be charged with any debt or debts, by any will, testament or codicil, and the creditor whose debt is so secured shall attest the execution of the same, such creditor shall, notwithstanding, be admitted as a witness to the execution thereof.(*j*)

We now turn to the record.

Mr. Jones gives forms for certificates of the proof of wills, which seem eminently proper as certificates of evidence in such matters when the will is proved in common form, *i. e.*, not contested in probate.(*k*)

STATE OF ILLINOIS, } *ss.* County court of   county. *In probate.*
County.

In the matter of the last will and }
testament of A B, deceased.

At a regular term of said court for probate business, and on the   day of   , A. D. 18   , personally appeared before me, J. S., judge of said court, the above-named O. P. and G. R., two credible witnesses, who, being duly sworn, on their oaths depose and say that * they were present and saw the above-named A B sign the above last will and testament in their presence; that they believed, and still believe, that the said A B was of sound mind and memory at the time of signing the same; and that they attested the signing of said last will and testament, in the presence and by the request of the said A B, and in presence of each other.

[L. S.]   In testimony whereof, I have hereunto set my hand and affixed the seal of said court, this   day of   , A. D. 18   .

J. S., *County judge, etc.*(*l*)

If the will was not signed by the deceased himself, but by some person for him, at his request, and acknowledged by him, then the proof will be as follows:

(*The certificate should be as before to the *, then as follows:*)
they were present at the signing of the above will, and that the said A B directed Mr.   to sign the same for him; and the same being signed in his presence, was acknowledged by the said A B to be his own act and deed; and that they then believed, and still believe, that the said testator, at the time of

(*i*) § 5, R. S. 1874, *p.* 1102.
(*j*) § 20, R. S. 1874, p. 1105.
(*k*) Jones' Forms, pp. 341, 342.
(*l*) This certificate should be signed by the judge, and not the clerk, the probate being a judicial act. (Compare *Ferguson* v. *Hunter*, 2 Gilm. 657, with § 2, R. S. 1874, *p.* 1101.)

Probate of wills.

acknowledging the same, was of sound mind and memory; and that they attested the acknowledging of the said last will and testament, in the presence and by the request of the said A B, and in the presence of each other.

[L. S.]

(*Teste*, as above.)

The certificate (or certificates if there be more than one) should be attached to the will and recorded as a part of it.(*m*) These certificates are like the certificates of evidence used here in chancery.(*n*) Whenever the subscribing witnesses appear in court, they may be examined, and, if parties in interest desire, cross-examined, and their testimony rebutted(*n*) and certificates made; the hearing, however, may take place at some subsequent time, upon this evidence and

(*m*) § 2, R. S. 1874, *p.* 1101.
(*n*) Hill's Ch. Pr., Hearing and Decree, p. 307. To entitle a will to probate four things must concur:
1. It must be in writing and signed by the testator, or in his or her presence by some one under his or her dictation.
2. It must be attested by two or more credible witnesses.
3. Two witnesses must prove that they saw the testator or testatrix sign the will in their presence, or that he or she acknowledged the same to be his or her free act and deed; and
4. They must swear that they believe the testator or testatrix to be of sound mind and memory at the time of signing and acknowledging the same. *Allison* v. *Allison* 46 Ill. 61; *Dickie* v. *Carter*, 42 id. 376; 80 id. 460.

In *Dickie* v. *Carter*, the heirs contested the will in the county court, and it was there rejected; Carter appealed; a jury trial was had, to whom the question, " Is this the will of (the testator), or not?" was submitted. The jury found in the affirmative; judgment was entered accordingly; a writ of error was sued out and the judgment was affirmed. See 3 Redf. Wills, 2d ed. pp. 40, 41.

The proviso of § 2 of the act of March, 1872 (R. S. 1874, *p.* 1101). prescribes that the probate shall be good and available in law for granting, conveying and assuring the lands, tenements, hereditaments, annuities, rents, goods and chattels therein and thereby devised, granted and bequeathed." But in *Ferguson* v. *Hunter*,* 2 Gilm. 657, where a will was proved in common form, *i. e.*, without notice to the parties interested, the probate was held to be a ministerial act, and subject to inquiry in collateral action. *Ackless* v. *Seekright*, Breese, 46.

In *Duncan* v. *Duncan*, 23 Ill. 364, it was held that our statute (and it is not in this respect changed by the acts of 1872) contemplated the contesting of the will in the county court as well as in chancery. We have already suggested the propriety of notice to the parties interested on the part of the executor or others seeking the probate of the will. If the heirs have the right to be heard they certainly should be notified, especially where titles to real property may be called in question; and the will thus, in the first instance, be proved in solemn form, *i. e.*, on notice to the parties interested. See *Ferguson* v. *Hunter, supra;* 3 Redf. Wills, 27, 30.*

---

* We have read the case of *Ferguson* v. *Hunter*, again and again, and compared it with recent statutes, and tried to reconcile it with the authorities. We are prone to think that the word *ministerial* was used without the consideration usually bestowed by the learned judge who gives the opinion. Is not the probate of a will a judicial act? See 2 Phil. Ev. 76.

other proofs and the files of the court. The order is made in the nature of a judgment.

If any of the proof should be taken under a dedimus, the county judge may indorse upon the deposition a certificate:

Received in evidence this   day of   , A. D. 18 .   J. S.,
County judge, etc.

9. PROOF OF THE EXECUTION OF A WILL, AND THE RECORD.

In the matter of the estate }
of John Doe, deceased.(*o*) }

On this day comes A B, of said county, and produces to the court an instrument in writing, purporting to be the last will and testament of John Doe, deceased, and attested by C D, E F and J K, as witnesses; and the said A B prays that said instrument in writing be admitted to record as the last will and testament of the said John Doe.

And it appearing to the court by the evidence of said A B, that said John Doe, late of said county of   , died on or about the   day of   , 18 , at the said county, the court proceeded to hear the proof of the execution of said instrument in writing.

And thereupon come C D and E F, two of the said attesting witnesses, who, being first duly sworn, say, respectively, that they were well acquainted with John Doe, late of said county, deceased, in his life-time. The instrument in writing so produced by said A B, purporting to be the last will and testament of said John Doe, being shown them, they each further say that they were present at the execution of said will, and saw the said John Doe sign it on the day of the date thereof, and heard said John Doe say then and there that said instrument in writing was his last will and testament; that they subscribed their names as witnesses thereto, at the request of the said John Doe, in his presence and in the presence of each other, and that they respectively believe that the said John Doe was then of sound mind and memory, and competent to make a will.

(If the probate be in solemn form, or contested, add, "and the said witnesses having also been cross-examined by X Y, of counsel for C D, E F, G H, parties interested in the estate of said A B, and proofs as follows: (*Here set out all testimony in rebuttal*) by the said C D, E F and G H, having also been adduced.")

And now the court being sufficiently advised by the evidence of said attesting witnesses, of the proper and legal execution of the said will, it is

ORDERED and adjudged, That said instrument in writing be considered proven, and be admitted to record as the last will and testament of said John Doe, deceased.

This day also appears A B, named in said last will and testatemt of said John

---

(*o*) After the probate of the will, this title should be used in all proceedings; before this the title should be as   at page 37, *supra*; see Probate Record, *infra*.

Probate of wills.

Doe, deceased, as the executor thereof, and prays that the court issue to him letters testamentary as said executor; and the court being now sufficiently advised touching the same, it is

ORDERED, That letters testamentary issue to the said A B, as such executor, upon his entering into bond in the penal sum of   dollars, conditioned and payable as the law requires.

And now again comes the said A B, and presents to the court his bond as executor, etc., with L M and O P as his securities thereon; and the court being advised concerning said bond and securities, it is

ORDERED, That the same be approved, which bond is in the words and figures as follows: (*Here set out the bond in full.*) And the said A B, having taken his oath of office as such executor, which oath is in the words and figures as follows: (*Here set out the oath in full.*) it is

ORDERED, That letters testamentary do now issue to him, which letters are in words and figures as follows: (*Here set out the letters in full*); and it is further

ORDERED, That (L M, O P and Q R) be appointed appraisers of the said estate.

This record is to be made by the clerk from time to time as the proceedings are progressing. The first order is, that the will be admitted to record. If it be rejected, the probate record, of course, is at an end.

When a will has been duly proved and allowed, the county court shall issue letters testamentary thereon to the executor named in such will, if he is legally competent and accepts the trust, and gives bonds to discharge the same; and when there is no executor named in such will, or the executor named therein dies, refuses to act, or is otherwise disqualified, the court shall commit the administration of the estate unto the widow, surviving husband, next of kin or creditor, the same as if the testator had died intestate. In all cases copies of the will shall go out with the letters.(*p*)

10. The form of the letters to be issued upon the probate is prescribed as follows:

LETTERS TESTAMENTARY.(*q*)

STATE OF ILLINOIS,
County of   . } *ss*:

The People of the State of Illinois, to all to whom these presents shall come, greeting:

Know ye, that whereas   , late of the county of   , and State of Illinois, died on or about the   day of   , A. D. 18   , as it is said, after having duly made and published   last will and testament, a copy whereof is

(*p*) § 1, R. S. 1874, *p.* 104. (*q*) § 10, R. S. 1874, *p.* 106.

Probate of wills.

hereunto annexed, leaving at the time of   death property in this State, which may be lost, destroyed or diminished in value if speedy care be not taken of the same; and inasmuch as it appears that   ha   been appointed execut   in and by the said last will and testament, to execute the same; and to the end that the said property may be preserved for those who shall appear to have legal right or interest therein, and that said will may be executed according to the request of the said testa   , we do hereby authorize   , the said   , as such execut   , to collect and secure all and singular the goods and chattels, rights and credits which were of the said   at the time of   decease, in whosesoever hands or possession the same may be found in this State; and well and truly to perform and fulfill all such duties as may be enjoined upon   by the said will, so far as there shall be property, and the law charge   , and, in general, to do and perform all other acts which are now, or hereafter may be, required of   by law.

Witness,   , clerk of the county court of said county, and the seal thereof, at the court-house, in the   of   , in said county, this   day of   , A. D. 18   .

, Clerk.

They are usually certified:

CERTIFICATE OF THE CLERK.

STATE OF ILLINOIS, } ss :
  County of   . }

I,   , clerk of the county court of   county, in the State aforesaid, do hereby certify that the within is a true and correct copy of the letters testamentary issued to   , now in force, and now of record in my office.

In witness whereof I have hereunto set my hand, and the seal of said county court, this   day of   , A. D. 18   .

[L. S.]

, Clerk.

And competent evidence of the appointment and confirmation of the executor.

This completes the record of the proceedings; armed now with his letters and a certified copy of the will and its probate, the executor is prepared to study and learn his duties, and ascertain and exercise his powers.

11. NUNCUPATIVE WILL. (1.) If the application be for letters testamentary upon the admission to probate of a nuncupative will, the heirs and legal representatives of the testator must be cited if they reside within the county, or notified if they live without, by advertisement.(r) As the statute of wills does not prescribe the length

---

(r) Coth. Ann'd. Stats., 1539, § 16.

CH. II.] TESTATE ESTATES. 51

Probate of wills.

of time during which the notice be published, in the event that publication is necessary, reference must be had to an act to revise the law in relation to notices, passed February 13, 1874, and which took effect July 1 of that year. By section 3 of that act it is provided "whenever notice is required by law or order of court and the number of publications is not specified, it shall be intended that the same be published for three successive weeks." By section 4 the publication may be in a weekly newspaper, and, by section 5, a proper newspaper is defined to be a secular newspaper of general circulation, published in the city, town or county, or some paper especially authorized to publish legal notices in the city, town or county. The publication may be proved by producing the certificate of the publisher, by himself or his authorized agent, with a written or printed copy of the notice annexed, stating the number of times which the same shall have been published, and the dates of the first and last papers containing the same. (s)

The following may be used as both a notice and a citation:

(2.) NOTICE TO HEIRS AND LEGAL REPRESENTATIVES OF TESTATOR, OR TESTATRIX, OF THE ISSUING OF LETTERS TESTAMENTARY, ON A NUNCUPATIVE WILL.

STATE OF ILLINOIS,⎱ ss.: In   court of   county, of the   term,
County of   ⎰   A. D. 18   .

The People of the State of Illinois, to A B, C D, E F and G H, heirs and legal representatives of J K, deceased:

Take notice that a nuncupative will of the said J K has been duly proven and recorded in said court, and that letters testamentary will be granted thereon to L M, on the   day of   , A. D. 18   , unless sufficient cause be shown to the contrary. You, and each of you, are, therefore, hereby cited and notified to appear before said court, to be holden on the day and year aforesaid, at the court-house in   , in said county, to show cause, if any you have, why such letters should not be granted to the said L M.

[L. S.]

[*Teste.*]

NOTE.— 1. Old age and disease are not to be treated as an absence of sanity. These are not of themselves sufficient to incapacitate a party from making a valid disposition of his property by will, when no undue influence is practiced. Even softening of the brain, two years prior to the making of the will, will not invalidate it, if

---

(s) Coth. Ann'd. Stats., 1009.

the testator at the time of making it was capable of transacting his ordinary affairs.(*t*) It is not required that a person, to make a valid will, shall possess a higher capacity than for the transaction of the ordinary affairs of life.(*u*) The testator need not have sufficient mental capacity to understand and know the extent of his property, who his relations are and their claims on his bounty, and how he wishes to dispose of his property, and also sufficient capacity to hold all these things in his mind at the same time.(*u*) If the mind and memory of the testator are sufficiently sound to enable him to know and understand the business in which he is engaged at the time of executing his will, then within the statute, he is of sound mind and memory.(*v*) The rule is that a person who is capable of transacting business is also capable of making a valid will; it is the same in the case of a sale of property and its disposition by will. The usual test is, that the party be capable of acting rationally in the affairs of life. The derangement or imbecility that incapacitates is of that character which renders him incapable of understanding the effect and consequences of his acts; it need not be a total obliteration of the mental faculties which prevents a party from reasoning correctly on all subjects, upon correct premises to arrive at correct conclusions, but it is that want of capacity which prevents a person reasoning correctly and from understanding the relation of cause and effect in ordinary business affairs.(*w*)

2. Fraud or undue influence, to avoid a will, must be directly connected with its execution. The fact that a testator was influenced by the devisee, in the ordinary affairs of life, does not show that the latter used undue influence in procuring the execution of a will subsequently made.(*x*) It is not unlawful for a man, by honest advice or persuasion, to induce a person to make a will, or to influence the disposition of his property by will; such advice or persuasion will not vitiate a will made freely.(*y*) The influence exercised over a testator to avoid his will, must be of such a nature as to deprive him of free agency and render his act more the offspring of the will of others than his own, and it must be specially directed toward the object of procuring a will in favor of particular parties, and must be still operating at the time the will is made.

(*t*) *Rutherford* v. *Morris*, 77 Ill. 397.
(*u*) *Carpenter* v. *Calvert*, 83 Ill. 63.
(*v*) *Yoe* v. *McCord*, 74 Ill. 33.
(*w*) *Meeker* v. *Meeker*, 75 Ill. 269.
(*x*) *Rutherford* v. *Morris*, 77 Ill. 397.
(*y*) *Yoe* v. *McCord*, 74 Ill. 33.

Influence and persuasion may be fairly used, and a will procured by honest means, by acts of kindness, attention and persuasion, which delicate minds would shrink from, will not be set aside on that ground alone. The influence, to vitiate the will, must not be the influence of affection or attachment.(z)

12. LOST WILL. No provision is made in the statute for the proof of a lost will in probate, but if known to exist the lost will may be proved. The question is not only one of evidence but also of jurisdiction. The proper jurisdiction, it seems, in such cases is in chancery.(a) The proceeding similar to that prescribed for the restoration of lost deeds, by the statute of records.(b)

SECTION III. — EXECUTORS.

I. Competency and appointment.
II. Powers and duties.
III. Renunciation, resignation and removal.

I. COMPETENCY AND APPOINTMENT.

1. Who may be executors.
2. Appointment of a debtor as executor.
3. A *femme couverte* may be.
4. A corporation.

1. WHO MAY BE EXECUTORS. An executor is one appointed by a testator (and whose appointment is confirmed by the proper court) to execute his will and to represent him in his personal rights and liabilities left at his death. Persons of the age of seventeen years, of sound mind and memory, may be appointed executors; but when a person appointed executor is, at the time of proving the will, under the age of twenty-one years, or of unsound mind, or convicted of any crime rendering him infamous, administration with the will annexed may be granted during his minority or other disability, unless there is another executor who accepts the trust, in which case the estate shall be administered by such other executor until the minor arrives at full age or the other disability is removed,

---

(z) *Rutherford* v. *Morris*, 77 Ill. 397; *Alimon* v. *Pigg*, 82 Ill. 149.
(a) See Hill's Chan. Pr , p. 646 ; 3
Redf. Wills, 6, 7 ; but see *Duncan* v. *Duncan*, 23 Ill. 364.
(b) Coth. Ann'd. Stats., 1202 *et seq.*

Executors.

when, upon giving bond as in other cases, he may be admitted as joint executor with the former. When a married woman is executrix her husband may give bond with her for her faithful performance of the trust as in other cases. (c)

When a will has been duly proved and allowed, the county court shall issue letters testamentary thereon to the executor named in such will, if he is legally competent and accepts the trust, and gives bond to discharge the same, unless by the request of testator and approval of the court, the giving of surety be waived; and when there is no executor named in such will, or the executor named therein dies, refuses to act, or is otherwise disqualified, the court shall commit the administration of the estate unto the widow, surviving husband, next of kin or creditor, the same as if the testator had died intestate. In all cases copies of the will shall go out with the letters. (d)

2. APPOINTMENT OF A DEBTOR AS EXECUTOR. In no case hereafter, within this State, where any testator or testatrix shall, by his or her will, appoint his or her debtor to be his or her executor or executrix, shall such appointment operate as a release or extinguishment of any debt due from such executor or executrix to such testator or testatrix; unless the testator or testatrix shall, in such will, expressly declare his or her intention to devise, bequeath or release such debt; nor even in that case, unless the estate of such testator or testatrix is sufficient to discharge the whole of his or her just debts over and above the debt due from such executor or executrix. (e)

3. A MARRIED WOMAN may be, if her husband consents, and will unite with her in the bond, with securities for her faithful performance as such, executrix. (f)

4. A CORPORATION AGGREGATE, it has been said, in England, (g) may be entitled to be executor; but the authorities are the other way in America. Corporations can exercise only such powers as are expressly conferred on them, and such implied powers as are necessary to enable them to perform their prescribed duties; they have none of the elements of sovereignty and having no soul cannot commit perjury.

Those who are not of sound mind and memory are incapable; as idiots, infants under the age of seventeen, and persons convicted of any infamous crime. What are infamous crimes is declared by section 279 of the Criminal Code. (h)

II. POWERS AND DUTIES.

1. The authority.
2. How appointed.
3. Executor *de son tort.*
4. Their principal duties.
5. Distinction between their duties and those of administrators.

(c) § 3, R. S. 1874, p. 104.
(d) § 1, R. S. 1874, p. 104.
(e) § 19, R. S. 1874, p. 1105.
(f) Cothran's Stats., 48, § 3; § 3, R.
S. 1874, p. 104; 2 Bl. Com. 503.
(g) Tol. Ex. 3; 8 Bac. Abr. 5.
(h) § 279, R. S. 1874, p. 394; Cothran's Statutes, p. 507.

Executors.

1. THE AUTHORITY of an executor is grounded upon the will and may be express or implied; absolute or qualified; exclusive, or in common with others.

2. HOW APPOINTED. He may be expressly nominated, either by a written or nuncupative will. He may be constructively appointed, merely by the testator's recommending or committing to him the discharge of those duties which it is the province of an executor to perform, only conferring on him those rights which properly belong to the office, or any other means from which the testator's intention to invest him with that character may be distinctly inferred.

His appointment is absolute, where he is constituted certainly, immediately, and without any restriction or limitation; it is qualified where his duties are limited to a restricted time, or to certain of the testator's property.

3. AN EXECUTOR *DE SON TORT* (in his own wrong) is one who, without lawful authority, undertakes to act as executor of a person deceased. A very slight circumstance will render a man executor *de son tort*, as where a man receives a debt of the deceased, or gives an acquittance for it. He is liable to all the trouble of an executorship, with none of the profit or advantage. Merely doing acts of necessity or humanity, as locking up the goods or burying the corpse of the deceased, will not amount to such an intermeddling as will charge a man as executor of his own wrong.(*i*)

But where there is a rightful executor or administrator, there can be no executor of this description. The doctrine relating to executors in their own wrong applies to chattels only.

4. DUTIES OF EXECUTORS. In the performance of his duties, he is required to act in good faith, and to use due diligence.

His principal duties are the following:

First. To bury the testator in a manner suitable to the estate he leaves behind him.

Second. To collect the goods of the deceased.

Third. To prove the will in a proper office, before the proper officer appointed by law.

Fourth. To make an inventory of all the goods and chattels which come to his hands and, under our statute, of the real estate of the testator, and return the same into the county or probate court which approved his appointment, within three months from the date of his testamentary letters, as well as to make such supplementary inventories, from time to time, as other assets or liabilities of the testator may come to his knowledge.

Fifth. To ascertain the state of the debts and credits of the estate, and endeavor to collect the claims with as little delay as possible, consistently with the interest of the estate.

Sixth. To reduce all the goods not specifically bequeathed, into assets.

(*i*) 1 Wms. on Exec. 210 *et seq.*

Executors.

Seventh. To pay the debts of the testator and the legacies bequeathed by him, in the order required by law.

Under our statute of wills, the power of the executor over the testator's estate, before the probate of the will, extends simply to the burial of the deceased, the payment of necessary funeral expenses, and the taking care and preservation of the estate.(*d*)

When the letters testamentary issue, the executor's authority over the estate relates back to the death of the deceased. His right to act generally, from the time of the testator's decease, is suspended until he complies with the law in producing the will, having it probated, and qualifies.(*d*)

He is to give bond, the same as an administrator, for the faithful performance of his duties, unless the will itself dispense with security; even then, if persons interested in the estate suspect fraud, or the court see cause, or the estate be insolvent, he will be required to give such bond. The suspicion of the creditors or legatees, under such circumstances, should be reasonable, not mere caprice.

The duties of an executor, AFTER LETTERS TESTAMENTARY have been granted to him, are identical with those of an administrator, in making the inventory, appraisement bill, account, setting apart to the widow her specific property, and settling up the estate before distribution. The law may be said to take possession of the goods, chattels, rights and credits, and the real estate of a person, as soon as he dies, whether he be testator or intestate, and to hold the estate for the purpose of paying his debts; hence, the mode of settling up the estate, so far as the creditors are concerned, is the same, whether the person invested with the trust for such purpose be nominated executor by the will of the deceased, or appointed administrator by the county court. No disposition that the testator may make of his property by will can affect the rights of creditors.

5. THE DISTINCTION between the duties of an executor and an administrator is this: After the administrator has made a complete

---

(*d*) POWER BEFORE PROBATE. The power of the executor over the testator's estate, before probate of the will and obtaining letters testamentary, shall extend to the burial of the deceased, the payment of necessary funeral charges, and the taking care of the estate; but in all such cases, if the will is rejected when presented for probate, and such executor thereby never qualifies, he shall not be liable as an executor of his own wrong, unless upon refusal to deliver up the estate to the person authorized to receive the same. *Provided*, that this section shall not be construed to exempt any person claiming to be executor as aforesaid, for any waste or misapplication of such estate. Sec. 4, R. S. 1874, *p.* 104.

settlement of all the debts due creditors of the estate, the surplus of the intestate's property is distributed among his heirs, according to the laws of descent, while, under a will, it goes in the direction desired by the testator. The executor looks to the will, the administrator to the law of descent, to ascertain his duties and powers. The will is consulted in the one case, the statute in the other.

All the law, instructions and precedents, therefore, concerning administrators, from the time of their appointment up to the time of distribution, which will be given in the next chapter, are equally applicable to executors. The forms there given may be used for an executor, by substituting for the words "administrator," etc., the words "executor of the last will and testament of." By reference to the synopsis of the statutes given in the appendix, the executor can readily see where his duties and those of an administrator are identical. This chapter contains only such matters as are peculiarly or exclusively applicable to executors.

III. — RENUNCIATION, RESIGNATION AND REMOVAL.

1. Renunciation.
2. Form of.
3. Record of.
4. Resignation.
5. Removal.
6. Superseding, petition for.
7. Revocation of letters testamentary.

1. RENUNCIATION OF EXECUTORS. If a person named in a will as executor be unwilling to act in that capacity, he may refuse by so declaring in writing, and having the same filed in the proper court. The following form may be used for this purpose:

2. FORM OF RENUNCIATION OF EXECUTORSHIP.

STATE OF ILLINOIS, } ss: County Court of   County,
        County.   Term, A. D. 18   .

To the Hon.   , Judge of said Court :

The undersigned herewith presents to the court a paper writing, purporting to be the last will and testament of   , who died at the county aforesaid, the same being his place of residence, on the   day of   last, in which said will the undersigned is nominated and appointed executor thereof. He hereby wholly refuses to accept the executorship thereof, and renounces all right and claim to the exercise of the duties of executor of the same. He further states that he has not intermeddled with the effects of the testator since his decease, nor in any manner acted as executor of the said will.

Dated   , 18 .   RICHARD ROE.

Executors.

A verbal declaration is not sufficient, but, to give validity to the renunciation, it must be solemnly entered and recorded.(e)

3. THE FACT OF RENUNCIATION SHOULD APPEAR OF RECORD, in order to give validity to the appointment of an administrator with the will annexed. Such an appointment is, in the supposed cases, based upon the renunciation. Taking possession and selling part of the personal estate of the testator, and paying some of the debts, are proof of his election to act, and renders a person chargeable as executor.(f)

If there be several executors, they must all renounce before administration can be granted. If the administration be committed before refusal, it will be void.* If several executors are appointed and one or more of them die before letters issue, or renounce or become disqualified, letters issue to the survivor, willing to undertake the trust.

4. RESIGNATION OF EXECUTORS. An executor may resign the executorship in the same manner as an administrator.

5. REMOVAL OF EXECUTORS. If any person named as executor or executrix in any last will and testament is, at the time when administration ought to be granted, under the age of seventeen years, or of unsound mind, or convicted of any crime rendering him or her infamous, or shall be a married woman, letters of administration or testamentary (as the case may require) may be granted in the same manner as if such person had not been named as executor in such will; unless, in the case of the married woman, her husband shall give bond with her, etc.: Under such circumstances, the appointment under the will is superseded by an appointment of the court. The person not being capable of the office, the nomination in the will is, in effect, a blank. But the person named is presumed to be competent until the contrary is made to appear; therefore, there should be some judicial proceedings before the person named is superseded by an appointment of an administrator with the will annexed. The court should be advised by competent evidence that the person is disqualified from some cause mentioned in the statute, and when so advised the consideration of the court thereon should be made a matter of record, so that the subsequent appointment of an administrator will be authorized and legal. The widow, next of kin,

(e) Toll. Ex. 40; 3 Redf. on Wills, 11 (n).
(f) Van Horn v. Fonda, 5 Johns. Ch. 388.
* But see § 5, R. S. 1874, p. 105.

Executors.

or other person interested in the estate should bring the question before the court, by petition, affidavit or suggestion, and the person represented to be disqualified should be cited to show cause why letters of administration, with the will annexed, should not be granted. The notice to the executor should be reasonable, so that he may have an opportunity to contest the question of disqualification.

The petition may be in the following form:

6. Petition to Supersede the Appointment of an Executor.

State of   , }
    County. } *ss*:   *County Court of   county. In Probate.*

To Hon. C D, Judge of said Court:

The petition of A B, of said county, respectfully represents, that she is the widow of C B, late of said county, deceased. That said C B died on the day of   , 18 , having made and published his last will and testament.

That said C B died seized of a large estate, consisting of real and personal property of the value of *ten thousand* dollars, as your petitioner believes, all of which is disposed of by said last will and testament, after the payment of all just debts of said testator. That the said estate is owing large sums of money to divers persons, the amount of which your petitioner does not know, but believes it to be *two thousand* dollars.

And your petitioner further represents, that in and by said last will and testament, one E F, of said county, is appointed executor thereof. That said E F was, at the   term of the circuit court of said county, held in   , A. D. 18 , convicted of the crime of burglary, and sentenced to imprisonment and hard labor in the penitentiary for two years, and served the said term (*or* is of unsound mind, *stating how unsound, or* is under the age of seventeen years, *or* is a married woman, *giving the name of her husband, as the case may be*.) Wherefore, your petitioner shows that the said E F is incapable of qualifying as such executor.

Therefore, in consideration of the premises, your petitioner prays that she may be appointed administratrix of the estate of said C B, with the will annexed, and that a citation may issue herein, requiring said E F to appear in this court at the next   term thereof, and show cause, if any he has, why such letters of administration should not be granted.

And your petitioner will ever pray, etc.   A B.
  Dated, this   day of   , A. D. 18   .

State of   , }
    County. } *ss*:

A B, the petitioner above named, being first duly sworn, says, that the matters and things in the foregoing petition stated are true of her own knowledge
                                                                             A B.

  Subscribed and sworn to this first }
day of   , A. D. 18   .   }
               J K, *County Clerk.*

Executors.

The petition should specify the facts which show that the executor named in the will is disqualified, in order that he may be advised particularly of what is charged against him, so that he can, accordingly, prepare his defense. It would be insufficient to say that he was convicted of an infamous crime, without further stating what such crime was, and when and where he was convicted.

The testator selects whom he desires to execute his will, and his appointment should not be overruled, unless the person whom he has selected be, in law, clearly incompetent. Therefore the evidence should be certain and convincing before the court should disregard the appointment of the testator. If, upon hearing the evidence, the court consider the person named as executor in the will, disqualified, it should be so entered of record, as a foundation for granting letters of administration with the will annexed.

7. REVOCATION. It is provided that the county court shall have power to revoke all letters testamentary or of administration, granted to persons who shall become insane, lunatic or of unsound mind, habitual drunkards, who may be convicted of any infamous crime, who waste or mismanage the estate, or who conduct themselves in such a manner as to endanger their co-executors or securities. The proceedings and precedents necessary under this section to revoke the letters of an executor, are substantially the same as those applicable to administrators.(*h*)

(*h*) See p. 100, *infra*.

CHAPTER III.

INTESTATE ESTATES.

Section I. Introduction.
  II. Appointment of administrators.
  III. Their powers and duties generally.
  IV. Resignation and removal.

SECTION I. — INTRODUCTION.

1. Estates generally.
2. Priority of the rights of creditors.
3. Testate estates and intestate estates distinguished.
4. Administration of estates.

1. ESTATES consist of real and personal property.(*a*)

2. ALL JUST DEBTS AND CLAIMS(*b*) against estates left by decedents, if enforced within a reasonable time, take precedence of legacies,(*c*) devises, and the rights of legatees, devisees or distributees(*d*) and their alienees or assigns.(*e*)

3. TESTATE ESTATES pass by will; they are the estates of deceased testators which we term testate estates.(*f*)

INTESTATE ESTATES consist of the real and personal property of resident and non-resident proprietors dying intestate.(*g*)

THEY DESCEND and are distributed, while testate estates are disposed of according to legacies and devises. All these estates fall, on the death of their proprietors, under the administration of the proper court in probate. For the purposes of administration of testate estates, where there is no executor, the court appoints one, and then the testate estate is in its management and control through an administrator *cum testamento annexo* or *de bonis non*, deemed an intestate estate; but the legacies, devises and provisions of the will are paramount rules in their disposition.

THE LAW OF DESCENT(*h*) may be regarded as the PUBLIC WILL for the distribution of estates, after paying all just debts and claims of creditors, among the relatives of the decedent; while the LAW OF

(*a*) Bl. Com.; Washburn's Real Prop.; act in regard to descent of property; R. S. 1874, p. 417.
(*b*) See page 215, *infra*.
(*c*) See page 233, *infra*.
(*d*) See page 251, *infra*.

(*e*) *Meyer* v. *McDougal*, 47 Ill. 278; § 1, R. S. 1874, p. 417; Hill's Ch. Pr. 513. Cothran's Statutes, p. 541.
(*f*) See pp. 10–60, *supra*.
(*g*) See page 1, *supra*.
(*h*) See chap. x, *infra*.

Introduction.

WILLS provides for the disposition of his property, after death, by the will of the proprietor, indicated, while living, in a formal manner, in an instrument termed a will.

4. ADMINISTRATION OF ESTATES. Death comes to all. The instant it comes to the proprietor of either real or personal property, the probate jurisdiction begins;* the authority of the proper judge

---

*Acting upon this doctrine, the supreme court of the United States hold all proceedings to sell lands of a deceased person in probate to be solely *in rem*. *Grignon* v. *Astor*, 2 How. 319. The preliminaries to the sale are not to be collaterally attacked. The supreme court of Illinois hold that such proceedings are partially *in rem* and partially *in personam*. *Botsford* v. *O'Conner*, 57 Ill. 72. But if the creditors have a prior lien upon the estate in administration, how are heirs or devisees to take the property discharged of this lien? Until creditors are paid, the property is in *custodia legis* by the statute, according to innumerable decisions.

Then, if we assume that a proceeding to subject the real property of an intestate to the payment of his debts is partly *in personam* and partly *in rem*, are we not begging the question? For, does not the estate, at the death of its proprietor, pass through the probate jurisdiction? Have not all the world notice of the attaching and province of this jurisdiction, at the death of the proprietor, *ipso facto?* Is it, then, not the better doctrine that every thing pertaining to the administration is *in rem*, and that all contests relative to the manner of administration should take place in the jurisdiction already attached, original and complete? If the doctrine which supports the case of *Ferguson* v. *Hunter, supra*, be correct, the whole administration may be impeached in the case of a will, or according to that held in *Botsford* v. *O'Conner, supra*, in case of intestacy in ejectment.

On the decease of the ancestor or benefactor, the heirs or beneficiaries know that, before they can receive their inheritance or devise, the estate must be settled in probate. Is it unreasonable or unjust to ask them to meet and settle all questions in probate or on appeal? Is it unreasonable or unjust to protect *bona fide* purchasers at judicial sales against the unskillful exercise of the probate jurisdiction, by insisting that all who are interested in it should be chargeable with notice of the attaching of the jurisdiction, when all they ultimately get comes directly through this very jurisdiction to them in the first instance? Is it just or reasonable that they, thus benefited by such a jurisdiction, fully notified of it in fact, should be treated as the owners of property, yet in *custodia legis* and brought *in personam* into the same court where they must eventually come to get their property? Having occasion to examine these questions heretofore with great care in closely litigated cases, we have taken the liberty of adding the points to show the necessity of a skillful and careful exercise of the probate jurisdiction in view of the cases *Ferguson* v. *Hunter* and *Botsford* v. *O'Conner*, and their kindred. The practitioner who would examine the matter critically by starting here and comparing them with *Grignon* v. *Astor*, and its kindred cases, will see the issue involved. To those who rely upon the former, and as counsel for parties interested in estates of the deceased, we would say, beware of the latter, and to those who rely upon the latter, and insist on original, complete jurisdiction in probate, we would say, beware of the former. They may, in Illinois, be said to be settled, but the questions involved, in view of the new constitution and changes in our statutes, are subject to re-examination. There is no position to which jurists, who have adhered to the doctrine that such proceedings are *in rem*, are more tenacious. They see the jurisdiction attaching at the decease of the proprietor. They start there, with the probate jurisdiction over all the estate, whether it be real or personal. And when we consider

Introduction.

then attaches to the estate. The production and probate of the will are the first things to do after the funeral of the deceased testator.(*i*) Application for letters of administration is the first step to be taken after the burial of the intestate. The statute (*j*) prescribes the mode of procedure in such cases for the court and all concerned in the administration of the estate which fortune or frugality may have conferred upon the one who has now been laid in the grave. Through the sorrow and anguish of death-bed scenes and funeral rites and ceremonies, the probate power of the county court beams forth to illumine the gloom, and well-drawn statutes now come in to guide in the proper disposition of the estate, according to the law of administration, and its distribution according to the will or the law of descent.

We have, for the present, disposed of the law of wills and the statute of administration, so far as relate exclusively to executors and their appointment, powers and duties generally, and their renunciation, resignation and removal. We now purpose to consider the law of administration, so far as it relates exclusively to administrators, their appointment, powers and duties generally, and their resignation and removal.

At the death of the intestate, as of the testator, the statute provides for the exigencies of the hour. Nothing should, however, be

---

(*i*) See page 14, *supra*.   (*j*) § 18, R. S. 1874, *p*. 107.

how far the policy of our law has been to ignore the old distinctions between real and personal property, and to assimilate them; how earnestly and strenuously the State tribunals have struggled against, but sooner or later have succumbed to, the doctrine promulgated by the United States supreme court in *Grignon* v. *Astor*, we must confess that we cannot regard such decisions as *Ferguson* v. *Hunter* and *Botsford* v. *O'Conner* as settling the law on this point even in the State of Illinois. In view of them, it behooves the probate courts to be more careful of the exercise of their jurisdiction. In view of the case of *Grignon* v. *Astor*, it behooves heirs and devisees to be more careful in watching the exercise of probate jurisdiction over the estates in which they are interested. Volumes might be written on the cases involving this issue. To our mind, the whole controversy turns on *the point of departure*. If it be true that real property passes at the death of the proprietor under the probate jurisdiction, then the exercise of such a jurisdiction ought not to be collaterally questioned. It is *in rem*. If the real estate goes immediately to heirs or devisees, thus to divest their title, they must, according to well-settled principles, be brought personally before the court by personal or constructive service. The jurisdiction is partly *in rem* and partly *in personam*. This brings us back to the point where we started, and shows that the text needs qualification when it is said that the probate jurisdiction attaches at the instant death comes to the proprietor of real estate in view of the cases *Ferguson* v. *Hunter*, and *Botsford* v. *O'Conner*. We shall discuss the subject further under chapter vii, *infra*.

Appointment of administrators.

done with unseemly haste. For sixty days(*k*) the claims of creditors are stayed. Their lien has attached, and if enforced within a reasonable time, is paramount.(*l*) Sixty days are allowed for the grief of mourning relatives to abate.(*m*) Then, if the relatives do not apply during the next fifteen days, the creditors become entitled to letters of administration. If relatives and creditors are wanting, the peculiar office of public administrator, with its powers and duties, intervenes; if relatives are absent and creditors lenient or neglectful, then the discretion is ample with the court in granting letters of administration to suitable persons. If the right of representation be contested, then a special administrator may be empowered, so that every possible contingency is fully provided for. Hence, we may consider the statute in hand as follows:

(1.) As it relates to the appointment, powers and duties, and the removal of the public administrator.

(2.) As it provides for the appointment, powers and duties, and the resignation and removal of an administrator to collect.

(3.) As it provides for the regular grant of administration to the persons preferred and in the law entitled thereto; the powers and duties of the administrator, and his resignation and removal.

(4.) As it relates to the recognition and exercise of the powers, rights and duties of an administrator appointed in another jurisdiction, or the foreign administrator.

In doing this, we shall refer to the decisions and former statutes as we proceed, and conclude the chapter with a *resume* of the decisions and statutes involved not already discussed and delineated.

SECTION II. — APPOINTMENT OF ADMINISTRATORS.

1. Administrators virtually executors.
2. Of several kinds, general and special.
3. An intestate
4. Special administrators.
5. Administrator *de bonis non*.
6. Administrator *pendente lite*.
7. Letters of administration are a grant of power.
8. Intestacy and death of decedent must be proved.
9. How proved.
10. The English Statutes, and

(*k*) § 18, R. S. 1874, *p.* 107.
(*l*) *Meyer* v. *McDougal*, 47 Ill. 278, R. S. 1874, *p.* 417.

(*m*) § 19, R. S. 1874, *p.* 108; Cothran's Annotated Statutes, *p.* 53.

Appointment of administrators.

11. Our statute compared.
12. The *jus representationis*.
13. Degrees of consanguinity according to the civil law.
14. The public administrator appointed by the governor, by and with the consent of the senate.
15. When the estate may be committed to the public administrator.
16. His duties in general.
17. His expenses preferred.
18. Removal in special cases on appearance of parties entitled within six months after his appointment.
19. To advertise on settlement, etc.
20. Administrator to collect.
21. Letters to collect.
22. Bond of administrator to collect.
23. His oath.
24. Who may be administrators generally.
    (1.) They should be of lawful age and legally competent.
    (2.) The preference conferred by statute.
    (3.) Waiver of *juris representationis*.
    (4.) Who to administer, on the death of surviving husband, as administrator *de bonis non* of his deceased wife's estate, *quære?*
    (5.) Next of kin — the relatives generally.
    (6.) Renunciation or relinquishment.
25. Venue — proper county.
26. Practice — how to be appointed administrator.
27. Petition for letters of administration.
28. Affidavit of death, intestacy, etc.
29. The administrator's bond.
30. And letters of administration.
31. The oath.
32. Form of bond by administrator with the will **annexed**.
33. Oath of.
34. Additional bond.
35. Decisions in Illinois.
36. Foreign executors and administrators, how, where and when they may act; limitations and restrictions.

1. AN ADMINISTRATOR is a person appointed or authorized to manage and distribute the estate of the intestate, or of a testator who has no executor(*n*) — virtually an executor; his duty is to settle the estate of a deceased person, either where no will appears, or if such appear, and for any reason there is no person to act as executor of the duties imposed by the will. If there be no will, he is simply an administrator to settle the estate according to the

(*n*) Bouvier.

Appointment of administrators.

requirements of the law applicable to the case. He has, in all respects, the same rights and duties, and is subject to the same responsibilities, as an executor; except that, where the testator directs that his executor shall act without giving sureties for his faithful administration, he cannot be required to do so unless, for special cause shown, the county court should consider that the rights of creditors and others make security indispensable to the ends of justice, or where the statute requires such security. The administrator, being an officer of the court, is required, in all cases, to give security for the faithful performance of his duties. Regularly, the administrator can do no act in regard to the estate before his appointment by the court, except such necessary acts as are indispensable to the preservation of the estate; and, as to such, there can be no question but they will be brought under the shield of a subsequent appointment from the court, and that as well in the case of an administrator as of an executor.(*o*)

2. ADMINISTRATORS ARE OF SEVERAL KINDS: (1.) General administrators, or those who have the right to administer the whole of the decedent's estate. (2.) Special administrators, or those who administer a part of an estate, or who act for a limited time or purpose.

General administrators are those who are appointed to administer the estate of an intestate, or who are administrators *cum testamento annexo*, with the will annexed.

3. AN INTESTATE is one who dies leaving no will, and whose assets are administered according to the law. On the death of a person who has made no will, his real estate descends to his heirs, subject to the payment of debts, after personal estate is exhausted, while his personal estate is vested in such persons as may be legally appointed by the proper officer or tribunal, in trust, to pay the debts of the deceased, and distribute the surplus to those by law entitled to it.(*p*) But such real estate is subject to the payment of the debts of the intestate, in case the personal estate be insufficient for that purpose.

Administration, *cum testamento annexo*, is granted when the deceased has made a will and no executor is named in the same, or the executor therein named shall die, refuse to act, or be otherwise disqualified. In that case, letters of administration are granted to some proper person, to which is attached a copy of the will.(*q*)

(*o*) 3 Redf. 21–23. (*p*) 2 Bouv. Inst. 141. (*q*) Id. 144.

Appointment of administrators.

4. SPECIAL ADMINISTRATORS are also of several kinds; administrator *de bonis non* of goods not previously administered is appointed when a former administrator has partially administered and has died, or has not fully administered for any cause. His duty is to complete the administration; and, so far as the estate is committed to him, he has all the power of a general administrator.

5. ADMINISTRATORS *DE BONIS NON, cum testamento annexo*, are those who are appointed to complete the execution of a will when the executor has commenced administering and dies, or otherwise becomes incapable or is removed.

An administrator, *durante minore aetate*, acting during minority, is appointed when the executor in a will is an infant and has not legal capacity to execute the will. His authority is limited to the time when the minor becomes capable, and is otherwise limited as to his acts.

6. AN ADMINISTRATOR *PENDENTE LITE*, pending litigation, is one appointed to do certain acts pending a contest in relation to the probate of a will, to the right of executorship, or the right to administer, etc. Under the statute, he is called *administrator to collect*. This administrator is but an officer of the court. His power extends to collecting and preserving the estate only. He may bring suits.(*r*)

There are also administrators *durante absentia*, etc., during absence. The foregoing enumeration will be sufficient for the purpose of this work.(*s*)

If the deceased leave no will, letters of administration will be granted of his personal estate.

7. LETTERS OF ADMINISTRATION ARE A GRANT OF POWER, and confer upon the grantee the qualified property in the personal estate pertaining to the trust. They clothe the recipient with the absolute title to this property.(*t*)

8. INTESTACY, PROOF OF, must be made before such a grant can be made. Proof of the death of the intestate, too, must be presented, and these facts found to obtain the letters.(*u*)

Intestacy may be absolute or qualified. It is absolute where no will is left; qualified where the deceased has made a will as regards

---

(*r*) § 11, R. S. 1874, *p.* 106.
(*s*) See Redf. on Wills, Administrators.
(*t*) See *p.* 83, *infra*.
(*u*) §§ 18, 20, R. S. 1874, *p.* 107.

Appointment of administrators.

his or her real estate only, (*v*) or has, by will, only disposed of his foreign property.(*w*)

9. DEATH, proof of, may be by affidavit of a member of the family generally, unless the point be contested; and proof of intestacy in the same manner.(*x*)

10. THE ENGLISH STATUTES. The persons preferred under the English statutes are "the next and most lawful friends of the deceased" (*y*) "the widow of the same person deceased or to the next of his kin, or both, as by the discretion of the same ordinary shall be thought good."(*z*)

The husband of *femmes couverte*, dying intestate, " may demand and have administration of their rights, credits and other personal estate, and recover and enjoy the same as they might have done before the making of the 22 and 23 Car. II, ch. 10,"(*a*) and the relatives (not next of kin) having distributive shares, *jure representationis* under the 22 and 23 Car. II, ch. 10, and 1 Jac. II, ch. 17, and also all persons having a cognizable beneficial interest in the intestate's estate, may become grantees on the relinquishment of the *potiores*.

Our statute in this respect is founded on these English statutes, and is as follows:

11. ADMINISTRATION shall be granted to THE HUSBAND upon the goods and chattels of his wife, and to the widow or next of kin to the intestate, or some of them, if they will accept the same and are not disqualified; but in all cases THE WIDOW SHALL HAVE PREFERENCE; and if no widow or other relative of the intestate applies within sixty days from the death of the intestate, the county court may grant administration to ANY CREDITOR who shall apply for the same. If no creditor applies within fifteeen days next after the lapse of sixty days, as aforesaid, administration may be granted to ANY PERSON whom the county court may think will best manage all the estate. In cases where the intestate is a non-resident, or without a widow, next of kin or creditors in this State, but leaves property within the estate, administration shall be granted to the PUBLIC ADMINISTRATOR of the proper county; *Provided*, that no administration shall, in any case, be granted until satisfactory proof be made before the county court, to whom application, for that

(*v*) *O'Dwyer* v. *Geare*, 1 Swab. & Trist. 466; *Jane Barden*, 1 L. R., P. & D. 325.
(*w*) *Coode*, 1 L. R., P. & D. 449.
(*x*) See p. 76, *infra*.
(*y*) 31 Edw. III, ch. 11.
(*z*) 21 Hen. VIII, ch. 5, § 3.
(*a*) 29 Car. II, ch. 3, § 25.

Appointment of administrators.

purpose, is made, that the person in whose estate letters are requested is dead and died intestate; *And provided further,* that no non-resident of this State shall be appointed administrator or allowed to act as such.(*b*)

12. *JUS REPRESENTATIONIS.* This right is oftentimes of great importance, and may be discussed in view of the English authorities.

BACHELOR DECEASED, OR A WIDOWER without issue. His father has this right exclusively, notwithstanding the deceased has left a mother. The father would thus seem to be the sole next of kin of the intestate. The *jure mariti* at common law and the statute gives administration of his deceased wife's estate to THE HUSBAND.

If the intestate has left no widow, the intestate's children (if qualified by age), or some or one of them, take the grant. They do so if there be a widow and she relinquish, has died since the decease of the intestate, or is excluded by the court as unworthy or disqualified, or fails to act or qualify.

If the intestate has left neither widow, husband, father nor children, the next of kin take administration.

Those persons only are to be ranked as next of kin of an intestate who were such at the time of the intestate's death.

If the widow renounce, or has died since the decease of the intestate, or is incapacitated or unworthy, administration will be granted to the next of kin to the intestate.

If the husband renounce and consent, administration will be granted to the next of kin to the intestate.(*c*)

If the intestate be a divorced woman, her next of kin take administration.

The court will grant administration to a person nominated by all the next of kin.(*d*)

Also to the husband of a sole next of kin, being the sole person entitled to the estate, on her renouncing or being cited and not appearing to the process.(*e*)

RECAPITULATION. It may be said that administration is granted to:

(1.) Husband or wife;
(2.) Child or children;

(*b*) § 18, R. S. 1874, p. 107.
(*c*) *Jane Bell,* 1 Swab. & Trist. 290.
(*d*) *Farrell* v. *Browbill,* 3 Swab. & Trist. 468.
(*e*) *Haynes* v. *Matthews,* 1 Swab. & Trist. 462; *Wenham* v. *Wenham,* 6 Notes of Cases, 17.

Appointment of administrators.

(3.) Grandchild or grandchildren;
(4.) Great-grandchildren or other descendants;
(5.) Father;
(6.) Mother;
(7.) Brothers and sisters;
(8.) Grandfathers or grandmothers;
(9.) Nephews and nieces, uncles, aunts, great grandfathers or great grandmothers.
(10.) Great nephews, great nieces, cousins german, great uncles, great aunts, great grandfather's father, and so on, according to the proximity of kindred; all those in the same degree being equally entitled.(*f*)

13. DEGREES OF CONSANGUINITY, ACCORDING TO THE CIVIL LAW, govern, except as modified by the law of descent, in these matters and in the distribution. We give further on the tables made use of frequently to illustrate the same.(*f*)

The granting of letters where there is a contest over the *jure representationis*, under our statute may be aided, if not satisfactorily settled, by reference to the English cases. No cases are to be found in our reports where the right has been severely contested.(*g*) The discretion of the court is broad, and its decision subject to review only on appeal.(*g*)

14. THE PUBLIC ADMINISTRATOR, HOW APPOINTED. This functionary is appointed by the governor of the State, by and with the consent of the senate. He is to take an oath before entering upon the duties of his office:

I do solemnly swear (or affirm as the case may be), that I will support the constitution of the United States and of the State of Illinois, and that I will faithfully discharge the duties of the office of public administrator of county, according to the best of my ability. One is appointed for each county.(*h*)

15. WHEN AN ESTATE MAY BE COMMITTED TO THE PUBLIC ADMINISTRATOR. Before the county court can obtain jurisdiction to commit an estate to a public administrator it should affirmatively appear, and be preserved of record, that there was not any relative or creditor within the State to whom administration might be committed; and

---

(*f*) See chap. x, *infra*.　　　　(*h*) §§ 44, 45, R. S. 1874, p. 112;
(*g*) But see *Schnell* v. *Chicago*, 38　Cothran's Annotated Statutes, p. 60.
Ill. 382, and page 74, *infra*.

Appointment of administrators.

that the application was made by a party interested in the estate.(*i*) The provisions of the first section of the act supplemental to the statute of wills, of March 1, 1833, in relation to the appointment of public administrators, is not restricted in its application to cases of the death of resident proprietors of real estate, but embraces all classes of persons.(*j*) A public administrator must give a bond and take out letters of administration in each particular case, before he can be invested with any control over an estate.(*k*) If the public administrator neglect, for sixty days, to qualify after it becomes his duty so to do, his office is thereby vacated and the governor is to fill the vacancy.*

16. GENERALLY the public administrator is to take such measures as he may deem proper to protect and secure the effects of non-resident intestates, and resident intestates, who have neither relatives nor creditors in the State, from waste and embezzlement until administration is granted.(*l*)

17. THE EXPENSES of the public administrator are to be allowed by the county court, and take preference of all other demands against the estate, funeral expenses excepted.(*l*)

He is to discharge the functions in particular cases in the same manner and under the direction and supervision of the court as any other administrator.

18. REMOVAL. The appearance within six months after grant of letters to him, of the widow, next of kin or other persons entitled thereto, is cause for the revocation of the grant to him and re-grant to the persons entitled.(*m*)

19. He is to advertise after settlement for claims and demands, and finally to pay over the balance as prescribed into the county treasury, to be paid over whenever the persons entitled thereto shall appear.(*n*)

20. ADMINISTRATOR TO COLLECT. During any contest in relation to the probate of any will, testament or codicil, before the same is recorded, or until a will which may have once existed, but is destroyed or concealed, is established, and the substance thereof com-

---

(*i*) § 46, id.; *Unknown Heirs of Langworthy* v. *Baker*, 23 Ill. 489; *Schnell* v. *Chicago*, 28 id. 382.
(*j*) *Bowles' Heirs* v. *Rouse, Adm'r*, 3 Gilm. 409.
(*k*) *Thomas, Adm'r*, v. *Adams*, 5 Gilm. 319.

(*l*) § 50, act April 1, 1872
(*m*) § 48, id.
(*n*) See p. 278, *infra*.
* See act January 10, L. 1825, p. 70; R. S. 1833, p. 659; Laws 1843, p. 10; 56–62, R. S. 1845 ' act April 1 1872, 44–50. R. S. 1874, pp. 112, 113.

Appointment of administrators.

mitted to record, with proof thereupon taken, or during any contest in regard to the right of executorship, or to administer the estate of any person dying either testate or intestate, or whenever any other contingency happens which is productive of great delay before letters testamentary or of administration can be issued upon the estate of such testator or intestate, to the person or persons having legal preference to the same, the county court may appoint any person or persons as administrators, to collect and preserve the estate of any such decedent, until probate of his will, or until administration of his estate is granted, taking bond and security for the collection of the estate, making an inventory thereof, and safe keeping and delivering up the same when thereunto required by the court, to the proper executor or administrator, whenever they shall be admitted and qualified as such.(o)

21. LETTERS TO COLLECT. The form of the letters to be granted to the person or persons so appointed to collect and preserve the estate of the decedent, as aforesaid, shall be as follows, viz.:

The People of the State of Illinois, to all to whom these presents shall come, greeting:

Know ye, that whereas A B, late of the county of   , and State of Illinois, deceased, as it is said, had, at his (or her) decease, personal property within this State, the administration whereof cannot be immediately granted to the persons by law entitled thereto, but which, if speedy care be not taken, may be lost, destroyed or diminished; to the end, therefore, that the same may be preserved for those who shall appear to have a legal right or interest therein, we do hereby request and authorize C D (and E F, if two shall be appointed), of the county of   , and State aforesaid, to collect and secure the said property, wheresoever the same may be, in this State, whether it be goods, chattels, debts or credits, and to make, or cause to be made, a true and perfect inventory thereof, and to exhibit the same, with all convenient speed, to the county court of the said county of   , together with a reasonable account of his collection, acts and doings in the premises aforesaid.

Witness, E F, clerk of the county court in and for said county of   , and the seal of said court, this   day of   , A. D. 18

E F, *Clerk.*(p)

22. BOND OF ADMINISTRATOR TO COLLECT. Before letters of administration to collect shall be granted as aforesaid, the person or persons so appointed shall give bond, with good and sufficient security, to be approved by the court, in the following form, to wit:

(o) § 11, R. S. 1874, *p.* 106.   (p) § 12, R. S. 1874, *p.* 106.

Appointment of administrators.

Know all men by these presents, that we, C D, E F and J K, of the county of   , and State of Illinois, are held and firmly bound unto the people of the State of Illinois in the penal sum of   dollars, current money of the United States, for the payment of which, well and truly to be made and performed, we bind ourselves, our heirs, executors and administrators, jointly, severally and firmly, by these presents.

Witness our hands and seals, this   day of   , A. D. 18   .

The condition of the above obligation is such, that if the above-bounden C D shall well and honestly discharge the duties appertaining to his appointment as administrator, to collect of the estate of A B, late of the county of   , deceased, shall make, or cause to be made, a true and perfect inventory of all such goods, chattels, debts and credits of the said deceased, as shall come to his or her possession or knowledge, and the same in due time return to the county court of the proper county; and shall also deliver to the person or persons authorized by the said county court, as executors or administrators, to receive the same, all such goods, chattels and personal estate as shall come to his or her possession, as aforesaid, and shall, in general, perform such other duties as shall be required of him (or them) by law, then the above obligation to be void; otherwise to remain in full force and virtue.

Which said bond shall be signed and sealed by such administrator and his securities, and filed with the clerk of the county court and spread upon the records.

23. OATH, ETC. Before any administrator to collect shall enter upon the duties of his appointment he shall take and subscribe the following oath or affirmation before the clerk of the county court, to wit:

"I do solemnly swear (or affirm) that I will well and honestly discharge the trust reposed in me as administrator to collect the estate of A B, deceased, according to the tenor and effect of the letters granted to me by the county court of the said county of   , to the best of my knowledge and ability: so help me God."

Which said oath shall be in writing, subscribed by the party making it, and filed in the office of the clerk of the county court before whom the same is taken.(r)

24. WHO MAY BE ADMINISTRATORS.

(1.) The person appointed should be twenty-one years of age, and in all other respects legally competent. Infants and persons *non compos mentis*, of unsound minds, are incapable of executing the trust. Until the enabling act of 1861, known as the married woman's act, *femmes couvert* were incapacitated.(r)

(r) *Huls* v. *Buntin*, 47 Ill. 396.

Appointment of administrators.

(2.) Of competent persons, the statute gives the following preference over others: In case of the death of the *wife*, the husband has the superior right to administer. In case of the death of the *husband*, the widow has the preference; then the next of kin, after whom creditors have the preference over those who are not relatives, and also over the public administrator. When there are several persons in the same degree, it is competent for the judge, in his discretion, to select any one of them who will accept the appointment. If the widow or other relatives do not apply for letters within sixty days after the intestate's death, any creditor applying may be appointed administrator. If no such application be made by a creditor within fifteen days after the lapse of the sixty days, then administration may be granted by the court to such other person as it may think will best manage the estate. The public administrator has the exclusive right to administer when the intestate was a non-resident of the State, and without a widow, next of kin, or creditor in this State.*

(3.) WAIVER. If the person having a prior right to letters of administration does not avail himself of his preference within the prescribed time, he is considered as having waived it, and the persons next entitled may be appointed. A person having a preference may renounce or waive it, which will have no different effect upon others than to bring forward those who are next in order in law. As the statute fixes the order of preference, the person first entitled cannot renounce and introduce another in his or her place, to the exclusion of those who have the next right to administration under the statute.

(4.) Upon the death of the husband, who has survived his wife, and partially administered upon her estate, his executor or administrator is entitled to be *administrator de bonis non* of unadministered goods of the wife, in preference to her next of kin.(s) But *quære*, since the enabling act of 1861.

Granting letters of administration to the next of kin of the deceased wife, where the husband has survived her and died, has sometimes been done, but such administrator is regarded as the trustee of the representatives of the husband.(t) The practice, however, has been regretted by many judges,(u) and the practice

---

* See pp. 70, 71. *supra*.
(s) 4 Munf. Rep. 231.
(t) *Elliott* v. *Collier*, 3 Atk. 521.
(u) Gill, in, etc., 1 Hagg. 341, 344.

Appointment of administrators.

seems finally abandoned,(v) and administration is only granted to the next of kin of the wife, when they were entitled to her effects by settlement.(w) And a similar rule obtains in many of the American States.(x)

(5.) By *next of kin*, is understood the nearest of blood. It is a term applied, in the laws of descent and distribution, to the nearest blood relatives of a deceased person, including only those who are entitled to have, under the statute of distributions or descent.

(6.) RENUNCIATION OR RELINQUISHMENT. The person who has the prior right to administer may renounce his or her claim. If the person not specifically entitled to administer applies for letters within seventy-five days after the decease of the intestate, he must produce satisfactory evidence that the persons having the preference (*potiores*) have relinquished or renounced it.(a)

RENUNCIATION.

STATE OF ILLINOIS,} ss: County court of ____ County,
_____ County.}   ____ term, A. D. 18 ____ .

To the Judge of said court:

I, A B, widow of C D, late of said county, deceased, do hereby relinquish and renounce all right, claim and preference which I may have to administer upon the estate of him, the said C D.   A B.

Dated ____ , 18 ____ .

Witnesses:

As to whom letters of administration may be granted and when.(b)

Personal property of a minor vests immediately in the next of kin, and there is no necessity of taking out letters of administration before instituting suit in equity against the sureties of a guardian for a discovery and an account on the ground of mal-administration.(c)

Husband may administer on his wife's estate.(d)

(v) *Fielder* v. *Hunger*, 3 Hagg. 769; 1 Wms. Ex'rs, 360.
(w) *Bunchley* v. *Lynn*, 9 Eng. L. & Eq. 583; S. C., 16 Jur. 292.
(x) *Ward* v. *Thompson*, 6 Gill. & J. 349; *Sheldon* v. *Wright*, 5 N. Y. 497; *Patterson* v. *High*, 8 Ired. Eq. 52; *Wilborn* v. *Hector*, id. 55; *Randall* v. *Shrader*, 17 Ala. 833.

(a) § 19, R. S. 1874, p. 108.
(b) *Schnell* v. *City of Chicago*, 38 Ill. 382.
(c) *Lynch* v. *Rotan*, 39 Ill. 15.
(d) *Townsend* v. *Radcliffe*, 44 Ill. 446.

Appointment of administrators.

Issue of a void marriage have no right to administer on the estate of the deceased father.(e)

The lapse of seven years after the death of a decedent constitutes a bar to granting letters of administration, but it may be removed by showing circumstances which prevented an earlier application.(f)

Surviving partner of the intestate should not be appointed administrator.(g) Administration is not always necessary.(g) Although letters of administration may be granted irregularly, yet the court having jurisdiction, the person appointed is administrator *de facto*, and the regularity of appointment cannot be questioned collaterally.(h)

25. VENUE OR THE PROPER COUNTY. A grant of administration in one country, confers on an administrator no title to the property of the intestate situate in another country. He has no authority over, nor is he responsible for, any effects of the estate that may be beyond the jurisdiction appointing him. If he wishes to reach property, or collect debts belonging to the estate in a foreign country, he must there obtain letters of administration, and give such security and become subject to such regulations as its laws may prescribe.(i)

THE PROPER COUNTY in which to take out letters of administration, in case of non-residents dying, leaving lands in this State, is the county where such lands or a part of them lie.(j)

26. PRACTICE — HOW TO BE APPOINTED ADMINISTRATOR. Obtain a petition and bond in blank from the clerk, fill them out, write on the back of the petition the names of two persons to serve as appraisers, file them with the clerk, pay his costs. Have at least two securities sworn, examined and accepted by the court. Present the bond in a penalty of double the value of the estate to be administered, get it approved and take the oath of office.

Previous to the appointment of administrators, the proof of intestacy should be made *to the court*. This proof may be made by any person cognizant of the facts, usually by the person applying for letters. This is indispensable to any action by the court.

(e) *Myatt* v. *Myatt*, 44 Ill. 473.
(f) *Fitzgerald* v. *Glancy*, 49 Ill. 465.
(g) *Heward* v. *Slagle*, 52 Ill. 336.
(h) *Wight* v. *Wallbaum*, 39 Ill. 555; *Duffin* v. *Abbott*, 48 id. 17.
(i) *Judy* v. *Kelley*, 11 Ill. 211; see *Harrison* v. *Nixon*, 9 Peters, 483; 10 id. 408; 4 How. 467, and 14 id.; Hill's Ch. Pr. 23

(j) *Bowles' Heirs* v. *Rouse, Adm'r*, 4 Gilm. 409; see p. 14, *supra*. Where a court of probate of one county has acquired a full jurisdiction of an estate, it retains that jurisdiction until the estate shall be fully administered. *The People* v. *White*, 11 Ill. 342.

Appointment of administrators.

It is the usual practice to present a petition to the court, praying that letters be granted. The following form is in general use:

27. PETITION FOR LETTERS OF ADMINISTRATION.

In the matter of the estate of   ,} *Petition of*
   deceased, for letters of administration.}

To the Hon.   , *Judge of the county court of*   *county, in the State of Illinois:*

The petition of the undersigned   respectfully represents that   late of the county of   aforesaid, departed this life at   , in said county on or about the   day of   , A. D. 18   , leaving no last will and testament, as far as your petitioners know or believe.

And this petitioner further shows that the said   died seized and possessed of real and personal estate, consisting chiefly of   , all of said personal estate being estimated to be worth about   dollars; that said deceased left him surviving   , his widow, and   , his children, his only heirs; that your petitioner (being   of said deceased, and) believing that the said estate should be immediately administered, as well for the proper management of said   , as for prompt collection of assets by virtue of   rights under the statute, therefore pray that your honor will grant letters of administration to   , in the premises, upon   taking the oath prescribed by the statute, and entering into bond, in such sums and with securities as may be approved by your honor.

28. PROOF OF INTESTACY.(*k*)

Before letters of administration issue, the person applying must make and file an affidavit with the proper county clerk, setting forth, as near as may be, the date of the death of deceased, the probable amount of the personal estate, and the names of the heirs and widow, if known.(*l*)

AFFIDAVIT OF DEATH AND INTESTACY.

STATE OF ILLINOIS,} *ss :*
   County.   }

       , being duly sworn, deposeth and saith, That   , late of   , in the county of   , departed this life at   , in said county, on or about the   day of   , A. D. 18   , and that he died leaving no last will and testament, to the best of   knowledge and belief, and that deceased left surviving him   , his widow, and the following named children (*as the case may be*):

29. BOND.

Upon this proof being made, the court appoints the person, if entitled, administrator of the goods, chattels, rights, credits and effects of the deceased, and requires him to enter into

---

(*k*) Laws of 1859, § 9, p. 95; §§ 18, 20, R. S. 1874, pp. 107, 108.

(*l*) The act of 1872 requires proof to be made before the court; this may be by affidavit. See Cothran's Ann'd Stats., 1880, p. 53.

bond in the sum of double the value of the estate, with good and sufficient security, to be approved by the court. The judge is to ascertain the value of the estate, in such manner as shall be satisfactory to himself. If, at any time afterward, the court shall be advised of the insufficiency of the bond, either as to the amount or the security, the administrator may be summoned to show cause why he should not give additional or other security; and in case he should refuse or fail to give such new bond, his letters may be revoked, and administration granted to some other person, who will, in effect, be administrator *de bonis non*. The form of the bond is prescribed in the statute of wills, and must be substantially followed, as near as the case will admit. The bond should be approved by the judge, and filed in the clerk's office. The form of this bond is as follows:

BOND BY ADMINISTRATOR.

KNOW ALL MEN BY THESE PRESENTS, that we, A B, C D and E F, of the county of , and State of Illinois, are held and firmly bound unto the people of the State of Illinois, in the penal sum of dollars, current money of the United States, which payment, well and truly to be made and performed, we, and each of us, bind ourselves, our heirs, executors and administrators, jointly, severally and firmly by these presents.

Witness our hands and seals, this day of , A. D. 18 .

The condition of the above obligation is such, that if the said A B, administrator of all and singular the goods and chattels, rights and credits of J K, deceased, do make, or cause to be made, a true and perfect inventory of all and singular the goods and chattels, rights and credits of the said deceased, which shall come to the hands, possession or knowledge of him, the said A B, as administrator, or to the hands of any person or persons for him; and the same so made, do exhibit, or cause to be exhibited, in the county court for the said county of , agreeably to law; and such goods and chattels, rights and credits, do well and truly administer according to law, and all the rest of the said goods and chattels, rights and credits, which shall be found remaining upon the account of the said administrator, the same being first examined and allowed by the court, shall deliver and pay unto such person or persons, respectively, as may be legally entitled thereto; and further, do make a just and true account of all his actings and doings therein, when thereunto required by the said court; and if it shall appear that any last will and testament was made by the deceased, and the same be proved in court, and letters testamentary or of administration be obtained thereon, and the said A B do, in such case, on being required thereto, render and deliver up the letters of administration granted to him as aforesaid, and shall in general do and perform all other acts which may at any time be required of him by law, then this obligation to be void; otherwise to remain in full force and virtue.

Appointment of administrators.

This bond must be signed and sealed by the administrator and his securities, and attested by the clerk and filed.(*m*)

30. LETTERS OF ADMINISTRATION.*

STATE OF ILLINOIS, } *ss:*
County of   .

The People of the State of Illinois, to all to whom these presents shall come, greeting:

Know ye, that whereas   , late of the county of   and State of Illinois, died intestate, as it is said, on or about the   day of   , A. D. 18 , having at the time of his decease duly made and published   , personal property in this State, which may be lost, destroyed or diminished in value, if speedy care be not taken of the same; to the end, therefore, that said property may be collected and preserved for those who shall appear to have a legal right or interest therein, we do hereby appoint   , of the county of   and State of Illinois, administrator of all and singular the goods and chattels, rights and credits, which were of the said   at the time of h decease: with full power and authority to secure and collect the said property and debts wheresoever the same may be found in this State; and in general to do and perform all other acts, which now are or hereafter may be required of by law.

Witness   , clerk of the county court of said county, and the seal thereof, at the   of   , in said county, this   day of   , A. D. 18 .

                                          , *Clerk.*

STATE OF ILLINOIS, } *ss:*
County of   .

I, A B, clerk of the county court of   county, in the State aforesaid, do hereby certify that the within is a true and correct copy of the letters of administration, *with will annexed*, issued to   , now in force, and properly on file in my office.

In witness whereof, I have hereunto set my hand, and the seal of said county court, this   day of   , A. D. 18 .

                                          , *Clerk.*

31. THE OATH. The person appointed must take an oath to perform all acts required of him as administrator by law, public administrators excepted. It is as follows:

OATH OF ADMINISTRATOR.

I do solemnly swear (*or* affirm) that I will well and truly administer all and singular the goods and chattels, rights, credits and effects of A B, deceased, and pay all just claims and charges against his estate, so far as his goods, chattels and effects shall extend, and the law charge me; and that I will do and perform all other acts required of me by law, to the best of my knowledge and abilities.(*n*)

(*m*) See § 23, R. S. 1874, p. 108.   (*n*) See § 22, id.

---

* These letters are to be adapted *mutatis mutandis* to all cases of administration. See § 21, R. S. 1874, p. 108; Cothran's Annotated R. S., p. 53.

Appointment of administrators.

Administrator with the will annexed, must enter into the required bond:

32. BOND BY ADMINISTRATOR, WITH WILL ANNEXED.

KNOW ALL MEN BY THESE PRESENTS, that we, A B, C D, and E F, of the county of   , and State of Illinois, are held and firmly bound unto the people of the State of Illinois, in the penal sum of   dollars, current money of the United States, which payment, well and truly to be made and performed, we, and each of us, bind ourselves, our heirs, executors and administrators, jointly, severally and firmly by these presents.

Witness our hands and seals, this   day of   , A. D. 18 .

The condition of the above obligation is such, that, if the above bounden A B, executor of the last will and testament of G H, deceased (*or* administrator with the will annexed, of G H, deceased, *as the case may be*), do make, or cause to be made, a true and perfect inventory of all and singular the goods and chattels, rights and credits, lands, tenements and hereditaments, and the rents and profits issuing out of the same, of the said deceased, which have or shall come to the hands, possession or knowledge of the said A B, or into the possession of any other person for him, and the same so made do exhibit in the county court for the said county of   , as required by law; and also make and render a fair and just account of his actings and doings as such executor (*or* administrator) to said court, when thereunto lawfully required; and to well and truly fulfill the duties enjoined on him in and by the said will; and shall, moreover, pay and deliver to the persons entitled thereto, all the legacies and bequests contained in said will, so far as the estate of the said testator will thereunto extend, according to the value thereof, and as the law shall charge him; and shall, in general, do all other acts which may, from time to time, be required of him by law, then this obligation to be void; otherwise to remain in full force and virtue.(*o*)

33. FORM OF OATH OF ADMINISTRATOR, WITH WILL ANNEXED.

I do solemnly swear (*or* affirm) that this writing contains the true last will and testament of the within named A B, deceased, so far as I know or believe; and that I will well and truly execute the same, by paying first the debts and then the legacies mentioned therein, as far as his goods and chattels will thereunto extend, and the law charge me; and that I will make a true and perfect inventory of all such goods and chattels, rights and credits, as may come to my hands or knowledge, belonging to the estate of the said deceased, and render a fair and just account of my executorship, when thereunto required by law, to the best of my knowledge and abilities: so help me God.(*p*)

34. ADDITIONAL BOND.

Where a new bond is required to be given by the administrator, the formal part should be as prescribed in other cases, with a condition thereto, in the form prescribed as follows: (*q*)

(*o*) See § 23, R. S. 1874, p. 108.
(*p*) § 6, R. S. 1874, p. 105.

(*q*) See § 1, act 1879; Cothran's Stats., p. 1016.

Appointment of administrators.

The condition of the above obligation is such, that whereas the above bounden A B, executor of the last will and testament of J K, deceased (*or* administrator of the goods and chattels, rights and credits of J K, deceased), has heretofore executed a bond, payable to the people of the State of Illinois, and conditioned for the discharge of his duties as executor (*or* administrator) as aforesaid, which said bond bears date on the   day of   , A. D. 18 ; and whereas, by an order of the county court, made on the   day of   , A. D. 18 , other bond and security has been required of the said executor (*or* administrator). Now, therefore, if the said executor (*or* administrator) shall well and truly have kept and performed, and shall well and truly keep and perform, the condition of the bond first given as aforesaid, in all respects according to law, and shall in all respects have performed, and shall continue to perform, the duties of his office as aforesaid, then this obligation to be void; otherwise to remain in full force and virtue.

Which bond must be signed, sealed, approved, filed and recorded as above.

And in cases where the form prescribed by the statute does not cover the particular state of facts, the statutory forms are to be followed, so far as applicable, with such variations as will be adapted to the particular case.(*q*)

35. DECISIONS RELATIVE TO SUCH BONDS. For a breach in the condition of the bond of an executor, an action may be maintained against any one or more of the obligors of the bond. The common law in this particular is changed by statute.(*r*) The statute gives an action against the obligors in an executor's bond in cases of neglect or refusal to comply with any of the provisions of the law governing the conduct of the executor, as also in cases where one or more of the covenants in his bond are violated.(*r*) For liability of security on administrator's bond, and for the conclusive effect on security of an order of the probate court on the administrator to pay over moneys in his hands to the heir.(*s*)

MERGER. If a judgment has been entered on an executor's or administrator's bond in the circuit court, it would merge the latter in the former, and the judgment would stand as security for any additional breaches of the bond. In such case, the remedy would be to suggest a breach, and have damages assessed in that court.(*t*) For effect of giving new bonds, or of revocation of the letters of administration, on liabilities of securities to the old bond.(*u*)

(*q*) § 34, R. S. 1874, p. 110.
(*r*) *People* v. *Miller*, 1 Scam. 83.
(*s*) See *Ralston* v. *Wood*, 15 Ill. 159.
(*t*) *People* v. *Summers*, 16 Ill. 173.
(*u*) See *The People* v. *Lott*, 27 Ill..215.

Appointment of administrators.

36. FOREIGN EXECUTORS AND ADMINISTRATORS. When any person has proved or may prove the last will and testament of any deceased person, and taken on him the execution of said will, or has obtained or may obtain administration of the estate of an intestate in any State in the United States, or in any territory thereof, such person shall be enabled to prosecute suits, to enforce claims of the estate of the deceased, or to sell lands to pay debts, in any court in this State, in the same manner as if letters testamentary or of administration had been granted to him under the provisions of the laws of this State; *Provided*, that such person shall produce a copy of the letters testamentary or of administration, authenticated in the manner prescribed by the laws of congress of the United States for authenticating the records of judicial acts in any one State, in order to give them validity in other States; *And provided*, that said executor or administrator shall give a bond for costs, as in case of other non-residents.(v)

A CITIZEN OF ANOTHER STATE, in which administration has been granted on an estate, may come to this State and cause administration to be taken out here, a claim to be allowed, and real estate sold for its payment; and, in such case, it is not necessary to show that the personal estate in the other State has been exhausted.(w)

Nothing contained in the preceding section shall be so construed as to apply to cases where administration is obtained upon the estate of any intestate, nor where letters testamentary are granted in this State; and when, after any suit is commenced by any administrator or executor, under the provisions of the preceding section, and before final judgment thereon, administration is had, or execution undertaken within this State, under the laws of the same, upon the estate of any decedent, upon suggestion of such fact, entered of record, the said resident, administrator or executor shall, upon motion, be substituted as party to such suit; and thereupon the court shall proceed to hear and determine the same, as if it had been originally instituted in the name of the said resident, executor or administrator, and the benefits of the judgment, order or decree shall inure to him, and be assets in his hands. (x)

(v) § 42, act April 1, 1872; *Keefer* v. *Mason*, 36 Ill. 406; see page 294, infra; Cothran's Stats., p. 59.

(w) *Rosenthal* v. *Renick*, 44 Ill. 202.
(x) § 43, R. S. 1874, p. 112.

Powers and duties of administrators.

SECTION III.—THE POWERS, DUTIES, RIGHTS AND LIABILITIES OF ADMINISTRATORS.

1. The scope of the office of administrator.
2. Administrators are personal representatives of their intestates.
3. Decisions of the supreme court of the State of Illinois.

1. THE ADMINISTRATOR REPRESENTS THE PERSON of his intestate in respect to his *personal estate*, the whole of which, generally speaking, vests in the administrator on the grant of letters of administration, and such grant has relation to the time of the intestate's death.(*y*)

The interest which the administrator has in the personal estate is only temporary, and qualified. He is intrusted merely with the custody and distribution of the effects.(*z*)

As the jurisdiction of the administrator extends only to the "goods and chattels, rights and credits, which were of the person at the time of his death," it may be important to know what the terms "goods," "chattels," "rights" and "credits" embrace. *Goods* strictly consist of movable inanimate property, such as may attend a man's person wherever he goes. The term *chattels* includes all that is expressed by the word *goods*, and something more; it includes all kinds of *property*, except the freehold or things which are a parcel of it.(*a*)

RIGHTS AND CREDITS, as distinguished from chattels, are mostly applicable to such matters as lie in action, as debts owing the intestate, etc. The administrator succeeds to all such rights of action against third persons as the intestate had at the time of his death, or would have been entitled to if living. Some actions of a personal character die with the person, as slander, case for assault and battery on the person of the intestate, false imprisonment, etc. By actions for torts are meant actions on wrongs, not actions on contract.

2. ADMINISTRATORS ARE THE REPRESENTATIVES OF THE PERSONAL PROPERTY of the deceased, and not of his wrongs, except so far as the tortious act complained of was beneficial to the estate.(*b*)

(*y*) Toller's Law of Ex'rs, 133. Com. Dig. Adm., B. 10, 11; Coke Litt. 209.
(*z*) Toller's Law of Ex'rs, 134.
(*a*) 2 Bl. Com. 384; 1 Bouv. Iust; see chaps. vi and x, *infra*.

(*b*) 2 Kent's Com. 416. See 1 Hill's C. L., p. 399; 2 id., p. 228; § 123. act April 1, 1872; *Smith* v. *Archer*, 53 Ill. 241; § 122, R. S. 1874, p. 126; Cothran's Ann'd Stats., 1880, p. 80.

Powers and duties of administrators.

3. DECISIONS OF THE SUPREME COURT OF THE STATE OF ILLINOIS. These general principles are fully illustrated by exhaustive opinions of the supreme court, to which we refer, and which we, assisted by the digests, collate for the purpose of this work.

An administrator or an executor, so long as he retains his office, is the sole representative of the personal estate of the deceased.(c)

THE ACTS OF AN EXECUTRIX, rightfully done in her official character, are binding upon the estate which she represents.(d)

AN EXECUTOR, ADMINISTRATOR OR GUARDIAN may dispose of the personal estate or assets of his testator, intestate or ward, to a *bona fide* purchaser, for a valuable consideration, and the contract will be obligatory, unless the purchaser knows, or has good reason to suspect, that the sale is made with a design to misapply the funds, to the prejudice of those interested in the estate; and the purchaser is not bound to see to the proper application of the money.(e)

MAY CALL UPON A FORMER ADMINISTRATOR TO ACCOUNT. Under our statute, the authority of an administrator *de bonis non* to call upon a former administrator, whose letters have been revoked, to account fully for his administration of the estate, is clear and unmistakable.(f)

AN ADMINISTRATOR *DE BONIS NON*, appointed to succeed an administrator whose letters have been revoked, has authority to call upon the removed administrator to account fully for his administration of the estate, and may maintain all necessary actions for the purpose, and may, moreover, make him answer in damages for any mal-administration of the estate. *Aliter*, where the former administrator dies.(g)

AN ADMINISTRATOR *DE BONIS NON* has no authority to call on the first administrator, or, in case of his decease, on his personal representative, for an account of assets already administered. He can only administer upon so much of the estate as remained unadministered. The distributee or creditor of the first intestate should prosecute the representatives of the first administrator for any waste or misapplication of assets.(h)

Whatever is honestly done by one acting in the character of an

---

(c) *Gold* v. *Bailey*, 44 Ill. 491.
(d) *Greene* v. *Grimshaw*, 11 Ill. 389.
(e) *McConnell* v. *Hodson*, 2 Gilm. 640; *Makepiece* v. *Moore* 5 id. 474.
(f) *Duffin* v. *Abbott*, 48 Ill. 17.

(g) *Marsh* v. *The People*, 15 Ill. 284.
(h) *Rowan* v. *Kirkpatrick*, 14 Ill. 1; *Newhall* v. *Turney*, id. 338; *Marsh* v. *The People*, 15 id. 284.

Powers and duties of administrators.

executor *de son tort,* and not contrary to law, is binding between the parties. A settlement made in good faith with such an executor is valid.(*i*)

In relation to covenants, the general rule is, that an administrator has no power to charge the effects of his intestate by any contract originating with himself; and his contracts, in the course of his administration, or for the debts of his intestate, render him liable *de bonis propriis.*(*j*)

AN ADMINISTRATOR MAY ASSIGN a promissory note payable to his intestate, so as to vest the legal interest in the assignee.(*k*)

TITLE TO PERSONAL ESTATE. An administrator succeeds to the legal title to the personal estate of his intestate; and the title takes effect by relation from the death of the latter.(*k*)

ASSIGNMENT OF A NOTE. One of several executors may assign a promissory note made to the testator.(*l*)

Executors and administrators may assign notes made to the testator or intestate. And if an executor or administrator make or indorse a note in his own name, adding thereto "as executor," "as administrator," he would be personally responsible.(*m*)

An administrator may legally sell and transfer, at a discount, negotiable paper, taken for the estate, before it falls due; and allowance to the assignee of such paper and payment thereof, within a year of taking out letters, is good, provided all the transaction was in good faith.(*n*)

If an administrator act honestly and prudently, though there be a loss to, or a total diminution of, the intestate's estate, he will not be liable.(*o*)

Where M., an administrator in Illinois, employed an agent in Virginia to collect a demand due the estate from a resident in Virginia, and the agent collected the money and appropriated it to his own use, and never accounted to M. for it. *Held,* that M. was not liable for the loss of the money.(*o*)

A judgment cannot be rendered against an executor "to be levied of the goods and chattels, rights and credits, lands and tenements of the testator in the hands of the executor to be administered." Judgment can only be rendered against the goods and

(*i*) *Riley* v. *Loughrey,* 22 Ill. 99.
(*j*) *Vincent* v. *Morrison,* Breese, 175.
(*k*) *Makepeace* v. *Moore,* 5 Gilm. 474.
(*l*) *Dwight* v. *Newell,* 15 Ill. 333.
(*m*) *Walker* v. *Craig,* 18 Ill. 125.
(*n*) Id. 116.
(*o*) *Christy* v. *McBride,* 1 Scam. 75.

Powers and duties of administrators.

chattels of the testator, in the hands of the executor to be administered. Neither the lands nor the credits of a deceased person can be reached by execution.(*p*)

INTEREST. An administrator is chargeable with interest whenever he receives it, uses the money, or unreasonably retains it.(*q*)

DILIGENCE. Administrators who have acted in good faith in the collection of debts due their intestates, exercising proper vigilance, directed by a reasonable judgment, ought not to be charged with debts they may have failed to collect.(*r*)

One of several administrators is liable for the acts done by either, while they all continue in office. This liability ceases to attach to such of them as are removed from office for all acts done after the removal.(*s*)

A person who is at the same time administrator and guardian, is not allowed to apply the funds received in one capacity to the interests of the other.(*t*)

THEIR RIGHTS. An administrator has the legal title to the personal estate of the decedent, as a trustee and for a particular purpose; but when the debts are paid the residue of such estate belongs to the heir.(*u*)

COMPROMISE OF DEBTS. If an administrator settles a claim against a debtor to the estate in good faith, his action cannot be called in question by a subsequent administrator.(*v*)

The administrator has power to compromise or stipulate for the dismissal of a suit brought to recover damages for the death of intestate, caused by negligence.(*w*)

THEIR DUTIES. It is the duty of administrators to interpose the presumptions and positive limitations of law against claims presented for allowance; but their omission to do so will not entirely debar others affected by the neglect from all protection.(*x*)

SALE MUST BE PUBLIC. An administrator has no power to sell the personal property of his intestate at private sale.(*y*)

FOR PROFITS. An administrator, like a trustee, must account to the estate for any profits arising out of the use of its funds; and he

(*p*) *Greenwood* v. *Spiller*, 2 Scam. 502.
(*q*) *Rowan* v. *Kirkpatrick*, 14 Ill. 1.
(*r*) Id. 2.
(*s*) *Marsh* v. *The People*, 15 Ill. 284.
(*t*) *Stillman* v. *Young*, 16 Ill. 318.
(*u*) *Lewis* v. *Lyons*, 13 Ill. 117.
(*v*) *Short* v. *Johnson*, 25 Ill. 489.

(*w*) *Henchey* v. *City of Chicago*, 41 Ill. 136.
(*x*) *McCoy* v. *Morray*, 18 Ill. 519; *Unknown Heirs of Langworthy* v. *Baker*, 23 id. 484.
(*y*) *Burnap* v. *Dennis*, 3 Scam. 478.

Powers and duties of administrators.

should satisfy claims with the smallest amount of assets, as by the purchase of bank bills at a discount. And his reasonable labor and expenses for that object, or interest upon the use of his own funds, should be allowed against the estate.(z)

NEGLECT TO DEFEND — SURETIES LIABLE. If the administrator has been guilty of laches in not defending a suit at law, the remedy is on his bond.(a)

Foreign administrators cannot sue in the courts of this State.(b)

The law is now changed so as to allow foreign executors and administrators to sue in the courts of this State.(c)

The act of the legislature giving foreign administrators the power "to prosecute suits in any court in this State," includes the power to sue out an execution on a judgment rendered in favor of the intestate in his life-time.(d)

HOW MADE A PARTY. For mode of procedure to make an executor or administrator a party on the death of plaintiff in an attachment suit, see *Singleton* v. *Wofford.*(e)

PRACTICE. A claim against the estate of the decedent should be presented either on the notice of his representative or of the claimant; and, if not allowed at the time fixed for hearing, should be continued to a day certain or withdrawn, so that the claim shall not be allowed against the estate without giving the executor or administrator an opportunity to appear and contest.(f)

Administrators of the estate of persons who died before the act of 1823, regulating administrations, etc., cannot be compelled to pay claims against the estate according to that act, but they are governed by the law as it existed before that act, in respect to judgments obtained against the person in his life-time, upon whose estate they are administering.(g)

If one of two administrators loans the money of the estate, he does it upon his own responsibility, and an action to recover it should be brought in his own name alone.(h)

If an executor fail or refuse to comply with the order of the court of probate, requiring him to pay over to the heirs and devi-

---

(z) *Wingate* v. *Pool*, 25 Ill. 118.
(a) *Gold* v. *Bailey*, 44 Ill. 491.
(b) *The People* v. *Peck*, 3 Scam. 118.
(c) § 42, act April 1, 1872.
(d) *Keefer* v. *Mason*, 36 Ill. 406.
(e) 3 Scam. 577.

(f) *Propst* v. *Meadows*, 13 Ill. 157; *Reitzell* v. *Miller*, 25 id. 67.
(g) *Jones' Adm'rs* v. *Bond*, Breese, 223.
(h) *Thornton* v. *Smiley*, Breese, 13.

Powers and duties of administrators.

sees their distributive portions of the estate, the remedy is by attachment for contempt of court.(*i*)

Notwithstanding the act of 1823, regulating the distribution of an intestate's estate, a judgment obtained before that time against the intestate in his life-time is entitled to preference in the payment of his debts out of his personal estate, even if the estate be insolvent.(*j*)

APPEARANCE BY HEIRS. Heirs appearing before the county court, by their guardian, to contest the validity of claims against the estate of their ancestor, should defend in the name of the administrator; and an appeal to the circuit court, if taken by the opposite party, should bring the administrator only into that court, and the heirs may equally contest there.(*k*)

Whatever defense an administrator may be allowed to make against the claims or demands of creditors, may be made by any person interested in the realty against an application of an administrator to sell such realty for the payment of the debts of the intestate.(*l*)

Heirs dissatisfied with the settlement of the estate by administrators should proceed by bill in chancery.(*m*)

FORUM. The creditor of an estate is not compelled to present his claim to the probate court for allowance, but may resort to the circuit court in the first instance if that court has jurisdiction.(*n*)

REMOVAL OF INCUMBRANCE. The administrator can apply for an order to sell the real estate to pay debts, but he must take the estate as he finds it; he cannot bring suit to remove an incumbrance.(*o*) The act of 1857 does not change the law.(*p*)

When a person renders service for the benefit of the estate of a decedent, at the instance of the executrix thereof, his claim for compensation is not a personal demand against the executrix; but, on the death of the executrix, may be enforced against the estate, for the benefit of which the services were rendered.(*q*)

WARRANTY. If an administrator takes upon himself to warrant personal property sold by him, the maker of the note given for

---

(*i*) *Piggott* v. *Ramey*, 1 Scam. 145.
(*j*) *Woodworth* v. *Paine's Adm'rs*, Breese, 294.
(*k*) *Motsinger* v. *Wolf*, 16 Ill. 71.
(*l*) *Dorman* v. *Lane, Adm'r*, 1 Gilm. 143.
(*m*) *Heward* v. *Slagle*, 52 Ill. 336.

(*n*) *Rosenthal* v. *Magee*, 41 Ill. 370; *Wells* v. *Miller*, 45 id. 33.
(*o*) *Phelps* v. *Funkhouser*, 39 Ill. 401.
(*p*) *Cutter* v. *Thompson*, 51 Ill. 390; id. 531; *Gridley* v. *Watson*, 53 id. 186.
(*q*) *Greene* v. *Grimshaw*, 11 Ill. 389.

Powers and duties of administrators.

such property may show failure of consideration under the warranty.(r)

Cannot submit a claim against the estate to arbitration.(s)

PAROL CONTRACT WITH INTESTATE. In an action against the administratrix on such a contract, plaintiff must show a readiness and willingness on his part to perform, and also a demand on defendant for the property contracted to be delivered.(t)

DEVASTAVIT. A judgment cannot be rendered against a security in an administration bond, nor is he liable to an action until a *devastavit* by a suit has first been established against the administrator.(u)

The statute authorizes several actions on an executor's bond.(v)

Where administrators have given several bonds, and there is a complication of interests, resulting from the death of one of the administrators, and of some of the sureties, whose legal representatives cannot be made parties in a joint action at law upon the bonds, a court of equity will entertain jurisdiction.(w)

[This rule is now changed by the act of 1829. Purples' Statutes, p. 1218, § 126; Scates' Comp., p. 1207.(x))

It is not necessary to establish a *devastavit* previous to instituting a suit on an executor's bond.(y)

In an action on a judgment against administrators, suggesting a *devastavit*, a judgment by default admits the truth of the allegations in the declaration, and a jury of inquiry is not necessary to ascertain the damages.(z)

The time of the *devastavit* of an administrator is properly ascertained from the return of *nulla bona* to the execution issued against him in his representative character.(a)

EVIDENCE THEREOF. Where an administrator, on the sale of property belonging to the estate, received the notes of the purchasers with security, and it resulted that the principals and sureties were insolvent, this will show, *prima facie*, that the administrator had neglected his duty, and was guilty of a *devastavit*.(b)

(r) Welch, Adm'r, v. Hoyt, 24 Ill. 117.
(s) Clark v. Hogle, 52 Ill. 427; Reitzell v. Miller, 25 id. 67.
(t) Pahlman v. King, 49 Ill. 266.
(u) Biggs v. Postlewait, Breese, 154.
(v) The People, use, v. Randolph, 24 Ill. 324.
(w) The People v. Lott, 27 Ill. 215.
(x) § 25, R. S. 1874, p. 109.
(y) The People v. Miller, 1 Scam. 83.
(z) Greenup v. Woodworth, Breese, 179.
(a) Greenup v. Brown, Breese, 193.
(b) Curry v. The People, 54 Ill. 263.

Powers and duties of administrators.

WHO MAY HAVE A REMEDY THEREFOR. In an action upon an administrator's bond, at the instance of a creditor, a *prima facie* right of recovery exists, if it appears that the person for whose use the suit is brought holds a claim against the estate, and that the administrator has been guilty of a *devastavit* to the extent of such claim. It is not essential to such right of recovery that the creditor shall prove there were no assets to which he could resort for the satisfaction of his claim.(*b*)

LIMITATIONS. A claim was filed by a creditor on the day appointed by the administrator, and within two years after his letters were granted. *Held*, a proper exhibition of the claim, and not barred, though, after the lapse of two terms, it was dropped from the docket for a period of three years before final adjudication.(*c*)

The running of the two years' limitation may still be prevented by presenting the claim or account to the administrator, notwithstanding the act of February 21, 1859.(*d*)

The claim having been presented to the administrator within two years, the judgment should direct payment to be made in due course of administration, though the suit was not commenced within the two years.(*e*)

Where an administratrix, in that capacity, loans money belonging to the estate to her husband by a subsequent marriage, for the use and benefit of her children by the former husband, until the youngest shall have reached majority, such children cannot maintain an action for the recovery of the money so loaned upon the majority of the youngest until after an order for distribution has been obtained.(*f*)

And after the order of distribution the action should be brought against the administratrix.(*f*)

And the creditor can recover costs against the estate in the circuit court, after the term appointed for prosecuting claims in the probate court, upon the expiration of a year from the taking out letters of administration, if he prove a demand before the commencement of suit.(*g*)

Delay of three years by a near relative in presenting a claim

---

(*b*) *Curry* v. *The People*, 54 Ill. 263.
(*c*) *Barbero* v. *Thurman*, 49 Ill. 283.
(*d*) *Wells* v. *Miller*, 45 Ill. 33; *Mason* v. *Tiffany*, id. 392.
(*e*) *Wells* v. *Miller*, 45 Ill. 33.
(*f*) *Neubrecht* v. *Santmeyer*, 50 Ill. 74.
(*g*) *Rosenthal* v. *Magee*, 41 Ill. 370.

against an estate may, under certain circumstances, be considered by the jury in determining the character of the claim.(*h*)

REVIVAL OF JUDGMENT. It is erroneous, in reviving a judgment against an administrator, to award an execution against the goods and chattels, lands and tenements of the intestate. The proper order would be to revive the judgment against the administrator, to be paid in the due course of administration.(*i*)

An order of a probate court against an administrator, ordering him to pay over money in his hands to an heir, is conclusive not only on the administrator, but on his sureties, though the latter were not parties to the proceedings. And if such order is not complied with, the person in whose favor it is made may have an action against the administrator and his sureties on their bond. Such suit on the bond is a collateral action, founded as well upon the judgment as the bond; and, where such judgment is offered in evidence, it cannot be inquired into except for fraud. It is as conclusive as any other judgment.(*j*)

A judgment rendered in the courts of a sister State against an administrator deriving his authority under and by force of the laws of this State, who voluntarily entered his appearance to the action in which such judgment was pronounced, cannot be enforced in our courts against the estate represented by such administrator. A judgment rendered under such circumstances is a nullity here, and the creditor must resort to his action upon the original contract.(*k*)

JUDGMENT NOT AN ADMISSION OF ASSETS. A judgment in this State against an administrator is not an admission of assets sufficient to satisfy the debt; its only effect is to establish a debt against the estate, to be paid in due course of administration.(*k*)

But a prior judgment rendered on the claim in the probate court is not affected by the void judgment rendered in the circuit court on the award.(*l*)

Judgment against an administrator binds the personal estate.(*m*)

Judgment for costs not to be rendered against the administrator personally.(*n*)

A judgment for costs cannot be rendered against an administra-

(*h*) *O'Connor* v. *O'Connor*, 52 Ill. 316.
(*i*) *Turney* v. *Gates*, 12 Ill. 141.
(*j*) *Ralston* v. *Wood*, 15 Ill. 159.
(*k*) *Judy* v. *Kelley*, 11 Ill. 211.
(*l*) *Clark* v. *Hogle*, 52 Ill. 427.
(*m*) *Gold* v. *Bailey*, 44 Ill. 491.
(*n*) *Hunter* v. *Bilyeu*, 39 Ill. 368.

Powers and duties of administrators.

tor in his personal character, but must be rendered against him in his representative character.(*o*)

The judgment against an administrator, upon foreclosure of a mortgage, should be such a judgment as could have been rendered against the mortgagor had he been living.(*p*)

A circuit court has no authority to render a judgment against the lands of an intestate in a proceeding *in personam* against his administrator.(*q*)

It is erroneous to award execution on a judgment against an estate of one deceased, which is founded on a claim exhibited and allowed against it. The proper judgment in such case is for the amount of the debt, and costs to be paid in the due course of administration.(*r*)

SCIRE FACIAS. A creditor having a judgment against an administrator cannot sue out a *scire facias* upon the judgment against an heir, to make it chargeable upon the land.(*s*)

An appeal bond by an executor, conditioned that he shall pay the debt in due course of administration, is good.(*t*)

ASSETS; WHAT ARE. The amount recovered in the statutory action, where the death of a person is caused by the wrongful act, default or neglect of another, is not to be treated as part of the estate of the deceased; creditors do not get any benefit from it. It is to be distributed among those to whom the personal estate would descend in the absence of a will according to the statute of descent.(*u*)

An administrator takes no estate, right, title or interest in realty. He takes only a power.(*v*)

Accruing rent descends to the heirs, and the administrator has no concern with it.(*w*)

Any saving or accumulations by the administrator, in the management of the estate, becomes assets, and liable to distribution.(*x*)

For a full discussion of the rights of the widow, and the conse-

(*o*) *Church* v. *Jewett*, 1 Scam. 55; *Gibbons* v. *Johnson*, 3 id. 61.
(*p*) *Swiggart* v. *Harber*, 4 Scam. 364.
(*q*) *McDowell* v. *Wight*, 4 Scam. 403.
(*r*) *Welch, Adm'r*, v. *Wallace*, 3 Gilm. 490; *Peck, Adm'r*, v. *Stevens*, 5 id. 127; *Judy* v. *Kelley*, 11 Ill. 211.

(*s*) *Stone* v. *Wood*, 16 Ill. 177.
(*t*) *Mason* v. *Johnson*, 24 Ill. 159.
(*u*) *City of Chicago* v. *Major*, 18 Ill 349.
(*v*) *Smith* v. *McConnell*, 17 Ill. 135.
(*w*) *Foltz* v. *Prouse*, 17 Ill. 487. See 1 Hill's C. L. 463.
(*x*) *Wingate* v. *Pool*, 25 Ill. 118.

Powers and duties of administrators.

quences of her electing to take their value, instead of the specific articles allowed by law, see *Cruce* v. *Cruce.(y)*

Where an administrator has purchased a CHATTEL REAL belonging to his intestate in his life-time, and charged himself with the rents and profits thereof, and treated it as assets of the estate, he will not be allowed afterward to claim it as his own property, but must account for it as assets.(*z*)

It is his duty to reduce the assets to money, and report the same to the court, to be paid upon debts and distributed among the parties entitled to receive it.(*z*)

If an executor loan the money of the estate without authority in the will, it operates as a *devastavit*, and creditors, legatees or distributees may sue and recover on his bond.(*z*)

For necessary food and clothing furnished by an executor for the support of minor heirs having no guardian, he should be allowed to charge a reasonable compensation.(*a*)

ADMINISTRATOR OF DECEASED PARTNERS; SURVIVORS; RELATIVE RIGHTS. Primarily, the administrator has nothing to do with the firm assets and debts. The surviving partners take the exclusive title to the former for the payment of the latter. If any assets remain in their hands after the payment of liabilities, the administrator takes the distributive share of the deceased.(*a*)

But if the survivors are guilty of delay or waste in the settlement of the firm accounts, the administrator may interpose in equity for an account and the appointment of a receiver to adjust and settle the partnership matters.(*b*)

Rent falling due after lessor's death does not go to the executor or administrator, but to the heir.(*c*)

Decedent, while taking lumber by river from Illinois to Tennessee, died on the Missouri shore. *Held*, that, as decedent's domicile was in this State, and as he had no other assets in Missouri or Tennessee, and that, as the persons alleged to have taken wrongful possession of the lumber resided in this State, the administratrix of decedent could sue such persons here.(*d*)

The personal assets of an estate become legally vested in the administrator, and the heirs cannot maintain an action at law, in

(*y*) 21 Ill. 46.
(*z*) *Willenborg* v. *Murphy*, 36 Ill. 344.
(*a*) *Johnston* v. *Maples*, 49 Ill. 101.
(*b*) *Miller* v. *Jones*, 39 Ill. 54.
(*c*) *Dixon* v. *Niccolls*, 39 Ill. 372.
(*d*) *Wells* v. *Miller*, 45 Ill. 382.

Powers and duties of administrators.

their own right, for any portion of such personal estate, until an order of court for distribution has been obtained.(e)

PERSONAL ESTATE. Money due a testator at his decease, upon contracts for the sale of real estate, made by him during his life, no deed having been executed, are to be considered a part of his personal estate, the same as other debts due the estate, and the fact that some of the contracts were liable to forfeiture at the death of the testator can make no difference, since the testator did not assert such right.(f)

LIABILITY OF SURETIES. Money paid to an administrator by a railroad company, upon whose road the intestate was killed, being paid as compensation therefor, is not assets in the hands of the administrator which he is bound to administer; and the sureties on the administrator's bond are responsible for its proper distribution. (g)

An administrator cannot affect the title of the heirs to real estate, descended to them from the intestate, except by a sale authorized by an order of court. He has no power to admit away the title to real estate which is held by heirs under the law of descent.(h)

As to limitation of the administrator's power over the real estate of decedent.(i)

The administrator has no power, nor is he bound to protect the realty in any manner, not even to the extent of paying the taxes.(j)

CHANCERY JURISDICTION. The thirty-fourth section of the conveyance act, which authorizes the executors, administrators or heirs of any deceased person, who shall have made a contract in writing, in his life-time, for the conveyance of land, to apply to a court of chancery for a decree that the conveyance be made, embraces only those cases where the purchase-money has been fully paid, and has no reference to a case where the consideration remains wholly or in part unpaid; yet a court of chancery will entertain a bill at the suit of the executors or administrators, and heirs or devisees of such vendor, where the consideration has not been paid, for the twofold purpose of enforcing the payment of the money and authorizing a conveyance of the land.(k)

MISTAKE. An administrator has no authority to apply to a court

(e) *Neubrecht* v. *Santmeyer,* 50 Ill. 74.
(f) *Skinner* v. *Newberry,* 51 Ill. 203.
(g) *Goltra* v. *The People,* 53 Ill. 224.
(h) *Walbridge* v. *Day,* 31 Ill. 379.
(i) *Phelps* v. *Funkhouser,* 39 Ill. 401; *Gridley* v. *Watson,* 53 id. 186; *Shoemate* v. *Lockridge,* id. 503.
(j) *Phelps* v. *Funkhouser,* 39 Ill. 401
(k) *Burger* v. *Potter,* 32 Ill. 66.

Powers and duties of administrators.

of chancery to reform a deed, made to his intestate in his life-time, on the allegation that there was a mistake therein in the description of the land intended to be conveyed.(*l*)

VOLUNTARY DEED; FRAUD. An administrator cannot avoid a voluntary deed of his intestate, nor can he take advantage of a fraudulent conveyance made by his intestate.(*m*)

An administrator cannot, in equity, obtain relief by the removal of adverse apparent titles to the lands of his intestate, or convert an equitable into a legal title.(*n*)

Where an administrator accepted from a debtor of the estate a mortgage upon land of which the intestate died seized in fee simple, and the title to which had fully vested in the heirs by descent, and a foreclosure and sale of the premises was had under such mortgage: *Held*, that these proceedings on the part of the administrator, while they were an admission by him that the mortgagor had some title in the premises, in nowise affected the title of the heirs, which they took by inheritance. Nor would such proceedings on the part of the administrator operate to estop a subsequent administrator of the same estate from purchasing the title of the heirs to these premises, and holding it, at least against the right of purchasers derived under such mortgage.(*o*)

By the statute of 1825, an executor or administrator was authorized to relinquish a part, and obtain a patent for the residue, of any tract of land which might have been purchased by the testator or intestate, and for which full payment might not have been made, whenever that could be done under the acts of congress; and the executor or administrator was likewise authorized to sell and assign a certificate of purchase of land partly paid for, when such sale might be necessary in order to pay the debts of the deceased.(*p*)

A, being at the point of death, made his will, directing, among other things, how his real estate should be disposed of, but omitted to name an executor. B was duly appointed administrator with the will annexed, who, supposing that he had authority, sold the land and executed a deed with intent to convey the fee. In an action of ejectment against the grantee, brought by the heirs of the testator, this deed was offered in evidence and excluded by the court.

(*l*) *Shoemate* v. *Lockridge*, 53 Ill. 503.
(*m*) *Choteau* v. *Jones*, 11 Ill. 300; *Alexander* v. *Tams*, 13 id. 221.
(*n*) *Smith* v. *McConnell*, 17 Ill. 135;
Gridley v. *Watson*, 53 id. 186; *Shoemate* v. *Lockridge*, id. 503.
(*o*) *Walbridge* v. *Day*, 31 Ill. 379.
(*p*) *Prevo* v. *Walters*, 4 Scam. 35.

Held, that, as the administrator had not the power to sell and convey by virtue of the will, either at common law or by the provisions of our statute of wills, the deed was properly excluded.(*q*)

PURCHASING AT THEIR OWN SALE. As to effect in law, also in equity.(*r*)

As to acquiescence of the heirs in such a purchase by the administrator, and delay in setting the sale aside.(*s*)

A court of chancery will not compel an heir to pay over money to an administrator when such administrator has no debts to pay, nor any use to make of it connected with the estate.(*t*)

SECTION IV. RESIGNATION AND REMOVAL OF EXECUTORS AND ADMINISTRATORS.

1. The statute of 1872.
2. Petition.
3. Order.
4. Notice.
5. Resignation.
6. Record.
7. Notice to security.
8. Assent.
9. Removal and revocation, grounds of.
10. Petition.

1. THE STATUTE OF 1872. The repealed statute required a notice to be published before presenting and asking for the acceptance of a resignation by an executor or administrator. The act of 1872 (*u*) provides "that the executor or administrator may, upon his petition, and upon giving such notice to the legatees, devisees or distributees as the court shall direct, be allowed to resign his trust when it appears to the county court to be proper."

2. PETITION.

In the matter of the estate of } *County court of   county,*
A B, deceased.   }   *term, A. D.* 18   .

To the Hon.   , Judge of said court:

Your petitioner respectfully shows that he is about to remove from the

(*q*) *Hall* v. *Irwin*, 2 Gilm. 176.
(*r*) *Lockwood* v. *Mills*, 39 Ill. 603;
Miles v. *Wheeler*, 43 id. 123; *Kruse* v.
Steffens, 47 id. 112.

(*s*) *Miles* v. *Wheeler*, 43 Ill. 123.
(*t*) *Lewis* v. *Lyons*, 13 Ill. 117.
(*u*) § 40, R. S. 1874, p. 111.

Of executors and administrators.

State, and is going to reside at San Francisco, in the State of California. He, therefore, asks leave to resign his trust as administrator (or executor) of the said estate (or of the last will and testament of said A B). C D.

Upon filing this petition, notice should be given as required by the court, in an order to be entered. If the legatees, devisees and distributees cannot be personally served, notice should be published as required in chancery.(*v*)

3. ORDER. On reading and filing the petition of C D, administrator (or executor, etc.), showing that he is about to remove from this State, and asking leave to resign, ordered, that notice of his application be given to all the distributees (or legatees and devisees) of said estate (*here specify if the notice is to be published — how*), and that said application be heard (*here state when the hearing is to be*).

4. NOTICE OF RESIGNATION.

STATE OF ILLINOIS, } *ss:*
County.

To the   term of county court of   county, A. D. 18   :

In the matter of the estate }   Notice of application to resign.
of A B, deceased.

To all persons concerned :

Take notice, that the undersigned, administrator of A B, deceased, will, at the   term of said court, holden at the court-house in the   of   , in said county, on the first Monday of   , 18   , present to said court, for acceptance, his resignation of the office of administrator of A B, deceased, and you are hereby notified and summoned to be and appear before said court on the   day of   , A. D. 18   , to show cause, if any you have, why said resignation should not be accepted, according to the statute in such case made and provided.   E F,

Clerk of said court.

Dated   , 18   .

A copy of the ADVERTISEMENT, with the publisher's certificate of the due publication thereof,(*w*) should be attached to, or presented to the court with, the resignation. Before the acceptance of the resignation, the administrator (or executor) must render a complete settlement of all matters in his hands up to the time of his resignation, and deliver into court all evidences of property, moneys, etc., in his possession. The resignation must be in writing, and may be in the following form:(*x*)

(*v*) See pp. 126-131, *infra*.   (*x*) §§ 40 41, R. S. 1874, p. 111.
(*w*) See p. 51, *supra*.

Resignation and removal

5. RESIGNATION.

STATE OF ILLINOIS, } ss :
 County.

County court of county.
 term, A. D. 18 .

In the matter of the estate }
of A B, deceased.

To , *Judge of said court :*

 The undersigned, administrator of A B, deceased, having given the notice thereof required by order of court, as will appear by proof of the same herewith filed, does hereby resign his office as administrator of the goods, chattels, rights, credits and effects of said A B, deceased, and prays that this, his resignation, be accepted, and that he be discharged from the further exercise of his said office. C D,
Administrator of A B, deceased.

April 2, 18 .

 6. THE ACCEPTANCE OF THE RESIGNATION may be entered in the following form :

In the matter of the estate } Resignation of administrator.
of A B, deceased.

 On this day came C D, administrator of A B, deceased, and presents to the court, for its acceptance, his resignation of the office of administrator of the goods, chattels, effects, rights and credits of the said A B, deceased; and, it appearing to the court that due notice of the presentation of said resignation has been given, and the said administrator having stated and adjusted with said court an account of his actions and doings as such administrator, and paid over all moneys, effects and choses in action, according to law, and the court being sufficiently advised in the premises, it is *ordered* and adjudged that the resignation of the said C D, as administrator of A B, deceased, be accepted, and the said C D be discharged from further exercise of his said office.

7. NOTICE TO SECURITY.

STATE OF ILLINOIS, } ss :
 County.

 County court of county, to term, 18 .

In the matter of the estate } Notice of resignation.
of A B, deceased.

To E F, *security on the bond of C D, administrator of A B , deceased :*

 Take notice, that the undersigned, administrator of A B, deceased, will, at the term of said court, to be holden at the court-house in the of , on the Monday of , 18 , tender to said court, for its acceptance, his resignation of the office of administrator of said A B, deceased.
                   C D,

Dated , 18 .   *Administrator of A B, deceased.*

 Copies of these notices should likewise be presented, and proof of service made, as above.

Of executors and administrators.

8. Where one of several administrators desires to resign, he may do so upon complying with the directions of the court, and filing the ASSENT OF HIS CO-ADMINISTRATOR.

8. FORM OF ASSENT TO RESIGNATION.

STATE OF ILLINOIS,
 County. } *ss.:*

In the matter of the estate }
of A B, deceased. }

To J H, Judge of the county court of county:

We, J K, co-administrator, and Y Z, security of C D, administrator of A B, deceased, do hereby assent to the resignation of C D as such administrator.

Witness our hands and seals this day of , A. D 18 .

[SEAL.]   J K,
[SEAL.]   Y Z.

9. REMOVAL OF ADMINISTRATORS FROM OFFICE. The letters of administration being a grant of power, which alone invests this officer with the right to act as administrator, if they be revoked or repealed, his right to act in such capacity is ended; and, consequently, all acts done by him subsequently thereto are void, as against the interests of others. If the administration be not *absolutely* void, but only *voidable*, before the repeal of his letters, his acts regularly done under color of his office are valid, and the repeal does not, in such case, act retrospectively to affect them.

Letters of administration may be revoked and repealed for various causes, among which may be named the following: The production and probate of a will; the non-residence or removal from the State of the administrator; removing intestate's property out of the State, and his refusal or neglect to render his account and make settlement; or where the person to whom letters have been issued shall become insane, lunatic or of unsound mind, or an habitual drunkard, or be convicted of an infamous crime, or shall waste or mismanage the estate, or conduct himself in such manner as to endanger his co-administrator or securities, or has procured letters upon the false and fraudulent pretense of being a creditor of the estate, or upon any false pretense whatever, etc.

In the revocation and repeal of letters of administration, the court generally acts upon the *application of some interested party.*

10. PETITION FOR REVOCATION OF LETTERS OF ADMINISTRATION.

STATE OF ILLINOIS, }
 Cook County. } *ss:* County court of county, term, 18 .

To Hon. , Judge of said court:

The petition of John Doe, of said county, respectfully represents to your

Resignation and removal

honor that your petitioner is an heir at law (*or, as the case may be*), of Richard Roe, late of said county, deceased, and, as such, is interested in the safe and proper administration of said deceased's estate, and entitled to distribution therein; "that the security of A B, administrator of said Richard Roe, has become insufficient; that E F, his security, has not property of sufficient value to secure the distributees and creditors of the estate against loss and damage which may occur in the administration of the said estate." (*In other cases, omit all between the quotation points, and insert the particular facts of the case upon which revocation is sought.*) Wherefore, your petitioner prays, that the said A B be required by this court to give other and sufficient security, and, in default thereof, that the letters of administration so granted to him be revoked and repealed, and administration be granted to some other person entitled to the same.

And your petitioners will ever pray, etc.

Dated   , 18   .   JOHN DOE.

The petition should be verified by the oath of the person making it.

Upon filing the petition, a citation will issue to the administrator to show cause against the application. Upon the return of the citation, the court, upon being satisfied of the insufficiency of the security, will require the administrator to give a new bond by a specified day, and, in case of default thereof, will order his removal.

GROUND OF REMOVAL. Where an administrator shows by his report that he has given an unauthorized preference to creditors in the payment of assets, it is sufficient to justify his removal.(x)

REVOCATION. The acceptance of the probate court of the resignation of an administrator amounts to a revocation of his letters; and if there are other administrators the burden of administration is cast on them.(y)

The refusal of an administrator to perform the duties of his trust is a sufficient cause for revoking his authority.(y)

REMOVAL OF ADMINISTRATOR FROM THE STATE. The act of 1847 on this subject, as reprinted in 1853, and as it appears in Scates' Compilation, page 1238, is not correctly copied from the original session laws, important words being omitted.(y) But the same is correctly printed in Gross' Statutes, page 811; also in Cothran's Statutes, page 56. A non-resident cannot legally be appointed administrator of an estate in this State, not even on the estate of a non-resident dying abroad and leaving effects in this State.(z)

(x) *Foltz* v. *Prouse*, 17 Ill. 487.
(y) *Marsh* v. *The People*, 15 Ill. 284.
(z) *Child* v. *Gratiot*, 41 Ill. 357; 3 Cothran's Stats., p. 50.

Of executors and administrators.

Where a non-resident is so appointed, it is the duty of the probate court to revoke the appointment on proper application.(z)

THE HEARING. On filing the petition for the removal of an executor or administrator for cause, as we have seen, process issues. The time for hearing should be fixed and continued from time to time until the executor or administrator is either actually or constructively served. No course of procedure is indicated, but the Chancery Practice in such cases affords ample precedents, if we are to consider the petition in the nature of a bill in chancery.

The decree should recite the facts upon which the same is made.

DECREE OF REMOVAL OF AN EXECUTOR OR ADMINISTRATOR.

THE PETITION of John Doe coming on this day to be heard, and it appearing that A B, the   aforesaid, has filed his answer herein, denying the facts stated in said petition, and it appearing to the court from the testimony that A B has mismanaged said estate as stated in said petition, and that all the facts stated in said petition are true and have been fully proved to the satisfaction of this court, and after argument by the respective counsel for said petitioner and said   , it is now here ORDERED, ADJUDGED AND DECREED, that said   accounts be forthwith closed; that all the estate of the said   which has come to the hands of the said A B, as such   , now remaining undisposed of, be delivered over to another   , to be by this court appointed, and that the letters   heretofore issued to the said A B be, and hereby are, revoked; and that the said A B attend before this court from day to day until this decree and the several orders herein are fully complied with, and until the further order of court.

Dated   , A. D. 18 .

Another executor or administrator is then to be appointed as before, and the estate unadministered, turned over to him.

In case of a will, the appointee of the court is sometimes termed " an administrator *cum testamento annexo de bonis non*" (with the will annexed of the unadministered estate); in case of an intestate, "administrator *de bonis non*" (of the unadministered estate).

(z) *Child* v. *Gratiot*, 41 Ill. 357.

Infants or minors.

CHAPTER IV.

PERSONS AND ESTATES OF INFANTS OR MINORS.

SECTION I. Infants or minors.
II. Competency and appointment of guardians.
III. Their powers and duties.
IV. Resignation and removal of guardians.

SECTION I. — INFANTS OR MINORS.

1. Females under eighteen years of age and males under the age of twenty-one, in this State, are minors.
2. Validity or invalidity of their acts generally.
3. Ratification of a sale of land, right to hold property, etc.
4. Estoppel and laches, not applicable to infants, generally.
5. Of their property.
6. Actions by and against.

1. MALES AT TWENTY-ONE, FEMALES AT EIGHTEEN, ARE OF LAWFUL AGE. Males of the age of twenty-one, and females of the age of eighteen years, are considered of full age for all purposes; and until these ages are attained they are considered minors.(*a*)

2. VALIDITY OR INVALIDITY OF THEIR ACTS. An infant cannot bind himself by bond,(*b*) but the implied contracts of an infant for necessaries are binding upon him; (*c*) the appointment of an attorney by an infant is absolutely void.(*c*)

A minor contracted to work nine months, but worked six weeks and quit; *held*, that he was not bound by the contract, and that he could recover the value of the services rendered.(*d*)

Contracts by infants for the improvement of their property are not binding upon them. Nor does the receipt of rents from the improved property, after they attain majority, amount to a ratification.(*e*)

Where a plaintiff relies on a new promise, made after the defendant became of age, the original contract having been made during infancy, he should declare on the new contract.(*f*)

(*a*) § 1, R. S. 1874, p. 558; *Stevenson* v. *Westfull*, 18 Ill. 209; *Harrer* v. *Wallner*, 80 Ill. 197; Cothran's Stats., p. 766.
(*b*) *Bliss* v. *Perryman*, 1 Scam. 484.
(*c*) *Cole* v. *Pennoyer*, 14 Ill. 158.
(*d*) *Ray* v. *Haines*, 52 Ill. 485.
(*e*) *McCarty* v. *Carter*, 49 Ill. 53.
(*f*) *Bliss* v. *Perryman*, 1 Scam. 484.

Infants or minors.

FRAUDS AND TORTS. For a discussion of the liability of infants for frauds and torts, see *Davidson* v. *Young.*(*g*)

An infant is not to be charged with laches for failing to bring an advancement into hotchpot.(*h*)

Conveyances made by an infant in person are voidable only, to be confirmed or repudiated at his discretion after he arrives at majority.(*h*) So, if a minor contracts to sell real estate, the contract cannot be enforced if he refuse after his majority to sanction it;(*i*) and, generally, a minor may revoke a conveyance within a reasonable time after he becomes of age. In this State, under the seven years' limitation act, if a conveyance by a minor is to be revoked by him, he must commence proceedings within three years after the disability is removed;(*j*) and a conveyance by a minor of real estate must be disaffirmed and repudiated within three years after his majority, or it will be upheld.(*k*)

3. RATIFICATION. As to what is necessary to constitute a ratification of a sale of lands.(*l*)

If an infant conveys his land, and on attaining his majority ratifies the conveyance, and then conveys to another person for a valuable consideration, the last grantee, having notice of the deed made in infancy, but no notice of the ratification, will hold the land.(*m*)

One has as perfect a legal right to purchase land which his grantor has conveyed during infancy, as to purchase land that has never been conveyed at all, and he is not to be denied the position of an innocent purchaser because he has notice of the deed made in infancy.(*n*)

4. ESTOPPEL AND LACHES. Infants are not estopped by failure to give notice or by acquiescence.(*o*)

5. THE PROPERTY OF INFANTS. SALE, ETC., OF REAL PROPERTY. A obtained money from B to purchase certain land. The land was purchased in the name of C, to secure B for the money loaned. A died before the time for payment of the money to B, leaving an infant son. *Held*, that the infant had an equitable estate in the

---

(*g*) 38 Ill. 145.
(*h*) *Barnes* v. *Hazelton*, 50 Ill. 429.
(*i*) *Walker* v. *Ellis*, 12 Ill. 470.
(*j*) *Cole* v. *Pennoyer*, 14 Ill. 159. See 1 Hill's C. L., Limitations.
(*k*) *Blakenship* v. *Stout*, 25 Ill. 132.
(*l*) *Davidson* v. *Young*, 38 Ill. 145.
(*m*) *Black* v. *Hills*, 36 Ill. 373.

(*n*) Id.; and *Cadwell* v. *Sherman*, 45 Ill. 348. See the case of *Parmelee* v. *Smith*, 21 Ill. 620, as to the right of a minor to hold property as his own.
(*o*) *Kane County* v. *Herrington*, 50 Ill. 232; *Williams* v. *Wiggand*, 53 id. 233; *C., R. I. & P. R. R. Co.* v. *Kennedy*, 70 id. 350.

Infants or minors.

land, and that a bill was properly filed to redeem the land; and that, as the infant averred that he had no means of redeeming but through this property, an account should be taken to determine the amount of the incumbrances, and that the money be raised by a sale or mortgage of the premises, or in such other appropriate way as might be most for the interest of the infant, and applied to the extinguishment of the incumbrances.(*p*)

Where it appeared that notice of an application for the sale of land, as recited in a decree pronounced thirty years since, was served upon infants instead of their guardians, as the statute required, no guardians *ad litem* having been appointed: *Held*, that the circuit court had not jurisdiction.(*q*)

As to how far infants are bound by sales of their real estate by executors, administrators and guardians, see *Gibson* v. *Roll*.(*r*)

ESTOPPEL. For the facts necessary to estop a party from asserting claim to lands sold by the administrator without due authority, during the minority of such party.(*s*)

6. ACTIONS BY AND AGAINST. Neither a default nor a decree *pro confesso* can be entered against an infant. Where infants are defendants in chancery proceedings, the proper and convenient practice is for the court to refer the matter which requires to be proved to the master in chancery, that he may take the evidence and report the facts to the court for its final determination.(*t*)

Laches are not imputable to an infant.(*u*)

Where the complainant chooses to proceed against infants, under the statute, without service of process, it is the duty of the court to exact of the guardian a vigorous defense of their interests; and it is wrong to take a bill for confessed against them under any circumstances.(*v*)

Nothing can be admitted, but every thing must be proved, against an infant.(*w*)

The right of action for services rendered by a minor is in the parent or guardian.(*x*)

(*p*) *Smith* v. *Sackett*, 5 Gilm. 534.
(*q*) *Whitney* v. *Porter*, 23 Ill. 445.
(*r*) 27 Ill. 90; *Williams* v. *Wiggand*, 53 id. 233.
(*s*) *Davidson* v. *Young*, 38 Ill. 145.
(*t*) *McClay, Adm'r,* v. *Norris,* 4 Gilm. 370; *Enos* v. *Capps*, 12 Ill. 255; *Cost* v. *Rose*, 17 id. 276; *Chaffin* v. *Heirs of Kimball*, 23 id. 36.

(*u*) *Smith* v. *Sackett*, 5 Gilm. 534.
(*v*) *Sconce* v. *Whitney*, 12 Ill. 150.
(*w*) *Hitt* v. *Ormsbee*, 12 Ill. 166; *Hamilton* v. *Gilman*, id. 260; *Tuttle* v. *Garrett*, 16 id. 354; *Reddick* v. *Pres. State Bank*, 27 id. 148.
(*x*) *Dufield* v. *Cross*, 12 Ill. 397.

Infants or minors.

An infant is not always bound to appear in a court of chancery by guardian, although one may be in existence. The bill may be filed by the next friend, and it rests in the sound discretion of the court whether the suit shall so proceed or in the name of the guardian. (*y*)

A party having a right of action against the ancestor is not to be delayed in his remedy, whether legal or equitable, because of the non-age of those on whom the law casts the liability. (*z*)

In all cases against infants, strict proof is required. The record must furnish proof to sustain a decree against them, whether the guardian *ad litem* answer or not. (*a*)

Where a special agreement has been made by a parent to pay the board of a child, the creditor cannot collect the board from the infant's estate, if the parent neglect to pay. (*b*)

A guardian *ad litem* must be appointed for infant defendants, or all proceedings against them will be erroneous. (*c*)

A judgment or decree against a minor without a guardian, or an appearance by attorney, is not void, but merely voidable. (*d*)

Such a judgment may be set aside in the court where it is rendered on motion; and, where the judgment has been set aside, the defendant may make any defense to which he may be entitled. (*d*)

It is error to permit a guardian *ad litem* to withdraw a plea and allow a judgment by default to be entered against the infant. (*e*)

If heirs be brought into court by *scire facias*, under the statute, to show cause why they should not be made parties to a judgment, it will be necessary to prove up the case *de novo* against them. But adults cannot demand that more shall be proved against them when there are infant parties than if all were adults. (*f*)

A party who is under eighteen years of age at the time of committing a larceny should be punished by imprisonment in the county jail, even though he is over eighteen when convicted. (*g*)

It is not every suit which has for its object to divest a minor of his estate that is against his interest so that he must be made a

---

(*y*) *Holmes* v. *Field*, 12 Ill. 422.
(*z*) *Enos* v. *Capps*, 15 Ill. 277.
(*a*) *Masterson* v. *Wiswould*, 18 Ill. 48; *Carr* v. *Fielden*, id. 77; *Cost* v. *Rose*, 17 id. 276; *Chaffin* v. *Heirs of Kimball*, 23 id. 36; *Tibbs* v. *Allen*, 27 id. 119.
(*b*) *Sinklear* v. *Emert*, 18 Ill. 64.
(*c*) *McDaniel* v. *Correll*, 19 Ill. 226.
(*d*) *Peak* v. *Shasted*, 21 Ill. 137.
(*e*) *Peak* v. *Pricer*, 21 Ill. 164.
(*f*) *Cox* v. *Reed*, 27 Ill. 434.
(*g*) *Monoughan* v. *The People*, 24 Ill. 340.

defendant, but only in those special cases arising under the statute. (*h*)

Where minors are defendants to a bill, a decree can only be rendered against them on full proof. Nor can their natural or legal guardians, by consent, waive this requirement. (*i*)

Where a decree has been rendered against a minor defendant, he is entitled to his day in court, whether the right is expressly reserved in the decree or not, and he may, even during his minority, by his next friend or guardian, file an original bill to impeach the decree either for fraud or for error appearing on its face. (*j*)

Delay after majority for the period which bars a writ of error would bar such bill. (*k*)

They cannot be brought into court by stipulation of attorneys. (*l*) Nor by entry of appearance by guardian. (*m*)

Where there are adult and infant defendants, and the writ of error is in fact prosecuted by the adults alone, they cannot assign for error those proceedings which only affect the interests of the infants. (*n*)

Decree against infants, without a guardian or an appearance, will be set aside. (*o*)

Defaults and decrees *pro confesso* cannot be entered against infants. (*p*)

The decree against infants must show that the material allegations of the bill were proved. (*q*)

A decree may be absolute in form in the first instance. The statute protects the minor by giving him five years after his majority to bring his writ of error. (*r*)

A day in court need not be given infants specifically in the decree. (*s*)

An infant defendant in chancery cannot consent, nor can his guardian *ad litem* for him, to the taking of testimony before a person not properly authorized to take it. A guardian *ad litem* cannot

---

(*h*) *Burger* v. *Potter*, 32 Ill. 66.
(*i*) *Waugh* v. *Robbins*, 33 Ill. 182; *Rhoads* v. *Rhoads*, 43 id. 239; *Quigley* v. *Roberts*, 44 id. 503; *Barnes* v. *Hazleton*, 50 id. 429.
(*j*) *Kuchenbeiser* v. *Beckert*, 41 Ill. 172; *Hess* v. *Voss*, 52 id. 472.
(*k*) *Kuchenbeiser* v. *Beckert*, 41 Ill. 172.

(*l*) *McDermaid* v. *Russell*, 41 Ill. 490.
(*m*) *Greenman* v. *Harvey*, 53 Ill. 386.
(*n*) *Rhoads* v. *Rhoads*, 43 Ill. 239.
(*o*) *Hall* v. *Davis*, 44 Ill. 494.
(*p*) *Quigley* v. *Roberts*, 44 Ill. 503.
(*q*) *Preston* v. *Hodgen*, 50 Ill. 56.
(*r*) *Barnes* v. *Hazleton*, 50 Ill. 429.
(*s*) *Hess* v. *Voss*, 52 Ill. 472.

Competency and appointment of guardians.

admit away any of the rights of an infant, or bind him by consent to an action which may be prejudicial to the infant. (*t*)

In order that a decree shall affect infants, they must be made parties to the bill, either complainants or defendants; and, if the latter, they must be served with process. (*u*)

INFANCY is not, at common law, a dilatory plea. (*v*)

SECTION II.—COMPETENCY AND APPOINTMENT OF GUARDIANS.

1. Guardians, jurisdiction of the county courts to appoint.
2. Construction of the statute.
3. The court of chancery in cases of divorce, etc.
4. When a minor may nominate, and when and how guardians may be appointed by the county courts.
5. The application for appointment.
6. Petition to be appointed.
7. Citation to minors.
8. Petition of minors to be appointed.
9. The bond.
10. Suits on bonds.
11. Appointment of a guardian of a minor's estate when the father is living; petition.
12. Other cases.
13. Letters of guardianship.
14. Guardian *ad litem* for a minor in a justice court.
15. Guardian *ad litem* in a common-law cause, in the county or circuit court, or in chancery.

1. DEFINITIONS, ETC. A guardian is a person to whom is delegated the authority to take care of a minor, or of his estate. The minor in such case is termed the *ward*.

There are several kinds of guardians : *First*. Guardians *by nature*, being the father, or, on his death, the mother. This guardianship only extends to the custody of the person, and terminates when the child attains the age of twenty-one years. (*w*)

Second. Testamentary guardians are such as are appointed by a will. Parents may dispose of the custody of their children by will. Such guardians supersede the claim of any other, and their authority extends over the person and estate of the child.

(*t*) *Fischer* v. *Fischer*, 54 Ill. 231.
(*u*) *Hickenbotham* v. *Blackledge*, 54 Ill. 316.
(*v*) *Greer* v. *Wheeler*, 1 Scam. 554.

See 2 Hill's C. L., Defenses. See Hill's Chan. Pr. 599.
(*w*) 3 Pick. 213 ; 7 Wend. 354.

Competency and appointment of guardians.

Third. Guardians *appointed by the court* under some statutory power. These are either guardians of the person or of the estate of the ward or of both.

Fourth. Guardians *ad litem* are such as are appointed by the court, where an infant is sued in a civil proceeding, to defend him in the same. Every court, when an infant is sued therein, may appoint a guardian of this character. His power and duty only extends to the suit in which he is appointed.

As the person appointed guardian acts for the infant on the account of *his* incapacity, such person should himself be capable. Minors, persons *non compos*, and persons infamous, are incompetent to act as guardians. Also such persons as have an interest in the property adverse to the ward.

In general, the guardian stands in the place of the parent to the ward, but not in all respects. He is bound to take care of the person of the ward; to represent him in all civil suits; to lease the real estate of the minor, and to perform all acts of simple administration ;(*x*) to put the money of the ward at interest; under the direction of the court, to superintend the nurture and education of the ward; and generally to act for and in place of the minor for his interest, and to render to the proper court an account of his administration.

When a guardian is appointed by a will, it is from *that* he derives his power to act. On the probate of the will, he will be entitled to letters of guardianship, which, in effect, amount to but an authentication of his appointment. No particular set of words are necessary in a will to constitute a guardian. Any language showing the intention of the testator to confer on a person designated the custody of the person or management of the estate of the ward will be sufficient. The will being the character of his authority, to that he must look for the particular manner in which he is to act.

JURISDICTION. Courts in probate, in their respective counties, may, when it appears necessary or convenient, appoint guardians to minors, inhabitants of, or residents in the same county, and to such as reside out of this State, and have an estate within the same, in the county where the real estate or some part thereof may lie; or, if they have no real estate, then in any county where they may have personal property. (*y*)

(*x*) 1 Bouv. Inst. 143.   (*y*) § 2, R. S. 1874, *p.* 558.

Competency and appointment of guardians.

2. THE STATUTE, in relation to guardians, does not constitute a complete code, but confers upon the county court power to appoint guardians, and to regulate their conduct in accordance with their duties at common law. Many of the powers and duties, rights and liabilities, of guardians are not specifically defined by statute. It contains such provisions as were necessary to define the nature of the jurisdiction conferred, prescribe the manner of its exercise, and correct some of the defects of the law as it then existed. In other respects, the common law regulating the powers and duties, rights and liabilities of guardians, is left in force. At common law, all guardians were regarded as trustees, clothed with such powers and rights as were necessary for the proper execution of the trusts imposed upon them, and they were held accountable for the faithful discharge of their duties. All except the guardian in chivalry might be compelled, in a court of chancery, to render an account before, as well as after, the guardianship terminated.(z) The guardian was required to take possession of his ward's property, and he was not only liable for such property as actually came into his possession, but for such as he might have taken possession of by the exercise of diligence and without any willful default on his part. So, in regard to the rents and profits of the ward's lands and tenements, and the income from every species of his property, the guardian was chargeable with what he actually received, and with what he might have received had he faithfully discharged his duties. (z)

The guardian should render to the county court yearly accounts, and, where he has used the money of his ward, he should charge himself with interest from the time he received it. At such rendering of an account, the interest should be made a part of the principal, and interest computed on the balance in the guardian's hands up to the next annual rendering of his account.(z)

Where the probate court appointed a guardian to two orphan minors, under the age of fourteen years, for the full time, until they should respectively attain the age of eighteen years: *Held*, that the appointment was valid. And, also, in case the minors, after they attained the age of fourteen years, neglected to choose guardians for themselves, the guardian already appointed by the

(z) *Bond* v. *Lockwood*, 33 Ill. 212.

Competency and appointment of guardians.

probate court would continue to act in his office until the said minors attained their majority.(a)

A, the testator, by his will, appointed his wife guardian to his infant daughter "*so long as she should remain his widow.*" After his decease, his widow took out letters of guardianship for the daughter from the probate court of the proper county. *Held*, that the appointment of the probate court was void for want of jurisdiction. The authority of the father to name a guardian for his children is greater than that conferred upon the probate court; and, when the former has exercised the right, the latter cannot act.(b)

3. In determining the fitness of the person to whom the custody of infants shall be given to act as guardian, the court of chancery is not bound down by any particular form of proceeding. The best interests of the child must be consulted.(c)

When the aid of a court of chancery is once invoked to provide for the guardianship of infants, in case of separation of the parents, such infants become the wards of the court, and it will not permit them to be removed beyond its jurisdiction, or permit either parent to alienate the affections of the infants from the other.(d)

4. GUARDIANS. If a minor is under the age of fourteen years. the county court may nominate and appoint his guardian. If he is above that age, he may nominate his own guardian, who, if approved by the court, shall be appointed accordingly; if not approved by the court, or if the minor reside out of the State, or if, after being cited, he neglects to nominate a suitable person, the court may nominate and appoint his guardian in the same manner as if he were under the age of fourteen years.(e)

5. APPLICATION FOR APPOINTMENT. Upon application being made for the appointment of a guardian, unless the proper persons are before it, the court shall assign a day for the hearing thereof, and shall direct such notice of the hearing to be given to the relatives of the minor residing in the county as he shall, on due inquiry, think reasonable. When any person shall, at the same time, be appointed guardian for several minors, the court may, if the estate

(a) *Young* v. *Lorain*, 11 Ill. 625.
(b) *Holmes* v. *Field*, 12 Ill. 424.
(c) *Cowls* v. *Cowls*, 3 Gilm. 435; *Petition of Smith*, 13 Ill. 139.
(d) *Miner* v. *Miner*, 11 Ill. 43.
(e) § 3, R. S. 1874, p. 558; Cothran's Statutes, p. 766.

Competency and appointment of guardians.

shall be so situated as to make it more convenient or advantageous to the interest of the ward, include all in one bond.

How to be appointed Guardian. If the minors are over fourteen years of age, bring them personally before the court to select their guardian; obtain petition and bond in blank from the clerk; fill them out; then file them with the clerk; pay his costs; call the court's attention to the petition; have two securities sworn and accepted by the court, and the bond approved. The penalty in the bond should be in no case less than double the amount of the minor's personal estate and six times the amount of the gross annual income of the minor's real estate. If, however, such real estate is improved, or is covered, in whole or in part, with timber, or is improved in part and in part covered with timber, the penal sum in said bond shall be increased by an amount at least double the value of the said improvements, or of said timber, or both, as the case may be.(z)

The following forms may be used:

6. Petition to be appointed Guardian of Minors.

State of Illinois,⎫
County of ,⎭ ss.:   *In the   Court of   county, term, A. D. 18 .*

To the Hon.   , judge of said court :

Your petitioner,   , who resides at No.   street,   , Illinois, respectfully represents that   , late of   , died, leaving his children, hereinafter named, who are all residents of said   county, and now living with   , at No.   street,   ; that they are all infants under fourteen years of age, to wit

  , aged   years, on the   day of   , A. D. 18 ; that said infants have no guardian, and that the names and residences of their relations are as follows: ; that they have real and personal estate, the entire value of which does not exceed   dollars; that it is composed of the following items: ; that the interest of each of said infants in said property is one   part.

Wherefore, your petitioner prays that your honor nominate and appoint your petitioner (or such other person as to your honor shall seem proper) guardian of the persons and estates of said infants, until they arrive at fourteen years of age, and until another guardian shall be appointed, and that all other orders necessary may be made.   , *Petitioner*

State of Illinois,⎫
County of ,⎭ ss.:

  , being duly sworn, deposes and says, that he knows the contents of the above petition, and that the statements therein are true.

Sworn to and subscribed before me   ,⎫
clerk of the county court of   county,⎬
this   day of   , A. D. 18 .   ⎭

                     , *Clerk.*

The person making such representation may state any other facts

---

(z) Cothran's Stats., 768.

ESTATES OF MINORS.

Competency and appointment of guardians.

showing the necessity or propriety for the appointment of a guardian, though the above form contains probably all that is required. Upon filing such representation in court, a citation will issue to the minor, and will be served upon him by the officer of the court.

7. CITATION TO A MINOR.

STATE OF ILLINOIS, } *ss*:
County.

The people of the State of Illinois to A B, C D, E F, minors, etc.:

Whereas, it has been represented by   to the county court of county, at the last   term thereof, that you, the said A B, C D, E F, are orphan minors above the age of fourteen years respectively, and have no guardian; you are, therefore, hereby cited to appear before the said court, at the next   term thereof, to be holden at the court-house in said county on the   day of   next, and choose a guardian; in default whereof, the said court will appoint one for you.

Witness my hand and the seal of said court, at   , in said [SEAL.] county, this   day of   , A. D. 18 .

E F, *Clerk County Court.*

This should be served by reading and leaving with each a copy. The officer serving such notice should return to the county court the original, with his return indorsed thereon.

On the return day, if the minor appear and make his choice, and the court deem the person so chosen capable, the selection is confirmed, and letters of guardianship are issued upon his qualifying. If the minor fail to appear, or, appearing, neglect to choose a guardian, then the court will appoint one for him, the same as if such minor were under fourteen years of age.

If the minor be under the age of fourteen, it is not necessary to issue a notification. The person desiring the appointment of guardian makes known to the court the fact that such minor is an orphan, the father being dead, is under the age of fourteen years, and is within the jurisdiction.

8. PETITION OF MINORS TO HAVE GUARDIAN APPOINTED.

STATE OF ILLINOIS, } *ss*:   *In the County Court of   county,*
County of   *term, A. D. 18 .*

To the Hon.   , Judge of said court:

Your petitioners respectfully represent, that   , late of   , died, leaving your petitioners his children, who are all residents of said   county,

Competency and appointment of guardians.

and now living with   , at No.   street; that they are all minors above fourteen years of age, to wit:

   , aged   years, on the   day of   , A. D. 18   ;
   , aged   years, on the   day of   , A. D. 18   ;
   , aged   years, on the   day of   , A. D. 18   ;

that your petitioners have no guardian, and that the names and residence of their relations are as follows: . ; that they have real and personal estate, the entire value of which does not exceed   dollars; that it is composed of the following items: ; that the interest of each of your petitioners in said property is one   part.

That your petitioners do hereby make choice of   , of No.   , as guardian of their persons and estates, subject to the approval of this honorable court; that he is a suitable person to be such guardian, and has consented to act if appointed. Wherefore, your petitioners pray that your honor appoint the said   (or such other fit and proper person as your petitioners may here after choose) guardian of the persons and estates of your petitioners during their minority, and that all other orders necessary may be made.

                   .A B,
                   C D, etc.

STATE OF ILLINOIS, } *ss*:
 County of   .}

  , being duly sworn, deposes and says, that he knows the contents of the above petition, and that the statements therein are true.

 Sworn to and subscribed before me,
clerk of the county court of   county, this
  day of   , A. D. 18   .
            , *Clerk*.

 I,   , the person named in the above petition, do hereby consent to become the guardian of the above-mentioned minors, pursuant to the prayer of the foregoing petition.   L. A. H

9. GUARDIAN'S BOND.

Know all men by these presents, that we,(1)   , of the county of   and State of Illinois, are held and firmly bound unto the people of the State of Illinois, for the use of   , minor , in the penal sum of   dollars, current money of the United States, which payment, well and truly to be made and performed, we and each of us do hereby bind ourselves, our heirs, executors, administrators and assigns, jointly, severally and firmly, by these presents.

 Witness our hands and seals, this   day of   , A. D. 18   .(2).

 The conditions of the bond are prescribed by statute. They are as follows :

---

(1) 1. INSTRUCTIONS FOR FILLING UP THE BOND. Write the names of all parties mentioned in the bond in full.
 2. There should be two securities in this bond, and it should be executed in the presence of the court. All parties to it must be present.

Competency and appointment of guardians.

"The condition of this obligation is such, that if the above bounden (name of guardian), who has been appointed guardian of (name of infant), shall faithfully discharge the office and trust of such guardian according to law, and shall make a true inventory of all the real and personal estate of the ward that shall come to his possession or knowledge, and return the same unto the court of   county, at the time required by law, and manage and dispose of all such estate according to law and for the best interest of said ward, and faithfully discharge his trust in relation thereto, and to the custody, nurture and education of said ward, and render an account, on oath, of the property in his hands,

and of the management and disposition of all such estate within one year after his appointment, and at such other time as shall be required by law or directed by the court, and, upon removal from office, or at the expiration of his trust, settle his accounts in said court, or with the ward or his legal representatives, and pay over and deliver all the estate, title, papers and effects remaining in his hands or due from him on such settlement to the person or persons lawfully entitled thereto, then this obligation shall be void; otherwise, to remain in full force and virtue."(g)

[SEAL.]
[SEAL.]
[SEAL.]

10. SUITS ON BONDS. Bonds may be put in suit in the name of the people of the State of Illinois, to the use of any person entitled to recover on a breach thereof, and damages assessed and proceedings had thereon as in other cases of penal bonds.(h)

11. APPOINTMENT OF A GUARDIAN OF A MINOR'S ESTATE WHEN THE FATHER IS LIVING. The proper mode of bringing such a case before the court is by the petition of some friend of the minor, viz.:

FORM OF PETITION FOR APPOINTMENT OF GUARDIAN OF A MINOR'S ESTATE.

STATE OF ILLINOIS, } ss.:
 County.   *County Court of   county,*
                 term, A. D. 18   .

To the Hon.   , judge of said court:

The undersigned, C D, respectfully represents that E F, of said county, is a minor, of the age of fourteen years, and is the child of G F, of said county, now living; that one D B, late of   county, deceased, by his last will and testament, which has been duly probated in said last-mentioned county, and a certified copy of which is hereto attached, marked "Exhibit A," granted and devised in fee to the said E F the following real estate, situate in the county of   aforesaid, to wit: (*Here describe the property.*) That the said real estate is improved, and, unless it be properly managed, the improvements thereon will become impaired, and the value of the property diminished.

And your petitioner further shows, that the said G F is not a proper per-

---

(g) Cothran's Anno. Statutes, 768, § 7.   (h) § 11, id.

son to have the charge and management of said estate, on account of drunkenness and vagrancy (*or whatever may be the case*); wherefore, your petitioner prays that a guardian be appointed for said minor, to manage the said estate, and that a citation issue to said G F, to show cause why such guardian should not be appointed, returnable to the next term of this court.

And your petitioner will ever pray, etc.

Dated   , 18 .   C D.

On filing such petition, THE CITATION should be served and returned as in other cases.

If good cause against the petition be not shown, and the charges therein be supported, the court will order that a guardian be appointed; and, in case the minor be over fourteen years of age, it will further order that a citation be issued to said minor, directing him to appear before said court, at a time to be therein specified, and choose a guardian. If he choose an unfit person, the court will not confirm his choice, and, if he persists in such improper choice, will treat it as a refusal or neglect to choose, and may proceed the same as if such minor had openly refused or wholly neglected to make a choice.

The father of an infant, though his natural guardian, has no power to lease his land, nor authority to demand and receive a legacy. The guardian by nature, the father, or, in case of his death, the mother, having no authority over the estate of his or her child, but only control over its person, the appointment of a guardian is necessary for the purpose of leasing lands or dealing on account of such minor's estate.

12. THERE ARE SOME OTHER CASES where it might be eminently proper that a guardian should be appointed, especially while the parents are yet living. By stating in plain, perspicuous language the grounds on which any one deems it "necessary or convenient" that a guardian of a minor should be appointed, in a petition similar in character and form to those already given, and verifying the petition, the court has full *original* jurisdiction to act. If the facts stated are denied, the court may settle the disputed questions by citing the interested parties before it, and taking testimony in a summary manner.(*i*)

The bond, of course, should be quite like the form given in the above cases.

(*i*) See p. 112, *supra* ; see p. 120, *infra*

Competency and appointment of guardians.

Upon granting the application, letters of guardianship issue.

13. LETTERS OF GUARDIANSHIP.

STATE OF ILLINOIS, } ss:
County of .}

The people of the State of Illinois to , of said county, greeting:

Whereas, you were, by the county court of said county, on the day of , A. D. 18 , appointed guardian of the person and estate of: , aged years, on the day of , A. D. 18 ; , aged years, on the day of , A. D. 18 ; minor of said county; and whereas, you have complied with the conditions of said appointment by giving bond, with two sureties, in the penal sum of dollars, which bond has been approved by said court.

Now, therefore, know ye, to whom these presents shall come, that the said is the duly constituted guardian of the person and estate of said minor , and is authorized and required to have the care and custody of h person and estate ; to present to said court, within three months from the date hereof, a just and true inventory, under oath, of all the real and personal estate belonging to said minor ; to lease the real estate of said minor, upon such terms and for such time as said court shall, by its order, direct; to render an account of h guardianship to said court for adjustment within one year from the date hereof, and every year thereafter, until discharged by order of said court; to put to interest the money of said minor upon security to be approved by said court; to superintend, under the direction of said court, the education and nurture of said minor, and for that purpose may pay out such portion of said minors' money as the said court shall, from time to time, by order, direct.

And also to do whatever else the law requires of a guardian of the persons and estates of minors.

Witness , clerk of said court, and the seal thereof, at the of , in said county, this day of , A. D. 18 . , *Clerk.*

STATE OF ILLINOIS. } ss:
County of .}

I, , clerk of the county court of county, in the State aforesaid, do hereby certify that the within is a true and correct copy of letters granted on , to , as guardian of the person and estate of , minor, and the same have not been revoked by this court.

In witness whereof, I have hereunto set my hand and the seal of the county court, at , in the State aforesaid, this day of , 18 .
, *Clerk.*

STATE OF ILLINOIS, } ss:
County of .}

, being duly sworn, deposes and says, that he knows the contents of the above petition, and that the statements therein are true.

Sworn to and subscribed before me,)
clerk of the county court of , county,}
this day of , A. D. 18)
, *Clerk.*

Competency and appointment of guardians.

I, , the person named in the above petition, do hereby consent to become the guardian of the above-mentioned minors, pursuant to the prayer of the foregoing petition.
L. A. H.

14. GUARDIAN *AD LITEM* IN A JUSTICE COURT. Where an infant is sued for necessaries in such a court, *he* cannot appear and defend; a guardian *ad litem* should be appointed, or his guardian should be sued if he have one of record.(*j*)

15. GUARDIAN *AD LITEM* AT COMMON LAW AND IN CHANCERY.(*k*) On filing an affidavit, or pleading properly verified, showing the infancy of a defendant, the court should appoint a guardian *ad litem* for such infant defendant.

In chancery, the complainant must see to it that the infant defendants are brought in by guardian *ad litem,* or that they appear by next friend.(*k*)

AFFIDAVIT OF INFANCY.
(Title of cause.)

(*Venue.*)

C D, being duly sworn, says that he is the defendant named in the above entitled cause, and is now but   years old; that he was born at   , on the   day of   , A. D. 18   , and is aged   years and   months.
(*Jurat.*)
C D.

The clerk should enter this order.

ORDER OF APPOINTMENT.

It appearing to the court that C D, named as defendant in this cause, is an infant, ordered, that E F, of   , be, and hereby is, appointed guardian *ad litem* for said C D, to appear and defend for him, the said C D, herein.

If the guardian *ad litem* then appear and plead, it is evidence of his accepting the trust. In a justices' court, the guardian should sign an acceptance on the docket.

ACCEPTANCE.

I hereby accept the appointment of guardian *ad litem* for C D in this cause.
E F.

(*j*) 1 Chitty's Pl.; Stephen's Pl. ; § 18, act April 10, 1872.

(*k*) See Hill's Chancery Pr., Infants See appendix, *infra*.

Powers and duties of guardians.

SECTION III.—THE POWERS AND DUTIES OF GUARDIANS.
1. Generally.
2. A guardian cannot appoint an attorney in fact to execute a deed; under decree or order of court of chancery, he may make compromises; the power to mortgage the ward's land is limited.
3. He may, under a decree, sell real estate.
4. Guardians are not allowed to make gain to themselves.
5. Supervision of the trust.
6. The husband of a guardian cannot act without express authority from the guardian.
7. Fraudulent proceedings instituted by a mother are open to attack, and how.
8. A third person, generally, cannot question the power and acts of the guardian. A guardian has no power to sell the real estate of his ward unless authorized by a court of competent jurisdiction, or by legislative enactment. The power must be strictly pursued, it is a naked power.
9. Fraud; *caveat emptor*, how applied.
10. To act for the ward generally.
11. Guardian *ad litem*.
12. Custody of child may be willed.
13. Removal from another State, and charge therefor.
14. Custody may be to one and guardianship to another.
15. Testamentary guardian.
16. Must be commissioned.
17. Frugally to manage the ward's estate.
18. And educate the ward.
19. If the guardian neglects to educate, the court may interfere.
20. To invest funds, or be chargeable with interest for neglect.

1. THE POWERS AND DUTIES OF GUARDIANS GENERALLY. The guardian of a minor shall have, under the direction of the court, the custody, nurture and tuition of his ward, and the care and management of all his estate. But the father of the minor, if living, and, in the case of his death, the mother, they being respectively competent to transact their own business, and fit persons, shall be entitled to the custody of the person of the minor and the care of his education. In case the father and mother shall live apart, the court may, for good reason, award the custody and education of the minor to the mother or other proper person.(*a*)

2. A guardian CANNOT APPOINT AN ATTORNEY to execute a deed.(*b*) He may make compromises under the direction of a court of chancery,(*c*) but he cannot make admissions to bind an infant.(*d*)

(*a*) § 4, R. S. 1874, p, 559.
(*b*) *Mason* v. *Wait*, 4 Scam. 127.
(*c*) *King* v. *King*, 15 Ill. 187.

(*d*) *Cochran* v. *McDowell*, 15 Ill. 10; *Reddick* v. *President State Bank*, 27 id. 148.

Guardian and ward.

Power to mortgage the ward's land is limited.(e) He may, under a decree, sell real estate.

3. The decree need not fix the precise day nor hour. It is sufficient if the court fixes certain reasonable limits within which the sale shall be held, and requiring the guardian to give due notice. The guardian may exercise some discretion in a mode favorable to the ward's interest.(f) And as to parties to sale, sufficiency of notice of application to sell, and method of masters reporting evidence.(f)

It is not necessary that it should appear that the probate court had, prior to the application to sell the land, ordered and directed the guardian to provide for the support and education of his ward, before the action of the probate court in the premises.(g)

In proceedings by administrator to sell real estate of decedent, a guardian cannot admit service of the summons for the minor heirs.(h)

4. GUARDIANS ARE NOT ALLOWED TO MAKE GAIN TO THEMSELVES of trust property in their hands. They are required to put on interest the moneys of their wards upon mortgage security or in U. S. securities when the sum loaned is over $100, for a time not to exceed three years. In this State, the statute permits the guardian to lease the real estate of the ward upon such terms and for such length of time, not extending beyond the minority of the ward, as the probate court shall approve. If a guardian neglects his duty in this respect, he will be chargeable with interest after a reasonable time has elapsed within which to make an investment. Six months from the receipt of the money has been deemed a reasonable time for that purpose.

5. SUPERVISION OF THE TRUST. It is a general rule of the common law that the expenses of an infant or ward shall be kept within the income or produce of his estate, but the statute provides that the court, sitting in probate, may order the sale of real estate of the ward for his support and education, when necessary, or for re-investment.(i)

6. The husband of a guardian has no right to possess or control the estate of the ward, and a payment to him on account of such

---

(e) *Merritt* v. *Simpson*, 41 Ill. 391.
(f) *Campbell* v. *Harmon*, 43 Ill. 18.
(g) *Mulford* v. *Stalzenback*, 46 Ill. 303.
(h) *Clark* v. *Thompson*, 47 Ill. 25.
(i) *Davis, Adm'r,* v. *Harkness*, 1 Gilm. 173; *Cummins* v. *Cummins*, 15 Ill. 33; Cothran's Statutes, 771, § 28.

estate is void, unless with the express sanction or direction of the guardian.(*k*)

7. Where a mother, in conjunction with the guardian of infants, presents a claim for their nurture, which is allowed, and proceeds thereupon to have the estate of the deceased father sold, and parceled out to the mother, in fraud of the children, the whole proceeding, even upon the motion of a stranger, may be set aside and held void. It is the duty of the guardian to contest such a claim, and he is an incompetent witness to establish it.(*l*)

8. A third person cannot question the power and acts of a guardian, except when such person's rights depend upon the existence and due exercise of the powers of the guardian.(*m*)

A GUARDIAN HAS NO POWER TO SELL THE REAL ESTATE OF HIS WARD, unless authorized by the court, or perhaps by the legislature.(*m*)

Such a power must be considered as a naked power, and be strictly pursued.(*m*)

9. FRAUD. The principle of *caveat emptor* applies to a guardian's sale; and a *suppressio veri* on the part of the guardian will not invalidate the sale or enable the purchaser to rescind it. *Aliter* of a *suggestio falsi*.(*m*)

10. TO ACT FOR THE WARD GENERALLY. The guardian shall settle all accounts of his ward, and demand and sue for, and receive in his own name as guardian, all personal property of, and demands due the ward, or, with the approbation of the court, compound for the same, and give a discharge to the debtor upon receiving a fair and just dividend of his estate and effects.(*n*)

11. *AD LITEM*. He shall appear for and represent his ward IN ALL LEGAL SUITS AND PROCEEDINGS, unless another person is appointed for that purpose, as guardian or next friend; but nothing contained in this act shall impair or affect the power of any court or justice of the peace to appoint a guardian to defend the interest of a minor impleaded in such court or interested in a suit or matter therein pending, nor their power to appoint or allow any person, as next friend for a minor, to commence, prosecute or defend any suit in his behalf.(*o*)

(*k*) *Holmes* v. *Field*, 12 Ill. 424.
(*l*) *Ex parte Guernsey*, 21 Ill. 443.
(*m*) *Mason* v. *Wait*, 4 Scam. 127.

(*n*) § 17, R. S. 1874, *p.* 560.
(*o*) § 18, id.

Guardian and ward.

12. CUSTODY OF CHILD MAY BE WILLED. The father, being of sound mind and memory, of a child likely to be born, or of any living child, being a minor and unmarried, may, by his last will, dispose of the custody and tuition of such child, to continue during its minority, or for a less time: *Provided*, no such will shall take effect to deprive the mother, during her life, of the custody and tuition of the child, without her consent, if she be a fit and competent person to have such custody and tuition. The mother being of sound mind and memory, and being sole or surviving the father of her child, may, in like manner, dispose of the custody and tuition of such child.(*p*)

13. Where a testator appointed a person permanently residing in another State guardian for his children, it will be inferred that he expected the guardian would remove the children to that State, and the expense of removing the children will be a proper charge against the estate.(*q*) Although it is generally necessary that an order should be obtained from the probate court before expenditures are made for wards, yet the rule may be deviated from under extraordinary circumstances.(*q*)

14. CUSTODY MAY BE TO ONE AND GUARDIANSHIP TO ANOTHER. The guardianship of the infant's estate may be appointed to one and the custody and tuition of the minor to another.(*r*)

15. A TESTAMENTARY GUARDIAN shall have the same powers and perform the same duties within the scope of his appointment as a guardian appointed by the county court.(*s*)

16. MUST BE COMMISSIONED. A testamentary guardian, except for the custody and tuition of the minor, shall, before he can act, be commissioned by the county court of the proper county, and give the bond prescribed in section seven of this act, except that, when the testator has requested in his will that a bond be not required, it shall not be required unless from a change in the situation or circumstances of the guardian, or for other sufficient cause the court shall deem it necessary to require it.(*t*)

17. FRUGALLY TO MANAGE THE ESTATE. The guardian shall manage the estate of his ward frugally and without waste, and apply the income and profit thereof, so far as the same may be nec-

(*p*) § 5, R. S. 1874, *p.* 559.
(*q*) *Cummins* v. *Cummins*, 29 Ill. 452.
(*r*) § 6, R. S. 1874, *p.* 559.
(*s*) § 8, R. S. 1874, *p.* 559.
(*t*) § 9, id.

essary, to the comfort and suitable support and education of his ward.(*u*)

18. He shall EDUCATE HIS WARD, and it is made the duty of all civil officers to give information to the county court of any neglect of the guardian to his ward.(*v*)

19. THE COURT MAY INTERFERE IF A GUARDIAN NEGLECTS TO EDUCATE HIS WARD. When there is not money of the ward sufficient to teach him to read and write and the elementary rules of arithmetic, and the guardian fails or neglects to have him so educated, the court shall have power to put out the ward to any other person for the purpose of having him so educated.(*w*)

20. To INVEST FUNDS. It shall be the duty of the guardian to put and keep his ward's money at interest, upon security, to be approved by the court, or invest the same in United States bonds, or other United States interest-bearing securities. Personal security may be taken for loans not exceeding one hundred dollars. Loans in large amounts shall be upon real estate security. No loan shall be made for a longer time than three years, nor beyond the minority of the ward: *Provided*, the same may be extended from year to year without the approval of the court. The guardian shall be chargeable with interest upon any money which he shall wrongfully or negligently allow to remain in his hands uninvested after the same might have been invested.(*x*)

SECTION IV.— RESIGNATION AND REMOVAL.

1. The court may permit a faithful guardian to resign.
2. Petition for permission to resign.
3. Settlement of accounts, surrender of estate, and acceptance of the resignation.
4. Guardians may be removed for cause.
5. Petition for removal; its form; petition to be verified and filed.
6. The summons; *alias*, *pluries*.
7. Constructive service.
    (1.) Non-resident guardian
    (2.) Absent guardian.
    (3.) Concealed guardian.
    (4.) Residence of guardian unknown.

(*u*) § 19,
(*v*) § 20, } R. S. 1874, *p.* 560.
(*w*) § 21,

(*x*) § 22, R. S. 1874, *pp.* 560, 561. See *p.* 119, *supra*.

Resignation and removal of guardians.

8. The notice.
9. The publication.
10. Jurisdiction to appoint another guardian, and to enforce orders in such matters.
11. The marriage of a female ward discharges her guardian as to custody and education, but not as to property.
12. The hearing.
13. The decree revoking the letters of guardianship.

1. THE FAITHFUL GUARDIAN MAY RESIGN. When it appears proper, the court may permit the guardian to resign his trust if he first settles his accounts and delivers over the estate as by the court directed.(y)

Prior to the passage of the act of the 13th of April, 1849, a guardian could not, as a matter of right, resign his trust. Still, when, previous to the passage of said act, a guardian tendered his resignation of his guardianship to the probate court, which resignation was accepted by the court and his letters of guardianship revoked, and another guardian appointed in his place: *Held*, that the validity of such revocation, and the appointment of another guardian, could not be collaterally called in question.(z)

Application showing the reasons for asking to resign must be made by petition.

2. PETITION FOR PERMISSION TO RESIGN.

STATE OF ILLINOIS,⎱ ss.: In the County Court of   county.
    County.   ⎰   To the   term, A. D. 18   .
In the matter of the estate⎱
   of C D, an infant.   ⎰

Your petitioner shows that, by the order and appointment of this court, on the   day of   , A. D. 18 , he was constituted guardian of C D, as by the records and files of this court will more fully and at large appear; that your petitioner is about to go to the State of New York to reside and there make his home, and leave the State of Illinois; that your petitioner is prepared to settle his accounts and deliver over the said estate now in his hands as this court shall direct. Whereupon, your petitioner here tenders his resignation of the office of guardian as aforesaid, and prays that, for the reasons above assigned, this court may accept said resignation and discharge your petitioner from said trust. And your petitioner will ever pray, etc.   A B, *petitioner*.

Add a verification and file the same.

(y) § 39, R. S. 1874, p. 562.   (z) *Young* v. *Lorain*, 11 Ill. 624.

Resignation and removal of guardians.

3. SETTLEMENT MUST BE MADE. Upon filing this petition, all parties interested, especially the ward and his relatives, should be summoned, together with the securities. The accounts should be examined and proved, and the estate turned over to a new guardian. When all is done to the satisfaction of the court, an order may be entered:

ACCEPTANCE OF RESIGNATION.

A B, who was, on the   day of   , A. D. 18 , appointed guardian of C D, a minor, being about to leave the State of Illinois, to make his home and to reside elsewhere, and having settled his accounts and delivered over all the estate that has come to his hands, and tendered his resignation as such guardian, ordered, that the said resignation be and is hereby accepted, and the said A B discharged from his said trust.

4. GUARDIANS MAY BE REMOVED FOR CAUSE. The county court may remove a guardian for his failure to give bond or security, or additional or counter security, when required, or for failure to make inventory, or to account and make settlement, or support or educate the ward, or when he shall have become insane, or have removed out of the State, or become incapable or unsuitable for the discharge of his duties, or for failure to discharge any duty required of him by law or the order of the court, or for other good cause.(*a*)

It was early held that a court of chancery may remove all guardians, whether appointed by the court itself, by the court of probate, by testament, or even by express act of the legislature, whenever it is satisfied that the guardian is abusing his trust, or the interests of the ward require it.(*b*)

GUARDIAN TO BE SUMMONED. But before removing a guardian, the court must summon him to show cause why he should not be removed for the cause alleged. If the guardian has left the State, or cannot be served with process, he may be notified in the same manner as non-resident defendants in chancery.(*c*)

5. PETITION FOR REMOVAL OF GUARDIAN.

STATE OF ILLINOIS, ⎱ *ss*:   *In the County Court of   county.*
      County.   ⎰   *term, A. D.* 18   .

To Hon. A B, Judge of said court:

The petition of E F, of said county, respectfully represents and shows to your honor that one J K, of said county. was, on the   day of   , A. D.

(*a*) § 87, R. S. 1874, *p*. 562.
(*b*) *Cowls* v. *Cowls*, 3 Gilm. 435. Sec. 37 seems to cover the whole ground, and the next section inaugurates in such matters the chancery practice.
(*c*) § 38, R. S. 1874, *p*. 562.

Resignation and removal of guardians.

18   , appointed by this court guardian of one C D, a minor (then) of the age of six years, as will appear by reference to the records of this court; that since his said appointment as such guardian, he has mismanaged the estate of the said ward by cutting, carrying off, selling and wasting the timber upon the land of the said minor, to the great injury in the value of the said land, and has, in other respects, mismanaged the estate of his said ward (*or, in place of this, insert, with a reasonable degree of certainty, the particular facts in the case, on account of which it is desired to remove the guardian*).

And your petitioner further states that he is the *brother* of the said ward.

Wherefore your petitioner prays that, on the final hearing hereof, the said guardian be removed, and his letters revoked; and that the guardianship of said minor be committed to some other person, and that said J K be cited to appear at the next term of this court, and show cause, if any he has, why he should not be so removed.

And your petitioner will ever pray, etc.   E F.
Dated   , 18 .

To which add a verification of the facts stated in the petition by the oath of the petitioner, and file it.(*d*)

Whenever any security of the guardian conceives himself in danger of suffering by the mismanagement of the guardian, he may petition the county court for relief, in writing, setting forth the cause of such apprehension. The court will examine the petition, and if it adjudge the causes therein stated and set forth to be sufficient, if true, to entitle such petitioner to relief, the guardian will then be summoned to show cause against the petitioner. On the hearing, the court may revoke the letters of guardianship, release such security, and require other security, or dismiss the petition. The foregoing form of petition, with slight alteration, may be used by the security.

The summons or citation should be served upon the person a reasonable time before the day for hearing the case, that he may have a fair opportunity to make his defense.

6. Summons to Guardian.

State of Illinois, }
    County.   } *ss* :

The people of the State of Illinois, to the sheriff of said county, greeting :

Whereas, it has been represented to the county court of said county, by the petition of C D, that J K, guardian of E F, a minor, has been guilty of mismanaging and wasting the estate of his said ward: These are, therefore, to command you to summon the said J K to appear before the county court of the county of   , at the next   term thereof, to be holden at the court-

(*d*) See p. 111, *supra*.

house in said county on the   day of   , A. D. 18 , and show cause, if any he has, why he should not be removed from his office of guardian of said E F, and his letters of guardianship be revoked. And you are to make return hereof according to law.

    Witness L O, clerk of the county court of   county, and the [SEAL.]   seal thereof, at his office in   , in said county, this   day of   , 18 .   L O, *Clerk county court.*

On the day stated in the summons, the court will proceed to hear the evidence in support of the allegations in the petition, and such proof as the guardian may offer to acquit himself thereof. If, upon such hearing, the judge shall decide from the evidence that there exist good and sufficient reason, he will cause the same to be entered upon the record, and an order removing the guardian, and also an order that he deliver up to his successor, to be appointed, all goods, chattels, moneys, title papers or other effects belonging to the ward, or which may be in his possession or under his control.

It is the duty of all civil county officers to give information to the court of the neglect of the guardian to educate his ward. Others interested in the welfare of the minors are not denied the privilege of doing this. If the guardian or other party be dissatisfied with the decision of the court, either may appeal to the circuit court of the county by entering into bond the same as in appeals from decisions of justices of the peace.

Guardians may be removed upon complaint of any person, in behalf of the minor, made to the circuit court of the county where such guardian may reside, on proof of malconduct or misbehavior in the performance of their duties. The same form before given may, with proper alterations, be used in the circuit court.

Upon the removal of the guardian, if the minor be above fourteen years of age, he may choose a guardian in place of the one removed. If he should neglect or refuse to do it, the court may unquestionably appoint one for him the same as if he were under fourteen years of age.

7. CONSTRUCTIVE SERVICE. Whenever any complainant or his attorney shall file in the office of the clerk of the court in which his suit is pending, an affidavit showing that any defendant resides or hath gone out of this State, or on due inquiry cannot be found, or is concealed within this State so that process cannot be served upon him, and stating the place of residence of such defendant, if known, or that, upon diligent inquiry, his place of residence cannot

Resignation and removal of guardians.

be ascertained, the clerk shall cause publication to be made in some newspaper printed in his county, and if there be no newspaper published in his county, then in the nearest newspaper published in this State, containing notice of the pendency of such suit, the names of the parties thereto, the title of the court, and the time and place of the return of summons in the case; and he shall also, within ten days of the first publication of such notice, send a copy thereof by mail, addressed to such defendant whose place of residence is stated in such affidavit. The certificate of the clerk that he has sent such notice, in pursuance of this section, shall be evidence.(e)

FOUR SUCCESSIVE WEEKS; FORTY DAYS. The notice required in the preceding section may be given at any time after the commencement of the suit, and shall be published at least once in each week for four successive weeks, and no default or proceeding shall be taken against any defendant not served with summons, or a copy of the bill, and not appearing, unless forty days shall intervene between the first publication as aforesaid, and the first day of the term at which such default or proceeding is proposed to be taken.(f)

The above provisions of the statute regulating the publication of notices in chancery are, perhaps, relevant to proceedings in probate courts or county courts sitting for the transaction of probate business, in so far as their equitable jurisdiction is called into action. It is true, however, that in the ordinary affairs of probate, the statute of 1874, in relation to notices, recited hereinbefore, has more special reference, the majority of cases in which notice is required to be given generally falling within the class of notices required, by law, to be published in which the number of publications is not specified. In matters of final accounting and resignation of executor or administrator, the probate court of Cook county has provided specific rules.(g)

PROCEEDINGS AT SUBSEQUENT TERM. If, for want of due publication or service, in time, the cause shall be continued, then the same proceedings may be had at a subsequent term of the court as might have been had at the term to which said summons is returnable.(h)

(e) § 12, Cothran's Stats., 185.
(f) § 13, Cothran's Stats., 186.
(g) *Post*, rules 8, 9.

(h) §§ 12, 13, Cothran's Stats., 185, 186; Hill's Chan. Pr. 18, 19.

Resignation and removal of guardians.

ALIAS, PLURIES, ETC. If in any suit in chancery the process shall not be returned executed on the return day thereof, the clerk, if required, shall issue an *alias, pluries* or other process, without an order of the court therefor. (*i*)

As between the parties to the suit and their privies, the summons or the affidavit, and advertisement with certificate of publisher must be in the record to confer jurisdiction over parties. (*j*) By the statute of 1845 the giving of notice or the making of constructive service materially differed from the present process. Under the then statute there was no provision made for mailing copy of the publication to the party to be affected by it. It was, however, provided that the proceeding to bring the party in by publication should "not dispense with the usual exertion on the part of the sheriff, to serve the summons." This clause of the law, the supreme court so construed that the procedure could not be resorted to until a return of *non est inventus* had been made by the sheriff. To remedy the necessary delay, as well as to avoid the useless performance of searching for parties sworn to be non-resident, a curative act was passed February 12, 1857. This in its turn has given place to the imposition of the duty, on the clerk of the court, of attempting to notify the non-resident, unless it be sworn that his place of abode is not known.(*k*)

SERVICE BY PUBLICATION rests on (1) the affidavit, (2) the notice, (3) the certificate of the printer or publisher (*l*), and (4) certificate of mailing. Such enactments are strictly construed.

IT SEEMS that a defective notice or certificate may be cured by the recitals of the decree, if not by the presumption *omnia rite esse acta, etc.,* which obtains in favor of courts of general jurisdiction, especially in cases where the decrees and judgments are called collaterally in question. (*m*) But the affidavit, being the foundation of this special proceeding, has always received most critical attention in the courts. (*n*)

(*i*) § 11, page 19, Hill's Ch. Pr.
(*j*) Compare *Randall* v. *Songer*, 16 Ill. 28 with *Reddick* v. *Bank*, 27 id. 148; *Smith* v. *Trimble*, id. 153.
(*k*) *Smith* v. *Trimble*, 27 Ill. 153; *McDaniel* v. *Correll*, 19 id. 227.
(*l*) *Tibbs* v. *Allen*, 27 Ill. 125; modifying *Randall* v. *Songer*, 16 id. 27; and *Varien* v. *Edmonson*, 5 Gilm. 272.
(*m*) *Reddick* v. *Bank*, 27 Ill. 148; *Tibbs* v. *Allen*, id. 125.
(*n*) *Tibbs* v. *Allen*, 27 Ill. 125; Jones' Forms, 281.

Resignation and removal of guardians.

A CAREFUL EXAMINATION of the authorities shows the requisites of such affidavits to be, (1) A suit pending when they are made; (2) Positive terms, not on information or belief; (3) They should be correctly entitled in the proper court; (4) They should contain facts, not conclusions of law; (5) They must be made by the party himself, or his attorney.(*o*)

Affidavit of the non-residence of a guardian may be made after the following precedent:

(1.) NON-RESIDENT GUARDIAN.

(*Title of matter.*)

STATE OF ILLINOIS, } ss.:
    County, }

A B, being duly sworn, upon his oath, says, that he is the petitioner, and that E F, guardian of C D, herein named in the above-entitled matter, resides at   , in the county of   , in the State of   , and further deponent saith not.

(*Jurat.*)   A B.

The court as well as the clerk can, from such an affidavit and the facts stated in it, draw the *legal conclusion* that E F resides out of this State, and determine the propriety of publication.

In case of filing such an affidavit, no action on the part of the sheriff, of course, could reach E F, and notice of publication may now issue at once without a return, *non est inventus*.(*p*) The intervention of the sheriff being no longer essential to jurisdiction in the court.

But in the four other cases: (1) Absence of a resident defendant, or (2), his concealment, or (3), where his residence is unknown or he cannot be found, and (4), where his name is unknown, or he is unknown, such a return was held essential to the validity of the notice of publication.(*q*) The following forms are suggested:

(*o*) 24 Ill. 281; 1 Daniel's Ch. Pr., ch. 22, § 10; 8 Paige, 414; *Campbell* v. *Morrison*, 7 Paige, 157; 41 Ill., 49; 3 Greenleaf's Evid., pp. 336, 342.

(*p*) Laws of 1874, 109, § 8.
(*q*) 19 Ill. 227; 27 id. 153.

(2.) Absent guardian.

(Title of cause, venue, etc.)

A B, being duly sworn, says, that he is the petitioner; that E F, guardian in this matter of C D, who resided recently (*or whose usual place of abode is*) at   , in the county of   , in this State, has departed from thence and gone (with all his family) (*on a journey to Europe*) (or to the State of   ) for the time being (or is now out of this State, and that upon diligent inquiry his place of residence cannot be ascertained), and further deponent saith not.

(*Jurat.*)   A B.

From such facts, coupled with the sheriff's return on file, it appears that ordinary service cannot be made on E F, although a resident guardian, on account of temporary absence.

(3.) Concealed guardian.

(Title of proceeding.)
(Venue.)

A B, being duly sworn, says, that he is the petitioner in this matter; that E F, guardian of C D herein, at the time of issuing of the summons herein, resided at   , in the county of   , in this State, but on learning that C D, the sheriff of said county, had such a summons, and was looking for said E F, he, the said E F, concealed himself within this State, and so continues to avoid the service of process herein, and that upon diligent inquiry his place of residence cannot be ascertained, and further deponent saith not.

(*Jurat.*)   A B.

(4.) Residence of guardian unknown.

Another case is provided for, to wit: where a guardian on due inquiry cannot be found, and where his residence is unknown and cannot, upon diligent inquiry, be ascertained. In this case also, the summons should be issued and returned "upon diligent search and inquiry made and had, I cannot find the within-named guardian E F in my county, nor can I learn where he is," etc.

Upon this return and an affidavit as follows:

(Title, venue, etc.)

A B, being duly sworn, says, that he is the petitioner in the above-entitled proceeding, and that the residence of the guardian E F herein is unknown, and cannot, upon diligent search and inquiry, which have been made, be ascertained, and that the said E F cannot, on due inquiry, be found, and further deponent saith not.

(*Jurat.*)   A B.

The publication notice will issue.

But few decisions have been made on the requisites of such affidavits. The importance of their sufficiency is forcibly stated in *Campbell* v. *McCahan*, 41 Ill. 49.(*s*)

The notice should be published immediately on filing the affidavit, and the affidavit must be filed as soon as it is made. Unreasonable delay in either case would prove fatal to the jurisdiction over the defendant.(*t*)

8. THE NOTICE. The form of a chancery notice, as used generally throughout the State, in cases of non-resident defendants, may be found at page 657, Hill's Chancery Practice, and in Jones' Forms, No. 472, page 282. It may be varied to meet the exigencies of any cause.

(1.) PUBLICATION NOTICE. Where defendants have not been served with process, the clerk may make publication of notice to them without an order of the court under the statute, and it will be sufficient.(*u*)

(2.) Where one of several defendants to a bill in chancery is a non-resident, and the notice by publication is insufficient to charge him, and the other defendants are personally served with notice, the latter cannot raise objections to the insufficiency of the notice by publication.(*v*)

NOTICE TO GUARDIAN.

STATE OF ILLINOIS,   *In the County Court of*   *county.*
county. } *ss:*   *term,* 18 .

In the matter of the }
guardianship of C D. }

Affidavit of the non-residence of the guardian above named, having been filed in the office of the clerk of said county court of   county, notice is hereby given to the said guardian that one E H filed his petition in said court, on the   day of   , 18 , and that a summons thereupon issued out of said court against said guardian   , returnable on the   Monday of   next (18), as is by law required.

Now, unless you, the said C D, shall personally be and appear before said county court of   county, on the first day of the next term thereof, to be holden in   in said county, on the third Monday of   , 18 , and (*w*) show cause against said petition, why you should not be removed from your trust as guardian of the said C D, and answer such other matters as are in said petition set forth, the same, and the matters and things therein charged and

(*s*) See Hill's Ch. Pr. 18.   Laws 1827, p. 48; 1833, p. 63; R. S. 47,
(*t*) *Campbell* v. *McCahan*, 41 Ill. 45.   P. 77 and 78, S. 81, Gross, 6. See p.
(*u*) *Ayres* v. *Lusk*, 1 Scam. 536.   51, *supra.*
(*v*) *Fergus* v. *Tinkham*, 38 Ill. 407;   (*w*) See page 133, *supra.*

stated, will be taken as confessed, and a decree entered against you, according to the prayer of said petition.

, *Complainant's solicitor.*   , *Clerk.*

9. DAILY PAPER. If published in a daily paper, publication on Sunday is forbidden by the policy of the law and prohibited by statute, and no greater amount is chargeable for costs for publication fee than would be sufficient to publish the same notice in a weekly paper.

In an adversary proceeding in the courts, the publication notices and all matters pertaining to them being usually directory, no questions collaterally can be raised relative thereto, but it is otherwise in special proceedings. In computation of time, Sunday is *dies non juridicus.*(x) In computing the time of the publication, the day of the publication should be excluded, and the day of the commencement of the term of the court included. When certified by the publisher or his agent and a copy of the notice filed with the certificate, these become a part of the record.(y) Proof of publication may be made otherwise, however, than by the publisher.

In collateral proceedings the notice cannot be impeached. A certificate, declaring that an advertisement was published "for four successive weeks, the first publication having been made on the 8th day of March, 1850," will, in a chancery proceeding against an unknown person, confer jurisdiction on the court, although the certificate proceeds to state, "and the last on the 26th of April, 1850," the inference being, that the certificate was published eight weeks; and, in a collateral proceeding, the presumption will be, that the court had other evidence that publication was duly made.(z)

10. ANOTHER GUARDIAN APPOINTED. Upon the removal, resignation or death of a guardian another may be appointed, who shall give bond and security and perform the duties of the office. And the court shall have power to compel the guardian so removed or resigned, or the executor or administrator of a deceased guardian, or the conservator of an insane person, or other person, to deliver up to such successor all the goods, chattels, moneys, title papers, and other effects in his custody or control, belonging to such minor; and upon failure to so deliver the same, to commit the person offending to jail until he shall comply with the order of the court.(a)

(x) *Scammon* v. *Chicago,* 40 Ill. 146; 12 id. 358.
(y) *Varien* v. *Edmonson,* 5 Gilm. 272; *Harper* v. *Ely,* 56 Ill. 179; *Tompkins* v. *Wiltberger,* id. 385; *Botsford* v. *O'Conner,* 57 id. 72.
(z) *Pile* v. *McBratney,* 15 Ill. 314.
(a) § 40, R. S. 1874, p. 562.

Resignation and removal of guardians.

11. THE MARRIAGE OF A FEMALE WARD shall discharge her guardian from all right to her custody and education, but not to her property. (*b*)

12. THE HEARING. On filing the petition for the removal of a guardian for cause, as we have seen, process issues. The time for hearing should be fixed and continued from time to time until the guardian is either actually or constructively served. No course of procedure is indicated, but the Chancery Practice in such cases affords ample precedents, if we are to consider the petition in the nature of a bill in chancery.

The decree should recite the facts upon which the same is made. (*c*)

13. DECREE OF REMOVAL OF GUARDIAN.

The petition of A B coming on this day to be heard, and it appearing that C D, the guardian of E F aforesaid, has filed his answer herein, denying the facts stated in said petition, and it appearing to the court from the testimony that C D has mismanaged said estate as stated in said petition, and that all the facts stated in said petition are true and have been fully proved to the satisfaction of this court, and after argument by the respective counsel for said petitioner and said guardian, it is now here   ordered, adjudged and decreed, that said guardian's accounts be forthwith closed; that all the estate of the said E F, which has come to the hands of the said C D, as such guardian, now remaining undisposed of, be delivered over to another guardian to be by this court appointed, and that the letters of guardianship heretofore issued to the said C D be and hereby are revoked; and that the said C D attend before this court from day to day until this decree and the several orders herein are fully complied with.

Dated   , A. D. 18 .

Another guardian is then to be nominated and appointed as before and the estate turned over to him. (*d*)

For further delineation of the law of guardian and ward, and the jurisdiction and practice, the reader is referred to subsequent chapters and to Hill's Chancery Practice, "Infants."

(1.) GUARDIAN *AD LITEM;* DECISIONS. An answer of a guardian *ad litem*, if it admit the truth of the charges in the complainant's bill, cannot affect the infant's rights; but, with respect to him, all allegations must be proved with the same strictness as if the answer had interposed a direct and positive denial of their truth. (*e*)

(*b*) § 41, R. S. 1874, p. 562.
(*c*) See Hill's Chan. Pr., Bill and Decree, Answer, Demurrer, Plea, etc., etc. But see *Bressler* v. *McCune*, 56 Ill. 565.
(*d*) See page 111, *supra*.
(*e*) *McClay, Adm'r,* v. *Norris,* 4 Gilm. 370; *Chaffin* v. *Heirs of Kimball,* 23 Ill. 36.

Resignation and removal of guardians.

(2.) WAIVER. A guardian *ad litem* cannot waive any of the rights of the defendant whom he represents, and when incompetent and illegal evidence is introduced without objection by the guardian, the court is bound to notice and exclude such evidence. (*f*)

(3.) Upon an application to sell the real estate of a decedent for the payment of debts, infant heirs, who have not guardians appearing for them, must be represented by guardians *ad litem*. (*g*)

(4.) It is not necessary that there should be a guardian, or *prochein ami*, for a minor at the time of suing out process. If the rule were otherwise, it should be taken advantage of by plea in abatement, or by motion to quash. (*h*)

(5.) It is the duty of the court to appoint a guardian *ad litem* to protect the interests of infant suitors. (*i*)

(6.) The failure of a guardian *ad litem* to answer for the infant does not take away the jurisdiction of the court over the infant. (*j*)

(7.) Where infants are not in court, owing to the fact that notice of publication is void, the appointment of a guardian *ad litem* is void. (*k*)

(8.) The appointment of, for minor defendants, not naming them, is inoperative, where the record likewise fails to show that any of defendants are minors. (*l*)

(9.) APPOINTMENT OF. As to, by the court, *sua sponte;* and whether and when on plaintiff's motion; need not be related to the infants. Executor not necessarily the guardian. (*m*)

(10.) Answer not binding on infants. (*m*)

(11.) Court should require answer of, before entering final decree. (*m*)

(12.) To vigorously defend the interest of the infants. (*m*)

(13.) A guardian *ad litem* must be appointed for infant defendants, or the proceedings against them will be erroneous. (*n*)

(14.) Jurisdiction is not conferred by answer of guardian *ad litem*, where there has been no service. (*o*)

(15.) The appointment of "the clerk of the court" without naming him is sufficient. (*p*)

(*f*) *Cartwright* v. *Wise*, 14 Ill. 417.
(*g*) *Herdman* v. *Short*, 18 Ill. 59.
(*h*) *Stumps* v. *Kelly*, 22 Ill. 140.
(*i*) *Loyd* v. *Malone*, 23 Ill. 43.
(*j*) *Goudy* v. *Hall*, 36 Ill. 313.
(*k*) *McDermaid* v. *Russell*, 41 Ill. 490.
(*l*) *Sullivan* v. *Sullivan*, 42 Ill. 315.
(*m*) *Rhoads* v. *Rhoads*, 43 Ill. 239.
(*n*) *Hall* v. *Davis*, 44 Ill. 494; *Quigley* v. *Roberts*, id. 503.
(*o*) *Clark* v. *Thompson*, 47 Ill. 25.
(*p*) *Hess* v. *Voss*, 52 Ill. 472.

CHAPTER V.

IDIOTS, LUNATICS AND OTHER INCAPACITATED PERSONS AND THEIR ESTATES.

SECTION I. The insane, etc.; decisions.
        II. Appointment of conservators — their powers and duties — restoration and removal.
        III. Commitment and detention of such persons.

SECTION I. — THE INSANE, ETC.; DECISIONS.

1. Evidence as to insanity, and presumptions as to sanity, *onus probandi*.
2. Lucid intervals, contracts, etc.
3. Questions relative to sanity and insanity, proper issues for a jury.
4. Facts indicating a disposing mind and *eo converso*.
5. Mere mental weakness insufficient to authorize equity to interfere in matters of contract.
6. Drunkenness producing inability or insanity, however, is sufficient.
7. Idiots and lunatics; conservators; their appointment and discharge.
8. Insanity as a defense against a criminal charge.

1. It cannot be presumed, against proof, that a person was insane merely because his mother had been so.(*a*) The law presumes every man to be sane, but when insanity is once proved to have existed, the law presumes it still to continue.(*b*) In questions of insanity, the affirmative testimony of those best acquainted with the person alleged to be insane should outweigh the testimony of those who merely testify, from interviews at or about the time of the act sought to be avoided for insanity, that they saw nothing indicating an insane mind.(*c*) In cases involving questions of insanity, the presumption is in favor of sanity, and the *onus* of proof is on the party seeking to impeach an instrument executed by a person of competent age and under no legal disabilities.(*d*)

2. A contract, entered into during the LUCID INTERVALS of one who is a lunatic, is valid.(*e*) A deed executed several years before the maker was, by inquest, found insane has the legal presumption

(*a*) *Snow* v. *Benton*, 28 Ill. 306.
(*b*) *Menkins* v. *Lightner*, 18 Ill. 282.
(*c*) *Emery* v. *Hoyt*, 46 Ill. 258.
(*d*) *Myatt* v. *Walker*, 44 Ill. 485.
(*e*) *Lilly* v. *Waggoner*, 27 Ill. 395.

of validity in its favor.(*e*) The evidence showing the insanity of a party at the time of the execution of a deed must preponderate, or the legal presumption in favor of sanity will sustain the act.(*e*) In an action upon a promissory note, the defendant, who alleges insanity when it was made, is not bound to overcome or pay any regard to a finding of an inquest in the county court that he was sane on a day prior to that on which the note was made.(*f*) When insanity is established in the maker of a contract, at times both before and after its execution, as a defense to an action to enforce the contract, the burden is on the plaintiff to show that it was made in a lucid interval. The fact that the consideration of the note was adequate would not of itself justify the inference that the maker was sane when he made it.(*f*)

3. Formerly the intervention of a jury was not an absolute necessity in dealing with the insane.(*g*) It is otherwise now.

4. HOMICIDE, FOLLOWED BY SUICIDE, and a disposition of property entirely at variance with long-declared intentions, and the exhibition of unnatural malice toward a child, are not of themselves sufficient to raise a presumption of insanity, and the want of a disposing mind.(*h*)

The rule which permits EVIDENCE AS TO THE PECUNIARY CONDITION, means and ability of the beneficiaries of a will, and of those who might be benefited by overthrowing it, with a view of determining whether the testator appreciates his relation to them, and exhibits a capable and disposing mind, has no application to the case of a gift accompanied with delivery.(*h*)

5. MERE MENTAL WEAKNESS will not authorize a court of equity to set aside an executed contract unless such weakness amounts to inability to comprehend the contract, and is accompanied by evidence of imposition or undue influence.(*i*)

6. The law will protect a party from the effects of his own acts done in a state of insanity, even though the INSANITY IS CAUSED BY DRUNKENNESS.(*j*) Evidence of a sober interval, after a long period of continued drunkenness and craziness, does not show that state of mind necessary to the validity of a contract.(*j*)

(*e*) *Lilly* v. *Waggoner*, 27 Ill. 395.
(*f*) *Emery* v. *Hoyt*, 46 Ill. 258.
(*g*) *Myatt* v. *Walker*, 44 Ill. 485.
(*h*) *Crum, adm'r*, v. *Thornly*, 47 Ill. 192.
(*i*) *Miller* v. *Craig*, 36 Ill. 109.
(*j*) *Menkins* v. *Lightner*, 18 Ill. 282

7. IDIOTS AND LUNATICS. Under the provisions of the Revised Statutes, concerning idiots and lunatics, application may be made by one who has been declared a lunatic, and for whom a conservator has been appointed, to the same court where the former proceedings took place for the discharge of the conservator, and the restoration of the property in his hands. (*k*) Where a conservator to a lunatic is sought to be appointed under the statute, the lunatic must have reasonable notice, or the inquisition will be set aside.(*l*)

8. INSANITY AS A DEFENSE. The presumption is that all men are of sufficient capacity to be responsible for crime; therefore, the prisoner must establish his insanity.(*m*) It need not, however, be established beyond a reasonable doubt; it is enough if the jury be reasonably satisfied thereof by the weight or preponderance of the evidence.(*m*) If the accused had, at the time of the offense, capacity and reason sufficient to enable him to distinguish between right and wrong, and understand the nature of the act, and his relation to the party injured, the defense of insanity is not made out.(*m*) The prosecution is not bound to prove the sanity of a defendant in a criminal case; but if evidence of insanity is introduced by the accused, and there is reasonable doubt of his sanity, he is entitled to the benefit of the doubt.(*n*) When a defendant, who is being tried upon a criminal charge, sets up insanity as an excuse for the act, he does not thereby assume the burden of the proof upon that question. Such a defense is only a denial of one of the essential allegations against him.(*o*) And in sustaining such a defense it is not necessary that the insanity of the accused be established, even by a preponderance of proof; but if, upon the whole evidence, the jury entertain a reasonable doubt of his insanity, they must acquit.(*o*) Where a party who is upon trial on an indictment for murder interposes the defense of insanity, the rule in regard to the degree of insanity which would demand an acquittal is, that whenever it shall appear from the evidence that, at the time of doing the act charged, the prisoner was affected with insanity, and such affection was the efficient cause of the act, and that he would not have done the act but for that affection, he ought to be acquitted.(*o*) But this unsoundness of mind must be of such a degree as to create an un-

(*k*) *Ayres* v. *Mussetter*, 46 Ill. 472.
(*l*) *Eddy* v. *People*, 15 Ill. 386.
(*m*) *Fisher* v. *People*, 23 Ill. 283.

(*n*) *Chase* v. *People*, 40 Ill. 352.
(*o*) *Hopps* v. *People*, 31 Ill. 385.

Conservators.

controllable impulse to do the act charged, by overriding the reason and judgment, and obliterating the sense of right and wrong as to the particular act done, and depriving the accused of the power of choosing between them.(*o*)

SECTION II. — APPOINTMENT OF CONSERVATORS; THEIR POWERS AND DUTIES.

1. When a conservator may be appointed.
2. Summons to be issued.
3. Conservator to give bond.
4. Bonds may be put in suit.
5. Duties of conservator, generally.
6. To take charge of the estate of his ward, and return inventories.
7. Requisites of an inventory.
8. Conservator to settle his account at least annually.
9. On final settlement to deliver estate and title papers.
10. The final accounting.
11. Conservator to settle all accounts of his ward, and sue in his own name.
12. May with consent of court perform the personal contracts of the ward.
13. To appear and represent his ward in all suits and proceedings.
14. Contracts of a lunatic after finding of a jury, void as to the lunatic.
15. Contracts made before such finding, when may be avoided.
16. Trading, bartering or gaming with a lunatic, etc., prohibited.
17. Conservator to frugally manage the estate.
18. Investments to be made.
19. Conservator may lease his ward's estate.
20. He may by leave of the county court mortgage the same.
21. Petition for leave to be filed.
22. Strict foreclosure prohibited and redemption prescribed.
23. Sale of real estate may on petition of the conservator be ordered by the county court.
24. The petition.
25. Notice of application.
26. Procedure as in chancery.
27. Notice of sale.
28. Report of sale and deed.
29. Account of proceeds.
30. Sureties of the conservator to be looked after and kept sufficient.
31. Conservator may be required to give counter security.
32. Conservator may be removed.

(*o*) *Hopps* v. *The People*, 31 Ill. 385.

Conservators.

33. To be first summoned.
34. He may in a proper case resign.
35. Another conservator may be appointed.
36. Fees and compensation of the conservator to be reasonable and just.
37. Conservator may be discharged and the property restored to the owner on his restoration to reason or reformation.
38. Notice of application to be given to the conservator.
39. Procedure on the application.
40. Appeals.
41. Conservator, guardian, curator, or committee of any non-resident idiot, lunatic, insane or distracted person, spendthrift or drunkard, may collect debts and recover property of ward in this State.
42. Application for sale of such ward's estate to be made to the circuit court.
43. Notice of application.
44. Bond may be required.
45. Bond for costs must be given.
46. Repeal of former laws.

1. Whenever any idiot, lunatic or distracted person has any estate, real or personal; or when any person by excessive drinking, gaming, idleness or debauchery of any kind so spends, wastes or lessens his estate as to expose himself or his family to want or suffering, or any county, town, or incorporated city, town or village to any charge or expense for the support of himself or his family, the county court of the county in which such person lives shall, on the application of any relative or creditor, or if there be neither relative or creditor, then any person living in such county, order a jury to be summoned to ascertain whether such person be idiot, lunatic or distracted, a drunkard or such spendthrift; and if the jury return in their verdict that such person is idiot, lunatic or distracted, or drunkard, or so spends, wastes or lessens his estate, it shall be the duty of the court to appoint some fit person to be the conservator of such person.(*p*) This jurisdiction has not been conferred on probate courts.

2. On an application for the appointment of a conservator of any person being filed, summons shall be issued and served upon the person for whom a conservator is sought to be appointed, in the same manner as summons is issued and served in cases in chancery. When the application is against an idiot or lunatic, the clerk of the court in which the application is filed shall also give not less than ten (10) days' notice thereof by at least one insertion in some newspaper published in the county.(*q*)

(*p*) Cothran's Stats, 955, § 1.   (*q*) § 2, id.

Conservators.

3. The conservator so appointed shall, before entering upon the duties of his office, give bond payable to the people of the State of Illinois, with at least two sufficient sureties, to be approved by the court, in double the amount of his ward's real and personal estate, with such condition as near as may be as provided in the case of the bonds of guardians of infants. Additional bonds and counter security may be required as hereinafter provided.(*r*)

4. Bonds given in pursuance of this act may be put in suit in the name of the people of the State of Illinois, to the use of any person entitled to recover on the breach thereof, and damages adjudged on proceedings had thereon as in other cases of penal bonds.(*s*)

5. Such conservator shall have the care and management of the real and personal estate of his ward, and the custody of his person unless otherwise ordered by the court, and the custody and education of his children, where no other guardian is appointed, unless the court orders otherwise; but this act shall not be so construed as to deprive the mother of the custody and education of the children without her consent, if she be a fit and competent person to have such custody and education.(*t*)

6. The conservator shall, immediately upon his appointment, take charge of the estate of his ward, and within sixty days after such appointment, or, if the court is not in session at the expiration of that time, at the next term thereafter, return to the court a true and perfect inventory of the real and personal estate of the ward, signed by him and verified by his affidavit. As often as other estates shall thereafter come to his knowledge he shall return an inventory thereof within sixty days from the time the same shall come to his knowledge.(*u*)

7. The inventory shall describe the real estate, its probable value and rental, and state whether the same is incumbered, and if incumbered, how and for how much; what amount of money is on hand, and contain a list of all personal property, including annuities and credits of the ward, designating them as "good," "doubtful," or "desperate," as the case may be.(*v*)

8. The conservator shall, at the expiration of a year from his appointment, settle his accounts as conservator with the county court, and at least once each one (1) year thereafter, and as much oftener as the court may require.(*w*)

(*r*) § 3, R. S. 1874, p. 685.
(*s*) § 4, id., p. 686.
(*t*) § 5, id.
(*u*) § 6, id.
(*v*) § 7, id.
(*w*) § 8, id.

Conservators.

9. Such conservator, at the expiration of his trust, shall pay and deliver to those entitled thereto all the money, estate and title papers in his hands as conservator, or with which he is chargeable as such, in such manner as shall be directed by the order or decree of any court having jurisdiction thereof.(*x*)

10. On every accounting or final settlement of a conservator, he shall exhibit and file his account as such conservator, setting forth specifically, in separate items, on what account expenditures were made by him, and all sums received and paid out since his last accounting, and on what account each was received and paid out, and showing the true balance of money on hand, which account shall be accompanied by the proper vouchers, and signed by him and verified by his affidavit.(*y*)

11. The conservator shall settle all accounts of his ward, and demand and sue for and receive in his own name, as conservator, all personal property of and demands due the ward, or with the approbation of the court compound for the same, and give a discharge to the debtor upon receiving a fair and just dividend of his estate and effects.(*z*)

12. The conservator, by permission and subject to the direction of the court which appointed him, may perform the personal contracts of his ward, made in good faith and legally subsisting at the time of the commencement of his disability, and which may be performed with advantage to the estate of the ward.(*a*)

13. He shall appear for and represent his ward in all suits and proceedings, unless another person is appointed for that purpose as conservator or next friend; but nothing contained in this act shall impair or affect the power of any court to appoint a conservator or next friend, to defend the interest of said ward impleaded in such court, or interested in a suit or matter therein pending, nor its power to appoint or allow any person as next friend for such ward, to commence, prosecute or defend any suit in his behalf, subject to the direction of such court.(*b*)

14. Every note, bill, bond or other contract by an idiot, lunatic, distracted person or spendthrift, made after the finding of the jury, as provided in section one of this act, shall be void as against the idiot, lunatic, distracted person, drunkard or spendthrift, and his estate; but the person making any contract with such idiot, lunatic, distracted person or spendthrift shall be bound thereby.(*c*)

(*x*) § 9, R. S. 1874, p. 686.
(*y*) § 10, id.
(*z*) § 11, id.
(*a*) § 12, id.
(*b*) § 13, id., p. 687.
(*c*) § 14, id.

Conservators.

15. Every contract made with an idiot, lunatic or distracted person before such finding, or with a drunkard or spendthrift made after the application for the appointment of a conservator, may be avoided, except in favor of the person fraudulently making the same.(*d*)

16. Whoever, by trading with, bartering, gaming or any other device, possesses himself of any property or valuable thing belonging to any idiot, lunatic or notoriously distracted person, drunkard or spendthrift, shall be deemed guilty of swindling, and upon conviction thereof be fined in a sum not exceeding two thousand dollars, or confined in the county jail not exceeding one year, or both.(*e*)

17. The conservator shall manage the estate of his ward frugally and without waste, and apply the income and profit thereof, so far as the same may be necessary, to the comfort and suitable support of his ward and his family, and the education of his children.(*f*)

18. It shall be the duty of the conservator to put and keep his ward's money at interest, upon security to be approved by the court, or invest the same in United States bonds or other United States interest-bearing securities. Personal security may be taken for loans not exceeding one hundred dollars. Loans in larger amounts shall be upon real-estate security. No loan shall be made for a longer time than three years, unless authorized by the court: *Provided*, the same may be extended from year to year, without the approval of the court.(*g*)

19. The conservator may lease the real estate of the ward, upon such terms and for such length of time as the county court shall approve.(*h*)

20. The conservator may, by leave of the county court, mortgage the real estate of the ward for a term of years, or in fee.(*i*)

21. Before any mortgage shall be made, the conservator shall petition the county court for an order authorizing such mortgage to be made, in which petition shall be set out the condition of the estate and the facts and circumstances on which the petition is founded, and a description of the premises sought to be mortgaged.(*j*)

22. No decree of strict foreclosure shall be made upon any such mortgage, but redemption shall be allowed, as is now provided by

(*d*) § 15, R. S 1874, p. 687.
(*e*) § 16, id.
(*f*) § 17, id.
(*g*) § 18, id.
(*h*) § 19, id.
(*i*) § 20, id.
(*j*) § 21, id.

Conservators.

law in cases of sales under executions upon common-law judgments.(*k*) That is within twelve months.

23. On the petition of the conservator, the county court of the county where the ward resides, or if the ward does not reside in the State, of the county where the real estate or some part of it is situated, may order the sale of the real estate of the ward for his support and that of his family when the court shall deem it necessary, or to invest the proceeds in other real estate, or for the purpose of otherwise investing the same or for the purpose of paying the debts of the ward or the education of the children of said ward.(*l*)

24. The petition shall set forth the condition of the estate and the facts and circumstances on which the petition is founded, and shall be signed by the conservator and verified by his affidavit, and shall be filed at least ten days before the commencement of the term of court at which the application shall be made.(*m*)

25. Notice of such application shall be given to all persons concerned by publication in some newspaper published in the county where the application is made at least once in each week for three successive weeks, or if no newspaper is published in such county, by setting up written or printed notices in three of the most public places in the county at least three weeks before the session of the court at which such application shall be made. The ward shall be served with a copy of such notice at least ten days before the hearing of such application. Such service may be proved in the same manner as the service of a copy of a bill in chancery.(*n*)

26. Such application shall be docketed as other causes, and the petition may be amended, heard or continued for further notice or for other cause. The practice in such cases shall be the same as in other cases in chancery.(*o*)

27. The court shall direct notice of the time and place of sale to be given, and may direct the sale to be made on reasonable credit, and require such security of the conservator or purchaser as the interest of the ward may require.(*p*)

28. It shall be the duty of the conservator making such sale, as soon as may be, to make return of such sale to the court granting the order, which, if approved, shall be recorded, and shall vest in the purchaser or purchasers all the interest of the ward in the estate so sold.(*q*)

(*k*) § 22, R. S. 1874, p. 687.
(*l*) § 23, id.
(*m*) § 24, id., p. 688.
(*n*) § 25, id.
(*o*) § 26, id.
(*p*) § 27, id.
(*q*) § 28, id.

Conservators.

29. An account of all moneys and securities received by any conservator for the sale of real estate of his ward, shall be returned on oath of such conservator to the county court of the county where letters of conservatorship were obtained, and such money shall be accounted for, and subject to the order of the county court in like manner as other moneys belonging to such ward. In case of sale for re-investment in this State, the money shall be re-invested under the direction of the court.(r)

30. It shall be the duty of the county court at each accounting of the conservator to inquire into the sufficiency of his sureties, and if at any time it has cause to believe that the sureties of a conservator are insufficient or in failing circumstances, it shall, after summoning the conservator if he be not before the court, require him to give additional security.(s)

31. Upon the application of the surety of any conservator and after summoning the conservator, the court may, if it believes him to be insolvent or in doubtful circumstances, require him to give counter security to his sureties.(t)

32. The county court may remove a conservator for his failure to give bond or security or additional or counter security when required; or for failure to make inventory or to account and make settlement, or support the ward, or when he shall have become insane, or have removed out of the State, or become incapable or unsuitable for the discharge of his duties, or for failure to discharge any duty required of him by law or the order of the court, or for other good cause.(u)

33. Before removing a conservator the court shall summon him to show cause why he should not be removed for the cause alleged. If the conservator has left the State or cannot be served with process he may be notified in the same manner as non-resident defendants in chancery, by publication.(v)

34. When it appears proper the court may permit the conservator to resign his trust, if he first settles his accounts and delivers over the estate as by the court directed.(w)

35. Upon the removal, resignation or death of a conservator another may be appointed who shall give bond and security and perform the duties prescribed by this act. The court shall have power to compel the conservator so removed or resigned, or the executor or administrator of a deceased conservator, to deliver up to such suc-

(r) § 29, R. S. 1874, p. 688.
(s) § 30, id.
(t) § 31, id.
(u) § 32, id.
(v) § 33, id.
(w) § 34, id., p. 689.

Conservators.

cessor all the goods, chattels, moneys, title papers and other effects in his custody or control belonging to the ward; and upon failure to so deliver the same, to commit the person offending to jail until he shall comply with the order of the court.(*x*)

36. Conservators on settlement shall be allowed such fees and compensation for their services as shall seem reasonable and just to the court.(*y*)

37. When any person, for whom a conservator has been or may be appointed under the provisions of this act, shall be restored to his reason, or in case such drunkard or spendthrift shall have become so reformed as to be a proper and safe person to have the care and management of his estate, such person may apply to the county court of the county in which such conservator was appointed to have said conservator removed and the care and management of his property, or so much thereof as shall remain restored to him.(*z*)

38. Notice of such intended application shall be given to the conservator ten days before the commencement of the term of the court to which the application shall be made.(*a*)

39. It shall be the duty of the court to which any such application, as provided in the foregoing section, is made, on proof that said conservator has been duly notified of such application, to cause a jury to be summoned to try the question whether said applicant is a fit person to have the care, custody and control of his or her property, and if the said jury return in their verdict that such person is a fit person to have the control of such property as aforesaid, then the court shall enter an order fully restoring such person to all the rights and privileges enjoyed before said conservator was appointed: *Provided*, that such conservator, so removed, shall be allowed a reasonable time to settle his accounts as such, and to pass over the money or property in his hands, and such removal shall not invalidate any contracts made in good faith by said conservator, while acting as such: *Provided, further*, that no application shall be entertained for the removal of any conservator appointed for any person under the provisions of this act, within less than one year from such appointment, unless for neglect of duty or mismanagement of his trust.(*b*)

40. Appeals shall be allowed to the circuit court from any order or judgment made or rendered under this act, upon the appellant

(*x*) § 35, R. S. 1874, p. 689.
(*y*) § 36, id.
(*z*) § 37, id.
(*a*) § 38, id.
(*b*) § 39, id.

Conservators.

giving such bond and security as shall be directed by the court; but no appeal from an order removing a conservator shall in any wise affect such order until the same be reversed. (c)

41. The conservator, guardian, curator, or committee of any non-resident idiot, lunatic, insane or distracted person, spendthrift or drunkard, appointed in any of the United States or territories, or any foreign country, in pursuance of the laws of any such State, territory, or country, may commence and prosecute in his name as such conservator, guardian, curator or committee, suits for the recovery of any real or personal property, or any interest therein in this State, belonging to any such idiot, lunatic, insane or distracted person, spendthrift or drunkard, or for any injury to any such property, in any of the courts of record in this State having jurisdiction in similar cases by persons in their own rights, and may collect, receive and remove to his place of residence any personal estate of his ward. (d)

42. It shall be lawful for any such conservator, guardian, curator, or committee of any non-resident idiot, lunatic, insane or distracted person, spendthrift or drunkard, who shall obtain an order from the proper court in the State, territory or country in which such conservator, guardian, curator or committee was appointed, authorizing him to make application for the sale of his ward's real estate or personal property in this State, upon filing a certified copy of such order for record in the office of the clerk of the circuit court of the county in this State in which the property, or the major part thereof, is situated, by petition to such court to obtain an order authorizing such conservator, guardian, curator or committee to sell and transfer any such property or interest therein, belonging to any such idiot, lunatic, insane or distracted person, spendthrift or drunkard, and to make deeds and conveyances thereof, which deeds and conveyances executed and acknowledged in pursuance of the laws of this State, or of the State, territory or country in which such conservator, guardian, curator or committee was appointed, shall be effectual in law and equity to pass to the grantee or grantees therein all the right, title and interest of such idiot, lunatic, insane or distracted person, spendthrift or drunkard therein. The court ordering the sale may authorize any person to act as auctioneer of the property, but the deed shall be executed by the conservator, guardian, curator or committee. (e)

(c) § 40, R. S. 1874, p. 689. (e) § 42, id., p. 690.
(d) § 41, id.

Conservators.

43. Notice of the time and place of presenting said petition to said circuit court shall be given by publication in the nearest newspaper, for four successive weeks, the first of which publication shall be at least forty days before the time fixed for the presentation of said petition, requesting all persons interested to show cause why the prayer of said petition should not be granted.(*f*)

44. The said circuit court may, in its discretion, require such conservator, curator, guardian or committee to file a bond, with sufficient securities, conditioned for the faithful application of the money which may be received for any such property, for the benefit, and to the use of such idiot, lunatic, insane or distracted person, spendthrift or drunkard.(*g*)

45. In all suits by non-resident conservators, guardians, curators or committees, they shall give a bond for costs as in cases of other non-residents.(*h*)

46. Chapter fifty of the Revised Statutes of 1845, entitled "Idiots and Lunatics," and an act entitled "An act to provide for the sale of the estates of insane persons," approved February 12, 1853, and an act entitled "An act to amend chapter L of the Revised Statutes of 1845," approved February 15, 1865, and an act entitled "An act to amend chapter fifty of the Revised Statutes, entitled 'Idiots and Lunatics,' and to extend the provisions thereof to habitual drunkards," approved April 19, 1869, and all other acts and parts of acts inconsistent with the provisions of this act are hereby repealed, except as herein re-enacted : *Provided,* that this section shall not be so construed as to affect any rights existing or actions pending at the time this act shall take effect.(*i*)

SECTION III. — COMMITMENT AND DETENTION OF LUNATICS.

1. Jurisdiction of the county court may be invoked by petition.
2. Petition to be filed, process to issue, and be served and returned.
3. Subpœnas may issue.
4. Jury, trial, continuance.
5. Verdict, its form.
6. Verdict to be recorded, order of commitment entered, and application for admission of respondent to superintendent of a state hospital for the insane to be made by the clerk.

(*f*) § 43, R. S. 1874, p. 690. (*h*) § 45, id.
(*g*) § 44, id. (*i*) § 46, act of March 21, 1874.

Commitment and detention of lunatics.

7. When commitment may be had.
8. Communication to be had between the clerk and superintendent relative to the reception of the respondent.
9. Mittimus may, if necessary, be issued by the clerk; its form.
10. Receipt to be given by the superintendent; its form.
11. Diseased persons and idiots not to be received.
12. Respondent may by order of court, pending proceedings, be restrained of his liberty.
13. Costs of the proceedings where respondent is not a pauper.
14. Costs where he is a pauper.
15. Bond to be given where he is not a pauper.
16. Clothing to be furnished each patient.
17. Clothing to be furnished where patient is a pauper by the county.
18. Patient to be removed when ordered to be discharged by the trustees.
19. Non-resident patient may be received.
20. Whenever reason is restored the patient may leave.
21. Insane pauper may be committed to a county hospital.
22. No one to be committed without a trial by jury.
23. Penalty for receiving or detaining any person not duly committed.

1. That when any person is supposed to be insane or distracted, any near relative, or in case there be none, any respectable person residing in the county may petition the judge of the county court for proceedings to inquire into such alleged insanity or distraction. For the hearing of such application and proceedings thereon, the county court shall be considered as always open.(*j*)*

2. Upon the filing of such petition, the judge shall order the clerk of the court to issue a writ directed to the sheriff or any constable, or the person having the custody or charge of the alleged insane or distracted person, unless he shall be brought before the court without such writ, requiring the alleged insane person to be brought before him at a time and place to be appointed for the hearing of the matter. It shall be the duty of the officer or person to whom the writ is directed to execute and return the same, and bring the alleged insane person before the court as directed in the writ.(*k*)

3. The clerk shall also issue subpœnas for such witnesses as may be desired on behalf of the petitioner, or of the person alleged to be insane, to appear at the time fixed for the trial of the matter.(*l*)

4. At the time fixed for the trial a jury of six persons, one of

---

(*j*) § 1, act March 21, 1874, in relation to the commitment and detention of lunatics; Cothran's Ann'd Stats., § 1, p. 950.

* This jurisdiction does not extend to probate courts.
(*k*) § 2, Cothran's Stats., 950.
(*l*) § 3, id. p. 951.

Lunatics.

whom shall be a physician, shall be impaneled to try the case. The case shall be tried in the presence of the person alleged to be insane, who shall have the right to be assisted by counsel, and may challenge jurors as in civil cases. The court may, for good cause, continue the case from time to time.(*m*)

5. After hearing the evidence, the jury shall render their verdict in writing, signed by them, which shall embody the substantial facts shown by the evidence, which verdict may be substantially in the following form: (*n*)

STATE OF ILLINOIS,⎱ *ss.*:
     County,⎰

"We, the undersigned jurors in the case of   (naming the person alleged to be insane), having heard the evidence in the case, are satisfied that said   is insane, and is a fit person to be sent to a state hospital for the insane; that he is a resident of the State of Illinois, and county of   ; that his age is   ; that his disease is of   duration; that the cause is supposed to be   (or is unknown); that the disease is (or is not) with him hereditary; that he is not (or is) subject to epilepsy, and that he does (or does not) manifest homicidal or suicidal tendencies. (If the person be a pauper, the fact shall also be announced in the verdict.)"*n*.

6. Upon the return of the verdict, the same shall be recorded at large by the clerk, and if it appears that the person is insane, and is a fit person to be sent to a state hospital for the insane, the court shall enter an order that the insane person be committed to a state hospital for the insane, and thereupon it shall be the duty of the clerk of the court to make application to the superintendent of some one of the state hospitals for the insane for the admission of such insane persons.(*o*)

7. If such insane person is a pauper the application shall be first made to the nearest hospital, but if he be not a pauper, application shall be made to such one of the state hospitals for the insane as the relatives or friends of the patient shall desire. In any case, if, on account of the crowded condition of any one of the hospitals, or for other good reason, the patient cannot be received therein, or it is not desirable to commit him thereto, he may be committed to any other of said hospitals. Upon receiving any such application, the superintendent shall immediately inform the clerk whether the patient can be received, and if so, at what time; and if not, shall state the reason why.(*p*)

(*m*) § 4, R. S. 1874, p. 681.   (*o*) § 6, id., p. 682.
(*n*) § 5, id.   (*p*) § 7, id.

Commitment and detention of lunatics.

8. Upon receiving notice at what time the patient will be received, the clerk shall, in due season for the conveyance of the person to the hospital by the appointed time, issue a warrant directed to the sheriff or any other suitable person, preferring some relative of the insane person when desired, commanding him to arrest such insane person and convey him to the hospital; and if the clerk is satisfied that it is necessary, he may authorize an assistant to be employed.(*q*)

9. The warrant may be substantially as follows:

STATE OF ILLINOIS, } *ss.:*
   County, }

"*The People of the State of Illinois to :*

"You are hereby commanded forthwith to arrest , who has been declared to be insane, and convey him to the Northern (or as the case may be) Illinois Hospital for the Insane (and you are hereby authorized to take to your aid an assistant, if deemed necessary), and of this warrant make due return to this office after its execution. Witness my hand and the seal of the county court of county, this day of , A. D.

[L. S.]   , Clerk of County Court County."(*r*)

10. Upon receiving the patient, the superintendent shall indorse upon said warrant a receipt as follows:

"NORTHERN (*or as the case may be*) ILLINOIS HOSPITAL FOR THE INSANE.

"Received this day, A. D. , the patient named in the within warrant.

                   , Superintendent."

This warrant, with a receipt thereon, shall be returned to the clerk, to be filed by him with the other papers relating to the case.(*s*)

11. No person having any contagious or infectious disease, and no idiot, shall be admitted to either of the state hospitals. When the trustees and superintendent shall find that an idiot has been received into the hospital, they may discharge him.(*t*)

12. If the court shall deem it necessary, pending proceedings and previous to verdict, or after verdict and pending admission to the hospital, temporarily to restrain of his liberty the person alleged to be insane, then the court shall make such order in that behalf as the case may require, and the same being entered of record, a copy

(*q*) § 8, R. S. 1874, p. 682. (*s*) § 10, id.
(*r*) § 9, id.   (*t*) § 11, id.

Lunatics.

thereof certified by the clerk shall authorize such person to be temporarily detained by the sheriff, jailer or other suitable person to whom the same shall be directed.(*u*)

13. When a person not a pauper is alleged to be insane, and is found by the jury not to be insane, the costs of the proceeding, including the fees of the jury, shall be paid by the petitioner, and judgment may be awarded against him therefor. If such person is found to be insane, such costs shall be paid by his guardian, conservator or relatives, as the court may direct. If the person alleged to be insane is a pauper, the costs of the proceeding, including the fees of the jury, shall be paid out of the county treasury: *Provided*, if such pauper is found not to be insane, the court may, in its discretion, award the costs against the petitioner.(*v*)

14. The expense of conveying a pauper to the hospital shall be paid by the county in which he resides, and that of any other patient by his guardian, conservator or relatives; and in no case shall any such expense be paid by the State, or out of any funds for the insane. The fees of the sheriff for conveying any person to a hospital shall be the same as for conveying convicts to the penitentiary.(*w*)

15. If the person be not a pauper, then one or more persons, relatives or friends of the patient shall, upon his admission into the hospital, become responsible to the trustees for finding the patient in clothes, and removing him when required; and shall execute a bond conditioned as follows, viz.:

"Know all men by these presents, that we   ·   and   , of the county of   , and State of Illinois, are held and firmly bound unto the trustees of the Northern (or as the case may be) Illinois Hospital for the Insane, in the sum of $100 (one hundred dollars) for the payment of which we jointly and severally bind ourselves firmly by these presents.

"The condition of this obligation is, that whereas,   insane person of the county and State aforesaid, has been admitted as a patient into the said hospital for the insane: Now, therefore, if we shall find said patient in suitable and sufficient clothing whilst   may remain in said institution, and shall promptly pay for such articles of clothing, as it may be necessary to procure for said   at the hospital, and shall remove   from said hospital when required by the trustees to do so, then this obligation to be void, otherwise to remain in full force.

"Witness our hands and seals, this   day of   , A. D.

"   [SEAL.]
"   [SEAL.]"(*x*)

(*u*) § 12, R. S. 1874, p. 682.
(*v*) § 13, id.
(*w*) § 14, id., p. 683.
(*x*) § 15, id.

Lunatics.

16. The clothing to be furnished each patient upon being sent to the hospital, shall not be less than the following: for a male, three new shirts, a new and substantial coat, vest, and two pairs of pantaloons of woolen cloth, three pairs of woolen socks, a black or dark stock or cravat, a good hat or cap, and a pair of new shoes or boots, and a pair of slippers to wear within doors. For a female, in addition to the same quantity of under garments, shoes and stockings, there shall be two woolen petticoats or skirts, three good dresses, a cloak or shawl, and a decent bonnet. Unless such clothing is delivered in good order to the superintendent, he shall not be bound to receive the patient.(*y*)

17. If the insane person be a pauper, it shall be the duty of the judge of the county court to see that he is furnished with the necessary amount of substantial clothing at the time he is sent to the hospital, and from time to time while he remains a patient in the hospital, and that he be removed therefrom when required by the trustees; the expense of such clothing and removal shall be paid out of the county treasury, upon the certificate of the judge of the county court.(*z*)

18. Whenever the trustees shall order any patient discharged, the superintendent shall at once notify the clerk of the county court of the proper county thereof, if the patient is a pauper, and if not, shall notify all the persons who signed the bond required in section fifteen of this act, and request the removal of the patient. If such patient be not removed within thirty days after such notice is received, then the superintendent may return him to the place from whence he came, and the reasonable expenses thereof may be recovered by suit on the bond, or in case of a pauper, shall be paid by the proper county.(*a*)

19. Whenever application shall be made for a patient not residing within the State, if the superintendent shall be of opinion that from the character of the case it is probably curable, and if there be at the time room in the hospital, the trustees may, in their discretion, order the patient to be admitted, always taking a satisfactory bond for the maintenance of the patient, and for his removal when required. The rate of maintenance in such cases shall be fixed by the trustees, and two months' pay in advance shall be required.

(*y*) § 16, R. S. 1874, p. 683. (*a*) § 18, id.
(*z*) § 17, id.

Lunatics.

But no such patient shall be detained without the order of a court of competent jurisdiction, or the verdict of a jury.(*b*)

20. When any patient shall be restored to reason, he shall have the right to leave the hospital at any time, and if detained therein contrary to his wishes after such restoration, shall have the privilege of the writ of *habeas corpus* at all times, either on his own application, or that of any other person in his behalf; if the patient is discharged on such writ, and if it shall appear that the superintendent has acted in bad faith or negligently, the superintendent shall pay all the costs of the proceeding. Such superintendent shall moreover be liable to a civil action for false imprisonment.(*c*)

21. This act shall not be construed to prevent the committing of any insane pauper to the hospital for the insane of the county in which he may reside, where such a hospital is provided.(*d*)

22. No superintendent, or other officer or person connected with either of the state hospitals for the insane, or with any hospital or asylum for insane or distracted persons, in this State, shall receive, detain or keep in custody, at such hospital or asylum, any person who shall not have been declared insane by the verdict of a jury, and authorized to be confined by the order of a court of competent jurisdiction; and no trial shall be had of the question of the sanity or insanity of any person before any judge or court without the presence of the person alleged to be insane.(*e*)

23. If any superintendent, or other officer or person connected with either of the state hospitals for the insane, or with any hospital or asylum for insane or distracted persons, in this State, whether public or private, shall receive or detain any person who has not been declared insane by the verdict of a jury, and whose confinement is not authorized by the order of a court of competent jurisdiction, he shall be confined in the county jail not exceeding one year, or fined not exceeding five hundred dollars, or both, and be liable civilly to the person injured for all damages which he may have sustained; and if he be connected with either of the insane hospitals of this State, he shall be discharged from service therein.(*f*)

(*b*) § 19, R. S. 1874, p. 683. (*e*) § 22, id.
(*c*) § 20, id., p. 684. (*f*) § 23, id.
(*d*) § 21, id.

FORMS.

Proceedings may be commenced by petition, as follows:

STATEMENT OF INSANITY.

STATE OF ILLINOIS, } ss:
County of ,

In the County Court of   County.

To the Honorable   , Judge of said court:

Your petitioner   , respectfully represents that   , of the county of   , and State of Illinois, is insane, and that for his benefit, and the safety of the community,   ought to be committed to the Illinois State Hospital for the Insane. The facts in h   case can be proven by   , county physician, and by   , all of whom reside in said county. That your petitioner believes the said   to be absolutely *non compos mentis*, and that   is incapable of governing   self. That your petitioner, after careful inquiry, believes that said insane person has no property, and is a pauper,*   , wherefore, your petitioner   , moved only by divers good and humane considerations, does request the interposition of this court in this behalf. Your petitioner, therefore, prays this honorable court to cause a writ to be issued, requiring the said   to be brought before this court, at a time to be fixed by the court, that a jury may be summoned to inquire into the truth of the matters alleged in this petition; that the said   may be adjudged *non compos mentis*, and that such orders and other proceedings may be made and instituted as to this court may seem meet and proper.

STATE OF ILLINOIS, } ss:
County of ,

    , being duly sworn, says that the foregoing petition, by him subscribed, is true.

Sworn and subscribed before me, }
    , clerk of the county court }
of   county, this   day of }
    , A. D. 18   .

                            , Clerk.

Whereupon a writ is issued to inquire into the facts alleged in the petition, as follows:

WRIT OF INQUISITION.

STATE OF ILLINOIS, } ss:
County of ,

The People of the State of Illinois to the sheriff of said county, greeting:

Whereas, it hath been represented to the Hon.   , judge of the county court of said county, by the petition of   , under oath, and filed in said

---

* The complaint or petition or application in case of a person of substance, may be made by a relative or creditor, and if there be neither in the county, then any person living in the county may make it. Care should be taken to show a cause within the statute. See p. 148, *supra*.

Forms — venire.

court, that   is insane, and that for   benefit, and for the safety of the community, he ought to be committed to the   Hospital for the Insane, and that a conservator ought to be appointed to take charge of   property; and the said judge having fixed the time of the hearing of the matters alleged in said petition for the   day of   , A. D. 18   , at   o'clock, . M., and ordered that a writ issue out of said court, directing the sheriff of said county to take and safely keep the said   so that he have him on said day last named at the court-house in said county, to answer said petition.

We do, therefore, hereby command you to take the body of the said   , if he shall be found in your county, and   safely keep, so that he be and appear before our county court of   county, on said   day of   , A. D. 18   , at   o'clock, . M., at the court-house in   , in said county, to answer unto said petition and to abide by what may be adjudged thereon. And have you then and there this writ, with an indorsement thereon in what manner you shall have executed the same.

Witness   , clerk of the county court of   county, and the seal of said court at   , in said county, this   day of   , A. D. 18   .

, *Clerk.*

Before any person not legally pronounced insane is admitted to the hospital as a patient alleged to be insane, the judge shall order a trial by jury, consisting of six persons, one of whom shall be a physician, to try the issue.

The following is the form of venire used:

VENIRE.

STATE OF ILLINOIS,
County of   , } *ss:*

The People of the State of Illinois to the sheriff of said county, greeting:

You are hereby commanded to summon six good and lawful men, one of whom, at least, is to be a physician, to appear before our county court of said county, on the   day of   , A. D. 18   , at   o'clock, . M., to serve as a jury in the case of   , alleged to be insane; hereof fail not to make due service and return as the law directs.

Witness   , clerk of our said court, and the seal thereof, at   , this   day of   , A. D. 18   .

, *Clerk of the county court of said county.*

County court of   county,
In the matter of   .

(*Indorsement.*)

Inquisition of Insanity.

VENIRE.

Filed   , 18   .

, *Clerk.*

Returnable   , at   o'clock, . M.

Forms — the record.

Served the within writ by summoning the following named persons, viz.:
. For service, $. Mileage, $. Return, $.
                                                           , *Sheriff*.
                                      By
                                                           , *Deputy*.

THE RECORD, WITH THE VERDICT AND CERTIFICATE.

STATE OF ILLINOIS, }
  County of   , } *ss*:

Be it remembered, that on this day, to wit, on the   day   , A. D. 18 , the same being one of the days of   term, 18 , of the county court of   county.

Present thereat
                                          Hon.   , *Judge*,
                                                        , *Sheriff*,
                                                        , *Clerk*.

The following, among other proceedings, were by and before said court had and entered of record, to wit:

In the matter of the alleged insanity of   . Now comes   , who is alleged to be insane, in the custody of   , sheriff of   county, also comes   , at whose instance he was arrested, also comes a jury of   , good and lawful men, one of whom is a physician, to wit: , doctor of medicine   , who, after being impaneled and sworn, and after hearing the evidence adduced and arguments of counsel, retire in charge of an officer to consider their verdict, and on their return, in the presence of the said   rendered their verdict in the words and figures as follows, to wit:

[See § 5, p. 149, *supra*, for the form of verdict.]

Whereupon it is considered by the court that the said   is an insane person. And that the said   be committed to and detained in a State hospital for the insane (see § 7, p. 149, *supra*, and § 23, p. 153, *supra*), pursuant to law.

STATE OF ILLINOIS, }
    county, } *ss*:

I,   , clerk of the county court of   county, in the State aforesaid, do hereby certify that the foregoing is a true and correct transcript of the record of proceedings had and taken by and before said court, in the matter therein set forth.

In testimony whereof, I have hereunto set my hand and affixed the seal of said county court, at   , in said county, this   day of   , 18 .
                                                                                  , *Clerk*.

In the hands of the executor or administrator.

CHAPTER VI.

PERSONAL ESTATE IN ADMINISTRATION.*

SECTION I. Collection and disposition of, by the executor or administrator.
II. In the hands of guardians or conservators.

SECTION I.— COLLECTION AND DISPOSITION OF, BY THE EXECUTOR OR ADMINISTRATOR.

1. The retrospect.
2. Personal property, in due course of administration, governed by the *law of domicile.*
3. The title of the personal representative of a decedent to the personal estate.
4. His trust.
5. The *cestuis que trust*, the widow, the children, the creditors, legatees, devisees and distributees or heirs, their relation to the proceedings in administration.
6. Special proceedings requisite to divest the title of the devisees or heirs to the real property.
7. Scope of this chapter.
8. The inventory to be made and returned within three months from the date of letters testamentary or of administration; how made; failure to make, subjects the delinquent to citation to make inventory and account.
9. Citation to exhibit inventory and account.
10. Form of inventory.
11. The appraisement, the warrant, the oath.
12. The bill of appraisement.

*PERSONAL PROPERTY; ASSETS.

1. Things personal.
2. Mercantile transactions.
3. Insufficiency of assets.
4. Distinctions between *things personal* and *things real.*
5. Conversion of real property; special proceedings necessary for the purpose, against the property and also against the heir.
6. The practice in such cases governed by the superior courts.
7. The absolute title and qualified right of the administrator or executor to the assets of the decedent.
8. The assets considered.
9. Contracts in general.
10. Contracts defined.
11. Consideration essential to.
12. Sale or exchange.
13. Fraud annuls all contracts which it infects.
14. Warranty.
15. Caveat emptor.
16. Guaranty, statute of frauds.
17. Bailment, pawn.
18. Lien.
19. Hiring and borrowing.
20. Debts.
21. Bonds.
22. Bills of exchange.
23. Cheques.
24. Promissory notes.
25. Insurance policies.

In the hands of the

13. Inventories and exemplifications thereof to be *prima facie* evidence.
14. Additional appraisement.
15. Care and diligence required of executors and administrators in getting in the estates of their testates and intestates.
16. Appraisers' fees two dollars per day each.
17. Proceedings in case the assets do not exceed the amount of the widow's allowance.
18. Collection and disposition of assets.
19. Sale of personal property.
26. Bottomry.
27. The care and judgment required in the management of the assets.

1. PERSONAL PROPERTY. "THINGS PERSONAL." Under this designation are included all goods and chattels — terms equally applicable to interests in lands less than a leasehold — money and other movables, and the rights and profits issuing out of them. Besides, all movables, shares in canals, railways, banks and other similar interests are, by various statutes, made personal property. They are oftentimes of an intangible or incorporeal nature, such as copyrights, patent-rights, trade-marks, etc.

2. MERCANTILE TRANSACTIONS. — Bonds, bills of exchange, checks or cheques, promissory notes, bank notes, coupons, insurance policies, mortgages, trust deeds, and the like, all come under the terms personal property, things personal, and constitute assets in the hands of the personal representatives of a decedent; while things real, or real property (subject to the just debts and charges of the decedent and his personal representatives), pass to the heirs or devisees.

3. INSUFFICIENCY OF ASSETS. If the assets are insufficient to pay such debts and charges, the real property is to be converted, on special application to the court and under its orders and decrees, into cash, and thus become assets.(a)

4. In administration, the broad distinction made between THINGS REAL and THINGS PERSONAL consists in their distribution, it being the general rule of the common law that the whole of the real estate goes to the heir, while things personal are distributed among the next of kin.(b)

Our statute,(c) however, gives the same direction to both real and personal property.

Then, again, the effect of the marriage contract upon chattels *real* and chattels *personal* (d) gave different rules of enjoyment and disposition. The statute both here and in England (e) has, to a great extent, obliterated these peculiar rules, so that to-day the differences between real and personal property in administration exist rather in name than in fact. The old effects of these differences still remain.

If we concede full jurisdiction over the personalty, it is difficult to see why the same should not be exercised over the realty until the debts of the deceased are paid.

5. CONVERSION OF REAL PROPERTY, SPECIAL PROCEEDINGS NECESSARY. It has, however, been so often held that the real property by descent goes to the heir, and that, in order to divest the title of the heir, he must be personally notified, that the county court, in dealing with the realty, to acquire jurisdiction over it, must also acquire jurisdiction over the person of the heir.(f) To convert the real property into assets to pay debts, in Illinois, the probate jurisdiction must proceed not only *in rem* against the property, but *in personam*. He must be proceeded against by summons, which must be served either personally or constructively upon him like a chancery summons.(g)

The litigation, relative to the exer-

(a) See p. 62, *supra*; pp. 159, 165, *infra*.
(b) See 22 and 23 Car. ii, ch. 10, explained by 29 Car. ii, ch. 3.
(c) See ch. x, *infra*.
(d) See Hill's Chancery, 610-638.

(e) Id.; 33 and 34 Vict., ch 93.
(f) *Ferguson* v. *Hunter*, 2 Gilm. 657; *Botsford* v. *O'Conner*, 57 Ill. 72; *Schnell* v. *Chicago*, 38 id. 382.
(g) See Hill's Chancery, Process.

Executor or administrator.

1. THE RETROSPECT. We have already become acquainted with the jurisdiction of the county courts in the administration of the estates left by persons who have deceased, and in matters concerning the persons and property of those incapable of caring for themselves and their substance.

We have carefully examined the means through which such courts act, by appointing and controlling executors, administrators, guardians and conservators. The powers, duties, rights and responsibilities devolved upon these functionaries have, to some considerable extent, been discussed in view of the statute law and in the light of the authorities. We come now to the subject-matter of this conservative or administrative jurisdiction, the estates themselves.

cise of this jurisdiction, in converting real property into assets, has mainly arisen collaterally, *i. e.*, the orders and decrees of the probate court have been attacked by the heir, either by bill in chancery or ejectment.

The supreme court of the United States in several cases (*h*) have utterly refused to collaterally question the probate jurisdiction. The supreme court of Illinois still adhere to the requirement that the heir must be notified; beyond this, collateral inquiry is, also, here denied.(*i*)

6. But all courts give the widest latitude to DIRECT INQUIRY BY APPEAL OR WRIT OF ERROR. Therefore, in the exercise of probate jurisdiction, although collateral inquiry is either denied or limited, yet direct inquiry is encouraged. Hence, the county courts are held to close rules and a well defined practice, by the superior courts, in all matters in administration, but particularly in the conversion of real property into assets by the administrator or executor.

7. After his qualification by giving bond and taking the oath, the TITLE TO THE PERSONAL PROPERTY of the estate becomes ABSOLUTE, in the executor or administrator. He has a QUALIFIED RIGHT—he holds an absolute title against all the world, but it is in trust. He should have a certified copy of his appointment, that is to say, if he be an executor, a complete exemplification, certified by the clerk and presiding judge, of the probate, with a copy of the will and letters testamentary; if an administrator, of his letters of administration, as the evidence of this title; after being clothed with the title and the power, the first inquiry of the executor or administrator is as to the property in possession, and next as to that in action.

8. GOODS AND CHATTELS. All kinds of visible property in possession are too well and generally known to require mention even, but that class of *things personal*, known to the law as *choses in action*, including all kinds of contracts and agreements, demands careful consideration here, for the executor or administrator usually finds a large portion of the estate committed to his charge invested or involved in these *choses in action*. They are assets in his hands, and to liquidate the claims allowed against the estate, it is necessary and a part of his duty to convert such assets into cash. He must *get in* the estate, reduce it to possession, and collect and convert into cash, not only the goods and visible property, but he must dispose of these choses in action; a large class of these, however, are mercantile contracts, most of them susceptible of immediate conversion. Those already mentioned(*j*) comprise this class. We will now more particularly describe contracts generally, and then consider mercantile contracts.

9. CONTRACTS may be considered as

(*h*) *Grignon* v. *Astor, Comstock* v. *Crawford.* See 2 Hill's Com. Law, 645.

(*i*) *Schnell* v. *Chicago,* 38 Ill. 382.
(*j*) See p 158, *infra*.

Collection and disposition of

The distinctions between the two great classes of property,(*a*) personal and real, and the different rules pertaining to them admonish us to consider them separately as they come under this jurisdiction for administration or conservation. Therefore, we shall discuss in this chapter the personal estate in administration, and in the succeeding chapter real property in administration.

2. PERSONAL PROPERTY, when viewed in this, the probate juristion, appertains to the person, has no *situs* in the law other than the domicile(*b*) of the proprietor; it ebbs and flows, goes and comes with him; like his mind and will, it accompanies him where ever he goes, is ambulatory till his death, when it rests in the place of his

---

(*a*) See chapter x, *infra*.
(*b*) Hill's Ch. Pr. 56–70; Hill's Municipal Officer, Domicile, Personal Property.

---

one of the species of title to things personal. In its widest and most general sense, the word "contract" signifies an engagement, obligation or compact; it may be *express* or *implied, executory* or *executed;* and there must be two or more contracting parties of sufficient ability to make a contract.

10. A CONTRACT is an agreement or undertaking, upon sufficient consideration to do, or not to do, a particular thing. *First,* then it is an agreement, a mutual bargain or convention, and, therefore, there must be at least two contracting parties of sufficient ability to make a contract, as where A contracts with B to pay him $100. A thereby transfers a property in such sum to B, which property, however, is not in possession, but in action merely, and recoverable by suit at law.

A contract or agreement may be either express or implied. Express contracts are where the terms of the agreement are openly uttered and avowed at the time of the making, as to deliver an ox or ten loads of timber, or to pay a stated price for certain goods. Implied contracts are such as reason and justice dictate, which, therefore, the law presumes that every man undertakes to perform. As, if I employ a person to do any business for me, or perform any work, the law implies that I undertook, or contracted to pay him as much as his labor deserves; and, if I do not make him amends, he has a remedy for bringing his action upon such implied promise, undertaking or assumpsit. Or where a person buys an article without stipulating for the price, he is presumed to have undertaken to pay its market value or its worth.

A contract may be either executory or executed. An executory contract is one in which a party binds himself *to do or not to do* a particular thing; a contract executed is one in which the object of contract is performed. As if A agrees to change horses with B and they do it immediately, in which case the possession and the right are transferred together. This is an executed contract; but if A and B agree to exchange horses next week, here the right only vests, and their reciprocal property in each other's horse is not in possession; a contract executory conveys only a chose in action, a thing in course of transmutation.

11. *Second.* A SUFFICIENT CONSIDERATION is necessary to the validity of a contract. A *nudum pactum* (bare promise), or agreement to do or pay any thing on one side without any consideration on the other, is totally void in law, and a man cannot be compelled to perform it; as if one man promises to give another $100; here there is nothing contracted for or given on the one side, and, therefore, there is nothing binding on the other. Any degree of reciprocity, however, which is held in law to be a sufficient consideration, will prevent the contract from being void.

Third. The thing agreed to be *done* or *omitted.* A contract is an agreement upon sufficient considera-

By the executor or administrator.

domicile. (c) Then the *lex loci* distributes it, if he die testate, according to the *testatio mentis*, manifested in the most formal manner by written directions, which go to make his will; if he die intestate, according to the course of the common law as modified by statute; in either case by due course of administration. (d)

3. Through the executor or administrator, as the case may be, this jurisdiction when death comes, at the place of his domicile (if he have none, then where the property is), stepping as it were into the shoes of the deceased, collects, cares for, inventories, and manages the estate left by him. The executor or administrator to a certain

---

(c) § 11, R. S. 1874, p. 1103.

(d) A last will is defined to be the *testatio mentis*, or testament; a declaration, provision or direction of a testator in that he would have to be done with his estate, or how it should go after his death, as the evidence of his mind on the subject, (Went. Off. Ex. 265; 8 L., 111 a, 322 b; Pl. 343; 1 Bulst. 223; Sheph. Touch. 399; Fitz. G. 239,) or the appointment of a testamentary heir. Swinb. 3, 12. The testator by the will has testified his mind or intention. It contains his direction and declaration, being a provision for the event in contemplation of which it was made, which must be carried into execution so far as its meaning can be ascertained from the words he uses, taken in connection with the law which directs how papers of the kind shall be expounded, and the evidence in the case, to which the law is to be applied according to such circumstances as may bear on the written declaration of intention. It is an acknowledged principle, that wills are to be construed according to the intention of the testator; which shall be carried into full effect in all cases which are not repugnant to the settled law and rules of policy of the country in which they are to be executed. The laws of every country prescribe the rules by which such intention is to be ascertained. See chapter II, *supra*.

---

tion to "do or not to do a particular thing." Among the kinds of contract are: (1) Sale or exchange; (2) bailment; (3) hiring and borrowing.

12. SALE OR EXCHANGE is a transmutation of property from one man to another, in consideration of some price or recompense in value; for there is no sale without a recompense; there must be *quid pro quo*. If it be a commutation of goods for goods, it is an exchange; but if it be a transferring of goods for money, it is called a sale.

If a man agrees with another for goods at a certain price, he may not carry them away before he has paid for them; for it is no sale without payment, unless the contrary be expressly stipulated; and, therefore, if the vendor says the price of a beast is $10, and the vendee says he will give $10, the bargain is struck, and neither of them is at liberty to be off the bargain, provided immediate possession be tendered; but if neither the money be paid, nor the goods delivered, nor tender made, nor any subsequent agreement be entered into, it is no contract, and the owner may dispose of the goods as he pleases. If any part of the price is paid down, if it be but a penny, or any portion of the goods delivered by way of deposit, the property in the goods absolutely passes, and the vendee may recover the goods by action, as well as the vendor may the price of them.

If there be a sale of goods which are to be sent by a carrier to the purchaser, and the goods perish or sustain damage while *in transitu*, in the absence of special circumstances, the rule of law applies; that is, delivery to the carrier is delivery to the consignee, who will, therefore, have to bear the loss. But if the parties agree that the vendor shall not merely deliver the goods to the carrier, but that they shall actually be delivered at their destination, and express such extent becomes the owner of this property. It is not absolutely his. He is an officer of the court; the trustee of an express trust. (*e*)

4. He holds it for the incapacitated; the widow and the orphan; for the creditors, for the friends and relatives; the beneficiaries, legatees, or distributees: all his *cestuis que trust*. His title to the personalty relates back to the date of the death of the decedent. For them all, he must discharge his duties and exercise his powers. Over the property in charge, he must ever exercise the same care and diligence that the prudent are presumed to bestow about their business and in the management of their property. The property is in court; he is, in and out of court, the personal representative of the deceased.

(*e*) Hill on Trustees; Perry on Trusts; Hill's Chan. Pr.; Trusts.

intention, in such a case, if the goods perish in the hands of the carrier, the vendor is not only liable for the loss, but for whatever damages may have been sustained by the purchaser in consequence of the breach of contract to deliver at the place of destination.

General rules may be modified by the expressed intentions of the parties. Where an offer to sell goods is made, and a letter accepting such offer, without qualification, is put into the post, the bargain is complete.

Where an unpaid vendor of goods has put them into the hands of a carrier to be by him conveyed and delivered to the vendee, and the vendee or consignee, before actual delivery to him, becomes bankrupt or insolvent, the vendor or consignor has a right to resume possession of the goods by stopping them *in transitu;* but his right to do so will be defeated if the vendee or consignee of the goods has assigned his interest in them to a *bona fide* purchaser.

13. FRAUD destroys a contract *ab initio*, so that a fraudulent seller is precluded from insisting upon the completion of the contract, and a fraudulent purchaser gets no title.

Willful *misrepresentation* to induce another to contract or to part with goods, under the belief that such representation was true, is not tolerated by law, and such misrepresentation may be alleged with a view to annulling the contract, and to compelling restitution of property transferred or money paid in pursuance of it.

14. WARRANTY. By the civil law an *implied* warranty was annexed to every sale in respect to the title of the vendor; and so, too, in our law, a purchaser of goods and chattels may have a satisfaction from the vendor if he sells them as his own and the title proves deficient, without any express warranty for that purpose. But, with regard to the goodness of the wares so purchased, the vendor is not bound to answer, unless he expressly warrants them to be sound and good; or unless it is proved that he knew them to be otherwise, and has used art to disguise them; or unless they turn out different from what he represented them to the buyer. Thus, if a man sells a horse, and expresses by warranty that it is sound, the contract is void if the horse is proved to be otherwise.

15. Where goods may be inspected by the buyer, and there is no fraud on the part of the seller, the maxim CAVEAT EMPTOR applies; the purchaser takes them, at his risk, even though the defect which exists in them is latent, and not discoverable on examination.

Where goods are bought by *sample*, the law implies that the goods shall *reasonably* answer the specified description. If the bulk does not reasonably answer the description in a commercial point of view, the seller is liable for the amount paid for the goods.

16. A GUARANTY is a mercantile instrument, which is usually evidenced by writing, not under seal, whereby one man contracts on behalf of another,

By the executor or administrator.

5. ALLOWANCES may be made by the court to the widow and children which shall take precedence of the claims of the creditors.

THE EXPENSES OF ADMINISTRATION first are to be paid. THE CLAIMS OF THE CREDITORS are then paramount. Until all debts, expenses and allowances are paid and satisfied, neither devisees, legatees, nor heirs or distributees have any beneficial interest in the estate, either real or personal. The title to the real property it is true passes to the heirs, but to the creditors they must respond or surrender the estate. (*f*) The legatees, devisees or distributees then to protect their own interests, must come into the county court, with the executor or administrator, unite with him in resisting the claims,

---

(*f*) EXTENT OF THEIR LIABILITY FOR DEBTS OF THE ANCESTOR. The liability of heirs for the debts of their ancestors, both at law and in equity, is to the extent of the full amount which came to them by descent. But it seems an heir should not be made liable beyond the amount he has thus received. So, in entering a decree in the supreme court against several heirs, for the debt of their ancestor, the court directed that neither of them should be subjected to a greater liability than to the extent of the amount which came to him by descent. *Vanmeter's Heirs* v. *Love's Heirs*, 33 Ill. 260.

an obligation to which he is made as liable as the proper and primary party. The Statute of Frauds enacts that no action shall be brought whereby to charge the defendant upon any special promise to answer for the debt, default or miscarriages of another, unless the agreement upon which action is brought, or some memorandum or note thereof, be in writing, signed by the party to be charged therewith, or some person thereunto by him lawfully authorized, if *verbal* only, no action shall be brought whereby to charge the defendant thereupon. § 1, R. S. 1874, p. 540.

17. *Bailment*, from the French *bailler*, to deliver, is a delivery of goods in trust, upon a contract expressed or implied, that the trust shall be faithfully executed on the part of the bailee; as if cloth be delivered, or, legally speaking, bailed to a tailor to make a suit of clothes, he has it upon an implied contract to render it again when made up, and that in a workmanlike manner. Or, if money or goods be delivered to a carrier, to be conveyed from O to L, he is under a contract in law to pay, or carry them to the person appointed. Or if a debtor bail or *pawn* his goods to his creditor, the pawnee has them on the condition of restoring them on the debt being discharged. Again, if a friend deliver any thing to his friend to keep for him, the receiver is bound to restore it on demand.

18. *Bailees* have in certain instances that right which is technically called a LIEN in respect of the goods committed to their charge; that is, the right of retaining the possession of a chattel from the owner until all legal claims upon it be satisfied. The rule of law is, that every person to whom a chattel has been delivered, for the purpose of bestowing his labor upon it, has a lien thereon, and may withhold it from the owner (in the absence, at least, of any special agreement to the contrary) until the price of the labor is paid. The *bailment* of goods to a common carrier is another class. A common carrier is one who conveys the goods of applicants from place to place. If a man professes to be a carrier, the law creates for him a duty to receive goods brought to him for carriage, and he is bound to deliver them safely, and within a *reasonable* time, "except when prevented by the act of God or of the King's enemies." A carrier is not liable for damage arising from any inherent defect in goods delivered to him for conveyance by improper packing; nor is he liable for

Collection and disposition of

for allowance, and of the creditors, and oppose his claims for expenses and commissions, and in all things compel a proper administration of the estate. After the allowance of expenses, award to the widow and children and of claims, if the personal estate be insufficient to pay the debts, then the executor or administrator is to proceed *in rem* against the real estate and in *personam* against the devisees or heirs, to whom the law gives the real property subject to the lien of the creditors of the decedent, and convert the same or enough of it to pay the debts and expenses of sale. The remainder of the estate then becomes subject to the will, or the law of descent.

leakage. He must, however, exercise due skill and care.

19. HIRING AND BORROWING are also contracts by which a qualified property may be transferred to the hirer or borrower. They are both contracts whereby the possession and a transient property is transferred for a particular time or use, on condition to restore the goods so hired or borrowed as soon as the time is expired or use performed. The hirer or borrower gains a temporary property in the thing, with an implied condition "to use it and not abuse it," and the owner or lender retains a reversionary interest in the same, and acquires a new property in the price or reward.

20. THE SUBJECT OF DEBT is closely connected with that of *contract;* a debt being a legal relation which frequently arises out of a contract.

A debt by simple contract is where the contract upon which the obligation arises is neither ascertained by matter of record nor by deed or special instrument.

A debt by *specialty* is where a sum of money becomes due by deed or instrument under seal; that is, by covenant, by deed of sale, or by bond or obligation.

A debt of *record* is a sum of money due by the evidence of a court of record, when any specific sum is adjudged to be due from the defendant to the plaintiff in an action or suit at law.

21. A BOND is a deed or instrument under seal, where the party from whom a security is intended to be taken declares himself bound to pay a certain sum of money to another on the day specified; but there is a condition added, that if the obligor does some particular act the obligation shall be void.

22. A BILL OF EXCHANGE is a negotiable instrument or security used among merchants and others for the more easy remittance of money from one country to another. It is in the form of an open letter of request from A to B, desiring B to pay a sum named therein to a third person on A's account, by which means a man at the most distant part of the world may have money remitted to him from any trading country. Thus, if A lives in Jamaica, and owes B, who lives in New York, $1,000, if C be going from New York to Jamaica, he may pay B this $1,000, and take a bill of exchange, drawn by B in New York, upon A in Jamaica, and receive it when he comes thither. Thus, B receives his debt at any distance of place, by transferring it to C, who carries over his money in paper credit, without danger of robbery or loss. The person who makes the bill of exchange is called the drawer; he to whom it is written the drawee, and, after acceptance by the person on whom it is drawn, the acceptor; and the third person, to whom it is payable, is called the payee; and the payee may indorse it to any other person, who becomes the payee; and thus it may be transferred to twenty persons or more before it arrives, as it is called, at *maturity.*

When a bill of exchange has been drawn, accepted and indorsed, the person who accepted the bill is primarily and absolutely liable to pay it; the

By the executor or administrator.

6. SPECIAL PROCEEDINGS. To divest the title of the devisees or heirs, a special proceeding in the nature of a suit in chancery is provided for. (*g*) For the purposes of his trust either the guardian or conservator also may need to apply for the sale of real property. A similar proceeding is provided for each of them. These proceedings will be disposed of in the next chapter.

7. SCOPE OF THE CHAPTER. The collecting, inventorying, appraisement, sale and management of the personal estate pertaining to their respective trusts by the executor, administrator, guardian and conservator, are the subjects immediately before us. The executor and administrator are in nearly all these matters, in the

---

(*g*) The personal representative, as a general thing, has no control over the real estate of the deceased, except where it is made assets for the payment of debts, and then only to the extent of the excess of the debts above the amount of personalty applicable to their payment. *Drinkwater* v. *Drinkwater*, 4 Mass. 354. But the only mode by which the personal representative can appropriate such real estate or the income arising from it, is by pursuing the mode pointed out in the statute, and proceeding under an order of sale. And the same rule obtains in most of the American States. *Botsford* v. *O'Conner*, 57 Ill. 72.

The personal representative may always recover possession of all effects in the hands of the deceased at the time of his death, unless the defendant is able to show a better title in some other party, to whom he will be liable to account for the same. *Reeves* v. *Matthews*, 17 Yerg. 449; 1 Redfield, p. 122.

Chattels real go to the executor and administrator, and not to the heir, and this includes terms for years. All mortgage interests due to the estate are regarded as mere personalty. See *Scott* v. *Moore*, 3 Scam. 319; *Griffin* v. *Marine Co.*, 52 Ill. 130; R. S. 1845, 110, § 39; id. 301, § 1; also see pp. 158, 159, *supra*.

As to the powers, liabilities and duties of the administrator, the following decisions in Illinois may be here considered:

The court knows of no power in an administrator, as such, to loan the money of the estate. If he does, it is on his own responsibility, and makes him liable to the estate. *Thornton* v. *Smiley*, Breese, 14.

The law of 1825 (R. L. 646) authorized him to sell and assign a certificate of purchase of land made by deceased from the United States, on which partial payments were made, and which was necessary to be sold to pay debts. *Prevo* v. *Walters*, 4 Scam. 37.

One of two executors may assign a note made payable to the testator, so

---

person who drew it is liable only upon the contingencies of default being made by the acceptor and of the holder, to whom it may have been indorsed, performing certain conditions precedent to his right of suit being complete, viz.: Presenting the bill, and giving due notice to the drawer of the failure of the acceptor to pay it upon presentment. Payment of the bill, when refused, must be demanded of the drawer without loss of time, as the holder must give the drawer notice thereof; and if the bill has passed through many hands and been indorsed by them, the last holder, by giving notice of dishonor without *loss of time* to the indorsers, is at liberty to call on *any* or all of them to make him satisfaction, for each indorser is in the nature of a new drawer, and is a warrantor for the payment of the bill.

23. A cheque is a sort of an inland bill of exchange drawn upon a banker, and made payable to the bearer or order. The banker is the depositary of the customer's money, which he, in compliance with usage, undertakes to pay out from time to time to the customer's order, evidenced by his cheque. The holder

county court governed by the same rules and must take the same steps in discharging their trusts. There are, however, some things which we shall point out wherein the executor is governed by rules which have no application to the administrator. In getting the estate into their hands respectively, the same proceedings are prescribed.

as to transfer the legal interest to the assignee. *Dwight* v. *Newell*, 15 Ill. 335. So can an administrator. *Makepeace* v. *Moore*, 5 Gilm. 476.

So a term of years passes by the assignment of one of several executors. A sale of a chattel by one transfers the title to a purchaser. Id. 335.

In absence of fraud, a purchaser at an administrator's sale must not only look out for the title, but the quality. The administrator cannot warrant but on his personal responsibility. *Ray* v. *Virgin*, 12 Ill. 218; *Burnap* v. *Dennis*, 3 Scam. 482.

When an administrator placed notes of his intestate, due in another State, in the hands of an agent to collect, who was a man of means at that time, but, having used the money, failed: *held*, the administrator was not liable; he had used proper diligence and ordinary care. *Christy* v. *McBride*, 1 Scam. 78. The court, in that case,

doubted whether the administrator is bound to collect in another State.

If the surviving partner fail to settle the partnership promptly with the administrator of the deceased partner, it is the duty of the administrator to compel settlement by bill in equity, enjoin the surviving partner, receive the outstanding debts, and have a receiver appointed. *People* v. *White*, 11 Ill. 350.

An administrator is chargeable with interest, on the rule that the trustee shall take no advantage to himself out of the trust fund; the profits belong to the *cestui que trust*. *Rowan* v. *Kirkpatrick*, 14 Ill. 11. So, a guardian who converts the funds of his ward to his own use is chargeable with compound interest. Id.

If an administrator, being ordered, fail to pay over to an heir, an action accrues on his bond. *Ralston* v. *Wood*, 15 Ill. 159. See pp. 80, 81, *supra*.

of the cheque is bound to present it for payment on the day after that on which he received it; or if the cheque be on a banker in a distant town, the holder is bound to send it for presentment the following day. A party holding the cheque over the time specified, loses all claim against the drawer, in the event of the failure of the bank.

24. A PROMISSORY NOTE, or note of hand, is a plain and direct engagement in writing to pay a sum or thing specified at the time therein mentioned to a person therein named, or to his order or to bearer. There are but two parties to such instrument, the maker (drawer) and the payee. Like bills of exchange in case of non-payment by the maker, the last holder has the same remedy upon the several indorsers, observing the rules of notice, as stated in respect of bills of exchange.

An ordinary *bank note* is a promissory note, payable to bearer on demand, passes from hand to hand by delivery, passes in currency like cash, and cannot be impugned upon proof that the note had, before coming for value into his hands, been stolen from its rightful owner. R. S. 1874, pp., 718–720.

25. A POLICY OF INSURANCE is a contract between A and B, that when A pays a premium equivalent to the hazard to be incurred, B will indemnify or insure him against a particular event then expressed. These insurances are either life policies, insurances against fire, or marine insurances against loss or damage by sea. As to life policies, it is held that no insurance shall be made on lives or any other event wherein the party insured hath no interest; and that in all policies the name of such interested party shall be inserted. Life insurances are also made available for effecting various useful objects, such as making a settlement upon marriage, or after-

By the executor or administrator.

8. INVENTORIES AND APPRAISEMENT. Whenever letters testamentary, of administration, or of collection are granted, the executor or administrator shall make out a full and perfect inventory of all such real and personal estate, or the proceeds thereof, as are committed to his superintendence and management, and as shall come to his hands, possession or knowledge, describing the quantity, situation and title of the real estate, and particularly specifying the nature and amount of all annuities, rents, goods, chattels, rights and credits and money on hand, and whether the credits are good, doubtful or desperate; which said inventory shall be returned to the office of the clerk of the county court within three months from the date of the letters testamentary or of administration. (*h*)

If, after making the first inventory, any other real or personal estate of the deceased come to his possession or knowledge, he shall file a similar additional inventory thereof. (*i*)

An inventory is a list, schedule or enumeration in writing, containing, article by article, a description of all the real and personal estate, rights and credits of the intestate. (*j*) In many instances, the administrator cannot, from want of knowledge, make an inventory

(*h*) § 51, R. S. 1874, p. 113. (*j*) Bouvier.
(*i*) § 52, id.

---

ward insuring a provision for wife and children.

26. BOTTOMRY is in the nature of a mortgage on a ship, when the owner or commander borrows money to enable him to carry on his voyage. This security is called a *bottomry bond*.

We have not, in this note, cited the authorities; the principles stated underlie the whole fabric of the law of personal property. They are fundamental principles, a knowledge of which is essential to a proper discharge of the trusts involved in the administration of such property, and are stated here as they have for ages been promulgated by the sages of the law.

27. In the execution of his trust, the foregoing, which are the leading principles of the law of contracts, will afford the executor or administrator, guardian or conservator, a general knowledge of the personal estate or assets which may have come to his hands. In dealing with such property he has a broad, general discretion. He is to inventory it, cause it to be appraised, file the appraisement bill, and do other needful acts, and report to the court, as will be more fully explained further on.(*k*)

This discretion is that CAREFUL JUDGMENT AND DISCRIMINATION OR CARE which a prudent business man is presumed to, and usually does, exercise over like property in its management and disposition.

As soon as the personal estate is found to be insufficient to pay the debts and charges, etc., application should be promptly made for an order to sell the real property. This is treated of in the next chapter. The real property, or enough of it, will then be under the direction of the court, subjected to sale, and converted into assets for the purposes of the trust.

(*k*) see pp. 169, 170, *infra*.

of all the property belonging to the deceased. But should he discover afterward any other property, he should make out an additional inventory or account.

Whether the intestate's title to the property be perfect or not, it should all be mentioned, as the administrator cannot be the judge of title. All real property to which the intestate had an apparent claim should be included in the list, and the nature of such claim carefully and fully stated.

It is also the duty of the administrator to inventory property fraudulently concealed by the intestate;(*k*) all mortgages or other securities for the payment of money or property, bonds, notes, contracts, judgments ; all debts on account or otherwise, stating whether the claims be *good, doubtful* or *desperate ;* all property in the hands of third persons, belonging to the estate, or in which the estate is interested. Moneys, even in the hands of the wife, and carried by her, or given to her by her husband before his death, are to be inventoried.(*l*) Where debts or claims for money are listed, the amount and nature of the debt should be stated ; also the name of the person indebted. He will be obliged to show good cause for not collecting the debts mentioned to be due, unless he had precaution to note them in the inventory as desperate or doubtful.(*m*) If he mark a debt doubtful or desperate, it will devolve on the creditor or distributee to show that the same was good and might have been collected. In the inventory of real estate the administrator should particularly describe the land, as stated in the deed or other evidence of title or interest. If the land be held under bond, or contract, or otherwise, it should be so stated. If a debt be secured by mortgage it should be so stated, and the land or chattels described-mortgages, leases, etc., should be inventoried. If a party administer without making an inventory, the law will suppose him to have assets for the payment of all the debts and legacies, unless he repel the presumption. Whereas, if he make an inventory, he shall not be presumed to have more effects of the deceased than are comprised in it, and the proof of any omission is then thrown on the opposite party.(*n*) Whether the presumption of assets, where no inventory is made, would be held to be the law here, is an open question. The statute requiring the inventory would lend many presumptions against

(*k*) *Andrus* v. *Doolittle,* 11 Conn. 283.　(*m*) 2 Kent's Com. 415.
(*l*) *Washburn* v. *Hale,* 10 Pick. 429 ;　(*n*) Toler Law Ex'rs, 250; 3 Harr. &
Rowan v. *Kirkpatrick,* 14 Ill. 13.　Johns. 373.

By the executor or administrator.

the administrator should he fail to comply with the law in this respect.

If an administrator fail to make out his inventory as required by law, the judge may summon or cite him at the instance of a party interested, or, it seems,(*o*) at his own discretion, to show cause why he should not file his inventory, and may then be proceeded against to the revocation of his letters of administration. If he do not make out a proper inventory, he would also be liable upon his bond.(*p*)

9. CITATION TO EXHIBIT INVENTORY AND ACCOUNT. Any person interested in an estate, whether as a next of kin, as being entitled in distribution, or as a legatee or a creditor, may call upon the administrator or executor who has become the legal representative of the deceased to exhibit an inventory of the estate and render an account of his administration.

A second administrator may call upon the original administrator to exhibit an inventory and account.

An inventory may be called for at any period after administration is due, *i. e.*, after the expiration of three months.

In regard to the account after three months also, there does not appear to be any time limited before which that may not be called for. The citation cannot issue until an affidavit in verification of the averments which it contains has been filed. Disobedience to the citation is followed by attachment.(*q*)

APPLICATION FOR CITATION TO THE ADMINISTRATOR, TO MAKE AN INVENTORY.

STATE OF ILLINOIS,
Cook county. } *ss* :

County Court of   county,
term, A. D. 18 .

To Hon. E F, *Judge of said court :*

The petition of E F, of said county, respectfully represents that your petitioner is security on the bond of C D, administrator of A B, deceased, as by reference to said administrator's bond will appear. That letters of administration were issued to said C D, on the day of , A. D. 18 , and that said C D has failed to make out and file in this court a full and perfect inventory of the real and personal estate of the said intestate, within three months from the date of said letters of administration; and your petitioner says that by reason of said E F's neglect to file such inventory, your petitioner is in great danger of being wronged thereby, wherefore he prays that said administrator may be cited to show cause why he should not file such inventory in this court, if any he has, and that such further proceedings be had thereon as may be consistent

---

(*o*) Toler Ex'rs, 240.   (*q*) See p. 16, *supra*.
(*p*) 2 Kent's Com. 415.

Collection and disposition of

with law and the rights of your petitioner. And your petitioner will ever pray, etc.

E F.

STATE OF ILLINOIS, } *ss:*
    county.

E F, being sworn, says, that the matters and things in the foregoing petition are true of his own knowledge in manner and form as therein stated.

(*Jurat.*)

When personal property of any kind, or assets, shall come to the possession or knowledge of the administrator after the making out of the inventory aforesaid, and the appraisement bill, an account or inventory of the same is to be returned to the court, appraised as in other cases, within three months after the discovery thereof.(*r*)

10. FORM OF INVENTORY.

The inventory of real and personal estate of A B, late of the county of and State of , deceased, intestate :

REAL ESTATE.

North-west quarter section 6, township 10 north, 7 east, in county, , 160 acres; lot 2, block 1, in the city of , Illinois, purchased of A Pease, homestead and farm of deceased, improved; value	$5,000 00
Title bond or contract for deed, to south-half section 10, township 8 north, 3 east, county, , made by , of , Illinois, to deceased, bearing date January 1, 18 ; payment of $500 due on same January 1, 18 , when the deed is to be made; unimproved prairie land; value	1,000 00
Lease of deceased with A B, for south-west quarter of south-east quarter 15 north, 3 east, in county, , dated April 1, 1870, for two years, rent payable quarterly in advance; accrued due on lease since intestate died	50 00

PERSONAL ESTATE.

Money in hand..	1,500 00
Judgment against Richard Roe, on docket of superior court, Cook county, with interest from January 1, 18 (doubtful)..........	560 00
Due on lease with A B (good)...................................	150 00

NOTES, CONTRACTS AND ACCOUNTS (GOOD).

E F's note, dated September 1, 1872, due January 1, 18	1,000 00
G H, account	91 89

(*r*) § 52, R. S. 1874, p. 113; See p. 169, *supra*.

By executor or administrator.

NOTES, CONTRACTS AND ACCOUNTS (DOUBTFUL).

Note of J K, June 1, 18 , due on demand	$2,100 00
Interest two years and two months (unpaid)...................	
L M, on contract with said intestate, dated August 1, 18	160 00

NOTES, CONTRACTS AND ACCOUNTS (DESPERATE).

Note of N O, dated August 1, 18 , payable January 1, 18 , with interest; indorsed by P Q.................................	1,590 60

GOODS AND CHATTELS.

One bay horse; one-third of twenty acres of corn growing on home farm.

The foregoing is a full and perfect inventory of all the real and personal estate, or the proceeds thereof, belonging to the estate of the said A B, deceased, that has come to the hands, possession or knowledge of   C D,

Administrator of John Doe, deceased.

Dated *August* 8, 18 .

The above illustrates the form of the inventory, which may be varied to suit any state of facts; and, with little change, may be used for an *additional* inventory if one should be requisite.(*s*)

11. THE APPRAISEMENT. On granting letters testamentary or of administration, a warrant shall issue, under the seal of the county court, authorizing three persons of discretion, not related to the deceased, nor interested in the administration of the estate, to appraise the goods, chattels and personal estate of the deceased, known to them, or to be shown by the executor or administrator; which warrant shall be in the following form, to-wit:

(*Venue, title, etc.*)

"*The people of the State of Illinois to A B, C D and E F, of the county of and State of Illinois, greeting:*

"This is to authorize you, jointly, to appraise the goods, chattels and personal estate of J K, late of the county of   and State of Illinois, deceased, so far as the same shall come to your sight and knowledge; each of you having first taken the oath (or affirmation) hereto annexed; a certificate whereof you are to return, annexed to an appraisement bill of said goods, chattels and personal estate by you appraised, in dollars and cents; and in the said bill of appraisement you are to set down in a column or columns, opposite to each article appraised, the value thereof.

"Witness: A B, clerk of the county court of   county, and the seal of said court, this   day of   , 18 .

[L. S.]   A B, *Clerk*.

And on the death, refusal to act, or neglect of any such appraiser, another may be appointed in his place.(*t*)

(*s*) See p. 175, *infra*.   (*t*) § 53, R. S. 1874, p. 114.

Collection and disposition of

The appraisement is the valuation of the goods and chattels of the deceased by persons appointed by the court for that purpose.

The appraisers, before they proceed to the appraisement of the estate, shall take and subscribe the following oath (or affirmation), to be annexed or indorsed on the said warrant, before any person authorized to administer an oath, viz.:

" We, and each of us, do solemnly swear (or affirm) that we will well and truly, without partiality or prejudice, value and appraise the goods, chattels and personal estate of J K, deceased, so far as the same shall come to our sight and knowledge, and that we will, in all respects, perform our duties as appraisers to the best of our skill and judgment."

After which, the said appraisers shall proceed, as soon as conveniently may be, to the discharge of their duty, and shall set down each article, with the value thereof, in dollars and cents as aforesaid. All the valuations shall be set down on the right hand side of the paper in one or more columns, in figures, opposite to the respective articles of property, and the contents of each column shall be cast up and set at the foot of the respective columns.(*u*)

Give a specific valuation to each article of property by itself. It would be incorrect to set down in the bill two or more articles in one valuation, *e. g.*, " Wagon and harness, $100," because creditors and others have a right to know what the wagon itself was valued at, independent of the harness. But the following would be correct: "Ten hogs, at $5 each, $50," because such would be a valuation of each hog as well as all.

There are no well defined rules to guide appraisers in fixing the *just* and *exact* valuation of the property, save good, sound judgment, enlightened as to the quality and market value of the kinds of articles to be appraised. The law provides that *disinterested* persons of discretion shall be appointed appraisers. A person of this description is presumed to be one who possesses that discernment, united with caution, which enables him to judge critically of what is correct and proper.

When the BILL OF APPRAISEMENT is completed, the appraisers shall certify the same under their hands and seals; and shall deliver the same into the hands of the executor or administrator to be, by him, returned into the office of the clerk of the county court, within three months from the date of his letters.(*v*)

If the appraisers or any of them die, or neglect to act, another warrant may issue forthwith for other appraisers.

(*u*) § 54, R. S. 1874, p. 114.   (*v*) § 55, id.

By executor or administrator.

12. Bill of Appraisement.

Bill of appraisement of the goods, chattels and personal estate of A B, late of   county, Illinois, deceased, intestate.

NO.	ARTICLES APPRAISED.	VALUATION.
1	Bay horse..	$100 00
1	Wagon	70 00
1	Harness	15 00
20	Shoats, at $1.25 each....................................	25 00
	Amount brought down.....................................	$210 00

[*On next page.*]

NO.	ARTICLES APPRAISED.	VALUATION.
	Amount brought over	$210 00
50	Bushels corn in crib, at 20 cents per bushel..................	10 00
	Undivided one-third of 20 acres standing corn	60 00
	Total valuation	$280 00

CERTIFICATE.

We, the undersigned appraisers, appointed and sworn to appraise the goods, chattels and personal estate of A B, deceased, do hereby certify that the foregoing bill of appraisement is a true, correct appraisement of the several articles of goods, chattels and personal estate of the said intestate, made by us, that have come to our knowledge, and that we have valued the same according to our best judgment.

Witness our hands and seals, this   day of   , A. D. 18 .

A B. [SEAL.]
C D. [SEAL.]   } *Appraisers.*
E F. [SEAL.]

(Here annex the certificate of the oath and the appraisers' warrant.)

All the appraisers should sign the appraisement bill and join in making the appraisement. An appraisers' fee is fixed at $2 per day.(*w*)

13. Inventories and bills of appraisement, and authenticated copies thereof, may be given in evidence in any suit by or against the executor or administrator, but shall not be conclusive for or against him, if any other testimony be given that the estate was really worth, or was *bona fide* sold for more or less than the appraised value thereof.(*x*)

14. Additional Appraisement. Whenever personal property of any kind, or assets, shall come to the possession or knowledge of any executor or administrator, which are not included in the first bill of appraisement as aforesaid, the same shall be appraised and return

---

(*w*) § 59, R. S. 1874, p. 114; see p. 174, *infra;* Costs and Fees, *infra.*   (*x*) § 56, id.

Collection and disposition of

thereof made to the office of the clerk of the county court, in like manner, within three months after discovery of the same. (*y*)

15. Executors and administrators shall be chargeable with so much of the estate of the decedent, personal or real, as they, after due and proper diligence, might or shall receive. (*z*)

16. Every appraiser appointed under this act shall be entitled to the sum of two dollars per day for each day's necessary attendance in making all such appraisements, to be allowed by the county court, and paid upon its order by the executor or administrator.

17. If the administrator or executor of an estate discover, at any time after the inventory and appraisement of the property is made, that the personal property and assets of the estate do not exceed the amount of the widow's allowance, after deducting the necessary expenses incurred, such administrator or executor shall report the facts to the court, and if the court find the report to be true, he shall order said property and assets to be delivered to the widow by the administrator or executor, and discharge the executor or administrator from further duty; but such executor or administrator shall first pay out of the property and assets the costs and expenses of administration. After the court orders the delivery of such property and assets to the widow, the clerk of said court shall make and deliver to her a certified copy of the order, under seal, which shall vest her with complete title to said property and assets, and enable her to sue for and recover the same in her own name and for her own use. Such widow shall not be liable for any of decedent's debts or liabilities, excepting the funeral expenses of the deceased. If, upon affidavit being filed with the clerk of said court, that such administrator or executor fails or refuses to report in any case provided for in this section, the court may order a citation and attachment to issue as in other cases of a failure of administrators to report. And on a discovery of new assets, administration may be granted as in other cases, and charged to the account of the estate. (*a*)

18. COLLECTION AND DISPOSITION OF ASSETS. If any executor or administrator, or other person interested in any estate, shall state upon oath to any county court that he believes that any person has in possession, or has concealed or embezzled, any goods, chattels, moneys or effects, books of account, papers, or any evidences of debt

(*y*) § 57, R. S. 1874, p. 114.   (*a*) § 50, id
(*z*) § 58, id.

By executor or administrator.

whatever, or titles to lands, belonging to any deceased person (or that he believes that any person has any knowledge or information of or concerning any indebtedness or evidence of indebtedness, or property titles or effects, belonging to any deceased person, which knowledge or information is necessary to the recovery of the same, by suit or otherwise, by the executor or administrator, of which the executor or administrator is ignorant, and that such person refuses to give to the executor or administrator such knowledge or information), the court shall require such person to appear before it by citation, and may examine him on oath and hear the testimony of such executor or administrator, and other evidence offered by either party, and make such order in the premises as the case may require.(b)

If such person refuse to answer such proper interrogatories as may be propounded to him, or refuse to deliver up such property or effects, or in case the same has been converted, the proceeds or value thereof, upon a requisition being made for that purpose by an order of the said court, such court may commit such person to jail until he shall comply with the order of the court therein.(c)

Upon suggestion made by an executor or administrator, to the county court, that any claim, debt or demand whatever belonging to the estate in his hands to be administered, and accruing in the lifetime of the decedent, is desperate on account of the insolvency or doubtful solvency of the person or persons owing the same, or on account of the debtor having availed himself of the bankrupt law of the United States, or on account of some legal or equitable defense which such person or persons may allege against the same, or for the cause that the smallness of such claim, debt or demand, and the difficulty of finding the debtors, owing to the remoteness of their residence, or such executor's or administrator's ignorance of the same, the said court may order such claim, debt or demand to be compounded or sold, or to be filed in the said court for the benefit of such of the heirs, devisees or creditors of such decedent as will sue for and recover the same, giving the creditors the preference if they or any of them apply for the same before the final settlement of such estate: *Provided,* that no order for the sale or compound-

(b) § 80, R S. 1874, pp. 118, 119.   (c) § 81, id.

ing of any such debts, claims or demands, or any of them, shall be made until two weeks' public notice* shall have been given to all whom it may concern, of the time and place when the said order will be applied for, which notice shall be given by the administrator or executor in a newspaper published in the county where such application is to be made; or if no such newspaper is published in such county, then by posting up such notices in not less than three public places in the county, of which one shall be at the office of the clerk of the county court, which notice shall be so posted at least two weeks previous to the time of said application. The executor or administrator shall report to the said county court, for its approval, the terms upon which he has settled or disposed of any such claim, debt or demand.(*d*)

And if such claim is compounded or sold, such executor or administrator shall be chargeable with the avails of such compounding, and if the same is taken by any of the creditors, heirs or devisees, he or they may maintain an action for the recovery thereof, in the name of such executor or administrator, for the use hereinafter mentioned; and upon recovering the same, or any part thereof, he or they shall be chargeable therewith, after deducting his claim or distributive share, with reasonable compensation for collecting the same; and upon such suits the executor or administrator shall not be liable for costs.(*e*)

COUNTY COURT MAY ORDER DEBTS COMPOUNDED. The county court may order claims, debts and demands, due at so remote a period as to prevent their collection within the time required for the final settlement of estates, and the collection or disposition of which

(*d*) § 82, R. S. 1874, p. 119.   (*e*) § 83, id.

---

* FORM OF NOTICE OF APPLICATION TO SELL OR COMPOUND DESPERATE CLAIMS. ADMINISTRATOR'S NOTICE.

To all whom it may concern:

Take notice, that the undersigned, administrator of the estate of C D, deceased, will apply to the county court of   county, in the State of Illinois, at the next term thereof, to be holden in the court-house in   , in said county, on the third Monday of   next, for leave to compound or sell all the desperate claims, debts and demands whatsoever due the estate of the said C D, deceased, which accrued in his life-time.   A B, *Adm'r*.

Dated,   .

Proof of the publication or posting of this notice should be made the same as in other cases. See p. 51, *supra,* 182, *infra.*

Before such notice is given, the administrator should properly make the

By the executor or administrator.

is necessary to the payment of the debts against the estate, to be compounded or sold in the same manner and upon like condition as though such claims, debts or demands were desperate or doubtful: *Provided,* that no such claims, debts or demands shall be sold or compounded for less than ten per cent below the par value thereof.(*f*)

No executor or administrator shall, without the order of the court, remove any property wherewith he is charged, by virtue of his letters, beyond the limits of this State. And in case any such executor or administrator shall remove such property without such order, the court shall, on notice, forthwith revoke his letters and appoint a successor, and cause a suit to be instituted on his bond,

(*f*) § 84, R. S. 1874, p. 119.

suggestion to the court mentioned in the law, that the persons interested may examine the schedule of such debts with a view of buying or otherwise. Such suggestion may be in this form:

SUGGESTION OF DESPERATE DEBTS.

STATE OF ILLINOIS, } *ss*:
County.

To A B, Judge of the county court of   county, Illinois:

The undersigned, administrator of the estate of C D, deceased, suggests and makes known to the court here that the following claims, debts and demands, belonging to the estate of the said C D, deceased, and which accrued in his life-time, are desperate, for the reasons here stated, to wit:

Note of E F, dated June 1, 1870, due on demand (debtor insolvent), for.......... $90 00
Account of J L (debtor absconded and gone to parts unknown), for............ 20 00
Account of O P, due since 1850 (barred by statute of limitations, which the undersigned is assured will be pleaded against it), for............................. 36 20

And the undersigned states that he has made all necessary efforts to collect said demands, but believes legal proceedings would be unavailing, and that the interest of the estate would be best promoted by compounding or selling them.

A B,
Administrator of C D, deceased.

This "suggestion" should particularize the demands, and state wherein they are desperate, assigning some of the causes mentioned in the law.

At the time mentioned in the notice, the administrator should apply to the court for an order to compound or sell the demands described in the suggestion. He should first file the proof of the publication or posting of the notices. The following short form may be used:

APPLICATION TO SELL OR COMPOUND DESPERATE DEMANDS.

STATE OF ILLINOIS, } *ss*:   County Court of   county.
County.   term, A. D. 18   .

To Hon.   , Judge of said court:

The undersigned, administrator of the estate of C D, late of said county, deceased, shows to your honor that he has given notice of his intended application, to the court, against him and his security, for the use of the persons interested in the estate; and if it shall appear, upon the trial of such cause, that the executor or administrator has so removed such property, judgment shall be rendered against the offender and his securities for the full value thereof, and such other damages as the parties interested may have sustained by reason thereof.(*g*)

PARTNERSHIP ESTATE. In case of the death of one partner, the surviving partner or partners shall proceed to make a full, true and complete inventory of the estate of the copartnership within his knowledge, and shall also make a full, true and complete list of all the liabilities thereof at the time of the death of the deceased partner. He or they shall cause the said estate to be appraised in like manner as the individual property of a deceased person.(*h*)

(*g*) § 85, R. S. 1874, pp. 119, 120.   (*h*) § 86, id.

at this term, for an order to sell or compound all desperate claims, debts and demands belonging to the estate of said C D, deceased, as will appear by the publication of said notice, proof whereof is herewith filed. Wherefore, the administrator prays that all the said debts, claims and demands, mentioned in the said schedule and "suggestions," heretofore filed in this court, be sold according to the statute in such case made and provided, except the said note of E F, which the undersigned prays leave to compound with said E F.   A B,
Administrator of C D, deceased.

Upon this application, the court will order the compounding or sale of the desperate claims, as the court, under the peculiar circumstances of the case, may deem most beneficial to the estate. The statute is silent as to the mode of selling, whether it be at private or public sale. An administrator may pass the legal interest of a note belonging to the intestate's estate, by indorsing the same as a person in his private capacity, and such transfer will enable the holder of it to sue on the same in his own name. If the sale be a public one, which would probably be the correct mode, the usual notice of the time and place of such sale should be given, as in other cases, by posting. The order of the court should direct the manner of sale. In compounding claims, the administrator should exercise his discretion, and settle on the best terms he can secure. If an administrator should return a collectible claim as desperate, and corruptly compound the same with the debtor, he would undoubtedly be liable to the amount of damages thereby done to the estate which he represents. He should deal in the same way for those for whom he is acting, as a reasonable, business-like man would do for himself, if he would exonerate himself from all liability; no other course would be honest or safe.

After the administrator has sold and compounded all such claims, he is required to report to the court, for approval, the terms upon which he has settled or disposed of such claims, debts or demands.

By the executor or administrator.

He or they shall return, under oath, such inventory, list of liabilities and appraisement, within sixty days after the death of the copartner, to the county court of the county of which the deceased was a resident or carried on the partnership business at the time of his death; if the deceased shall have been a non-resident, then such return shall be made to the county court granting administration upon the effects of the deceased. Upon neglect or refusal to make such return, he shall, after citation, be liable to attachment.(*i*)

Such surviving partner or partners shall have the right to continue in possession of the effects of the partnership, pay its debts out of the same, and settle its business, but shall proceed thereto without delay, and shall account with the executor or administrator, and pay over such balances as may, from time to time, be payable to him in the right of his testator or intestate. Upon the application of the executor or administrator, the county court may, whenever it may appear necessary, order such surviving partner to render an account to

(*i*) § 87, R. S. 1874, p. 120.

REPORT OF SALE OF DESPERATE CLAIMS.

STATE OF ILLINOIS, } *ss*: *County Court of   county,*
County.   *term*, 18 .

To the Honorable the Judge of said court:

The undersigned, administrator of C D, deceased, respectfully submits the following report of the sale and compounding of the desperate claims, debts and demands belonging to the estate of said C D, made in pursuance of the order of this court at the term thereof:

That he succeeded in settling with E F, and obtained the amount on his
note upon discounting the interest of.......................... .... $75 00

That after giving the notice required in said order (as per proof herewith filed), he sold the following claims, as here stated:

Account of J L, $12.75, to L M, for 5 00
Account of O P, $36.20, to B C, for 20 00

Total amount received for desperate claims........................... ..... $100 00

That he could obtain no bid for I P's account of $28, and he herewith returns the same into court.

A B,
Administrator of C D, deceased.

Dated   , 18 .

If the court be satisfied with the report, it will order the same approved, and charge the administrator with the amount so received by him.

If such claims are taken by the heirs or creditors, they are authorized by the statute to sue on them, in the name of the administrator, for their use. If an administrator sells an account or other indebtedness, not negotiable, it is presumed that the person buying may maintain an action for the recovery of the amount due on the same.

Collection and disposition of

said county court, and in case of neglect or refusal, may, after citation, compel the rendition of such account by attachment.(*j*)

Upon the committal of waste by the surviving partner or partners, the court may, upon proper application, under oath, setting forth specifically the facts and circumstances relied on, protect the estate of the deceased partner, by citing forthwith the surviving partner or partners to give security for the faithful settlement of the affairs of the copartnership, and for his accounting for and paying over to the executor or administrator of the deceased whatever shall be found to be due, after paying partnership debts and costs of settlement, within such time as shall be fixed by the court; the giving of such security may be enforced by attachment, or upon refusal to give such security, the court may appoint a receiver of the partnership property and effects, with like powers and duties of receivers in courts of chancery; the costs of proceedings under this section to be paid by the executor or administrator, out of the estate of the deceased or surviving partner, or partly by each, as the court may order.(*k*)

19. SALE OF PERSONAL PROPERTY. When it is necessary for the proper administration of the estate, the executor or administrator shall, as soon as convenient, after making the inventory and appraisement, sell at public sale all the personal property, goods and chattels of the decedent, when ordered to do so by the county court (not reserved to the widow, or included in specific legacies and bequests, when the sale of such legacies and bequests is not necessary to pay debts), upon giving three weeks' notice* of the time and place of such sale, by at least four advertisements, set up in the most public places in the county where the sale is to be made, or by inserting an advertisement in some newspaper published in the county where the sale is to be made, at least four weeks successively, previous thereto. The sale may be upon a credit of not less than six nor more than twelve months' time, by taking notes with good security of the purchasers at such sale. The sale may be for all cash, or part cash and part on time. *Provided*, that any part or all of such personal property may, where so directed by the court, be sold at private sale.(*l*)

If any testator directs that his estate shall not be sold, the same shall be preserved in kind, and distributed accordingly, unless such

(*j*) § 88, R. S. 1874, p. 120. (*l*) § 90, id.; act Feb. 9, 1874.
(*k*) § 89, id.

* See note on page 181, *infra*.

By the executor or administrator.

sale become absolutely necessary for the payment of the debts and charges against the estate of such testator.(*m*)

If the sale of the personal property be not necessary for the payment of debts, or legacies, or the proper distribution of the effects of the estate, the court may order that the property be preserved and distributed in kind.(*n*)

If any executor or administrator be of opinion that it would be of advantage to the estate of the decedent to dispose of the crop growing, and not devised at the time of his decease, the same shall be inventoried, appraised and sold, in like manner as other personal property; but the executor or administrator may, if he believe it would be of more advantage to the estate, cultivate such crop to maturity, and the proceeds of such crop, after deducting all necessary expenses for cultivating, gathering and making sale of the same, shall be assets in his hands, and subject to the payment of debts and legacies, and to distribution as aforesaid.(*o*)

In all public sales of such property, the executor or administrator may employ necessary clerks, and a crier, who shall be allowed such compensation, not exceeding three dollars per day, as the court may deem reasonable, to be paid by such executor or administrator, and charged to the estate. All such sales shall be made between the hours of ten o'clock in the forenoon and five o'clock in the afternoon of each day; and any sale made before or after the time herein limited shall be voidable at the instance of heirs, devisees or creditors prejudiced thereby.*(*p*)

All executors and administrators shall, immediately after making such sales, make, or cause to be made, a bill of the sales of said estate, under oath, describing particularly each article of property

(*m*) § 91, R. S. 1874, p. 121. (*o*) § 93, id.
(*n*) § 92, id. (*p*) § 94, id.

---

* The first step is to give the notice required by law. The following form may be used:

NOTICE OF ADMINISTRATOR'S SALE.

Administrator's Sale.

Notice is hereby given that the undersigned, administrator of C D, deceased, will, on the   day of   , A. D. 18 , between the hours of 10 o'clock, A. M., and 5 o'clock, P. M., of said day, sell at public sale, on the premises lately occupied by said decedent, in the town of   , county of   , all the personal property, goods and chattels belonging to the estate of the said deceased, consisting of horses, hogs, etc. (*the property for sale should be specifically described*), upon a credit of   months; purchasers giving notes and approved security for all sums of five dollars and upwards; cash in sold, to whom sold, and at what price ;(q) which sale bill, when thus made and certified by the clerk of such sale and the crier thereof, if any such were employed, as true and correct, shall be returned into

(q) § 95, R. S. 1874, p. 121.

(q) The sale being a public one, where all persons competent to make contracts may become purchasers, each article by itself should be put up, and sold to the highest bidder who can comply with the terms of the sale. All sales made before 10 o'clock, A. M., and after 5 o'clock, P. M., are voidable. The crier is the agent of the administrator in selling, and also of the purchaser in buying ; so, if the crier, in selling, make false and fraudulent representations, they will be taken as the fraud of the administrator.

In an action on a note given for goods bought at an administrator's sale, it was held that the purchaser may show, in defense to the note, that the administrator, knowing the contrary, fraudulently represented the goods to be sound. *Ray* v. *Virgin*, 12 Ill. 216.

The administrator cannot sell any of the property of the deceased at private sale. *Burnap* v. *Dennis*, 3 Scam. 481. Nor can he delegate his power to sell; he must himself be present to direct and control. *Kellogg* v. *Wilson*, 80 Ill. 357. If an administrator purchases the goods of the deceased at a public sale at

hand for all sums under five dollars. No property to be removed until the terms of the sale are complied with.

                                                                 A B,
                            Administrator of   , *deceased*.
Dated   ,18 .

If posted, there must be at least four copies put up in the most public places in the county. The administrator should keep a copy of the notice, upon which should be indorsed his affidavit of posting, and returned with the sale bill. The following form of an affidavit may be used for this purpose:

AFFIDAVIT OF POSTING NOTICES.

STATE OF ILLINOIS, } *ss*:
      County. }

A B, administrator of   , deceased, being sworn, says, that on the   day of   , instant, he posted four notices, of which the within (or foregoing) is a copy, at the following places, the same being the most public places in said county, viz.: one at the court-house in   , one at   , in the town of   , one at   , in the town of   , and one at   , in the town of   .
                                                                            A B.

(*Jurat*.)

If the notice be published in a newspaper, the certificate of the publisher that the same was inserted, stating the facts, attached to the notice, will be sufficient evidence of publication. See p. 51, *supra*.

The advertisement is the process upon which the administrator makes the sale of the intestate's property. It should specify the *time, place* and *terms* of the sale, with legal certainty.

By the executor or administrator.

the office of the clerk of the county court in the like time as is required in cases of inventories and appraisements.*(r)

(r) § 95, R. S. 1874, p. 121.

a less price than their appraised value, he will be accountable for the difference. *Griswold* v. *Chandler*, 5 N. H. 492.

Public sale is one made by auction to the highest bidder, and is not in general subject to all the rules of other sales; for example, there is no warranty of title of personal property, either express or implied. Bouvier.

A bidding at an auction may be retracted before the hammer is down; it is not binding upon either party till assented to. 2 Kent's Com. 587.

The sale should be conducted fairly. The estate is not liable on a warranty made by the administrator, in general, though the administrator may be personally liable. There is no implied warranty of title in sales made by administrators. 2 Harr. & Gil. 176.

The rule of *caveat emptor* is strictly applicable to sales by administrators. In the absence of fraud, the purchaser at such sales must not only look out for the title of the property, but for the quality of the article which he purchases. 12 Ill. 216; 15 id. 294. A purchaser at the sale buys at his own risk as to title and quality of property.

If there be no bidders (and perhaps on the sound discretion of the administrator), the sale may be postponed. The statute is silent in regard to such postponement; but it is presumed the law would admit of and justify it where it is best for the interests of the estate. Notice of the postponed sale should be co-extensive with the original notices as to the posting and publication.

Immediately after the sale, the administrator should make, or cause to be made, a bill of the sales of said personal estate, the truth and correctness of which is to be certified to by the clerk and crier.

*BILL OF SALE.

A bill of the sales of goods, chattels and personal estate of A B, late of the county of , Illinois, deceased, made on the day of , A. D. 18 , in pursuance of notice thereof, a copy of which is hereto attached.

NO.	ARTICLES SOLD.	TO WHOM SOLD.	FOR WHAT PRICE.
1	Two-horse wagon	James Godard	$80 00
1	Harness	do do	10 00
20	Hogs, at $1.50 each	Joseph Farmer	30 00
10	Acres of wheat, standing	do do	25 00
	Total amount of sales		$145 00

We, the undersigned, clerk and crier at the said sale, do hereby certify that the foregoing is a true and correct bill of the sales of the goods and chattels of the said A B, made on the day and year first aforesaid.

Witness our hands and seals, the day of , A. D. 18 .

E F, *Clerk.* [SEAL.]
G H, *Crier.* [SEAL.]

In the sale bill, as in the appraisement bill, *each* article is to be specifically

In the hands of guardians or conservators.

SECTION II. — IN THE HANDS OF GUARDIANS OR CONSERVATORS.

1. The guardian to return an inventory within sixty days after his appointment, and additional inventory.
2. Contents of inventory.
3. Form of inventory.
4. Conservators are required to do the like.

1. INVENTORY TO BE RETURNED. The guardian shall, within sixty days after his appointment, or if the court is not in session at the expiration of that time, at the next term thereafter, return to the court a true and perfect inventory of the real and personal estate of the ward, signed by him and verified by his affidavit. As often as other estate shall thereafter come to his knowledge, he shall return an inventory thereof, within sixty days from the time the same shall come to his knowledge.(s)

2. CONTENTS OF INVENTORY. The inventory shall describe the real estate, its probable value and rental, and state whether the same is incumbered, and, if incumbered, how and for how much; what amount of money is on hand; and contain a list of all personal property including annuities and credits of the ward, designating them as "good," "doubtful," or "desperate," as the case may be.(t)

(s) § 12, R. S. 1874, p. 560.   (t) § 13, id.

described, and not grouped with others, as, "a covered buggy and harness," for the buggy is to be sold by itself, and the name of the person to whom sold, and the price for which it sold, set opposite; and so of the harness. Persons interested in the estate have a right to know, from the sale bill, what each individual article was sold for. It is questionable whether hogs can be sold in a drove, even on a bid of so much for each hog, taking the lot. The whole of the personal estate might, with equal propriety in law, be sold *en masse*, as hogs by the drove. A field of growing wheat, consisting of ten acres, might, with propriety, be sold as an entirety, while it would be doubtful whether three distinct fields of wheat could be put up at once and included in one sale. The interests of the creditors and heirs might be seriously affected by such sales *en masse*. Each article of personal property should be put up, sold and entered in the sale bill separately, unless one person should purchase several of the same kind of articles in succession, then it might be convenient to enter them as illustrated in the foregoing form of sale bill, as, "20 hogs at $1.50 each, to Joseph Farmer, $30."

When the bill of sale is made out as aforesaid, the notice, with affidavit of posting (or proof of publication), should be attached to it, and returned within three months to the court.

PERSONAL ESTATE IN ADMINISTRATION.

In the hands of guardians or conservators.

The following may be used as a form for such inventory:

3. GUARDIAN'S INVENTORY.

An inventory of the estate, real and personal, belonging to C A D, a minor of the county of , and State of Illinois.

ARTICLES.	VALUATION.
Money received of J K, administrator of T F D, deceased.........	$500 00
4 Horses of the value of $100 each.....	400 00
1 Wagon, of the value of..	80 00
160 acres of land, being N. E. qr. of sec. 10, T. 11 N., R 3 E., of the value of............................	1,000 00
Undivided two-thirds of 80 acres of land, being S. hf. of N. W. qr. of sec. 10, T. 11 N., R. 3 E., said share is worth................	600 00
Amount due on lease of said first described land made by T F D in his life-time, to R S...	65 00
Total..	$2,045 00

STATE OF ILLINOIS, } ss:
County.

I, E B M, guardian of the said C A D, do certify that the foregoing is a true and perfect inventory of all the real and personal estate, goods, chattels and effects belonging to the said C A D, so far as the same have come to my possession and knowledge, and that I believe the foregoing to be a fair and just valuation of the same.

June 1, 187 . E B M,
Guardian of C A D.

4. CONSERVATORS are to do the same thing in like manner.(*u*)

(*u*) See p. 138 *supra.*

CHAPTER VII.

REAL ESTATE IN ADMINISTRATION.

SECTION I. Through the executor.
      II. Through the administrator.
     III. Through the guardian.
     IV. Through the conservator.

SECTION I.—ADMINISTRATION OVER REAL ESTATE THROUGH THE EXECUTOR.

1. Power of executor to sell land valid, if given in the will.
2. Implied power of sale.
3. Power vests in those who qualify, where several are appointed and part refuse.
4. Conveyance to a person as executor, his heirs, etc., conveys a fee.
5. Co-executor may call a co-executor to account in chancery.
6. Mortgages and leases by executors, on petition to the county court.
7. Foreclosure of such mortgages confined to the county court having jurisdiction over the property, *i. e.*, in the county where it is, or a greater part of it is, situated.
8. Decree of strict foreclosure in such case prohibited, and redemption as upon judgments at law prescribed.
9. Actions which survive, specified.
10. General directions; practice indicated; suggestions.

1. SALE OF REAL ESTATE.* In all cases where power is given in any will to sell and dispose of any real estate or interest therein,

---

* Says Chancellor KENT, in speaking of tenures, 4 Com. 3: "The technical language of the common law was too deeply rooted in our usages and institutions to be materially affected by legislative enactments." With the other parts of the English jurisprudence, the intricate doctrines and the complex and multifarious learning connected with landed property, were introduced into this country and subsisted in force before the Revolution. Resort then, in order to acquire a proper and clear understanding of the subject, must be had to the text-books (Blackstone's Com.; Kent's Com.; Bouv. Institutes; Washburne on Real Property), though modern legislation has, to a great extent, in practice, if not in theory, lessened the necessity for the vast fabric of learning which surrounds almost every thing connected with either the acquisition or disposition of real property. Personal property, on the death of the proprietor, passes to the executor or administrator, such being one of the qualities which pertain to it. On the other hand, real property passes at the death of an intestate to the heir, subject only to the debts of the deceased. *Vansycle* v. *Richardson*, 13 Ill. 171. The title, by the common law, vests instantly in the heir. The law casts the title of the realty upon the heir, at the death of the ancestor, if intestate;

Through the executor.

and the same is sold and disposed of in the manner and by the persons appointed in such will, the sales shall be good and valid; and where one or more executors shall fail or refuse to qualify, or depart this life before such sales are made, the survivor or survivors shall have the same power, and their sales shall be as good and valid as if they all joined in such sales.(a)

2. WILL; POWER OF EXECUTORS TO SELL LAND UNDER. Where a testator directed his land to be sold and the proceeds to be distributed among certain persons, without directing by whom such sale

(a) § 96, R. S. 1874, p. 121.

upon such estate the descent is then cast. See chap. x, *infra.* So that, in cases of intestacy, it is a familiar doctrine that the administrator has, as such, nothing whatever to do with the real property of the estate over which he is appointed, while in cases of wills unless power be given by the will, the executor is equally powerless, taking neither title nor power by virtue of the law, except it be conferred by the will; although this may all be theoretically true, yet, practically, both the executor and administrator may have more or less to do with the real property in administration. But in doing this they are exercising, strictly speaking, only a power. In dealing with personal property on the other hand, they have the absolute dominion over it. Over real property the law gives to the probate jurisdiction ample power, but the title which has descended to the heir as an inherent quality of the estate—one of its incidents, must be divested before this power can be brought to bear in disposing of the real estate of the decedent. The personal property proving insufficient for the purposes of administration, a SPECIAL PROCEEDING, of which the heir must be notified either actually or constructively, is to be instituted, in order to convert the real estate, or enough of it, into assets to complete the administration. *Botsford* v. *O'Conner*, 57 Ill. 72.

A license to sell the real property must be applied for, the heir must be made party defendant, and notified. It must be made to appear that the personal property is insufficient. The administrator in this represents the creditors, and is oftentimes in open antagonism to the heir.

The proceeding is in its nature very much like a suit in chancery, the heir may contest the matter from its inception to its close, in the probate court. He then has the right of appeal. He may collaterally attack the record so far as to question the jurisdiction of the probate court both over the estate and his person, but no further. 57 Ill. 72; see pp. 6, 62, 63, *supra.* So, to the conservator or guardian, the appointment gives no title to the real property. They, too, are equally bound to institute special proceedings in order to reach the real estate of their wards. These proceedings in form and in substance will be considered further on. See chap. xiv, *infra.* But here we must first study the nature of real property, for it makes little difference whether we are considering it as controlled by and through a power or by title, if we are to deal with it at all. To learn what real property is becomes now the all-important inquiry, and which requires much learning and research to fully comprehend. We, therefore, endeavor briefly and as plainly as possible for our present purpose, to define real property and explain what is, and what is not, real property:

REAL PROPERTY was early defined to be something which may be held by tenure, or that will pass to the heir of the possessor at his death, instead of his executor, including lands, tenements, and hereditaments, whether the latter be corporeal or incorporeal. 1 Atkinson Conv. In respect to property, *real* and *personal* correspond very nearly with *immovables* and *movables* of the civil law. By the latter, " biens " is a general term for property; and these are classified into movable and was to be made, and appointed executors who qualified, and sold the land at auction in good faith for a fair consideration, public notice by advertisement being first given, *held*, that the will was to be considered as a bequest of a fund distributable by the executors among the legatees, and that the executors have power to sell the land in order to raise the fund, without procuring a decree from a court of chancery for that purpose.(*b*) If a testator directs his estate to be sold for certain purposes, without declaring by whom the sale is to be made, if the proceeds are distributed by the executor, he takes the power to sell by implication. Money directed to be employed in the purchase of land, and land directed to be sold and turned into money, are to be considered as that species of property into which they are directed to be converted.(*b*)

Where deeds conveying lands in this State are executed by executors, duly qualified in pursuance of the power vested in them by will, executed and proved out of this State, the same shall be evi-

(*b*) *Rankin* v. *Rankin*, 36 Ill. 293.

---

immovable, and the latter are subdivided into corporeal and incorporeal. Guyot, Repert. *Biens*. By immovables the civil law intended property which could not be removed at all, or not without destroying the same, together with such movables as are fixed to the freehold, or have been so fixed and are intended to be again united with it, although at the time severed therefrom. Taylor's Civ. Law, 475. The same distinction and rules of law as to the nature and divisions of property are adopted in Scotland, where, as by the Roman law, another epithet is applied to immovables. They are called *heritable*, and go to the heir, as distinguished from movables, which go to executors or administrators. So rights connected with or affecting heritable property, such as tithes, servitudes, and the like, are themselves heritable; and in this it coincides with the common law. Erskine's Inst. 192. In another respect the Scotch coincides with the common law, in declaring growing crops of annual planting and culture not to be heritable, but to go to executors, etc., although so far a part of the real estate that they would pass by a conveyance of the land. Erskine's Inst. 193; Williams' Exec. 600. Though the term *real*, as applied to property, in distinction from *personal*, is now so familiar, it is one of a somewhat recent introduction. While the feudal law prevailed, the terms in use in its stead were lands, tenements or hereditaments; and these acquired the epithet of *real* from the nature of the remedy applied by law for the recovery of them, as distinguished from that provided in case of injuries, contracts broken, and the like. In the one case the claimant or demandant recovered the *real thing* sued for — the land itself — while, ordinarily, in the other he could only recover recompense in the form of pecuniary damages. The term, as a means of designation, did not come into general use until after the feudal system had lost its hold, nor till even as late as the commencement of the seventeenth century. *Wind* v. *Jekyl*, A. D. 1719, 1 P. Wms. Ch. 575; Williams' Real Prop. 6, 7.

Under the term *real property* or *estate*, so as to have heritability and other incidents of lands, tenements or hereditaments, it may be stated, in general terms, that it includes land and whatever is erected or growing upon the same, with whatever is beneath or above the surface.

Through the executor.

dence of title in the vendee or grantee, to the same extent as was vested in the testator at the time of his death; unless at the time of executing such deed, letters testamentary or of administration on the estate of decedent had been granted in this State and remain unrevoked. (c)

3. Power vests in those executors who qualify to act, even if a part refuse to qualify. (d)

4. A conveyance to a person, who is an executrix, her heirs, assigns, and successors, passes to her the fee. and she may sell and dispose of the land, although received in satisfaction of a debt due her testator. The words " successors " and " executrix," as employed in the deed, were held not to limit or control the estate conveyed. (e)

(c) Cothran's Statutes, 317, § 34.
(d) *Clinefelter* v. *Ayres*, 16 Ill. 330; *Wardwell* v. *McDowell*, 31 id. 364;
Wisdom v. *Becker*, 52 id. 342. See Jurisdiction.
(e) *Greer* v. *Walker*, 42 Ill. 401.

This would, of course, include houses standing and trees upon the land, and would not embrace chattels like stock upon a farm, or furniture in a house. But not only may houses or growing trees acquire the character of *personal*, but various chattels, originally personal movables, may acquire that of *real* property. Thus, if one erect a dwelling-house upon the land of another by his assent, it is the personal estate of the builder. 6 N. H. 555; 6 Me. 452; 8 Pick. (Mass.) 404. So, if a nurseryman plant trees, for the purpose of growing them for the market, upon land hired by him, they would be personal estate. 1 Metc. (Mass.) 27; 4 Taunt. 316.

So crops, while growing, planted by the owner of the land, are a part of the real estate; but if sold by him when fit for harvesting, they become personal (5 Barnew. & C. 829); and a sale of such crops, though not fit for harvest, as personal, has been held good. 4 Mees. & W. Exch. 343; 2 Dana (Ky.), 206; 2 Rawle (Penn.), 161.

So trees growing, though not in a nursery, may be changed into the category of personal estate, if sold to be cut without any right to have them stand to occupy the land. 4 Metc. (Mass.) 584; 9 Barnew. & C. 561; 7 N. H. 523. But if the owner of land in fee grant the trees growing thereon to another and his heirs, to be cut at his pleasure, the property in the trees would be *real*. 4 Mass. 266. The same rule would apply to property in fee in a dwelling-house, though the owner only have a right to have it stand upon the land of another. And one may own a chamber in a house as his separate real estate. 1 Term, 701; 1 Metc. (Mass.) 541; 10 Conn. 318.

So a large class of articles originally wholly movable, and which may be at the time even disconnected with the land, may be regarded as *real* property, from having been fitted for and actually applied to use in connection with real estate, such as keys to locks fastened upon doors, mill-stones and irons, though taken out of the mill for repairing, window blinds, though temporarily removed from the house, and fragments of a dwelling-house destroyed by a tempest. Williams' Exec. 613–615; 11 Coke, 50; 10 Paige's Ch. 162; 30 Penn. St. 185. And a conveyance of " a saw-mill " with the land was held to pass iron bars and chains then in it which had been fitted for and used in operating it. 6 Me. 154.

In case of corporations, the same property may assume the character both of *real* and *personal*. Thus, if the corporation hold real estate, such as a mill or banking house, it would be in the hands of the body corporate real estate, but as constituting a part of the property owned and represented in the form of stock by the members consti-

Through the executor.

5. Where there are two or more executors or administrators of an estate, and any one of them takes all or a greater part of such estate and refuses to pay the debts of the decedent, or refuses to account with the other executor or administrator, in such case the executor or administrator so aggrieved may have his action of account or suit in equity against such delinquent executor or administrator, and recover such proportionate share of said estate as shall belong to him; and every executor being a residuary legatee may have an action of account or suit in equity against his co-executor or co-executors, and recover his part of the estate in his or their hands. Any other legatee may have the like remedy against the executors: *Provided*, that before any action shall be commenced for legacies as aforesaid, the court shall order them to be paid.(*f*)

(*f*) § 118, R. S. 1874, p. 122.

---

tuting the body of the corporation, it is personal. 3 Mees. & W. Exch. 422; Angell & A. on Corp., § 557. But the shares in corporate property may be real estate when declared to be so by the charter creating it, or when the corporation is merely constituted to hold and manage lands, like proprietors of common lands in the New England States. 2 P. Wms. 127; 2 Conn. 567; 10 Mass. 150.

Manure made upon a farm in the usual manner, by consumption of its products, would be a part of the real estate; while if made from products purchased and brought on to the land by the tenant, as in case of a livery stable, it would be personal (21 Pick. [Mass.] 371; 3 N. H. 503; 6 Me. 222; 2 N. Chipm. [Vt.] 115; 11 Conn. 525); though in England the out-going tenant may claim compensation for manure left upon the farm under such circumstances. 1 Cromp. & M. Exch. 809.

There is a large class of articles known to the law as *fixtures*, which are real or personal according to circumstances. Whatever is fitted for and actually applied to real estate, if of a permanent nature, is real estate, and passes from the vendor to the vendee as such. 20 Wend. 368; 2 Smith's Lead. Cas. (Am. ed.) 168. And the same rule applies between mortgagor and mortgagee. 19 Barb. 317; 4 Metc. (Mass.) 311; 3 Edw. Ch. 246. The same is the rule as between heir and executor upon the death of the ancestor, and between debtor and creditor upon a levy made by the latter upon the land of the former. 10 Paige's Ch. 163; 7 Mass. 432. Whereas, such fixtures as between a tenant and a landlord are personal estate, and may be removed as such, unless left attached to the realty by the tenant at the close of his term, in which case they become a part of the realty. 2 Pet 143; 7 Cow. 319; 1 Wheat. 91; 17 Pick. (Mass.) 192.

The law of burials. 1. In this country corpses and their burials are not matters of ecclesiastical cognizance. 2. The right to bury a corpse or preserve it is a legal right, belonging, in the absence of testamentary disposition, exclusively to the next of kin, and includes the right to select and change at pleasure the place of sepulture. 3. If the place of burial be taken for public use, the next of kin may claim indemnity for the expense of removal and suitable re-interment. *Matter of Beekman Street*, 4 Brad. 503. 532; *Bogert* v. *Indianapolis*, 13 Ind 134; *Matter of Brick Church*, 3 Edw. Ch. 155.

Pews in churches are sometimes real and sometimes personal estate, depending, generally, upon local statutes; though in the absence of statute law it would seem they were clearly interests in real estate, and partake of the character of such estate. 1 Pick. (Mass.) 104; 16 Wend. 28; 5 Metc. (Mass.) 132

Through the executor.

6. MORTGAGE OF REAL ESTATE BY EXECUTORS. Real estate may be mortgaged in fee or for a term of years, or leased by executors: *Provided*, that the term of such lease, or the time of the maturity of the indebtedness secured by such mortgage, shall not be extended beyond the time when the heirs entitled to such estate shall attain the age of twenty-one years, if a male, or eighteen years, if a female: *And provided also*, that before any mortgage or lease shall be made, the executors shall petition the county court for an order authorizing such mortgage or lease to be made, and which the court may grant if the interests of the estate may require it: *Provided*,

Even *money* often has the character of realty attached to it, so far as being heritable, and the like, by equity, where it is the proceeds of real estate wrongfully converted into money, or which ought to be converted into real estate. 3 Wheat. 577; 1 Brown's Ch. 6, 497; 13 Pick. (Mass.) 154.

Slaves, in some of the States, were so far regarded as real estate as to descend to heirs, instead of passing to personal representatives. 2 Dana (Ky.), 43.

There is one class of interests in lands, etc., which, from relating to lands which are *real*, and from being governed as to succession by the rules which apply to *personal* property, or, as that is called, chattels, takes the name of *chattels real*. Of this class are terms for years in lands. Upon the death of the tenant of such a term, it goes to his personal representatives, and not to his heirs. 2 Blackstone's Com. 386.

There is a very large class of interests in lands however, which, at common law, at the death of the proprietor, goes to the personal representative and not the heir. (2 Bl. Com. 386.) These are terms for years, termed lease-hold interests, or real property held by virtue of a lease; without sufficient consideration of the subject, in Vol. I Common Law, at page 456, we said: "On the death of lessee his interest descends to his heirs;" referring to the 453d page, see 1 Hill's C. L., pp. 453, 456, and 52 Ill. 130. But see *Scott* v. *Moore*, 3 Scam. 319; 2 Bl. Com. 386. The importance of this question, to the proper administration of estates, is apparent if we look at it as jurisdictional. The title of the heir does not become absolute until after administration. He takes a defeasible estate, liable to be defeated by a sale made by the administrator in due course of administration. *Vansycle* v. *Richardson*, 13 Ill. 171; *Meyer* v. *McDougal*, 47 id. 278; see chap. x, *infra*. But he must be notified before his title can be divested. *Botsford* v. *O'Conner*, 57 Ill. 72.

It is necessary then for the administrator to know whether a lease-hold is his, by an absolute title as with personalty, or whether he can reach it only by a special proceeding through a power as in case of a free-hold—whether the term goes to the heir or to the personal representative.

Whether our statute (R. S., ch. 57, p. 301, § 1; § 3, R. S. 1874, p. 622; 2 Hill's C. L. 593), has gone so far as to change the common law in this respect, as to leasehold estates or terms, may perhaps be doubted. For it would seem that the conveyance act (R. S., ch. 24, § 39, p. 110; § 38, R. S. 1874, p. 280), set all doubts at rest on this point were it not for the next section (§ 39, R. S., p. 110; § 38, R. S. 1874, p. 280), or exception, that the act of conveyances shall not be construed so as to embrace last wills and testaments (as we read it) — the law pertaining to last wills and testaments including the entire statute of wills. If our reading be correct, the common-law rule, relative to the disposition of terms at the death of the termor or lessee, is still the rule in Illinois. But see *Griffin* v. *Marine Co.*, 52 Ill. 130; *Scott* v. *Moore*, 3 Scam. 306; *Nicoll* v. *Mason*, 49 Ill. 358; *Nicoll* v. *Ogden*, 29 id. 323; *Nicoll* v. *Miller*, 37 id. 387; *Vansycle* v. *Richardson*, 13 id. 171; *Cook* v. *Foster*, 2 Gilm. 652.

Through the administrator:

further, that the executor making application as aforesaid, upon obtaining such order, shall enter into bond, with good security, faithfully to apply the moneys to be raised upon such mortgage or lease to the payment of the debts of the testator; and all moneys so raised shall be assets in the hands of such executor for the payment of debts, and shall be subject to the order of the court in the same manner as other assets.(*g*)

7. Foreclosures of such mortgages shall only be made by petition to the county court of the county in which the premises, or a major part thereof, are situated; and any sale made by virtue of any order or decree of foreclosure may, at any time before confirmation, be set aside by the court for inadequacy of price or other good cause, and shall not be binding upon the executor until confirmed by the court.(*h*)

8. No decree of strict foreclosure shall be made upon any such mortgage, but redemption shall be allowed as is provided by law in cases of sales under executions issued upon common-law judgments.(*i*)

9. ACTIONS WHICH SURVIVE. In addition to the actions which survive by the common law, the following shall also survive: Actions of replevin, actions to recover damages for an injury to the person (except slander and libel), actions to recover damages for an injury to real or personal property, or for the detention or conversion of personal property, and actions against officers for misfeasance, malfeasance or nonfeasance of themselves or their deputies; and all actions for fraud or deceit.(*j*)

10. General directions, the practice and suggestions will be given further on.(*k*)

SECTION II.— ADMINISTRATION OVER REAL ESTATE THROUGH THE ADMINISTRATOR.

1. When realty may be sold.
2. Proceedings to be commenced by petition; parties.
3. Requisites of the petition.
4. Cause to be prosecuted according to the practice in chancery.
5. Summons to issue, requisites of.

(*g*) § 119, Cothran's Stats., 1880, 79.
(*h*) § 120, id., p. 80.
(*i*) § 121, id.
(*j*) § 122, id., p. 80.
(*k*) See ch. xiv, *infra*.

Through the administrator.

6. Service of summons.
7. Cases for constructive service; affidavit of non-residence, etc.
8. Publication notice.
9. Guardian *ad litem*.
10. The hearing, order and decree of sale.
11. The sale to divest title of defendants.
12. Preliminaries and regulations for making sale, the notice, penalties, etc.
13. Proceeds of sale, assets in the hands of the administrator.
14. Equitable estates; how sold or made legal estates and sold.
15. The practice indicated.
16. Forms for pleadings, affidavits, process, orders, decrees, etc., etc.

An administrator has no power over the real estate of a decedent, other than to obtain a decree of court and sell the same thereunder, to pay debts, when the personal property is insufficient. *LeMoyne* v. *Quimby*, 70 Ill. 399; *Walker* v. *Diehl*, 79 id. 473.

1. WHEN SALE MAY BE HAD. When the executor or administrator has made (1) a just and true account of the personal estate and debts to the county court, and (2) it is ascertained that the personal estate of a decedent is insufficient to pay the just claims against his estate, and (3) there is real estate to which such decedent had claim or title, such real estate, or such portion as may be necessary to satisfy (1) the indebtedness of such decedent, and (2) the expenses of administration, may be sold in the manner provided by statute. (*l*)

2. The mode of commencing the proceedings for the sale of real estate in such cases shall be by the FILING OF A PETITION by the executor or administrator, in the county court of the county where letters testamentary or of administration were issued. The widow, heirs or devisees of the testator or intestate, and the guardians of any

(*l*) § 97, R. S. 1874, p. 121. For discussion of all the sections of the repealed statutes giving power to the administrator to affect decedent's real estate, see *Phelps* v. *Funkhouser*, 39 Ill. 401. A sale cannot be made under an act of the legislature, without judicial inquiry as to the existence of debts. *Rozier* v. *Fagan*, 46 Ill. 404. There must be debts existing. An order to sell the real estate of a decedent will not be made unless it is shown that there are existing debts against the estate. *Dorman* v. *Yost*, 13 Ill. 127. Upon a deficiency of assets to pay the debts of the estate, he may apply, in connection with the heir, for an order to sell the realty. The parties in such cases are not in privity; the admissions of an administrator do not bind the heir, and the heir may contest an application for the sale of the realty. *Hopkins* v. *McCan*, 19 Ill. 113. Debts, how established. A judgment against an administrator is *prima facie* evidence of the existence of a debt against the estate, as against an heir. *Stone* v. *Wood*, 16 Ill. 177. Probate of the claims. It is not sufficient to show that the claims exist or have been allowed by the probate court in

Through the administrator.

such as are minors, and the conservators of such as have conservators, and the actual occupants of the premises, where the same or any part thereof are occupied, shall be made parties defendants. If there are persons interested in the premises whose names are not known, then they shall be made parties by the name of unknown owners.(*m*)

3. THE PETITION SHALL SET FORTH THE FACTS AND CIRCUMSTANCES on which the petition is founded, in which shall be stated the amount of claims allowed, with an estimate of the amount of just claims to be presented, and it shall also contain the amount of personal estate which has come to his hands, and the manner in which he has disposed of the same, with a statement of the amount of claims paid. The petition shall be signed by the executor or administrator, and verified by his affidavit, and shall be filed at least ten days before the commencement of the term of court at which the application shall be made.(*n*)

(*m*) § 98, R. S. 1874, p. 122.
(*n*) § 99, id. Petition. The proceedings will be reversed if the record does not show any petition by the administrator. *Monahon* v. *Vandyke*, 27 Ill. another State. *Hobson* v. *Payne*, 45 Ill. 158. Debts created by the administrator after the death of intestate will not justify a proceeding to sell the land. *Fitzgerald* v. *Glancy*, 49 Ill. 465. A creditor cannot, by an allowance of his claim, or by obtaining judgment against an estate or an administrator, thereby acquire any specific lien upon the lands of the intestate, nor could he enforce the collection of a judgment by the levy of an execution upon the land. *Stillman* v. *Young*, 16 Ill. 318. Where the legislature passed a special act, authorizing the administrator to sell the real estate of a party, to pay debts, and reinvest the surplus, with the approval of the probate judge, for the benefit of the widow and heir: *Held*, that the power was conferred for the purpose of paying debts, and could not be exercised until required for that purpose. *Davenport* v. *Young et ux.*, 16 Ill. 548. Where an administrator applies for leave to sell the real estate for the purpose of paying a judgment, the judgment is not conclusive as against an heir, and he may contest the application, unless he has been

154. The petition should show that the contingency exists which authorizes this proceeding. *Hobson* v. *Payne*, 45 Ill. 158. The petition need not give the names of the heirs who are the made a party to the judgment, by joining in taking an appeal from it to a superior court. *Stone* v. *Wood*, 16 Ill. 177; *Hopkins* v. *McCan*, 19 id. 113; *Moline Water Power & Manf. Co.* v. *Webster*, 26 id. 234. See *contra*, *Gibson* v. *Roll*, 27 id. 90. All real estate, by statute, may be sold for the payment of the debts of intestates, but administrators have no power to sell or incumber without an order of court. The lands descend to the heirs *sub modo*, subject to this liability. *Stillman* v. *Young*, 16 Ill. 318. Appraisement bill. It is not essential that it appear an appraisement bill was filed by an administrator, to authorize the court to grant his petition for an order to sell land to pay debts. *Shoemate* v. *Lockridge*, 53 Ill. 503. *Held*, on objection to a petition in the circuit court, that the statement as to the personal assets was incorrect; that where the judge of the probate court has properly certified the amount of assets and claims, showing a deficiency of personal assets, such evidence will justify an order of sale. *Madden* v. *Cooper*, 47 Ill. 359.

Through the administrator.

4. SUCH APPLICATION SHALL BE DOCKETED as other causes, and the petition may be amended, heard or continued for notice, or for other cause. The practice in such cases shall be the same as in cases in chancery.(*o*)

5. Upon the filing of the petition, the clerk of the court where the same may be filed shall issue a SUMMONS, directed to the sheriff of the county in which the defendant resides, if the defendant is a resident of this State, requiring him to appear and answer the petition on the return day of the summons; and where there are several defendants, residing in different counties, a separate summons shall be issued to each county, including all the defendants residing therein. Every summons shall be made returnable to the first term of the county court after the date thereof, unless the petition is filed within ten days immediately preceding any term, in which case the summons shall be returnable to the next term thereafter.(*p*)

(*o*) § 100, R. S. 1874, p. 122; see Hill's Chan. Pr.

(*p*) § 101, id. The intervention of six weeks' notice between the first day of publication and the day of the term at which application for an order to sell is made, is sufficient. *Madden* v. *Cooper*, 47 Ill. 359. After the expiration owners of the land sought to be sold. *Gibson* v. *Roll*, 27 Ill. 92; *Stow* v. *Kimball*, 28 id. 93. But see § 99, act 1872. If the administrator files the petition and dockets the cause at the term named in the notice, it would be competent for the court to continue the cause to a subsequent term and then grant an order to sell the real estate. *Schnell* v. *City of Chicago*, 38 Ill. 383; *Shoemate* v. *Lockridge*, 53 id. 503. In a proceeding by an administrator for leave to sell real estate, the petition, notice of sale, and deed to the purchaser, described the premises correctly, as being in section *thirty*-three; the abstract from the county court, the inventory, and the order of sale described the land as being in section *twenty*-three. *Held*, in a collateral proceeding, involving the title, that the misdescription was a mere clerical error. *Shoemate* v. *Lockridge*, 53 Ill. 503. Requisites of petition. In a proceeding by an administrator, under the act of 1857, for leave to sell real estate to pay debts, the petition should allege, in order to give the court jurisdiction to order the sale, that an account of the personal estate and debts had been made, as mentioned in the act, or that the decedent left no personal estate of which an account could be made. *Bree* v. *Bree*, 51 Ill. 367. And where the petition alleges that the decedent left no personal estate, and the finding of the court is, that all the material allegations of the petition had been proved, the court will, in the absence of any thing in the record rebutting such finding, presume that it was warranted by the evidence. The evidence need not all be preserved in the record. *Bree* v. *Bree*, 51 Ill. 367; *Shoemate* v. *Lockridge*, 53 id. 503. Not necessary to show that the personal estate in another State has been exhausted. *Rosenthal* v. *Renick*, 44 Ill. 202. The proper course to be pursued upon an application to sell real estate for the payment of debts indicated. *Stow* v. *Kimball*, 28 Ill. 93. A petition for the sale of realty for the payment of debts must clearly show that there are debts of the estate existing and allowed, and that the personalty is exhausted. *Moffitt* v. *Moffitt*, 69 Ill. 641. It must appear and be proved that such debts are legally chargeable upon the estate in order to support a decree of sale. *Walker* v. *Diehl*, 79 Ill. 473. In a case where no assets came to the hands of the administrator, but he paid of his own money, taxes, insurance, court costs, etc., it was held the decree for the sale of land could not be sustained. *Walker* v. *Diehl*, 79 Ill. 473.

Through the administrator.

6. THE SERVICE OF SUMMONS shall be made by reading thereof to the defendant, or leaving a copy thereof at the usual place of abode, with some member of the family of the age of ten years and upward, and informing such person of the contents thereof, which service shall be at least ten days before the return of such summons.(*q*)

7. Whenever any petitioner or his attorney shall file, in the office of the clerk of the court in which his petition is pending, an affidavit showing that any defendant resides or hath gone out of this State, or on due inquiry cannot be found, or is concealed within this State, so that process cannot be served upon him, and stating the place of

(*q*) § 102, R. S. 1874, p. 122.

of one year from the final settlement of the account of an intestate in the court of probate, by the administrator, no application on the part of the administrator to sell the real estate of the intestate, to satisfy debts still due, will be sustained, as a general rule. *Dorman* v. *Lane*, 1 Gilm. 143. Notice of intention to apply. An administrator may give a general notice by publication of his intention to apply for leave to sell real estate for the payment of decedent's debt, without naming particular persons as defendants, the statute having regard to *all* persons interested, whether defendants or not. *Bowles' Heirs* v. *Rouse, Adm'r*, 3 Gilm. 409; *Gibson* v. *Roll*, 27 Ill. 89. Parties interested are bound, after proper notice, to appear and contest the application to sell lands, on the day specified; but if the petition be not then presented, they are not required to wait from day to day to see whether any move will be made in the case. But after the presentation of the petition, the court may fix a subsequent day for the hearing of proofs or other action in the case. *Gibson* v. *Roll*, 30 id. 172. Want of service—decree not binding. If notice of such a proceeding is not served or given to the heirs, in some mode known to the law, a decree licensing the executor or administrator to sell lands of the testator to pay debts will be void, and may be questioned in both direct and collateral proceedings. *Morris* v. *Hogle* 37 Ill. 150; *Schnell* v. *City of Chicago*, 38 id. 383; *Clark* v. *Thompson*, 47 id. 25. Statute must be followed. In a proceeding by an administrator to sell the real estate of his decedent, unless the mode pointed out by the statute for bringing the parties interested before the court is pursued, there will be such a want of jurisdiction as will vitiate the order for sale. *Herdman* v. *Short*, 18 Ill. 59; *Gibson* v. *Roll*, 27 id. 92; *Bree* v. *Bree*, 51 id. 267. Notice by an administrator of an application to sell lands must be published for three successive weeks, the first publication to be at least six weeks before the presenting of the petition. If this be not done, parties are not bound to take notice of such application. And although a petition may not be presented in fact until a later day than the one fixed by the notice, nor till after the six weeks required by the statute have expired, yet that fact does not cure the defect. *Gibson* v. *Roll*, 30 Ill. 172. Where the statute requires six weeks' notice, a publication of only thirty days is a fatal error. *Monahon* v. *Vandyke*, 27 Ill. 155. At the term specified. The application must be made at the term specified in the notice published by the administrator. If not made at that term, the proceeding is abated, and the parties in interest must be brought into court by another notice. *Turney* v. *Turney*, 24 Ill. 625. The notice given of such application need not specify the day of term on which the petition will be presented. Id.; *Finch* v. *Sink*, 46 Ill. 169; *Madden* v. *Cooper*, 47 id. 359; *Shoemate* v. *Lockridge*, 53 id. 503. An administrator published notice in a newspaper in Shelby county that he would present a petition "at the next term of the Shelby circuit court, to be holden in

residence of such defendant, if known ; or that, upon diligent inquiry, his place of residence cannot be ascertained, the clerk shall cause publication to be made in some newspaper printed in his county, and if there is no newspaper published in his county, then in the nearest newspaper published in this State, containing notice of the filing of the petition, the names of the parties thereto, the title of the court, and the time and place of the return of summons in the case, and a description of the premises described in the petition ; and he shall also, within ten days of the first publication of such notice, send a copy thereof by mail, addressed to such defendant whose place of residence is stated in such affidavit. The certificate of the clerk that he has sent such notice in pursuance of this section shall be evidence.(r)

8. The notice required in the preceding section may be given at any time after the filing of the petition, and shall be published at least once in each week for four successive weeks, and no default or proceeding shall be taken against any defendant not served with summons, and not appearing, unless forty days shall intervene between the first publication, as aforesaid, and the first day of the term at which such default or proceeding is proposed to be taken.(s)

9. When it appears that any of the persons required to be made parties defendant, who have been served with summons or notified as aforesaid, are minors under the age of twenty-one years, if males, or eighteen years if females, without a guardian resident in this State, or are persons having conservators, or where such guardian, if any, or conservator shall not be personally served with summons or

---

(r) § 103, R. S. 1874, p. 122.   (s) § 104, id.

the court-house in Shelbyville, on," etc. Objection was made that the notice failed to show the county and State where the application was to be made. The notice was *held* sufficient. *Moore* v. *Neil*, 39 Ill. 256. Where the notice specifies that the administrator " will apply at the December term of the county court of the county of Mercer, State of Illinois, for an order," etc., and the notice bears date " September 6, 1852," it will be presumed that the application would be made at the December term, A. D. 1852. *Finch* v. *Sink*, 46 Ill. 169. Sale of additional land. Where the original proceeding had terminated at a former term, by the report and approval of the sale, a supplemental petition without new notice cannot be entertained. *Cromine* v. *Tharp*, 42 Ill. 120. Leave to sell real estate. Where an order of a county court, rendered on a notice that the executor would apply at the December term of the court for license to sell real estate, to pay debts, is not made at that time, but the application is made and the order rendered on a petition filed, without further notice, at the next February term, it is not binding on the heirs for want of notice. *Morris* v. *Hogle*, 37 Ill. 150. So also in application of administrator to county court. *Schnell* v. *City of Chicago*, 38 Ill. 383.

shall not appear, the court shall appoint a guardian *ad litem*, who shall appear and defend in behalf of such minors, and be allowed such compensation as may be fixed by the court.(*t*)

10. Upon hearing the cause upon the issues formed or taken, the court shall hear and examine the allegations and proofs of the parties and of all other persons interested in the estate who may appear and become parties; and if, upon due examination, the court shall find that the executor or administrator has made a just and true account of the condition of the estate, and that the personal estate of the decedent is not sufficient to pay the debts against such estate, the court shall ascertain, as nearly as can be, the amount of deficiency, and how much of the real estate described in the petition it is necessary to sell to pay such deficiency, with the expenses of administration then due or to accrue, and make a decree for the sale thereof: *Provided*, that where any houses and lots, or other real estate, are so situated that a part thereof cannot be sold without manifest prejudice to the heirs, devisees or owner, the court may order the sale of the whole or such part as it may deem best; and the overplus arising from such sale shall be distributed among the heirs and devisees, owners, or such other person as may be entitled thereto.(*u*)

In such proceedings, the court may order the lands to be surveyed and subdivided, and a plat to be made of the same. The costs are taxed. (Cothran's Annotated Statutes, p. 1088.)

(*t*) § 105, Coth. Stats., 75. Answer of guardian not sufficient. In an application for the sale of real estate to pay debts, the answer of the guardian *ad litem* is not a sufficient foundation for an order of sale. The record should show, further, that the court heard proof which satisfied it of the truth of the allegations of the petition. *Fridley* v. *Murphy*, 25 Ill. 146.

(*u*) § 106, id. When and how ordered. The act of 1827 did not, like the act of 1829, require that an application to sell real estate by administrators should be made to the circuit court of the county in which administration was granted. Under that act, an application to the circuit court of the county in which the real estate was situated was sufficient. *Smith* v. *Hileman*, 1 Scam. 323. It is error for the court to license an executor to sell so much real estate as he may deem for the best interest of the estate. He should be licensed to sell as much as may be required to pay the debts of the estate. *Morris* v. *Hogle*, 37 Ill. 150. A decree on a petition by an administrator for the sale of lands, directed the sale of the whole of the land, or so much thereof as would pay the debts. *Held* to be sufficient; and further, that it was unnecessary to state therein the particular interest the deceased had in the land ordered to be sold. *Bowles' Heirs* v. *Rouse, Adm'r.*, 3 Gilm. 409. Where an administrator *de bonis non* dies after he obtained an order to sell real estate, his successor should perfect the sale; and if his authority be doubted, or if he needs advice, a court of equity, and not a court of law, is the proper resort. *Baker* v. *Bradsby*, 23 Ill. 632. Not in chancery. A proceeding by an administrator to sell real estate is not a

Through the administrator.

11. All such sales of real estate shall be made and conveyances executed for the same by the executor or administrator applying for such order, and shall be valid and effectual against the heirs and devisees of such decedent, and all other persons claiming by, through or under him or them. In case of the death of the executor or administrator applying for an order of sale before conveyance is made, the administrator *de bonis non* shall proceed in the premises and make conveyance in the same manner as if he had originally applied for such order, which conveyance shall be good and valid.

The statute does not require the approval of the sale as a necessary step to vesting title in the purchaser. (*v*)

(*v*) *Moffitt* v. *Moffitt*, 69 Ill. 641.

---

chancery proceeding. *Moline Water Power & Manuf. Co.* v. *Webster*, 26 Ill. 233; *Shoemate* v. *Lockridge*, 53 id. 503. Order—credit. An order for the sale of the real estate of the decedent must specify whether it shall be sold for cash or on a credit, and on what credit. *Shoemate* v. *Lockridge*, 53 Ill. 503. Administrator's sale—what title passes. A purchaser of land at an administrator's sale acquires only such title as was then vested in the heirs of the intestate. So, if the land was subject to the lien of a prior judgment against the grantor of the intestate, the purchaser will take the title with that infirmity. *Walden* v. *Gridley*, 36 Ill. 523. The doctrine of *caveat emptor* applies to such sales, and the purchaser will be presumed to have examined the records in relation to the title, and if he neglects to do so, he must abide the consequences of his omission. *Walden* v. *Gridley*, 36 Ill. 523; *McConnell* v. *Smith*, 39 id. 279; *Bingham* v. *Maxey*, 15 id. 295. See *Moore* v. *Neil*, 39 id. 256; *McConnell* v. *Smith*, id. 279; *Shoemate* v. *Lockridge*, 53 id. 503. Sale—must follow the order. Where an order of court directs the manner of sale of real estate of a deceased person, it is the duty of the executor or administrator to conform strictly to its requirements. *Reynolds* v. *Wilson*, 15 Ill. 394. May be on credit. A court may, if deemed beneficial to the estate, order the sale by an executor or administrator to be on credit. *Reynolds* v. *Wilson*, 15 Ill. 394. Where an administrator made a bond, and subsequently a conveyance, which did not recite the power to sell, nor that the estate belonged to the decedent: *Held*, that the deed did not operate to pass the title of the decedent. *Davenport* v. *Young et ux.*, 16 Ill. 549. Report of sale is not necessary to the validity thereof, as to purchasers. *Moore* v. *Neil*, 39 Ill. 256. What is a reasonable time within which the heir should apply to set aside the sale. *Kruse* v. *Steffens*, 47 Ill. 112. For facts *held* to show a collusion between administrator and purchaser, and invalidating the title in the hands of a party having notice. *Lockwood* v. *Mills*, 39 Ill. 603. Proceeds. Under proper circumstances, a court of equity will provide for the administration of assets in cases of intestacy. In doing so, the court should have all the creditors before it, and make such disposition of the property as is required by the statute respecting estates. *Vansycle* v. *Richardson*, 13 Ill. 171. Conveyance. The court will allow and compel an administrator to amend a defective deed. *Thorp* v. *McCullum*, 1 Gilm. 614. Where a sale has been regularly and fairly made by an administrator, under an order of court, for a valuable consideration, and the deed executed by one administrator only, where there are two, the court will not permit advantage to be taken of such defective execution of a power, but will compel the co-administrator to join in the execution of the power. If it were a mere power, the court would

Through the administrator.

12. No lands or tenements shall be sold by virtue of any such order of the county court unless such sale is at public vendue, and between the hours of ten o'clock in the forenoon and five o'clock of the afternoon of the same day; nor unless the time, place and terms of holding such sale were previously published for the space of four weeks, by putting up notices thereof in at least four of the most public places in the county where such real estate shall be sold, and also by causing a similar notice thereof to be published four successive weeks prior to the sale in some newspaper published in such county, or, if there be no such newspaper, then in such other newspaper in this State as the court shall direct; nor unless such real estate shall be described with common certainty in such notices. And if any executor or administrator, so ordered to make sale of any real estate, shall sell the same contrary to the provisions of this act, he shall forfeit and pay the sum of five hundred dollars, to be recovered by action of debt, in the name of THE PEOPLE OF THE STATE OF ILLINOIS, for the use of any person interested, who may prosecute for the same: *Provided*, that no such offense shall affect the validity of such sale : *And provided, further*, that such executor or administrator may sell the same on a credit of not less than six nor more than twelve months, by taking note, with good personal security and a mortgage, or sale mortgage on the premises sold, to secure the payment of the purchase-money. It shall be the duty of the executor or administrator making such sale, on or before the first day of the next term of the court thereafter, to file in the office of the clerk of said court a complete report of said sale, giving a description of the premises sold, to whom, where and upon what terms sold and a general statement of the manner in which the terms of the decree were executed. Any person interested in the premises sold, and any creditor of the estate, may file exceptions to such report, and upon the hearing thereof the court may approve such report and confirm the sale, or disapprove the same and order the premises to be resold.

The power to sell cannot be delegated by the executor or administrator to another. If he be not present the sale will not meet

not; but where there is a duty and trust to be performed by the poper exercise of the power, the court will compel it. *Thorp* v. *McCullum*, 1 Gilm. 614. In an action of ejectment, an administrator's deed, made under a decree of court, cannot be excluded as evidence because the probate court erred in granting him letters. *Wight* v. *Wallbaum*, 39 Ill. 555; *Schnell* v. *City of Chicago*, 38 id. 383.

Through the administrator.

judicial sanction. *Chambers* v. *Jones,* 72 Ill. 275; *Sebastian* v. *Johnson,* id. 282; *Kellogg* v. *Wilson,* 89 id. 357.(*w*)

13. When real estate is sold, the moneys arising from such sale shall be received by the executor or administrator applying for the order to sell, and shall be assets in his hands for the payment of debts, and shall be applied in the same manner as assets arising from the sale of personal property.(*x*)

14. In all cases where a decedent is seized of a legal or equitable title to real estate, the payment whereof has not been completed, and the estate of such decedent is unable to make complete payment therefor, with advantage to such estate, the administrator or executor may sell or dispose of such real estate upon the order of the county court, and the money arising from such sales shall be assets in the hands of such executor or administrator, as in other cases. But in all cases where the estate of any such decedent shall be solvent, and such lands as aforesaid may be paid for without prejudice to the creditors, heirs or devisees of the estate, the executor or administrator shall complete the payment for the same out of the proceeds of the personal property, in the name of the heirs or legal representatives of the decedent entitled thereto; and he shall be allowed a credit for the amount of such payments, and all reasonable expenses incurred in making the same, upon final settlement of such estate: *Provided,* that the provisions of this section shall, in nowise, interfere with the provisions of any last will or testament.(*y*)

15. THE PRACTICE. The proceeds of sale are declared to be assets in the hands of the administrator.(*z*) The statute, in effect, reserves a lien on the lands of an intestate, to secure the payment of any excess of indebtedness beyond the proceeds of the personal estate. This lien is to be enforced by the administrator for the benefit of creditors generally.(*a*) The real estate descends to the heir with this charge resting upon it. He cannot incumber or alien it, to the prejudice of the rights of creditors.(*b*)

Again, when special proceedings are authorized, by which the real estate of one may be divested and transferred to another, every material step in the course of the proceedings must be pursued.(*c*)

(*w*) Cothran's Anno'd Stat. 76. § 108.
(*x*) § 109, id.
(*y*) § 110. id., 77.
(*z*) § 109, id., 76.
(*a*) See chap. x, *infra.*

(*b*) *Vansycle* v. *Richardson,* 13 Ill. 171; 4 Kent's Com. 419, 421; *Meyer* v. *McDougal,* 47 Ill. 278.
(*c*) *Reynolds* v. *Wilson,* 15 Ill 394. See *Botsford* v. *O'Conner,* 57 id. 72.

Through the administrator.

A deficiency of assets to pay the indebtedness of the estate must first exist, to authorize the sale. This deficiency should appear from the records of the county court. The court to which the petition for the sale is addressed should be advised, by the best evidence, of the amount of indebtedness and assets, so as to determine how much of the real estate should be subjected to sale.

This evidence is the just and true account of the personal estate and debts, required by section ninety-eight to be made, by the executor or administrator, to the county court, and which must be filed in that court. The following form of account may be used.

16. ACCOUNT OF PERSONAL ESTATE AND DEBTS.

A just and true account of the personal estate and debts of A B, late of —— county, deceased.

PERSONAL ESTATE.

The undersigned, administrator of A B, deceased, charges himself as follows:

DR.

To amount of Sale Bill, all collected..........................	$500 00
" collected of A B on note..............................	50 00
" " of C D on account..........................	90 00
" (*and so on, specifying the amount of money received, from whom received, etc.*)	
Total amount received from all sources....................	$640 00

Contra.

The administrator credits himself with the following disbursements, made pursuant to order of court, as appears by receipts herewith filed:

1872. Nov. 1. By cash paid to C. T. Dutton......................	$75 00
" Nov. 16. " " J K, on his claim.................	475 00
" Dec. 2. " ". M J, "	78 00
" Dec. 2. " " J. J. S., clerk's fees...............	12 00
Total amount paid out.........	$640 00

Amount of Debts due said Estate, not collected. (See Inventory.)

Note of N O (doubtful)	$45 68
Account of C B (desperate).......................................	70 00
Note of H G, discovered after filing inventory, dated Oct. 1, 1872, payable on demand (desperate)..............................	25 00
Account of X Y (desperate).......................................	13 25
Total amount due the Estate, doubtful and desperate.........	$153 93

Through the administrator.

Amount of Claims allowed aginst the Estate, as appears from the Records of the County Court.

E H........	$690 00
L S	380 00
Amount forward............	$1,070 00
Brought forward............	$1,070 00
L K	890 00
L M	105 00
W C............	100 00
J K............	1,000 00
M R (*and so on, stating all claims, whether allowed or not*).	
Total amount of claims allowed............	$3,165 00
Estimated amount of liabilities of estate not yet allowed, but probably valid............	800 00
Total indebtedness of estate............	$3,965 00
Deducting amount paid out............	640 00
	$3,325 00
Deduct probable amount that may be collected or received on doubtful and desperate debts............	75 00
Leaving as deficit of assets............	$3,250 00

I, C D, administrator of the estate of A B, deceased, do certify that the foregoing is a true and just account of the personal estate and the debts of said deceased, as far as I have been able to discover.

Dec. 3, 18 .

C D,
Administrator of A B.

The administrator must, before applying for a sale of the real estate, file such an account in the county court, have it approved and recorded. It then will be evidence—a proper basis for a valid sale of the real estate. A *true account* requires something more than a general statement of the amount of assets and indebtedness of the estate—a statement of the particular debts and credits.

Before application to sell the real estate, the inventory, appraisement bill and sale bill should also be filed in court, and all the available personal estate, or its proceeds, applied toward the payment of the debts of the decedent.

The following then are the necessary proceedings preliminary to an order of sale of real estate :

First. The filing of the inventory, appraisement bill, and sale bill.

Through the administrator.

Second. Rendering a just and true account of the personal estate and debts of the deceased.

Third. The petition and the evidence required.

Section 103, of the Statute of Wills, required a notice and was repealed by the 12th section of the law of 1857.

The decision in *Bowles' Heirs* v. *Rouse, Adm'r,*(d) prepared the way for the law of 1857,(e) substantially re-enacted in 1872.(f)

The following form of petition may be used:

PETITION FOR SALE OF REAL ESTATE.

STATE OF ILLINOIS, } ss: *In the County Court of* county, to County. term, 18 .

To the Hon. , *the judge of said court:*

The petition of C D, of said county of , administrator of the goods, chattels and effects of A B, late of said county, deceased, intestate, respectfully represents:

That your petitioner was, on the day of , A. D. 18 , appointed by the county court of county aforesaid, administrator of the goods and chattels, rights and credits of said intestate, as will appear by letters of administration, ready here in court to be shown.

And your petitioner further shows that he has filed in the county court of said county, as such administrator, his inventory, and the appraisement bill and sale bill, of the estate of said intestate, as required by law, and has also rendered to said court a just and true account of the personal estate and debts of the said deceased, a certified copy of which account is hereto annexed, and made part of this petition, market " Exhibit A." That the personal estate of the said intestate is insufficient to pay the just claims against the said estate, as will appear by reference to the said account, and also (*here set forth any other matter of import for the court to know in the case.*)

And your petitioner shows, more particularly, that the amount of money received by your petitioner as such administrator, from all sources, is *six hundred and forty* dollars, as will appear from said account (Exhibit A), and ; that he has paid out, by order of said court, on claims allowed, the sum of *six hundred and forty* dollars, as will also appear from said exhibit; that he has faithfully applied such part of the personal estate and the proceeds thereof as have come to his possession toward the payment of the debts of the said deceased, which will more particularly and fully appear by reference to said Exhibit A, and the said .

And your petitioner further represents unto your Honor, that the claims allowed against and the liabilities of the said estate amount to the sum of dollars, as will also appear by said exhibit and , of which he has paid *six hundred and forty* dollars; that there are doubtful and desperate claims in his hands in favor of said estate amounting to *one hundred and forty-three*

(d) 3 Gilm. 419.
(e) *Gibson* v. *Roll*, 27 Ill. 90.

(f) §§ 97–108, R. S. 1874, pp. 121–124.

Through the administrator.

dollars, of which he will probably collect or receive the sum of   dollars, after placing which as of the assets, there is a deficiency of personal property to pay the debts of the deceased, all which will more fully and particularly appear from said account marked "Exhibit A," and said   .

And your petitioner further represents, that the said intestate died seized in fee of the following described real estate, situated in the said county of   , and State of Illinois, to wit: The north-east quarter of Section No.   , in Township No.   , north of Range No.   , east of the 4th principal meridian; that the said real estate is reasonably worth the sum of $.

And your petitioner further represents that the said intestate died, leaving him surviving his widow J B, and the following named children (*here insert names of children*), who are his only heirs at law; that the said   and   are minors under the age of twenty-one years, and have no guardians residing in said   county. (*Here insert the names of minor children who have guardians, naming such guardians; also the names of devisees; also the names of actual occupants, if known, if not known, then make them parties by the name of "unknown parties"—all of whom, to wit (naming widow, heirs, devisees, minors having guardians, and guardians, and those not having such, and occupants), are hereby made parties hereto, and are interested herein.*

Wherefore, in consideration of the premises, your petitioner prays that the said (*here naming them again*), may be summoned and required to answer all the matters herein stated and charged, though not on oath, the necessity of answer under oath being hereby expressly waived, and for the order and decree of this honorable court, granting him leave to sell the said real estate, or so much thereof as may be necessary to pay the debts of the said intestate, and that a guardian *ad litem* be appointed for the said minor heirs, and for such other or further order or decree in the premises as may be deemed necessary, pursuant to the statute in such case made and provided, and the custom and practice of this honorable court.

And your petitioner will ever pray, etc.

C D,
Administrator of A B, deceased.

The usual chancery summons, *mutatis mutandis*, will be sufficient, stating the nature of the suit.

An affidavit is required to be made in three distinct cases:

(1.) Where a defendant is a non-resident of the State, or has gone out of it, or, on due inquiry, cannot be found.

(2.) Where he is concealed within the State, so that process cannot be served on him.

(3.) Where defendants are unknown.

On filing the necessary affidavit, a notice like the following may be published, as directed:

Through the administrator.

NOTICE OF PENDENCY OF SUIT.

STATE OF ILLINOIS, } ss: *In*   *County Court.*
     County.   *To the*   term, A. D. 18 .

C D   )   Petition for order of sale of real estate, to pay the
    v.   }   debts of the estate of A B, deceased, late of   , in-
E F, G H, I J, etc.)   testate.

Public notice is hereby given to the said E F, of, etc., that a petition has been filed in the office of the clerk of said court in the above-entitled cause, by C D, administrator of, etc., against the defendants above named, praying for sale of the real estate of said A B, deceased, which is described as follows: (*Here describe, with legal certainty, the lands to be affected*), to pay debts, and that an affidavit has been filed in said office, stating that you, the said E F, are a non-resident of this State (*or any of the grounds above stated*), and was such non-resident at the time of the commencement of this action, and that a summons has been issued in this cause, returnable on the first day of the next   term of said court, to be holden at   , on the third Monday of   , A. D. 18 . Now, unless you, the said E F, shall be and appear at said court, on the said first day of the   term thereof, to be holden as above, and plead to and answer said petition, the said petition will be taken as confessed by you, the said E F, and a decree for sale of said real estate as prayed will be entered for payment of said debts.

[L. S.]   Witness G H, clerk of, etc., and the seal of said court, this   day of   , A. D. 18 .

The proceedings in matters of process compelling appearance and preparing the issues are prescribed to be according to the chancery practice.

We shall give a complete record of an application contested at every step further on under the PROBATE RECORD. (*g*)

Rules and orders may, after the parties are in court, be made with great facility as occasion requires.

In these proceedings, from their inception to their close, the advice or judgment of the county judge having jurisdiction should be taken at every turn. He is the arbiter, the impartial conservator of these estates. If the application be resisted, then notice of every step in the cause should be given, unless in the minor matters of the suit.

Counsel will be required, and the admirable decisions of our supreme court in chancery and in administration and conservation will guide to a correct course of procedure in such cases. (*h*)

The county judge sitting quite like a chancellor in cases involving these high trusts, and the rights and property of the orphan, the widow, the absent, the unknown, and the incapacitated — those

(*g*) See Hill's Chan. Pr., Process, Pleadings, etc.   (*h*) Hill's Chan. Pr. 6, 7.

Through the guardian.

incapable of protecting either themselves or their property, is an exercise of administrative and judicial power, equal to any known to the court of chancery. Such provisions indicate the wise statesmanship that prompted them, and the confidence in our lesser courts which the integrity and ability of their learned judges, from the earliest period of our judicial history, have inspired.

For our idea of the form which such proceedings should wear, and the necessary steps to be taken throughout such a course, we would respectfully refer the reader to the probate record further on.(i)

From the filing of the petition for forms, see chapter XIV, *infra*.

SECTION III.—ADMINISTRATION OVER REAL ESTATE THROUGH THE GUARDIAN.

1. The guardian may lease the ward's real estate with the approval of the court.
2. He may by leave of court mortgage the same.
3. Petition for order must be filed however.
4. Foreclosure of such mortgages only to be made by petition to the court in which letters of guardianship were granted.
5. Decree of strict foreclosure not to be entered, and redemption as in case of judgments prescribed.
6. Proceedings prescribed for the sale of the ward's real estate; petition; venue, etc., etc.
7. The petition; its requisites, to be verified and filed.
8. Notice to be published and served.
9. Cause to be docketed and proceed as if a case in chancery. (See Hill's Chan. Pr.)
10. The sale, notice of the time and place to be given; sale may be on credit; credit how given, securities required.
11. Report of sale to be forthwith made and approved and recorded, and to vest in the purchasers the title of the property.
12. Guardian to account for proceeds of sales of real estate on oath.
13. Duty of court to keep the securities of the guardian good.
14. Guardian, if insolvent or in doubtful circumstances, may be required to give to his securities counter-securities.
15. The practice indicated.
16. Forms for pleadings, affidavits, process, orders, decrees, etc., etc.
17. Foreign guardians may sell when.
18. And under like process and procedure.

(i) See chap. xiv, *infra*.

Through the guardian.

19. Sales to invest purchasers with the title.
20. Foreign guardians must give security for costs, before commencing any proceeding.

1. The guardian may lease the real estate of the ward upon such terms and for such length of time, not extending beyond the minority of the ward, as the county court shall approve.(j)

2. The guardian may, by leave of the county court, mortgage the real estate of the ward for a term of years not exceeding the minority of the ward, or in fee; but the time of the maturity of the indebtedness secured by such mortgage shall not be extended beyond the time of minority of the ward.(k)

3. Before any mortgage shall be made, the guardian shall petition the county court for an order authorizing such mortgage to be made, in which petition shall be set out the condition of the estate, and the facts and circumstances on which the petition is founded, and a description of the premises sought to be mortgaged.(l)

4. Foreclosures of mortgages authorized by this act shall only be made by petition to the county court of the county where letters of guardianship were granted, or in case of non-resident minors, in the county in which the premises, or some part thereof, are situated, in which proceeding the guardian and ward shall be made defendants; and any sale made by virtue of any order or decree of foreclosure of such mortgage may, at any time before confirmation, be set aside by the court for inadequacy of price, or other good cause, and shall not be binding upon the guardian or ward until confirmed by the court.(m)

5. No decree of strict foreclosure shall be made upon any such mortgage, but redemption shall be allowed as is now provided by law in cases of sales under executions upon common-law judgments,(n) that is, within twelve months.

6. On the petition of the guardian, the county court of the county where the ward resides, or if the ward does not reside in the State, of the county where the real estate, or some part of it, is situated, may order the sale of the real estate of the ward, for his support and education, when the court shall deem it necessary, or to invest the proceeds in other real estate, or for the purpose of otherwise investing the same.(o)   *Provided*, the said county court shall make

(j) § 23, R. S. 1874, p. 561.
(k) § 24, id.
(l) § 25, id.
(m) § 26, R. S. 1874, p. 561.

(n) § 27, id.
(o) § 28, as amended May 21, 1877; Cothran's Stats., 1880, 771.

Through the guardian.

no order for a sale, under said petition, until the said guardian shall have executed and filed a bond, payable to the people of the State of Illinois, with at least two sufficient sureties, to be approved by the court, in double the value of the real estate by said petition sought to be sold, conditioned for the due and faithful accounting for and disposition of the proceeds of all real estate that may be sold by him under such order, in the manner provided by law; which bond may be put in suit, in the name of the people of the State of Illinois, to the use of any person entitled to recover on a breach thereof, and damages assessed and proceedings had thereon, as in other cases of penal bonds.

7. The petition shall set forth the condition of the estate and the facts and circumstances on which the petition is founded, and shall be signed by the guardian and verified by his affidavit, and shall be filed at least ten days before the commencement of the term of court at which the application shall be made. (*p*)

8. Notice of such application shall be given to all persons concerned, by publication in some newspaper published in the county where the application is made, at least once in each week for three successive weeks, or by setting up written or printed notices in three of the most public places in the county, at least three weeks before the session of the court at which such application shall be made. The ward shall be served with a copy of such notice at least ten days before the hearing of such application. (*q*)

9. Such application shall be docketed as other causes, and the petition may be amended, heard or continued for further notice, or for other cause. The practice in such cases shall be the same as in other cases of chancery. (*r*)

10. The court shall direct notice of the time and place of sale to be given, and may direct the sale to be made on reasonable credit, and require such security of the guardian or purchaser as the interest of the ward may require. (*s*)

11. It shall be the duty of the guardian making such sale, as soon as may be, to make return of such sale to the court granting the order, which, if approved, shall be recorded, and shall vest in the purchaser or purchasers all the interest of the ward in the estate so sold. (*t*)

(*p*) § 29, Cothran's Stats., 771.
(*q*) § 30, id. p. 772.
(*r*) § 31, id.
(*s*) § 32, Cothran's Stats., 772.
(*t*) § 33, id.

Through the guardian.

12. An account of all moneys and securities received by any guardian, for the sale of real estate of his ward, shall be returned on oath of such guardian to the county court of the county where letters of guardianship were obtained, and such money shall be accounted for, and subject to the order of the county court, in like manner as other moneys belonging to such minor. In case of sale for re-investment in this State, the money shall be re-invested under the direction of the court. (*u*)

13. It shall be the duty of the county court, at each accounting of the guardian, to inquire into the sufficiency of his sureties, and if at any time it has cause to believe that the sureties of a guardian are insufficient or in failing circumstances, it shall, after summoning the guardian if he be not before the court, require him to give additional security.(*v*)

14. Upon the application of the surety of any guardian, and after summoning the guardian, the court may, if it believes him to be insolvent or in doubtful circumstances, require him to give counter security to his sureties. (*w*)

15. THE PRACTICE INDICATED. See chapter XIV, *infra*.

16. FORMS, ETC. See chapter XIV, *infra*.

17. SALE OF REALTY BY FOREIGN GUARDIAN. Where any person residing in any other State of the United States, or any territory thereof, shall have been or may hereafter be appointed guardian, in the State or territory in which such person resides, of any infant or other person owning real estate within this State, not having any guardian in this State, it shall and may be lawful for every such guardian to file his or her petition in the circuit court of the county in which said real estate, or the major part thereof, may lie, for sale of said real estate, for the purpose of educating and supporting such infant, or other persons under guardianship, or for the purpose of investing the proceeds of such real estate in such manner as the court which appointed such guardian may order and direct; and the said circuit court is hereby fully authorized and empowered to order a sale of such real estate conformably to the prayer of said petition. *Provided*, that every such guardian applying for such sale shall file with his or her petition an authenticated copy of his or her letters

---

(*u*) § 34, R. S. 1874, p. 562.
(*v*) § 35, id.
(*w*) § 36, R. S. 1874, p. 562.

Through the guardian.

of guardianship. *And provided, further,* that the said circuit court shall make no order for a sale under said petition until the said guardian shall have executed and filed in the court which appointed said guardian, a bond, with sufficient security, approved by said last-mentioned court, for the due and faithful application of the proceeds of every such sale, in such manner as the said last-mentioned court may direct; an authenticated copy of which said bond, and the approval thereof, shall be deemed and taken by the circuit court as sufficient evidence of the execution and filing of the same.(*x*)

18. Every guardian, applying for an order of sale under the foregoing section, shall be required to give notice of his or her petition in the same manner as is now required by law in cases of application for sales of lands belonging to minors by resident guardians; and in every order for the sale of real estate under this act, it shall be the duty of the court to prescribe the terms of said sale, and the notice which shall be given thereof, and the place where such sale shall be made.(*y*)

19. All sales of real estate, under the provisions of this act, are thereby declared to be good and valid; and all deeds executed by such guardian to the purchaser or purchasers under such sales shall convey to and vest in such purchaser or purchasers all the estate, right, title and interest, in law or equity, of said infant or others in and to the land so sold.(*z*) If the court authorizing the sale have jurisdiction, the sale will not be invalidated by the irregularity of the proceedings of the guardian in executing the order of sale The purchaser is not bound to see to the application of the funds.(*a*)

20. In all suits and petitions by non-resident guardians, they shall give a bond for costs, as in cases of other non-residents.(*b*)

A subsequent deed, executed by a guardian for the purpose of explaining a former deed, and correcting mistakes therein, made some years after the first deed, is improper, as it amounts only to the declarations of the guardian made when he could not, by such declaration, affect the interest of his wards. The guardian's power was exhausted when he had made the sale and the first conveyance, and his acts were approved by the court.(*c*)

WHEN TITLE INURES; COVENANTS. Where a ward subsequently

(*x*) § 47, R. S. 1874, p. 563.
(*y*) § 48, R. S. 1874, pp. 563, 564.
(*z*) § 49, id.

(*a*) *Mulford* v. *Beveridge,* 78 Ill. 455
(*b*) § 50, R. S. 1874, pp. 563, 564.
(*c*) *Young* v. *Lorain,* 11 Ill. 625.

Through the guardian.

acquires from the government of the United States a patent for the premises which had been sold by his guardians, at a guardian's sale, under the statute. *Held*, that his independent title, subsequently acquired, did not inure to the benefit of a previous purchaser at a guardian's sale; nor was he estopped by the guardian's deed from setting up such subsequent title. *Held*, also, that the guardian could not insert any covenants in the deed which would be binding on his ward. If the guardian chooses to insert covenants in the deed, he may be held personally upon them, and to him alone must the grantee look.(*b*)

Upon a sale of land by a guardian, the title is defective, unless the guardian makes a report of his proceedings, and has the same confirmed by the order of the court authorizing the sale.(*c*) As to what stage of the case the report is to be made, the statute is silent.(*d*)

For a case where the minors were held to be estopped from attacking such an unconfirmed sale.(*e*)

CONFIRMING SALES. The discretion to be used by the court, in confirming sales of guardians, must conform to established principles.(*f*)

The English practice of opening biddings at such sales is not a sufficient cause for setting aside a sale.(*f*)

A sale by a guardian of his ward's land will not be sustained, unless it be shown that it was necessary for the infant's education and support. And applications by a guardian, for the sale of his ward's real estate, must be made in the county where the ward resides, although the estate may lie in a different county, and should state affirmatively such residence.(*g*)

A guardian must follow the directions of the probate court; and if, on an order being made, he finds he has no funds, he may then make application for a sale of his ward's land.(*g*) .

Minors need not be made parties to a proceeding asking an order of sale of their property for their support and education. Such an application is for their benefit, and not adverse to them.(*h*)

(*b*) *Young* v. *Lorain*, 11 Ill. 625.
(*c*) *Young* v. *Keogh*, 11 Ill. 642; *Ayres* v. *Baumgarten*, 15 Id. 444; *Young* v. *Dowling*, id. 481. (Defective in equity.)
(*d*) *Mulford* v. *Beveridge*, 78 Ill. 455.

(*e*) *Penn* v. *Heisey*, 19 Ill. 295.
(*f*) *Ayres* v. *Baumgarten*, 15 Ill. 444.
(*g*) *Loyd* v. *Malone*, 23 Ill. 43.
(*h*) *Fitzgibbon* v. *Lake*, 29 Ill. 165; *Smith* v. *Race*, 27 Id. 387.

Through the conservator.

Where the legislature authorizes a guardian to sell the land of his ward, under the direction and sanction of the judge of probate, a sale made without such sanction and direction is void.(*i*)

The jurisdiction of the circuit court, to order a sale of the real estate of a ward, on the application of the guardian, cannot be questioned collaterally where the contingency provided for by the statute existed. And all objections taken to the notices of the sale, posting them, and other matters involved in the adjudication of the circuit court, either in granting the order of sale or in the final order confirming the report of the guardian, can avail nothing in a collateral action.(*j*)

Whether one or two guardians named in a will had authority to apply for an order of sale, and whether the sale was regular, were questions for the court to determine where the application was made, and cannot be inquired into collaterally.(*k*)

An order entered by mistake, dismissing the proceeding after decree, and before the confirmation of sale, would not vacate the order of sale, nor revoke the authority of the guardian.(*k*)

The only power a guardian has over his ward's lands is to lease the same upon such terms and for such length of time as the county court shall approve. He is not entitled, nor is it made his duty, to take possession of the real estate of his ward.(*l*)

DOWER. It is the duty of a guardian to institute proceedings for the assignment of dower.(*m*)

It is equally his duty to lease such portion of the estate as is set apart to the wards; and his estate is liable for whatever might have been received by a faithful discharge of those duties.(*m*)

CONVERSION. If a guardian severs rails in a fence on the land of his wards and the widow, and converts them to his own use, his estate is answerable directly to the heirs for their value.(*m*)

SECTION IV.—ADMINISTRATION OVER REAL ESTATE THROUGH THE CONSERVATOR.

The law on this subject may be found at pp. 138, *et seq.*, *supra*. See Cothran's Annotated Statutes, 1880, p. 955.

(*i*) *Mason* v. *Wait*, 4 Scam. 127.
(*j*) *Young* v. *Lorain*, 11 Ill. 625;
Harvey v. *Sweet*, 16 Id. 127.
(*k*) *Fitzgibbon* v. *Lake*, 29 Ill. 165.
(*l*) *Muller* v. *Benner*, 69 Ill. 108.
(*m*) *Clark* v. *Burnside*, 15 Ill. 62.

Demands classified.

CHAPTER VIII.

EXPENSES, ALLOWANCES, CLAIMS AND LEGACIES.

SECTION I. Demands classified, the widow's award, funeral expenses, and expenses of last illness.
    II. Claims against estates.
    III. Legacies.

SECTION I. — DEMANDS CLASSIFIED, WIDOW'S AWARD, AND EXPENSES.

1. Demands classified.
2. To be classed in order as prescribed, and paid class by class, when insufficient, demands paid *pro rata*.
3. Demand of executor or administrator to be filed and defended against: how.
4. Demands to be entered and classed, papers to be filed and preserved.
5. Award to the widow and children, or the "widow's award."
6. Duty of appraisers in making the award.
7. Renouncing or failing to renounce under the will by the widow, not to affect her award.
8. Award to be to the children if there be no widow when decedent was a householder.
9. The widow or surviving husband may renounce in writing all benefit under the will, and receive property as if the decedent had died intestate.
10. Legacies and bequests, if diminished by renunciation, to be equalized.
11. Widow, when liable for waste.
12. Relinquishment of specified articles and further selection by the widow.
13. Statement thereof to the court.
14. Estimate of specific property.
15. Expenses attending the last illness.

1. DEMANDS CLASSIFIED. All demands against the estate of any testator or intestate shall be divided into classes, in manner following, to wit:

First. Funeral expenses.

Second. The widow's award, if there is a widow, or children, if there are children and no widow.

Third. Expenses attending the last illness, not including physician's bill.

Demands classified.

Fourth. Debts due the common school or township fund.

Fifth. All expenses of proving the will, and taking out letters testamentary or of administration, and settlement of the estate, and the physician's bill in the last illness of the deceased.

Sixth. Where the decedent has received money in trust for any purpose, his executor or administrator shall pay out of his estate the amount thus received and not accounted for.

Seventh. All other debts and demands of whatsoever kind, without regard to quality or dignity, which shall be exhibited to the court within two years from the granting of letters as aforesaid: and all demands not exhibited within two years as aforesaid, shall be forever barred, unless the creditors shall find other estate of the deceased, not inventoried or accounted for by the executor or administrator, in which case their claims shall be paid *pro rata* out of such subsequently discovered estate, saving, however, to *femmes couverte,* infants, persons of unsound mind, or imprisoned, or without the United States in the employment of the United States or of this State, the term of two years after their respective disabilities are removed to exhibit their claims.(*a*) Generally it is no part of an administrator's duty to pay a claim against an estate before it is allowed by the court. If he does so he must take the risk of its proof and allowance.(*b*)

2. All claims against estates, when allowed by the county court, shall be classed and paid by the executor or administrator, in the manner provided in this act, commencing with the first class; and when the estate is insufficient to pay the whole of the demands, the demands in any one class shall be paid, *pro rata,* whether the same are due by judgment, writing obligatory, or otherwise, except as otherwise provided.(*c*)

3. When an executor or administrator has a demand against his testator or intestate's estate, he shall file his demand as other persons; and the court shall appoint some discreet person to appear and defend for the estate, and, upon the hearing, the court or jury shall allow such demand, or such part thereof as is legally established, or reject the same, as shall appear just. Should any executor or administrator appeal in such case, the court shall appoint some person to defend as aforesaid.(*d*) No allowance for burdens voluntarily assumed by an administrator or executor, on behalf of the estate, while under no duty to act or protect it, may be allowed.(*e*)

4. The county court shall make an entry of all demands against estates, classing the same as above provided, and file and preserve the papers belonging to the same. If an executor or administrator

---

(*a*) § 70, R. S. 1874, p. 116.
(*b*) *Walker* v. *Diehl,* 79 Ill. 473.
(*c*) § 71, R. S. 1874, p. 117.

(*d*) § 72, R. S. 1874, p. 117.
(*e*) *Ex parte Allen, Adm'r.,* 89 Ill. 474.

Award to widow or children.

pays a claim before the same is allowed as aforesaid, said court shall require such executor or administrator to establish the validity of such claim by the like evidence as is required in other cases, before the same is classed, and be credited therewith.(*d*)

Funeral expenses are too well known to require specification; the coffin, the shroud, the carriages, the sexton, etc., familiar to all.

5. AWARD TO WIDOW OR CHILDREN. The widow, residing in this State, of a deceased husband whose estate is administered in this State, whether her husband died testate or intestate, shall in all cases, in exclusion of debts, claims, charges, legacies and bequests, except funeral expenses, be allowed as her sole and exclusive property forever, the following, to wit:

First. The family pictures and the wearing apparel, jewels and ornaments of herself and her minor children.

Second. School books and family library of the value of one hundred dollars.

Third. One sewing machine.

Fourth. Necessary beds, bedsteads and bedding for herself and family.

Fifth. The stoves and pipes used in the family, with the necessary cooking utensils; or, in case they have none, fifty dollars in money.

Sixth. Household and kitchen furniture to the value of one hundred dollars.

Seventh. One milch cow and calf for every four members of her family.

Eighth. Two sheep for each member of her family, and the fleeces taken from the same, and one horse, saddle and bridle.

Ninth. Provisions for herself and family for one year.

Tenth. Food for the stock above specified, for six months.

Eleventh. Fuel for herself and family for three months.

Twelfth. One hundred dollars worth of other property suited to her condition in life to be selected by the widow.

Which shall be known as the widow's award, or the widow may, if she elect, take and receive in lieu of the foregoing, the same personal property, or money in place thereof, as is or may be exempt

(*d*) § 73, R. S. 1874, p. 117.

Award to widow or children.

from execution or attachment against the head of a family residing with the same.(*e*)

6. The appraisers shall make out and certify to the county court an estimate of the value of each of the several items of property allowed to the widow; and it shall be lawful for the widow to elect whether she will take the specific articles set apart to her, or take the amount thereof out of other personal property at the appraised value thereof, or whether she will take the amount thereof in money, or she may take a part in property and a part in money, as she may prefer; and in all such cases it shall be the duty of the executor or administrator to notify the widow as soon as such appraisement shall be made, and to set apart to her such article or articles of property, not exceeding the amount to which she may be entitled, and as she may prefer or select, within thirty days after written application shall be made for that purpose by such widow. And if such executor or administrator shall neglect or refuse to comply with the above requisition, when application shall be made for that purpose, he shall forfeit and pay for the use of such widow the sum of twenty dollars per month for each month's delay to set apart said property so selected, after the said term of thirty days shall have elapsed, to be recovered in the name of the People of the State of Illinois, for the use of such widow, in any court having jurisdiction of the same. When there is not property of the estate, of the kinds mentioned in the preceding section, the appraisers may award the widow a gross sum in lieu thereof, except for family pictures, jewels and ornaments.(*f*)

7. The right of a widow to her award shall in no case be affected by her renouncing or failing to renounce the benefit of the provisions made for her in the will of her husband, or otherwise.(*g*)

8. When the person dying is at the time of his death a housekeeper, the head of a family, and leaves no widow, there shall be allowed to the children of the deceased, residing with him at the time

---

(*e*) § 74, R. S. 1874, p. 117. The widow takes, in addition to dower in the realty, one-third of the net personalty, after all claims are paid (*Sisk* v. *Smith*, 1 Gilm. 503), also the specific allowance under this act where the estate is solvent. If it is not solvent, then for any deficiency of the personalty to pay her separate allowance, she ranks as a creditor of the estate. *Cruce* v. *Cruce*, 21 Ill. 47. Chap. x, *infra.* See chap. 52, R. S. 1874, p. 497.

(*f*) § 75, R. S. 1874, p. 117. In *Cruce* v. *Cruce*, 21 Ill., the court held that where the intestate leaves no property of the kind specified in the statute, the widow shall be entitled to other property of equal value, and that it is the duty of the administrator to set apart to her such property. See *Tyson* v. *Postlethwaite*, 13 Ill. 727.

(*g*) § 76, R. S. 1874, p. 118.

Award to widow or children.

of his death (including all males under eighteen years of age, and all females), the same amount of property as is allowed to the widow by this act.(*h*)

9. WIDOW OR SURVIVING HUSBAND MAY RENOUNCE THE WILL. The widow or surviving husband of a testate may, at any time within one year from the time at which the will of her or his testate husband or wife was admitted to probate, renouncing in writing all her or his claim to the legacies and bequests made for her or him in such will, in which case she or he shall be allowed the same property as if the husband or wife had died intestate.(*i*)

10. In all cases where a widow or surviving husband shall renounce all benefit under the will, and the legacies and bequests therein con-

---

(*h*) § 77, R. S. 1874, p. 118. In the case of *Lesher* v. *Wirth*, 14 Ill. 39, it appeared, that on the 25th of September, 1840, one Henry Fox died intestate, leaving Adelia Fox his widow, and a number of children his heirs at law; that his estate was settled in due course of administration, and his widow allowed her separate provision under the statute; that she died September 25, 1848, leaving personal estate to the amount of about $150 or $200; that Lesher, a physician, attended her during her last illness. The probate court ordered the whole of the property to be distributed among the children, under the section in question. Appeal was taken to the circuit court, and the judgment below affirmed. Lesher brought writ of error against Wirth, the administrator. The court said, the only question in this case is, whether the children, where the intestate is a widow, who was at the time of her death a householder, and the head of a family, shall take under the provisions of this section the same as if the intestate had been a widower. "To me," said the court, CATON, J., "it seems exceedingly clear that the children are entitled to take the property left by a mother, the same as if left by a father." Widow's claim to the specific articles allowed her. Immediately on the death of the husband, the right of the widow accrues, and if she die before she receives the specific articles, and they not having been set off to her administrator, their value must be accounted for to him as assets of her estate. *York* v. *York*, 38 Ill. 522. In *Viele* v. *Koch* it was held that A was not a housekeeper within the meaning of the fourth section of the act entitled "An act to amend an act relative to wills," etc., and that his children could not receive the same amount of property that would have been allowed by law to his widow. 27 Ill. 129. A widow, whose husband died intestate, leaving no children or descendants, may recover in assumpsit for the property of her deceased husband, which she has sold, although letters of administration have never issued upon the estate. *Cross* v. *Carey*, 25 Ill. 562. The statute providing for an allowance to a widow of such beds, bedsteads, bedding, and household and kitchen furniture as may be necessary for herself and family, and provisions for a year for herself and family, is to be construed in reference to the circumstances of the parties; and in fixing such allowance, the appraisers should take into view the condition and mode of life in which the widow was left by the death of her husband, and regard as necessary that furniture which is the ordinary and appropriate furniture for such homesteads. *Strawn* v. *Strawn*, 53 Ill. 263. The widow of a person who dies intestate is entitled, as her sole and separate property, to certain specified articles of the intestate's estate, or their value. The children of a widow who dies intestate, a housekeeper, and the head of a family, take the same articles of property that they would take if the intestate were a widower. *Lesher* v. *Wirth*, 14 Ill. 39.

(*i*) Coth. Rev. Stats., p. 550, § 10–12.

Award to widow or children.

tained, to other persons, shall, in consequence thereof, become diminished or increased in amount, quantity or value, it shall be the duty of the court, upon settlement of such estate, to abate from or add to such legacies and bequests in such manner as to equalize the loss sustained or advantage derived thereby, in a corresponding ratio to the several amounts of such legacies and bequests, according to the amount or intrinsic value of each.(*j*)

11. If the widow commits waste in the lands and tenements, or the personal estate of the deceased, she shall be liable to an action by the heir or devisee, or his or her guardian, if of real estate, or by the executor or administrator if of personal estate; and if she marry a subsequent husband, he shall be answerable with her in damages for any waste committed by her, or by the husband himself, after such marriage.(*k*)

12. If the widow (or children, as the case may be) elect to take other articles than those specified in the statute, she (or they) should RELINQUISH THE RIGHT to the specified articles, and signify to the administrator what particular articles mentioned in the appraisement bill she desires to retain in lieu thereof, and the articles relinquished are then to be sold as the other property of the deceased. The following form will be found convenient for such relinquishment and selection:

WIDOW'S (OR CHILDREN'S) RELINQUISHMENT OF SPECIFIC PROPERTY.

I, M B, widow of A B, deceased, do hereby relinquish all my claim to the following articles, mentioned in the "estimate of specific property," allowed me, viz.: 10 sheep, 1 cow, etc., the aggregate value of which, as estimated, is $; and in lieu of the same I desire to retain the following articles, named in the "appraisement bill of personal property" of said A B, deceased, viz.: 1 buggy, 1 harness, etc., the total value of which, as appraised, is $, and the balance I prefer to have in money.

Witness my hand and seal, this   day of   , A. D 18 .
[L. S.]   M. B.

After such relinquishment and selection has been made known to the administrator, he should proceed to set out such articles to her, and withdraw from sale what she has selected, and sell what she has relinquished.

He should file in court the relinquishment, and a statement of the property actually taken by the widow (or children), with its appraised value, which may be in the following form:

(*j*) § 79, R. S. 1874, p. 118.   (*k*) § 80, R. S. 1874, p. 118.

Award to widow or children.

13. Articles of specific property set off to M B, widow of A B, deceased.

State of Illinois, } ss:
County.   In the County Court of   county,
                                    term, 18 .

To the Judge of said   court:

The undersigned, administrator of A B, deceased, would respectfully submit the following report of specific property set off to M B, widow of A B, in accordance with her relinquishment and selection, and pursuant to the statute in such case made and provided, as follows:

ARTICLES.	APPRAISED VALUE.
1 Buggy	$50 00
1 Harness	15 00
1 Cow	30 00
Beds	10 00
Total value	$105 00

Value of specific property as estimated and allowed by law .. $500 00
Balance due said A B in money. .... $

                                      C D,
                        Administrator of A B, deceased.

14. Estimate of specific property.

An estimate of the specific property allowed M B, widow (*or* E B and G B, children) of A B, deceased.

NAMES OF ARTICLES.	VALUATION.
2 Beds, at $5 each	$10 00
2 Cows, at $30 each	60 00
2 Calves, at $5 each	10 00
1 Horse	40 00

(And so on through the list. The one hundred dollars' worth of other property is not a subject for the estimation of value.)

Total value of specific property left by deceased................. $

Value of articles named in the statute of which the said A B did not die seized:

ARTICLES.	ESTIMATION.
10 Sheep, at $2 per head	$20 00
Necessary fuel for three months	15 00
Provisions for one year	200 00
Total	$

Total value of specific articles left by deceased brought down........
Add $100 worth of other property................................. 100 00

    Total.. $

Claims against estates.

The undersigned, appraisers of the personal estate of A B, deceased, do certify that the family of the deceased consists of the said widow and four children; that the foregoing is a complete schedule of all articles of personal property specified in the statute left by deceased, and a true estimate of the value of the same respectively; and that the articles named in said statute not left by the deceased, suitable to the condition in life of the said widow and her family, are of the value as above estimated.

Witness our hands and seals, this   day of   , A. D. 18   .
[L. S.]   A B.
[L. S.]   R S,
[L. S.]   T W,
                                         Appraisers.

15. THE EXPENSES ATTENDING THE LAST ILLNESS, NOT INCLUDING THE PHYSICIAN'S BILL. These depend upon the length and character of the illness, and the circumstances of each case. They are the necessary and usual expenses in taking the steps to prolong the life or soothe the pillow of the dying.

SECTION II. — CLAIMS AGAINST ESTATES.

1. Notice of term fixed by executor or administrator for adjustment of; procedure prescribed; jury trial, etc.
2. When a creditor may file his claim, summons to issue to the executor or administrator.
3. Return term, cause to be continued if summons be not served ten days before.
4. Procedure prescribed.
5. Claimant may be compelled to make oath that his "claim is just and unpaid."
6. Evidence.
7. Counter-claims.
8. Claims not yet due may be proven.
9. Appeal may be taken by either party to the circuit court.
10. Change of venue to circuit court if county judge be interested or a witness in any case or matter pending in his court.
11. Adjudication of claims, instructions to executors or administrators.
12. Administrator's notice.
13. Creditor's rights, how enforced.
14. Time in which claims are to be presented.
15. The decisions collated.

1. CLAIMS AGAINST ESTATES. Every administrator or executor shall fix upon a term of the court, within six months from the time

CH. VIII.] EXPENSES, ALLOWANCES AND CLAIMS. 223

Claims against estates.

of his being qualified as such administrator or executor, for the adjustment of all claims against such decedent, and shall publish a notice thereof, for three successive weeks, in some public newspaper published in the county, or if no newspaper is published in the county, then in the nearest newspaper in this State, and also by putting up a written or printed notice on the door of the courthouse, and in five other of the most public places in the county, notifying and requesting all persons having claims against such estate to attend at said term of the court for the purpose of having the same adjusted (the first publication of said notice to be given at least six weeks previous to said term), when and where such claimant shall produce his claim, in writing; and if no objection is made to said claim by the executor, administrator, widow, heirs or others interested in said estate, and the claimant swears that such claim is just and unpaid, after allowing all just credits, the court may allow such claim without further evidence, but if objection is made to such claim, the same shall not be allowed without other sufficient evidence. The court may allow either party further time to produce evidence in his favor, and the case shall be tried and determined as other suits at law. Either party may demand a jury of either six or twelve men, to try the issue, and it shall be the duty of the county clerk, when a jury is demanded, to issue a *venire* to the sheriff of the county to summon a jury, to be composed of the number demanded.(*l*)

2. Whoever has a claim against an estate, and fails to present the same for adjustment at the term of court selected by the executor or administrator, may file a copy thereof with the clerk of the court; whereupon, unless the executor or administrator will waive the issuing of process, the clerk shall issue a summons, directed to the sheriff of the county, requiring such executor or administrator to appear and defend such claim at a term of court therein specified, which summons, when served, shall be sufficient notice to the executor or administrator of the presentation of such claim.(*m*)

3. If the summons is not served ten days before the first day of the term to which it is returnable, the cause shall be continued until the next term of the court, unless the parties shall, by consent, proceed to trial at the return term.(*n*)

4. Upon the trial of such cause, the same proceedings may be had as if the claim had been presented at the time fixed for the adjust-

(*l*) § 60, R. S. 1874, p. 115. (*n*) § 62, R. S. 1874, p. 115.
(*m*) § 61, id.

ment of claims against the estate, but the estate shall not be answerable for the costs of such proceeding : *Provided*, that when defense is made the court may, if it shall deem just, order the whole or some part of the costs occasioned by such defense to be paid out of the estate.(*o*)

5. The court may, in its discretion in any case, before giving judgment against any executor or administrator, require the claimant to make oath that such claim is just and unpaid : *Provided*, that the amount of such judgment shall not in such case be increased upon the testimony of the claimant.(*p*)

6. A judgment regularly obtained, or a copy thereof duly certified and filed with the court, shall be taken as duly proven ; and all instruments in writing, signed by the testator or intestate, if the handwriting is proven and nothing is shown to the contrary, shall be deemed duly proved.(*q*)

7. When a claim is filed or suit brought against an executor or administrator, and it appears on trial that such claimant or plaintiff is indebted to such executor or administrator, the court may give judgment therefor, and execution may issue thereon in favor of the executor or administrator.(*r*)

8. Any creditor, whose debt or claim against the estate is not due, may, nevertheless, present the same for allowance and settlement, and shall thereupon be considered as a creditor under this act, and shall receive a dividend of the said decedent's estate, after deducting a rebate of interest for what he shall receive on such debt, to be computed from the time of the allowance thereof to the time such debt would have become due, according to the tenor and effect of the contract.(*s*) (See *Hall, Adm'r*, v. *Hoxsey*, 84 Ill. 616.)

9. In all cases of the allowance or rejection of claims by the county court, as provided in this act, either party may take an appeal from the decision rendered to the circuit court of the same county, in the same time and manner appeals are now taken from justices of the peace to the circuit court, by appellant giving good and sufficient bond with security to be approved by the county judge; and such appeals shall be tried *de novo* in the circuit court.(*t*)

10. In all cases and matters pending in the county court, where the judge of that court shall be interested in the same, or is a mate-

(*o*) § 63, R. S. 1874, p. 116.
(*p*) § 64, id.
(*q*) § 65, id.
(*r*) § 66, R. S. 1874, p. 116.
(*s*) § 67, id.
(*t*) § 68, id.

Claims against estates.

rial and necessary witness, the case shall be transmitted to the circuit court of the proper county, and there determined as in the county court, and the papers, with the order or judgment of the circuit court thereon, shall be duly certified and filed in the county court, and have the same effect as if determined in the county court.(*u*) It is further provided in the act giving jurisdiction to county courts, which is a later act, whenever the county judge of any county is interested in the estate of any deceased person, and the letters testamentary or of administration shall be grantable in the county of said judge, such facts shall be entered upon the records of such court, and certified to the circuit court of such county. *Provided,* that in case the judge is interested only as a creditor no change need be made except in relation to his claim.

11. ADJUDICATION OF CLAIMS. The administrator or executor should write on the back of all claims, before the same are called by the court at the regular adjudication, " no objection," or " objected to," and sign his name. Claims thus objected to are liable to be dismissed, unless the claimant appears and moves the court to set them down for trial. Claims, not so objected to, will be allowed in the discretion of the court.

The general adjudication is brought on by the —

12. ADMINISTRATOR'S NOTICE.

Public notice is hereby given, that on the first day of   next, I shall attend before the   court of   county, at   , Illinois, at 10 o'clock A. M. of said day, for the purpose of settling and adjusting all claims against the estate of   , late of said county, deceased, when and where all claimants are notified and requested to attend, and present their claims in writing against said estate for adjustment. All persons indebted to said estate are also notified to make payment to the undersigned without delay.

    , 18   .   A B, *Administrator.*(*v*)

At the time mentioned in said notice, all persons having claims against the estate may present them without giving notice to the administrator, and such claims may be adjusted at that time, though the administrator should actually be absent, for the law presumes him to be in court.(*w*) The claim should be presented in writing. If it be in a note or contract, or transcript of a judgment, the filing of such note, etc., would be sufficient.

If the claim be presented at any other time than that mentioned

(*u*) § 69, R. S. 1874, p. 116.   (*w*) *Propst* v. *Meadows*, 13 Ill. 166.
(*v*) See p. 51, *supra.*

in the administrator's notice, the administrator is to be notified of the time in the mode prescribed when the claimant intends to exhibit his demands. Ten days notice is to be given him before the time, by summons. In computing the ten days, the day of service is to be excluded.

The administrator may waive the service of notice or summons, and appear without it, which would give the court jurisdiction. The estate will not be liable for costs or claims filed after the time fixed by the administrator for the general adjustment of accounts.

EVIDENCE REQUIRED TO ESTABLISH A CLAIM. If no objection be made by the administrator, or any other person interested in the estate, the claimant shall be permitted to swear that the claim is just and unpaid. If objections be made, previous to the claim being sworn to, the account shall be adjudicated as is now required by law; that is, it is to be established by legal evidence, the same as similar matters in controversy in suits at law.

As estates of deceased persons are peculiarly exposed to imposition, and as the administrator is acting in a fiduciary capacity for the heirs and creditors, and not dealing for himself, he should not be too ready to admit the correctness of claims. Many claims, that would never be presented against a person while living, are brought forward against his estate when dead, because the ill-designing persons who hold them are aware that the knowledge of facts which would bar the claim is locked up in the grave of the deceased. The administrator is rarely familiar with the complete history of the accounts of the deceased, hence he should be satisfied, by proper evidence, of the correctness of all claims. The admission of the claimant as a witness to prove his own demand, where the administrator does not object, is a grant of discretion to the administrator, that he should exercise only in cases where he has convincing evidence to his own mind that the claim is just. He should not, in justice to the estate he represents, waive his right to object, only where he has personal knowledge or reliable assurance that the claim is just, legal and unsatisfied. The court may, in its discretion, in addition to the evidence heard on the claim, require the claimant to make oath that such claim is just and unpaid. *Provided*, that the amount of such judgment shall not be increased upon the testimony of the claimant. The law thus throws guards around the estate to protect it from the unscrupulous rapacity of

Claims against estates.

those who would despoil the widow and orphan by preying upon the estate of the dead.

In the case mentioned in this section of the law, the court may, after hearing the evidence produced by the claimant, which is not unfrequently the testimony of those whom the plaintiff has sought out as knowing but his side of the case, require the claimant himself to purge his conscience upon it. The undoubted spirit of the law is, to exact of the claimant such proof of the merits of his demand as would be required in case the suit were contested by the deceased, if living; unless the administrator, in the exercise of a sound discretion, should admit its legality, for the purpose of saving the estate the costs of unsuccessful litigation. Certified copies of unsatisfied judgments prove themselves, while the execution of notes of hand and other instruments in writing, purporting to be executed by the deceased, is to be proven; that is, the *handwriting* of the deceased is to be proved. The rule in this case differs from the law, in ordinary suits between the living, where the execution of a written instrument need not be proved, except the person denies such execution under oath. The law here does not presume the execution by the intestate, but throws the burden of its proof upon the person claiming under it.

The supreme court, in the case of *Propst* v. *Meadows*,(y) in regard to the presentation of claims against an estate, and their consideration, says: "The various provisions of these sections (z) must be considered together as regulating the practice of courts of probate, when entertaining claims against estates and adjudicating thereon. When a claim is presented at a term of the court, as designated in the notice given under the 95th section, the executor is presumed to be present, and the claimant is, therefore, not required to notify him of his intention to present his claim at that time.

"The adjudications of the court at that term upon claims must, therefore, be presumed to have been regular, and to have been made upon the proper proofs in the presence of both parties. In that section no express provision is made for the postponement of the consideration of such claims to any subsequent term. If they are not then finally disposed of, they must be continued, by an order of the court, to some specified time, or be again presented under the 118th

---

(y) 13 Ill. 157.   (z) Rev. Stat., ch. 109, §§ 95, 116, 117, 118. See R. S. 1874, p. 115.

Claims against estates.

section. This section, it will be observed, requires the person intending to present a claim to the court of probate against an executor or administrator, to give ten days' notice of the time that he intends to present the same, when the court may allow or reject the claim, or grant further time for either party to prepare for trial, according to the exigencies of the case. This section provides an intelligent and just practice for that court, and was, no doubt, intended by the legislature to be pursued in all cases of claims against estates, whether presented under a notice from the claimant or the executor, or filed under the law. (*a*) There is as much reason and propriety in allowing parties further time to prepare for the investigation of claims presented to the court by producing the necessary proofs, when the claim is presented in pursuance of the notice given by the executors to all creditors, as when the claim is presented under a notice from the creditor to the executor. It is this notice which justifies the court in taking cognizance of claims, and which requires the executor to appear and contest them. When the parties are thus before the court, its adjudication is final and conclusive upon them. What would constitute such final adjudication in all cases, it is not now necessary to determine. We are not prepared to say that the omission of the court to make an order, either disallowing the claim or continuing it for further investigation, would constitute such an adjudication as would bar the right of the claimant to prosecute it further."

It is the duty of the administrator to interpose any defense to a claim which exists, if he is aware of such defense.

Merely filing the claim is not sufficient. At final closing of his account at the end of two years, the administrator will or ought to have the claim, so filed, but not prosecuted, presented for allowance. In that case, the administrator's duty is, under the statute, to have such claim, if thus unprosecuted, dismissed. The safe course is, if the claim has not been presented on adjustment day, to file the same, or rather a copy, and have summons issued, and the claim prosecuted to allowance.

13. A CREDITOR'S RIGHT to enforce the payment of a debt by suit against the person determines at the latter's death, and his only course is to follow the deceased person's property into the

---

(*a*) § 116, R. S., ch. 109. See §§ 61, 62, R. S. 1874, p. 115.

Claims against estates.

hands of his personal representatives. The administrator, upon his appointment, takes the personal property of the deceased in trust for the payment of his debts, and to pass the surplus to his heirs. The proper mode, then, to seek the payment of a claim against a deceased person, is to look to the administrator of his goods, chattels, rights, credits and effects, or, rather, through him, to the property or assets in his hands. Before the payment of claims against an estate, they should be proved, in the mode pointed out by the statute. Though the person administering may be satisfied in his own mind that a claim is legal and just, yet he cannot safely pay it until such claim is presented to the court, and there allowed, on proof of its correctness. If an administrator should pay a claim before it is allowed, he does it at his own risk, and himself assumes the responsibility of proving the correctness of the claim in court.

14. THE TIME IN WHICH CLAIMS ARE TO BE PRESENTED. Creditors are required to exhibit their demands within two years after the grant of administration. Those free from disability, who neglect to comply with this requisition of the statute, must rely for the satisfaction of their debts on subsequently discovered estate. (*b*) The time is computed from the date of the letters of administration. The omission of the administrator to give notice of final settlement does not relieve creditors from the necessity of presenting their claims.(*c*) *Femmes couverte*, infants, persons of unsound mind, imprisoned, or beyond seas, may present their claims at any time within two years after their respective disabilities shall be removed. This provision, however, has reference only to such demands as are required to be exhibited to the court. It does not embrace the widow's award.(*d*)

15. DECISIONS. Presentation of claim by copy to one S., at the request of the administratrix, and again by giving the attorney of the estate a copy, *held* a sufficient presentation.(*e*)

PRESENTING AND REFERRING CLAIMS. An account was filed against an estate after the expiration of two years from the time of granting letters of administration upon the estate. *Held*, that the creditor had the right to have his claim passed on, and a judgment presently for the amount due, to be satisfied *pro rata* out of any

---

(*b*) 15 Ill. 49; 11 id. 341; 5 Gilm. 26; 14 Ill. 9.
(*c*) 11 Ill. 216, 349.
(*d*) *Miller* v. *Miller*, 82 Ill. 463.
(*e*) *Wells* v. *Miller*, 45 Ill. 382.

estate that might afterward be found not inventoried or accounted for by the administrator.(e)

The filing of a claim against an estate in the probate court does not arrest the general statute of limitations.(f)

It is a sufficient exhibition of a claim against an estate to file the same, or a copy thereof, with the probate court.(g)

Equitable claims against an estate may be allowed by the probate court.(h)

PARTNERSHIP DEBTS, WHEN. No claim should be allowed against an estate for a partnership debt till it is shown that all the partnership assets have been exhausted.(h)

PARTNERSHIP DEBTS — PAYMENT OF, BY ADMINISTRATOR. While the individual creditors of an estate can insist on the full payment of their debts, before the partnership creditors can receive anything from the individual assets, yet, as to the heirs, the mere order of payment is a matter of no moment, provided the partnership debts and the individual debts together fairly absorb all the partnership assets and the assets of the estate.(i)

An administrator's claim, if just, is as much entitled to payment as that of any other creditor.(j)

MARSHALLING ASSETS. The personal estate is primarily liable for the payment of the debts, and must be exhausted before resort can be had to the real estate.(k) This is so whether the debt claimed be secured or not, and the heirs and devisees have a right to enforce this rule.(l)

ARBITRATION. All claims against an estate must be presented to the probate court, and be, there, adjusted before they can be legally paid out of the assets of the estate. They cannot be submitted to arbitration by an executor or administrator.(m)

ALLOWANCE OF CLAIMS AGAINST ESTATES. The ninety-fifth section of the statute of wills contemplates that the heirs are parties, or

---

(e) *Thorn* v. *Watson, Adm'r*, 5 Gilm. 26.
(f) *Reitzell* v. *Miller*, 25 Ill. 67.
(g) *The People* v. *White*, 11 Ill. 342.
(h) *Moline Water Power & Manuf. Co.* v. *Webster*, 26 Ill. 233.
(i) *The People* v. *Lott*, 36 Ill. 447.
(j) *Johnson* v. *Gillett*, 52 Ill. 358.
(k) *Ryan* v. *Jones*, 15 Ill. 1.
(l) *Sutherland* v. *Harrison*, 86 Ill. 363.
(m) *Reitzell* v. *Miller*, 25 Ill. 67; *Wingate* v. *Pool*, id. 118; *Clark* v. *Hogle*, 52 id. 427.

Claims against estates.

may become parties to the proceedings in the county court on the presentation and allowance of claims against an estate. Under this section, the heirs have a right to be present and contest the justice of the claim. The heirs having this right to appear and resist the allowance of the claim, the adjudication of the court in making the allowance must be held *prima facie* binding upon them, though they neglect to avail themselves of such right. But the allowance is conclusive upon the executor and administrator, and has the force and effect of a judgment until it is reversed.(*n*)

LIMITATION. The time within which claims must be presented against an estate is to be computed from the date of the letters of administration, and not from the date of the notice requiring creditors to exhibit them ; and those who fail to exhibit their claims within two years after the grant of letters of administration are precluded from all participation in the estate inventoried or accounted for during that period.(*o*)

If an administrator does not return an inventory of the real estate of the intestate within two years, a creditor who presents his claim before the return of the inventory, but after the expiration of two years from the granting of letters of administration, may share in the proceeds of the inventory.(*p*)

LACHES OF CREDITOR. In determining the question whether a creditor has waived his lien upon the property of an intestate, by failing to pursue his remedy within a reasonable time, in the absence of legislative rule, each case must be left to depend largely upon its own circumstances.(*q*)

HEIRS — LIMITATION. The failure of an administrator to plead the limitation of two years on claims against the estate, will not preclude the heirs from pleading it on settlement with the administrator.(*r*)

LIEN — LIMITATION. A creditor will be considered to have waived his lien upon the property of an intestate if he does not pursue his remedy in a reasonable time. If prosecuted in a reasonable time, the lien will be good, against purchasers from heirs or devisees. By

---

(*n*) *Mason* v. *Bair*. 33 Ill. 195.
(*o*) *The People* v. *White*, 11 Ill. 342 ; *Stillman* v. *Young*, 16 id. 318 ; *Wingate* v. *Pool*, 25 id. 118.
(*p*) *Sloo* v. *Pool*, 15 Ill. 47.

(*q*) *Rosenthal* v. *Renick*, 44 Ill. 202 ; *Moore* v. *Ellsworth*, 51 id. 308 ; *Clark* v. *Hogle*, 52 id. 427.
(*r*) *Stillman* v. *Young*, 16 Ill. 318.

Claims against estates.

analogies of the law, it would seem that seven years from the death of the intestate should bar such liens. (*s*)

In a suit against an executor, after the expiration of two years from the date of his letters testamentary, upon a demand which had not been presented for allowance within that time, the judgment should direct the levy to be made out of property belonging to the estate which has not been inventoried, whether found previous or subsequent to the judgment.(*t*)

Where a person died in Ohio, having devised all his real estate in Ohio, Indiana and Illinois, to R., first to pay all his debts and then to convey it to his son H., and subsequently such trustee and devisee, died, the devisee H. leaving a will, and administrators with the will annexed were appointed in each of the States of Ohio and Illinois. *Held*, that the lien of a creditor upon the property of the testator was not barred by the failure to pursue his remedy within seven years after the death of the testator, it appearing that the property against which the lien was sought to be enforced, and of which the devisee H. died seized, had never been aliened by the devisee, nor any improvements made thereon by *him*, and that the estate was still unsettled in Ohio.(*u*)

LIMITATION. Where the plaintiff has failed to exhibit his demand against the estate within the two years limited by the statute, he is, nevertheless, entitled to a judgment against the administrator for the amount found to be due him, to be satisfied out of such assets as may thereafter be discovered, and which have not been inventoried or accounted for by the administrator.(*v*)

As between the wards and the widows of an intestate. (*w*)

How the widow may lose her priority of preference, and to what extent.(*w*)

(*s*) *McCoy* v. *Morrow*, 18 Ill. 519; *Unknown Heirs of Langworthy* v. *Baker*, 23 id. 484.
(*t*) *Bradford* v. *Jones*, 17 Ill. 93.
(*u*) *Rosenthal* v. *Renick*, 44 Ill. 202; *Moore* v. *Ellsworth*, 51 id. 308.

(*v*) *Judy* v. *Kelley*, 11 Ill. 211; *Rowan* v. *Kirkpatrick*, 14 id. 1; *Peacock* v. *Haven*, 22 id. 23.
(*w*) *Cruse* v. *Cruce*, 21 Ill. 46.

Legacies.

SECTION III. — LEGACIES.

1. Refunding bond to be given.
2. Duty of legatee to refund; refusal on citation and demand deemed a breach of the bond.
3. Payment of legacies.
4. The bond.
5. Decisions.

1. Whenever it shall appear that there are sufficient assets to satisfy all demands against the estate, the court shall order the payment of all legacies mentioned in the will of the testator, the specific legacies being the first to be satisfied. (*x*)

Executors and administrators shall not be compelled to pay legatees or distributees until bond and security is given by such legatees or distributees to refund the due proportion of any debt which may afterward appear against the estate, and the costs attending the recovery thereof; such bond shall be made payable to such executor or administrator, and shall be for his indemnity and filed in the court.(*y*)

2. When, at any time after the payment of legacies or distributive shares, it shall be necessary that the same or any part thereof be refunded for the payment of debts, the county court, on application made, shall apportion the same among the several legatees or distributees according to the amount received by them, except the specific legacies, which shall not be required to be refunded, unless the residue is insufficient to satisfy such debts; and if any distributee or legatee refuses to refund according to the order of the court, within sixty days thereafter, and upon demand made, such refusal shall be deemed a breach of his bond given to the executor or administrator as aforesaid, and an action may be instituted thereon for the use of the party entitled thereto; and in all cases where there is no bond, an action of debt may be maintained against such distributee or legatee, and the order of the court shall be evidence of the amount due.(*z*)

3. PAYMENT OF LEGACIES. After the executor has paid all the debts of the deceased, and settled the accounts of the estate, his next duty is to execute the will of the testator by paying the legacies of the will, and generally to fulfill the wishes of the testator.

(*x*) § 115, R. S. 1874, p. 125. (*z*) § 117, R. S. 1874, p. 125.
(*y*) § 116, id.

Legacies.

A *legacy* is a bequest or gift of personal property by will. It is general or specific. General, where the legacy is not described, as a particular fund or article of property; where it is so described, it is specific. Although the courts are averse to construing legacies to be specific, yet, if the words clearly indicate an intention to separate the particular thing bequeathed from the general property of the testator, they shall have that operation.

A legacy is sufficiently specific if the money or property is indicated in such a way as to be identified as distinct from the general funds or property.

The executors must be careful to pay the legacy into the hand which has authority to receive it.

An executor cannot pay a legacy to a minor, to his parents, or other relatives, without sanction of a court of equity. (*a*)

If a legacy be given to a married woman, it must not be paid to her husband. (*b*) It is a general rule that a legacy given by a debtor to his creditor, which is equal to or greater than the debt, shall be considered a satisfaction of it, but on this point the intention of the testator is the criterion. (*c*)

In case of a deficiency of assets to pay debts, specific legacies, although not liable so long as there are other assets, abate in proportion among themselves. (*d*)

An executor has no right to give himself the preference in regard to a legacy.

4. BOND BY LEGATEE OR DISTRIBUTEE.

KNOW ALL MEN BY THESE PRESENTS, That we, A B and C D, of the county of , in the State of , are held and firmly bound unto J K, executor of the last will and testament of E F, deceased, in the penal sum of five hundred dollars, for the payment of which well and truly to be made, we bind ourselves, our heirs, executors and administrators, jointly and severally, firmly by these presents.

Witness our hands and seals, this day of , 18 .* .

The condition of the above obligation is such, that whereas the above bounden A B, as one of the legatees of the estate of E F, deceased, this day received of the said J K, executor of the last will and testament of said E F, the legacy in the last will and testament of the said E F, deceased, bequeathed to him the said A B, being the sum of . Now should the said A B, legatee as aforesaid, well and truly refund his due proportion of any and all debts

---

(*a*) Toll. Ex. 319.
(*b*) Toll. Ex. 320. See Hill's Chan. Pr. 610.
(*c*) Toll. Ex. 335.
(*d*) Toll. Ex. 340.

Legacies.

which may hereafter appear against the estate of the said E F, deceased, and the costs attending the recovery thereof, to the said J K, executor as aforesaid, well and truly refund his due proportion of any and all debts which may hereafter appear against the estate of the said E F, deceased, and the costs attending the recovery thereof, to the said J K, executor as aforesaid, well and truly refund his due proportion of any and all debts which may hereafter appear against the estate of the said E F, deceased, and the costs attending the recovery thereof, to the said J K, executor as aforesaid, when thereunto requested, then the above obligation to be void; otherwise to be and remain in full force and virtue.

A B, [SEAL.]
C D. [SEAL.]

5. DECISIONS — THE ADMINISTRATOR IN POSSESSION. A grantee or purchaser is liable to account for rents and profits in excess of taxes, necessary repairs, debts of estate paid by him, and other proper charges.(e)

A legacy payable to a minor on his attaining his majority, goes to his administrator at the point of time at which, if living, he would have become of age. (*Ruffin* v. *Farmer*, 72 Ill. 615.)

Pecuniary legacies must be paid from the personal property of testator. In case of deficiency of personal property, the legatees must abate unless by will the realty is charged with their payments. (*Heslop* v. *Gatton*, 71 Ill. 528.)

REFUNDING BOND — DEMAND. Where an administrator died and no administrator was appointed for him, the distributees alleged that on final settlement the accounts of the administrator showed that there was money in his hands belonging to the estate, that the county court thereupon ordered him to pay the same to the heirs, specifying the sum due to each, that the administrator was dead, and the money unpaid; the securities demurred. *Held*, that, as demand on the administrator was rendered impossible, and as there was no one in existence to whom the refunding bond could be given, neither the proof of a demand nor the giving of such bond should be required.(g)

(e) *Kruse* v. *Steffens*, 47 Ill. 112.   (g) *The People* v. *Admire*, 39 Ill. 252.

Legacies.

Acceptance of a draft drawn by distributee in such case, for his share, binds the executor in his individual capacity only. (*h*)

Payment of distributive share not enforced till after order made by probate court, and execution of refunding bond if needed.(*i*)

In the distribution of the assets of deceased persons, judgment creditors and simple contract creditors are placed upon an equal footing; and this rule applies to an administrator who is a judgment creditor.(*j*)

Creditors and distributees, but not an administrator *de bonis non*, may charge an antecedent administrator with a *devastavit*. An administrator *de bonis non* can only administer upon such estate as has not been administered upon by others.(*k*)

The husband administering on his wife's estate must distribute the estate according to the statute of distribution. (*l*)

A creditor obtaining judgment after the lapse of the two years is not to be confined to assets discovered after his judgment is rendered, but is entitled to participate in assets discovered and inventoried after the lapse of two years from the granting of letters of administration. (*m*)

EXHIBITING CLAIM NOT MATURED. A executed a bond of indemnity to B, the damages depending on a contingency that did not happen until after lapse of two years from the granting of letters on the estate of A, deceased. *Held*, no suit could be instituted within the two years, and the claim was barred except as to future discovered property.(*m*)

If a party having a claim against an estate is sued by the representative of it after two years from the granting of letters of administration, he can plead his claim by way of set-off; and if any balance is adjudged to him, it will be paid out of any estate thereafter discovered and inventoried.(*n*)

FINAL ACCOUNTINGS. When an administrator's acts have been approved, and his resignation accepted, and his discharge granted, these matters become *res ajudicata*, and are binding until they shall be set aside.(*o*)

(*h*) *The People* v. *Admire*, 39 Ill. 252.
(*i*) *Wisdom* v. *Becker*, 52 Ill. 342.
(*j*) *Paschall* v. *Hailman*, 4 Gilm. 285; *Turney* v. *Gates*, 12 Ill. 141.
(*k*) *Rowan* v. *Kirkpatrick*, 14 Ill. 8; *Short* v. *Johnson*, 25 id. 489; *Stoss* v. *The People*, id. 600.
(*l*) *Townsend* v. *Radcliffe*, 44 Ill. 446.
(*m*) *Stone* v. *Clarke's Adm'rs*, 40 Ill. 411.
(*n*) *Peacock* v. *Haven*, 22 Ill. 23.
(*o*) *Short* v. *Johnson*, 25 Ill. 489.

Legacies.

Where the wife and the surviving partner of intestate were appointed administrators, the estate not owing a dollar, and being a large estate, no full account of their transactions having been exhibited by the administrators, and upon their final report and petition for a discharge, a mere pittance is shown to be left for the heirs, the order approving the settlement will not be sustained.(*p*)

ADMINISTRATOR — PROOF REQUIRED TO SET ASIDE SETTLEMENT. Before a court of equity will set aside as fraudulent or illegal a settlement of his accounts, made by an administrator more than sixteen years before the filing of the bill, and approved by the probate court, it will require clear proof of the alleged fraud or illegality.(*q*)

ORDERS OF PROBATE COURT — EFFECT OF, AS PROOF. The allowance against an estate, of partnership debts, must be considered as at least *prima facie* proof that the firm assets were wholly insufficient for their payment, and the approval by the court of an account showing their payment as at least *prima facie* proof that the firm assets had been exhausted.(*q*)

(*p*) *Heward* v. *Slagle*, 52 Ill. 336.   (*q*) *The People* v. *Lott*, 36 Ill. 447.

CHAPTER IX.
ACCOUNTS.

SECTION I. By the executor or administrator.
II. By the guardian and conservator.

SECTION I. — ACCOUNTS BY THE EXECUTOR OR ADMINISTRATOR.

1. General instructions to the executor or administrator.
2. Settlements to be made annually at least.
3. Apportionments to be made.
4. Settlement may be enforced.
5. Devastavit, etc.
6. Administrator's account.
7. Procedure for administrator or executor when cited to account.
8. Form of account.

1. INSTRUCTIONS TO THE EXECUTOR OR ADMINISTRATOR. (1) Present to the court an inventory and appraisement of the estate within three months from the date of your letters.

(2) Post notices, and publish for an adjudication of claims, within six months from the date of your appointment, and be present on the day named in the notice.

(3) Sell the personal property at public auction as soon as convenient after the inventory and appraisement are approved, unless it is selected by the widow or specially bequeathed.

(4) Pay no claims that accrued during the life-time of the deceased until they have been allowed by the court.

(5) Take and carefully keep receipts for all payments respectively.

(6) Make application for the sale of real estate as soon as you find that the personal estate will not be sufficient to pay the claims against the estate.

(7) At the end of one year from the date of your appointment, render your account to the court, and every year thereafter, until the estate is fully settled.

2. SETTLEMENT BY ADMINISTRATORS AND EXECUTORS. All executors and administrators shall exhibit accounts of their administration for settlement, to the county court from which the letters testamentary or of administration were obtained, at the first term

By the executor or administrator.

thereof after the expiration of one year after the date of their letters; and in like manner every twelve months thereafter, or sooner, if required, until the duties of their administration are fully completed. *Provided*, that no final settlement shall be made and approved by the court, unless the heirs of the decedent have been notified thereof, in such manner as the court may direct.(*a*)

3. Upon every such settlement of the accounts of an executor or administrator, the court shall ascertain the whole amount of moneys and assets belonging to the estate of the deceased, which have come into the hands of such executor or administrator, and the whole amount of debts established against such estate; and if there is not sufficient to pay the whole of the debts, the moneys aforesaid shall be apportioned among the several creditors *pro rata*, according to their several rights, as established by this act; and thereupon the court shall order such executor or administrator to pay the claims which have been allowed by the court, according to such apportionments; and the court, upon every settlement, shall proceed in like manner until all the debts due are paid, or the assets exhausted.(*b*)

4. The county courts of this State shall enforce the settlements of estates within the time prescribed by law, and upon the failure of an executor or administrator to make settlement at the next term of the court after the expiration of said time, the court shall order a citation to issue to the sheriff of the county where the executor or administrator resides, or may be found, requiring said executor or administrator to appear at the next term of the court and make settlement of the estate, or show cause why the same is not done; and, if an executor or administrator fails to appear at the time required by such citation, the court shall order an attachment requiring the sheriff of the county where the executor or administrator resides, or may be found, to bring the body of said executor or administrator before the court; and upon a failure of an administrator or executor to make settlement, under the order of the court, after having been so attached, he may be dealt with as for contempt, and shall be forthwith removed by the court, and some discreet person appointed in his stead; the costs of such citation or attachment to be paid by the delinquent executor or administrator, and the court shall enter a judgment therefor, and a fee bill may issue thereon. All moneys, bonds, notes and credits, which any administ-

(*a*) § 111, R. S. 1874, p. 124.   (*b*) § 112, R. S. 1874, p. 124.

By the executor or administrator.

trator or executor may have in his possession or control as property or assets of the estate, at a period of two years and six months from the date of his letters testamentary or of administration, shall bear interest and the executor or administrator shall be charged interest thereon from said period at the rate of ten per cent, or after two years and six months from any subsequent time that he may have discovered and received the same, unless good cause is shown to the court why such should not be taxed.(c)

When any administrator or executor shall have made final settlement with the court, it shall be the duty of the court to order said administrator or executor to deposit with the county treasurer such moneys as he may have belonging to any non-resident or unknown heir or claimant, taking his receipt therefor, and have the same filed at the office of the county or probate court where such settlement has been made. The person or persons entitled to the same may, at any time, apply to the court making said order and obtain the same, upon making satisfactory proof to the court of his, her or their right thereto. (Act of 1877, Cothran's Ann'd Stats., 82, 134.)

5. If any executor or administrator shall fail or refuse to pay over any moneys or dividend to any person entitled thereto, in pursuance of the order of the county court, lawfully made, within thirty days after demand made for such moneys or dividend, the court, upon application, may attach such delinquent executor or administrator, and may cause him to be imprisoned until he shall comply with the order aforesaid, or until such delinquent is discharged by due course of law; and, moreover, such failure or refusal on the part of such executor or administrator shall be deemed and taken in law to amount to a *devastavit*, and an action upon such executor's or administrator's bond, and against his securities, may be forthwith instituted and maintained; and the failure aforesaid to pay such moneys or dividend shall be a sufficient breach to authorize a recovery thereon.(d)

6. ADMINISTRATOR'S ACCOUNT. This embraces a statement of the amount of moneys received from all sources, and the amount paid out.

STATE OF ILLINOIS, } ss:
  County,

To the Hon.   , Judge of the   court of   county,   Term, A. D. 18   .

The account of C D, administrator of the goods, chattels, rights and credits of A B, late of the county of   , and State of Illinois, deceased.

The said administrator charges himself as follows:

19 . Jan.	1.	To all the personal property as per appraisement bill,	$875	63
		To excess of amount produced at the sale	90	00
Jan.	10.	To cash collected of E F on note	05	00
"		To cash collected of G H on account................	37	00
March	1.	To cash received from sale of real estate as per report of sale filed..............	965	00

(c) § 113, R. S. 1874, p. 124.   (d) § 114, R. S. 1874, p. 125; Cothran's Stat., 1880, p. 78.

By the executor or administrator.

To amount of sale notes due Feb. 10, 1869, not collected, to wit:		
E D's note	$45	00
P K's note	34	65
Total amount of money received and collected	$2,112	28

Contra.

By the following payments to creditors of deceased, to wit:

18 . Feb. 1. To John Doe, Voucher No. 1	$95	00
" " 12. To Richard Roe, Voucher No. 2	40	00
March 1. By cash paid clerk of court for his fees, as per Voucher No. 3	25	00
March 1. By cash paid Chicago Journal, printers' fees, Voucher No. 4	2	50
March 1. By cash paid J. V., Esq., attorney's fees, Voucher No. 5	40	00
	$202	50

Recapitulation.

Total amount received and notes collected	$2,112	28
Total amount disbursed	202	50
Balance on hand subject to the order of court	$1,909	78

Amount of claims allowed against the estate unpaid, due as follows:

To L Q	95	00
To P Q	876	00
To R S	975	00
To O P	297	00
Total amount allowed against the estate up to this date	$2,243	00
From which deduct amount of assets	1,909	78
Exhibiting a deficit of assets	$333	22

All of which is respectfully submitted.

C D,
Administrator of A B, deceased.

March 3, 18 .

This account should specify particularly each sum of money received or paid, from whom, and when received.

The administrator should always take a receipt from the person to whom he pays money. He must file the receipts in court when he exhibits his account.

7. PROCEEDINGS ON CITATION TO ACCOUNT. Prepare your account by charging yourself in separate items with all the money you

By the executor or administrator.

have received, giving dates and stating from whom and for what the same was received. Credit yourself with all that you have paid out, giving the items, but include no claim that existed in the lifetime of the deceased, until it has been allowed by the county court. Number your vouchers. Draw up a report on a separate paper to accompany your account, in which give a brief history of the estate from the date of your letters, or from your last accounting, as the case may be, stating what accounts, if any, remain uncollected, and why such accounts have not been collected; the personal property unsold, if any, and why it has not been disposed of. Answer the citation in writing, under oath, stating why you have not presented your account as required by the statute.

When you have thus prepared your papers, present them to the county judge in open court. Obtain his approval of your account, and your discharge from the citation. All of the above should be done at or before the hour named in the citation.

8. Your account may be in the following form:

Geo. Strong, Adm'r, in account with the estate of Henry Jones, Dr.

To all the personal property at its appraised value................	$800 00
To cash collected of John Smith, on note.........................	400 00
To cash collected of Wm. Wilson, in full of ac't	150 00
To cash on hand at time of death.................................	2,000 00
	$3,350 00

Cr.

By cash paid clerk for letters, voucher No. 1.....................	$3 20
By cash paid to clerk for costs, voucher No. 2....................	2 00
All of the personal property taken by Jane Jones at the appraised value, on her award, voucher No. 3............................	800 00
By cash paid Jane Jones, balance on her award, voucher No. 4.....	75 00
By cash paid claim of Dr. J. N. Banks, allowed, voucher No. 5.....	20 00
By cash paid claim of Wm. Smith, voucher No. 6.................	40 00
By cash paid appraisers, voucher No. 7...........................	2 52
By cash paid for printing adjudication notice, voucher No. 9......	10 00
By commissions on $3,350, at four per cent......................	134 00
By balance in hands of administrator...................	2,263 28
	$3,350 00

Give the date of each entry.

By the guardian and conservator.

SECTION II. — ACCOUNTS BY THE GUARDIAN AND CONSERVATOR.

1. Guardian must account once every year.
2. He must pay over to those entitled at the expiration of his trust.
3. Accounts must be filed.
4. Instructions in general to guardians and conservators.
5. Accounts, how kept.
6. Form of report to the court in accounting.
7. Another form.

1. The guardian shall, at the expiration of a year from his appointment, SETTLE HIS ACCOUNTS as guardian* with the county court, and at least once every three years thereafter, and as much oftener as the court may require. (e)

2. GUARDIAN TO PAY OVER. At the expiration of his trust, he shall pay and deliver to those entitled thereto all the money, estate and title papers in his hands as guardian, or with which he is chargeable as such. (f)

3. ACCOUNT TO BE FILED. On every accounting and final settlement of guardian he shall exhibit and file his account as such guardian, setting forth specifically, in separate items, on what account expenditures were made by him, and all sums received and paid out since his last accounting, and on what account each was received and paid out, and showing the true balance of money on hand, which account shall be accompanied by proper vouchers, and signed by him and verified by his affidavit. (g)

4. INSTRUCTIONS TO GUARDIANS AND CONSERVATORS. (1) Present to the court an inventory of the estate of your wards within three months from the date of your letters.

(e) § 14, R. S. 1874, p. 560.   (g) § 16, R. S. 1874, p. 560.
(f) § 15, id.

---

* TO ACT FOR WARD, GENERALLY. The guardian shall settle all accounts of his ward, and demand and sue for, and receive in his own name as guardian, all personal property of and demands due the ward, or with the approbation of the court compound for the same, and give a discharge to the debtor upon receiving a fair and just dividend of his estate and effects. § 17, id.

AND IN SUITS. He shall appear for and represent his ward in all legal suits and proceedings, unless another person is appointed for that purpose as guardian or next friend; but nothing contained in this act shall impair or affect the power of any court or justice of the peace to appoint a guardian to defend the interest of a minor impleaded in such court or interested in a suit or matter therein pending, nor their power to appoint or allow any person as next friend for a minor to commence, prosecute or defend any suit in his behalf. § 18, id.

By the guardian and conservator.

(2) Obtain an order of court to appropriate not to exceed a certain sum, for the nurture and education of your wards.

(3) Make no lease of the land of your wards, except under the order of court.

(4) Before loaning any of the money of your wards, have the security approved by the court.

(5) Procure an account book and enter therein an account of all moneys expended and received with dates, and take a receipt for all payments.

(6) At the end of one year from the date of your letters of guardianship, render your account to the court, and every year thereafter until your wards become of age, and then obtain your discharge.

5. How KEPT. The guardian is required to render an account and should therefore keep one, containing debts and credits, or of his receipts and disbursements, from whom received, and to whom paid and on what account. If there be several wards a separate account with each must be kept similar in form to the accounts kept by business men, but, if possible, with more care. He should take a voucher from every person to whom he pays the ward's money, to be carefully numbered, filed, and with the account presented, that the court may see that the money has been paid, and for articles suitable and necessary to the condition in life of his ward. The court has power to cite the guardian to make an inventory and account, upon oath for adjustment, but without waiting to be cited, the

---

DUTIES OF GUARDIAN. The guardian shall manage the estate of his ward frugally and without waste, and apply the income and profit thereof, so far as the same may be necessary, to the comfort and suitable support and education of his ward. § 19, R. S. 1874, p. 560.

The guardian shall educate his ward, and it is made the duty of all civil officers to give information to the county court of any neglect of the guardian to his ward. § 20, Id.

When there is not money of the ward sufficient to teach him to read and write, and the elementary rules of arithmetic, and the guardian fails or neglects to have him so educated, the court shall have power to put out the ward to any other person for the purpose of having him so educated. § 21, Id.

It shall be the duty of the guardian to put and keep his ward's money at interest, upon security, to be approved by the court, or invest the same in United States bonds, or other United States interest-bearing securities. Personal security may be taken for loans not exceeding one hundred dollars. Loans in large amounts shall be upon real estate security. No loan shall be made for a longer time than three years, nor beyond the minority of the ward. *Provided*, the same may be extended from year to year without the approval of the court. The guardian shall be chargeable with interest upon any money which he shall wrongfully or negligently allow to remain in his hands uninvested after the same might have been invested. § 22, Id.

By the guardian and conservator.

inventory should be promptly made and accounts presented and adjusted with the court, annually at least.

6. THE ACCOUNT may be substantially in the following form:

GUARDIAN'S ACCOUNT.

STATE OF ILLINOIS, } ss.:   In the County Court of   county,
County.   term, A. D. 18 .

To the Judge of said court:

The undersigned, guardian of C A D, would respectfully submit to the court the following account of his guardianship, from his appointment to   , 18 .

Account of E B M, Guardian of C A D.

Dr.

Jan. 16, 1871.	To cash received of L M, administrator of T F D...	$500 00
Jan. 23, "	To cash for rent of J B D, on lease of lot 10, bl. 19, etc...............	300 00
Mar. 19, "	To cash of W J B on his note.................	35 00
		$835 00

Cr.

April 1, 1871.	By cash paid Field, Leiter & Co., for merchandise as per bill and receipt......... .	$95 96
May 16, "	By cash paid V L H for medical attendance as per bill and receipt.................	130 00
June 1, "	By cash paid for U. S. government bond..........	500 00
	By cash on hand.................	109 04
		$835 00

STATE OF ILLINOIS, } ss.:
County.

E B M, guardian of C A D, being duly sworn, says that the foregoing is a just, full and perfect account of all his dealings and transactions, and of all moneys and effects received and paid out by him on account of the said minor, from the time of his appointment to the   day of   , 18 .

                                                                  E B M.

Subscribed and sworn to before me, this }
    day of   , A. D. 18 .
                         , *Clerk.*

7. Or in the following form:

EXPENSE ACCOUNT.[*]

William Page, Mary Page and John Page, Wards,
               To Andrew H. Dalton, their Guardian,   Dr.

To cash paid John G. Gindele, Clerk of Court, for letters of guardianship, voucher 1.....	$2 40

---

[*]The date of each entry in the account should be given.

By the guardian and conservator.

To cash paid U. S. stamps...	60
To cash paid taxes on No. 12 Lake street, for 1868, voucher 2......	$80 00
To cash paid insurance on No. 12 Lake street, for 1868, voucher 3..	40 00
To cash paid for attorney's fees, voucher 4.......................	10 00
To cash paid repairing sidewalk, voucher 5........................	81 00
	$214 00

ANDREW H. DALTON, *Guardian.*

Andrew H. Dalton, in account with (his Ward), John Page,	*Dr.*
To cash received of Joseph Page, Adm'r...........................	$1,000 00
To interest on same one year, at 10 per cent.....................	100 00
To cash received for rent of house No. 12 Lake street, from 1st of May, 1868, to 1st of May, 1869.................................	600 00
	$1,700 00
	Cr.
By cash paid for board from 1st of May, 1868, to 1st of May, 1869, at $2.00 per week, voucher 1......................................	$104 00
By cash paid for 6 months' tuition, voucher 2....................	25 00
By cash paid for 1 coat, $15, 1 pr. boots, $5, voucher 3.........	20 00
By cash paid for 1 hat, voucher 4................................	5 00
By cash paid Dr. Banks for professional services, voucher 5......	20 00
By commissions on $1,700, at 3 per cent, voucher 6...............	51 00
By one-third common expense account allowed...................	71 33
By balance in hands of guardian..................................	1,403 67
	$1,700 00

ANDREW H. DALTON, *Guardian.*

Attach the usual affidavit.

If you are guardian but for one minor, or the items of your expenses common to all your wards are few, the expense account may be dispensed with, and an account, similar to the account last given, kept with each ward, will alone be sufficient. Your account should be accompanied with a written report.

CONSERVATOR'S ACCOUNTS should be made in the same way, using the word *conservator* in lieu of *guardian.*(*h*)

A guardian is liable to account to his ward, although five years may have elapsed after the ward became of age before the ward commenced proceedings. (*i*) Though the guardian may be out of office,

---

(*h*) See p. 138, *supra.* (*i*) *Gilbert* v. *Guptill,* 34 Ill. 112.

By the guardian and conservator.

he is still liable to account, and this liability continues so long as his bond is in force. A guardian loaning money of ward on insufficient security is responsible for the amount with interest. He should be charged with the moneys he received belonging to his ward, and compound interest thereon, at six per cent from the day he received it, until his ward became of age, and interest on the amount from the day of demand by the administrator of the ward to the time of entering the final order.(*j*) See 81 Ill. 103.

A guardian must testify before probate court, if required, as to estate of ward.(*j*)

The powers of the county court, to compel guardians to render an account of their guardianship from time to time, are co-extensive with those of a court of chancery. The accounts are to be rendered upon oath, and the court may require their settlement. The court may allow or disallow an account in whole or in part, and for that purpose may examine witnesses, may require the production of vouchers, and do all other acts necessary to enable it to arrive at a correct conclusion as to whether or not the account ought to be allowed. When allowed, it is required to be entered of record.(*k*)

The allowance of a guardian's account is a judicial act, and although it is necessarily made during the minority of the ward, still it is to be presumed the act was properly performed until the contrary appears. It is *prima facie* evidence of the correctness of the account allowed. The authority of the county court in this regard is similar to that of a court of chancery. If an account has been stated erroneously, the ward may have it restated correctly. If the guardian has omitted to charge himself with any thing, or with a proper sum, the ward may make additional charges of such matters. If the guardian has obtained an allowance in his account apparently regular upon its face, the ward should be required to rebut the *prima facie* presumption of its regularity before the guardian can be called upon to establish its correctness; but, if it appears from the face of the account that items were improperly allowed, no such presumption will sustain them.(*k*)

Guardians are chargeable with waste committed or suffered by them. In England it was considered waste to cut growing trees, or to permit them to be cut. Any act or omission which diminished the value of the estate or its income, or increased the burdens upon

(*j*) *Gilbert* v. *Guptill*, 34 Ill. 112.   (*k*) *Bond* v. *Lockwood*, 33 Ill. 213.

By the guardian and conservator.

it, or impaired the evidence of title thereto, was considered waste. Many acts which, in England, would be waste, are not such here, in consequence of the difference in the condition of the two countries. In this country, whether the cutting of any kind of tree is waste, depends upon the question whether the act is such as a prudent farmer would do, having regard to the land as an inheritance, and whether the doing of it would diminish the value of the land as an estate.(*l*)

Where a trustee or guardian employs trust funds in a trade or adventure of his own, whether he keeps them separate or mixes them with his own private moneys, and notwithstanding difficulties may arise in the latter case in taking the account, the *cestui que trust*, if he prefers it, may insist upon having the profits made by, instead of interest upon the amount of, the trust funds so employed. It is sometimes impracticable, in applying this rule, to trace out and apportion the profits derived by a trustee from the employment of trust funds along with his own, and in such cases the court fixes upon a rate of interest as the supposed measure or representative of the profits, and assigns it to the trust fund.(*l*)

In determining what expenditures are necessary or proper, courts are exceedingly jealous of encroachments upon the principal of the ward's estate; and in reference to them it has been repeatedly held that they will not be allowed, except for necessaries, without an order of court is procured before making the expenditure, unless the guardian can show such a state of facts as would have entitled him to the order had he applied for it at the proper time, and a reasonable excuse for his neglect in that regard. (*l*)

Where a guardian has made a gift to his ward, and entered a credit to the ward in his account therefor, the county court, in view of it, may, with great propriety, allow larger expenditures in behalf of the ward than it would otherwise do; and where such appears to have been the case, it would be a gross fraud to allow the guardian to recall the gift.(*l*)

Commissions will not be allowed to a guardian for money of his ward in his hands which he has employed in his own business. Commissions are allowed to guardians for services rendered, and not for neglect of their duties.(*l*)

The statute directs the expenditure to be made by the guardian

(*l*) *Bond* v. *Lockwood*, 33 Ill. 213.

By the guardian and conservator.

under the order and direction of the court of probate, and requires that the rents and profits arising from the ward's real estate, and the interest on his money, should be first resorted to for his education and maintenance. (*m*)

A died, leaving an estate, a widow and two children. The widow administered, and afterward married B, who collected money belonging to the estate of A, and died without accounting therefor. A's children lived with B, and were supported by him until his death. In a suit by the heirs of A against the administrator of B, for an account, the court held that B had made himself liable as guardian, by intruding on the children's estate. That as B had nurtured and educated the children during his life, he should be allowed the interest on the money collected by him during his life; but as he had failed in duty in not giving bond, his estate must be held accountable for the principal sum collected by him, and interest thereon since his death. (*m*)

Upon a settlement of his account, the guardian, by order of court, gave his note for what was due the ward. The guardian paid part of the note in money and part in lumber, which was received. *Held*, that the payment in lumber should be allowed as a credit.(*n*)

Persons paying money to the guardian are not responsible for its application.(*n*)

It is the duty of a guardian to procure an order of the proper court before making expenditures; and that duty existed as well before the passage of the statute imposing such obligation upon him as afterward. A guardian may support his ward without any order of court, and all payments which he can show were necessary for that purpose will be allowed to him. Any one in the possession of the ward's property, or a stranger, may do it and have a like allowance; but it will only be made upon proof showing the necessity of the expenditure, and for what it was made. Expenditures not required for necessaries should be approved by the court before they are made.(*o*)

If an administrator or guardian, in his representative capacity, make a contract or covenant which he has no right to make, and

---

(*m*) *Davis, Adm'r,* v. *Harkness,* 1 Gilm. 173.

(*n*) *Mortimer* v. *The People,* 49 Ill. 473.

(*o*) *Bond* v. *Lockwood,* 33 Ill. 213.

By the guardian and conservator.

which is not binding on the estate or ward, he is personally bound to make it good.(*p*).

A guardian, who converts money of his ward to his own use, is chargeable with compound interest.(*q*)

To change a ward's property from personal to real is not ordinarily permitted.(*r*)

Where a guardian, to preserve the estate unimpaired until the heirs become of age, leases for a less sum than could be obtained from ordinary yearly rents, first securing the approval of the probate court, and acts in manifest good faith, he is not liable for having failed to secure a higher rent.(*s*)

A guardian cannot, by his own contract, bind the person or estate of his ward, but, if he promises, on a sufficient consideration, to pay the debt of his ward, he is personally bound by it, although he expressly promises as guardian. He may indemnify himself out of the ward's estate, or if discharged, may have an action against the ward for money paid to his use.(*t*)

GUARDIAN'S BOND. If the guardian fail to account, his sureties are liable.(*u*)

(*p*) *Mason* v. *Caldwell*, 5 Gilm. 196.
(*q*) *Rowan* v. *Kirkpatrick*, 14 Ill. 2.
(*r*) *Altridge* v. *Billing*, 57 Ill. 480.
(*s*) *McElheny* v. *Musick*, 63 Ill. 328.
(*t*) *Sperry* v. *Fanning*, 80 Ill. 371.
(*u*) *Wann* v. *The People*, 57 Ill. 202.

Estates of intestates to be distributed.

CHAPTER X.

DESCENT.

1. Estates both real and personal of intestates, after paying all just debts and claims, descend and are to be distributed:
    (1) To the children and their descendants, in equal parts; descendants of a deceased child taking the share of their parents in equal parts among them.
    (2) If there be no children, nor descendant of children, and no widow or surviving husband, then to the parents, brothers and sisters of the deceased, and their descendants, in equal parts, each parent taking a child's part, or to surviving parent, if one only be living, a double portion; and if no parent be living, then to the brothers and sisters of the intestate, and their descendants.
    (3) If there be a widow or surviving husband, and no child or children, or descendants of a child or children of the intestate, then one-half of the real and the whole of the personal estate shall descend to the surviving consort in fee.
    (4) If there be a widow or surviving husband, and a child or children, or descendants of a child or children of the intestate, to the surviving consort one-third of all the personal estate.
    (5) If there be no child or descendant of such child, no parent, brother or sister, or descendant of them, and no surviving consort, then to the next of kin to the intestate in equal degree, computing by the rules of the civil law; no representation among collaterals except with the descendants of brothers and sisters of the intestate, and no distinction between kindred of the whole or half blood.
    (6) If there be a surviving consort and no kindred, then the estate descends to the survivor.
    (7) If there be no surviving consort or kindred, then the estate escheats to the State.
2. Illegitimate issue to inherit on the mother's side; rules for specified cases.
3. Illegitimate issue may be legitimatized by subsequent marriage and acknowledgment by the father.
4–9. Advancements and rules relating thereto.
10. Posthumous heirs placed on an equal footing with the other heirs.
11. Issue of deceased, devisee or legatee to inherit, and how.
12. Undevised and unbequeathed real and personal property of any testator to be deemed and distributed as intestate estate; administrator *cum testamento annexo* preferred in administration.
13. Repealed laws enumerated; saving clause.
14. Computation of the civil law adopted.
15. Proof of heirship.
16. After accruing rent, an hereditament.

Estates of intestates to be distributed.

17. Husband and wife in no case next of kin to each other.
18. If the intestate die without issue leaving only a mother, the estate goes to her.
19. The interest of a posthumous child not affected by a decree and sale to satisfy debts of relatives, *e. g.*, his mother and uncle.
20. A posthumous child takes directly from the parent.
21. Distribution of personal estate not known to the common law except under the rules of the civil law.
22. Common-law rules as to the descent of real property, discussed in the light of the authorities.
23. The word *heir* taken in a double sense: 1. Designating the person to take the estate; 2. Limiting the estate transmitted or conveyed; title by descent or purchase.
24. The custom of gavel-kind.
25. The rule in Shelley's case.
26. Common-law rules prevail unless the provisions of an act of the assembly embrace the very case in controversy.
27. Heir at common law and statutory heir.
28. Distribution.
29. Proof of heirship before distribution.
30. Decisions in Illinois collated.

1. ESTATES, BOTH REAL AND PERSONAL, OF RESIDENT AND NON-RESIDENT PROPRIETORS in this State dying intestate, or whose estates or any part thereof shall be deemed and taken as intestate estate, after all just debts and claims against such estate are fully paid, shall descend to and be distributed in manner following, to wit:

(1) RULES OF DESCENT THEREOF.(*a*) To his or her children and their descendants, in equal parts; the descendants of the deceased

---

(*a*) An act in regard to the descent of property, April 9, 1872.* DESCENT hereditary succession. Title by descent is the title by which one person, upon the death of another, acquires the real estate of the latter as his heir at law. 2 Blackstone's Com. 201; Comyn's Dig. *Descent.* (A.) It was one of the principles of the feudal system that on the death of the tenant in fee, the land should *descend* and not *ascend*. Hence, the title by inheritance is in all cases called descent, although by statute law the title is sometimes made to ascend. The English doctrine of primogeniture, by which by the common law the eldest son and his issue take the whole real estate, has been universally abolished in this country. So with few exceptions has been the distinctions between male and female heirs. 2. The rules of descent at common law are applicable only to real estates of inheritance. Estates for the life of the deceased, of course, terminate on his death; estates for the life of another are governed by peculiar rules. Terms of years, and other estates less than freehold, are regarded as personal estates, and on the death of the owner vest in his executor or administrator. Gilb's Dev. 156; Fitzg. 245. Our statute here opens by making "estates, both real and personal," on an equal footing in this respect.

* See chap. 39, R. S. 1874, pp. 417-419.

Estates of intestates to be distributed.

child or grandchild taking the share of their deceased parents in equal parts among them.

(2) When there is no child of the intestate, nor descendant of such child, and no widow or surviving husband, then to the parents, brothers and sisters of the deceased, and their descendants, in equal parts among them, allowing to each of the parents, if living, a child's part, or to the survivor of them if one be dead, a double portion; and if there is no parent living, then to the brothers and sisters of the intestate, and their descendants.

(3) When there is a widow or surviving husband, and no child or children, or descendants of a child or children of the intestate, then (after the payment of all just debts) one-half of the real estate and the whole of the personal estate shall descend to such widow or surviving husband as an absolute estate forever, and the other half of the real estate shall descend as in other cases, where there is no child or children, or descendants of a child or children.

(4) When there is a widow or a surviving husband, and also a child or children, or descendants of such child or children of the intestate, the widow or surviving husband shall receive as his or her absolute personal estate, one-third of all the personal estate of the intestate.

(5) If there is no child of the intestate, or descendant of such child, and no parent, brother or sister, or descendant of such parent, brother or sister, and no widow or surviving husband, then such estate shall descend in equal parts to the next of kin to the intestate, in equal degree (computing by the rules of the civil law),(*d*) and there shall be no representation among collaterals, except with the descendants of brothers and sisters of the intestate ; and in no case shall there be any distinction between the kindred of the whole and the half blood.

(6) If any intestate leaves a widow or surviving husband and no kindred, his or her estate shall descend to such widow or surviving husband.

(7) If the intestate leaves no kindred, and no widow or husband, his or her estate shall escheat to and vest in the county in which said real or personal estate or the greater portion thereof is situated.

2. An illegitimate child shall be heir of its mother and any

(*d*) See p. 268, *infra*.

Illegitimate issue may be legitimatized.

maternal ancestor, and of any person from whom its mother might have inherited, if living; and the lawful issue of an illegitimate person shall represent such person, and take, by descent, any estate which the parent would have taken, if living.

(2) The estate, real and personal, of an illegitimate person shall descend to and vest in the widow or surviving husband and children, as the estate of other persons in like cases.

(3) In case of the death of an illegitimate intestate leaving no child or descendant of a child, the whole estate, personal and real, shall descend to and absolutely vest in the widow or surviving husband.

(4) When there is no widow or surviving husband, and no child or descendants of a child, the estate of such person shall descend to and vest in the mother and her children, and their descendants—one-half to the mother, and the other half to be equally divided between her children and their descendants—the descendants of a child taking the share of their deceased parent or ancestor.

(5) In case there is no heir as above provided, the estate of such person shall descend to and vest in the next of kin to the mother of such intestate, according to the rule of the civil law.

(6) When there are no heirs or kindred, the estate of such person shall escheat to the State, and not otherwise.

3. An illegitimate child, whose parents have intermarried, and whose father has acknowledged him or her as his child, shall be considered legitimate.

4. Any real or personal estate given by an intestate in his life-time as an advancement to any child or lineal descendant, shall be considered as part of the intestate's estate, so far as it regards the divisions and distributions thereof among his issue, and shall be taken by such child or other descendant toward his share of the intestate's estate; but he shall not be required to refund any part thereof, although it exceeds his share.

5. If such advancement is made in real estate, and the value thereof is expressed in the conveyance or in the charge thereof made by the intestate, or in the written acknowledgment thereof by the party receiving it, it shall be considered as of that value in the divisions and distribution of the estate; otherwise, it shall be estimated according to its value when given.

6. If such advancement is made in personal estate of the intestate,

Issue of deceased to inherit.

the value thereof to be estimated the same as that of real estate; and if, in either case, it exceeds the share of real or personal estate, respectively, that would have come to the heir so advanced, he shall not refund any part of it, but shall receive so much less of the other part of the intestate's estate as will make his whole share equal to the shares of other heirs who are in the same degree with him.

7. No gift or grant shall be deemed to have been made in advancement unless so expressed in writing, or charged in writing by the intestate as an advancement, or acknowledged in writing by the child or other descendant.

8. If a child, or other descendant so advanced, dies before the intestate, leaving issue, the advancement shall be taken into consideration in the division or distribution of the estate of the intestate, and the amount thereof shall be allowed accordingly by the representatives of the heirs so advanced, as so much received toward their share of the estate, in like manner as if the advancement had been made directly to them.

9. A posthumous child of an intestate shall receive its just proportion of its ancestor's estate, in all respects as if it had been born in the life-time of the father.

10. If, after making a last will and testament, a child shall be born to any testator, and no provision be made in such will for such child, the will shall not on that account be revoked; but, unless it shall appear by such will that it was the intention of the testator to disinherit such child, the devises and legacies by such will granted and given shall be abated in equal proportions to raise a portion for such child equal to that which such child would have been entitled to receive out of the estate of such testator if he had died intestate, and a marriage shall be deemed a revocation of a prior will.

11. Whenever a devisee or legatee in any last will and testament, being a child or grandchild of the testator, shall die before such testator, and no provision shall be made for such contingency, the issue, if any there be, of such devisee or legatee shall take the estate devised or bequeathed as the devisee or legatee would have done had he survived the testator, and if there be no such issue at the time of the death of such testator, the estate disposed of by such devise or legacy shall be considered and treated in all respects as intestate estate.

12. All such estate, both real and personal, as is not devised or

bequeathed in the last will and testament of any person, shall be distributed in the same manner as the estate of an intestate; but in all such cases the executor or executors, administrator or administrators, with the will annexed, shall have the preference in administering on the same.

13. REPEAL. The following acts and parts of acts are hereby repealed, to wit: Sections thirteen, fourteen, forty-six, forty-seven, fifty-one, fifty-two, fifty-three, fifty-four and one hundred and twenty-eight, of chapter one hundred and nine of the Revised Statutes of 1845; an act entitled "An act to amend an act concerning 'Wills,'" approved February 11, 1847; an act entitled "An act entitled 'An act concerning the descent of property in this State,'" approved February 12, 1853; an act entitled "An act to amend an act concerning the descent of real property in this State," approved February 12, 1853, approved February 11, 1857; also all other acts inconsistent with the provisions of this act: *Provided*, that nothing contained in this section shall be so construed as to affect any suits that may be pending, or any rights that have accrued at the time this act shall take effect.

14. THE COMPUTATION OF THE CIVIL LAW is adopted in ascertaining who are the next of kin to an intestate.(*e*)

15. PROOF that certain children are the only ones that survived their father, does not establish their claim to be his only heirs, unless it is also shown that none of those who died before their father left children or husbands or wives.(*f*)

16. RENT ACCRUING OUT OF LAND, upon a lease granted by the owner in fee, and which does not become due till after the death of the lessor, is a chattel real, which descends to the heir as a part of the inheritance, and does not go to the executors.(*g*)

17. THE NEXT OF KIN to a deceased intestate wife, who dies without issue, take all her property except one-half of her real estate, which goes to her husband. In no sense are husband and wife next of kin to one another.(*h*)

18. Where a person dies without children or father, but leaving a mother, and brothers and sisters, his whole estate goes to his mother.(*i*)

(*e*) *Hays* v. *Thomas*, Breese, 136; see p. 245, *supra*.
(*f*) *Skinner* v. *Fulton*, 39 Ill. 484.
(*g*) *Green* v. *Massie*, 13 Ill. 363.
(*h*) *Townsend* v. *Radcliffe*, 44 Ill. 446.
(*i*) *Hays* v. *Thomas*, Breese, 136. But see p. 245, *supra*, and p. 255, *infra*.

Common-law rules discussed.

19. The interest of a posthumous child in real estate is not divested by a decree against his mother and uncle, under which a sale was made to satisfy the debts of his relatives and ancestors.(*j*)

20. A posthumous child takes directly from the parent, his estate remaining meanwhile in abeyance, so that he is not bound by a decree had against the other heirs before his birth.(*k*)

21. Until the enaction of statutory provisions at a comparatively late period in the English law, THERE WAS NO MODE OF COMPELLING THE DISTRIBUTION OF THE PERSONAL EFFECTS of a decedent among his descendants or next of kin; THE WHOLE SUBJECT WAS REGULATED BY THE CIVIL LAW, according to which they became vested in the ordinary, as the successor to an intestate, and the ordinary appointed an administrator, who was his deputy. Where there was a will, the property vested in the executor as completely as it had been in the testator;(*l*) he represents his person, "and the estate he hath by his executorship is said to be in him, to the use of the testator and his right, and that he doth, in the disposition of his estate, is said to be in the right and to the use of the testator also."(*m*) The will is the declaration of the uses, for which the effects are held in trust by the executor, for the persons and purposes declared; the statute of distributions is a direction to the executor how to administer the assets.(*n*) As trustee the legal ownership is in the executor; the next of kin have a right only by statute,(*o*) nor by the civil law could even children claim them by right. After the payment of debts and legacies, the executor held the surplus to his own use; when his trust was executed, he was the legal owner, bound to account to no one.

22. THE REAL ESTATE of a person who dies intestate descends to and vests, ACCORDING TO THE COURSE OF THE COMMON LAW, in the person who, by the act of God, and in the right of blood, succeeds to the estate of one who dies seized of an inheritable interest in land. The course of descent is prescribed by definite rules or canons of the law, which designate the person who is nearest and worthiest of blood to the deceased owner, as *hæres sanguinis;* who, by right of inheritance, is heir to himself and estates of inheritance. The person on whom this right devolves is the eldest son of the father who dies seized; or, if he dies without lineal descendants, his eldest

(*j*) *Detrick* v. *Migatt,* 19 Ill. 146.
(*k*) *McConnel* v. *Smith,* 23 Ill. 611.
(*l*) Gilb's Dev. 156; Fitzg. 245.
(*m*) Sh. To. 400-2; Went. O. E. 95.
(*n*) 4 Burns' E. L. 58.
(*o*) Fitzg. 245.

The word "heir" taken in a double sense.

brother and their oldest sons, and their lineal descendants in perpetual succession; if males, to the oldest son; if females, to them equally as parceners.(*p*)

23. THE WORD "HEIR" IS TAKEN IN A DOUBLE SENSE, as relates to the person of the ancestor and to his estate. His personal heir is the one who is nearest in blood to him, and descended from the same ancestor on the side of the father, as the worthiest in blood. If a male descendant, it is one person only who is his heir at common law; he is also heir to his estate, if it is held and descends according to the course of the common law. But if the estate is in lands which are held by any particular tenure, and descend according to any local or customary law, the heir as to the land is the person to whom it descends by the custom. The difference is very forcibly and perspicuously exemplified by Lord HOBART, in *Counden* v. *Clerke:*

"Heir is sometimes taken absolutely or simply, or according to or by accident; sometimes in the abstract, standing naked by itself and of itself; and sometimes in the concrete, clothed with land or rent, in respect of which he may be heir, that is, not right heir, as the word is here. For example, the younger son in borough English is heir and all the sons in gavel-kind, whereof the reason is, because the custom is, and so must be pleaded, that the custom of those lands is, that they must descend to the younger son or all the sons; so they are heirs *secundum quid* of those lands in point of descent, or where they descend, for then they are within the custom that gives the inheritance. *Sum demum sumus cum per causas primus.* But now make the limitation, even of land of that nature, to heirs not in point of descent, and it will be clearly otherwise. And, therefore, if I give land, in gavel-kind, or borough English, to one for life, the remainder to the right heirs of I. S., the true heirs shall take it, for that is out of the case of custom, and so must run to the heir at common law. Note, also, that warranties and estoppels do always descend upon the right heirs general, as being to simple heirs. If there be a warrantor who hath lands in gavel-kind, the eldest son shall be vouched alone, but the tenant may also vouch the others for the possession; that the heir general shall take such advantage of such warranty and none other."(*q*)

"Nay, more; if I convey lands that I have on part of my mother

---

(*p*) L. 7, 6; L. 10 *a.*, 13 *b.*; G. Dev.   (*q*) Hob. 31.
156.

The word "heir" taken in a double sense.

or in borough English, and declare the use to me and my heirs, or reserve a rent to me and my heirs, it shall go to my heirs at the common law, for it is not within the custom; but it is a new thing divided from the land itself, and that is the reason of another difference, that land by descent falling upon one shall be taken from him by a nearer heir born. Not so of these purchases.(*r*)

The same distinction is taken by Lord COKE,(*s*) and illustrated by Lord MANSFIELD in *Doe ex dem. Lansing* v. *Long*.(*t*) He says: "Now the term 'heirs' (in the plural), in the case of gavel-kind land, answers to the term 'heir' (in the singular), in the common case of lands which are not gavel-kind; for the word 'heir' (in the singular) would not serve for gavel-kind lands, it must be heirs (in the plural). Therefore, all the arguments and reasonings that are applicable to the word 'heir' (in the singular) in the common case of lands not being gavel-kind, hold with equal strength and propriety when applied to the plural termination 'heirs,' when the lands are gavel-kind."

24. THE CUSTOM OF GAVEL-KIND was peculiar to the county of Kent; where, by the custom and use, time out of mind, lands descend to all the sons.(*u*) The people of this county made it a condition of their submission to the conqueror, that this custom should continue as the law of tenures and descent, notwithstanding the establishment of the feudal system as the general law of the kingdom; it remained, therefore, an exception to that law, as it had before been an exception to the general rules of the common law, unless since disgaveled by statute.(*v*)

There is no branch of the law in which the courts of England, and many of the States of the Federal Union, have been more anxious to adhere to established landmarks than in the meaning given to the words "heir" and "heirs," and none on which the security of titles so much depends.

Subtle as the distinctions on which some cases turn may be thought to be, they will be found, on investigation, to be founded in the strongest reasons of policy and good sense; which have stood the test of time, admired for their wisdom by all who will understand them, and never departed from without the most pernicious

(*r*) Hob. 31.
(*s*) L. 10 *a*.
(*t*) 2 Burr., 1106, 10.

(*u*) Litt., § 210, 1, 140, *a*, *b*.
(*v*) Litt., § 210, 1, 140, *b*.

The word "heir" taken in a double sense.

consequences to the peace of society and the safe enjoyment of estates.

The legal meaning of the word "heir" or "heirs" depends, at common law, on the intention of the party who uses them in a deed or will. They are used in one of two senses, as words of limitation or purchase. In the first sense, they denote the quantity of estate given to the person named; in the other, the person designated to take the estate; but they never operate in both ways. Where they operate by way of limitation, the whole estate vests in the first taker, and on his death intestate, descends to his heir according to the common law, as an estate descendible forever in fee, or in tail, according to the form of the gift. In these cases the word "heir" is *nomen collectivum;* not as a name of numbers, but as a word denoting the continuance and succession of the estate in the heir by inheritance from ancestor to heir, and from heir to heir.(*w*) Where they are used as words of limitation, heir or heirs mean the same thing.(*x*) So is the term right "heir" or "heirs;" it means only one person, who is right heir by the common law. So of the words "heir at law," "heir at common law," "heir general" or "lawful heir;" they mean the person who is heir *jure hereditatis.* These words are *prima facie* words of limitation, unless the words are express or have a different meaning, by necessary implication, from the whole sense and tenor of the writing.(*y*)

The word "heir" cannot be a name of purchase unless the devisor parts with the whole estate which is in him,(*z*) nor when the heir takes that, after the death of his ancestor, which the ancestor could enjoy while living; for that is descent, and not purchase.(*a*) A man cannot raise a fee simple to his own right heirs, by the name of heir, as a purchase.(*b*) So of a devise to a person who is his next heir, and his heirs; it works by descent,(*c*) because he is simply heir to the ancestor, and the devise does not break or alter the course of descent, whatever mode of expression is adopted. If it denotes the person who is to take by the term "heir" in the capacity of heir to an ancestor, and not a person designated as the heir of some one, as a

---

(*w*) L. 145; 2 Dane's Ab. 556; 2 R. A. 253, H. pl.; 1 Gil. D. 20; 1 Bulst. 219.
(*x*) L. 22 *b*, denoting the estate; 1 Bulst. 22, '3.
(*y*) Litt., 12 *a;* 2 Rawle, 33.

(*z*) L. 22 *b;* 2 R. A. 253.
(*a*) L. 13 *b*, 14 *a;* 2 Dane, 557; Gilb. Dev. 113; 1 *c* 95, etc.
(*b*) Hob. 30.
(*c*) Hobart, 30.

The rule in Shelley's case.

term describing the person to take, he takes by descent. A strong and clear illustration of this rule of the common law is in the principal case, *Counden* v. *Clerke*,(d) which was a devise of socage lands "unto the right heirs male and posterity of me and my name forever." The testator left a son, a daughter and brother; the son died without issue; the daughter married and had issue, two daughters; so that the contest was between the brother and granddaughters of the testator. It was held that the brother could not take, because he was not the heir; and the granddaughters could not take because they were not heirs male of his name.

25. Adverting to THE RULE IN SHELLEY'S CASE,* as to the meaning of the word "heir," and the innumerable cases which have arisen upon it, it will suffice to take the remarks of Lord THURLOW, as a summary of the laws on this point :(e)

"I take that rule to be, that where the heir takes in the character of heir, he must take in the quality of heir; I take that question always to have been as to the import of the word "heir" in the proposed case. I never heard it contended that the testator could vary the sense of the law; whether heirs general, heirs male, or heirs female, are to take by those words, they must take in that quality; therefore, you must prove that the second taker was not intended to take in that character but in some other."(f)   "All heirs, taking as heirs, must take by descent."(g)   The word "heirs" must be intended as a description of the persons to take by such "declaration plain," as would overturn the legal constructions, or it must be adopted.(h)

There is no difference, in this respect, between wills and deeds, or other writings, on questions of intention, except this : That where the words relate to the quality of the estate, as whether it is for life,

(d) Hob. 29.
(e) 3 Binney, 154.
(f) 1 Bl. Com. 216.

(g) 1 Bl. Com. 219.
(h) 1 id. 221, 224.

---

* Shelley's case. The following is the rule established in this case:

"When the ancestor, by any gift or conveyance, taketh an estate of freehold, and in the same gift or conveyance an estate is limited, either mediately or immediately, to his heirs, in fee or in tail, the heirs are words of limitation of the estate, and not words of purchase." 1 Coke, 104.

PURCHASE, in the law includes every mode of acquiring property known to the law, except that by which an heir on the death of his ancestor becomes substituted in his place as owner by operation of law. Washb. Real Prop. 401.

The acquisition of property, by a person, through a will or devise, is one of the modes of title by purchase, by deed is another.

The other mode of acquiring property is by descent.

The rule in Shelley's case.

or one of inheritance, certain words are necessary in a deed to carry a fee, they must be such as to effect their object by their legal operation; whereas, to have been designed by the testator, the intended effect being the legal effect.(*i*) Where the words relate to the person or persons who are to take under the limitation of the estate, in a deed or will,(*j*) the rules of construction are the same; the intention will be anxiously sought and faithfully asserted. The rule, as adopted(*k*) by all the judges,(*l*) is: "And here, first, I do exceedingly commend the judges that are curious and almost subtle, astute, to invent reasons and means to make acts according to the just intent of the parties, and to avoid wrong and injury which, by rigid rules, might be wrought out of the act.(*m*) The case of *Moore* v. *Magrath* is a strong but authoritative illustration of the principle which the supreme court of the United States, in the case of *The United States* v. *Arredondo*, have extracted from the law of construction common to England and this country :(*n*) "The words of a grant are always construed according to the intention of the parties as manifested in the grant, by its terms, or by the reasonable and necessary implication to be adduced from the situation of the parties, and of the thing granted, its nature and use."(*o*) But, while the court will take all these circumstances into their consideration, it must be remembered that it is to carry the plainly declared intention into effect, which must be apparent on the written instrument; when it is so, courts will be astute in effectuating it from every source of information, and by the most liberal and benign construction; nay, more, they will sometimes give a subtle construction to the words, in order to carry into execution the manifest object and intention of the testator. This, however, can only be done when there is some writing to construe; the intention must not be wholly *dehors*, it must appear on the instrument in some part of it. The court will examine the whole; the four corners as well as the body.(*p*) If it is expressed, however defectively, the court will aid it by extrinsic circumstances, and be astute in supplying defects and curing all ambiguities which appear.(*q*) In the absence of any apparent defect or inaccuracy of expression of any potent ambi-

(*i*) Sh. To. 437, 439.
(*j*) Fearne, 89.
(*k*) From Hobart, 277.
(*l*) In Willes, 333.
(*m*) 6 Pet. 739.
(*n*) Cowp. 9, 10, etc.
(*o*) 6 Pet. 640, and cases cited.
(*p*) Sh. To. 85; 2 J. & W. 89.
(*q*) *Vide* Sh. To. 86, *et seq.*; Went. Off. Ex. 271; Sh. To. 434; Gil. Dev. 21, 112; Fitzg. 236.

Heir at common law and statutory heir.

guity or doubt, as to the legal or intended meaning of the words used, they must be left to their legal meaning and effect; when legal words are used, without superadding words of intention which qualify them, or denote an intent to use them in any other sense, the law deems them to be so intended by the testator; to this rule there are no exceptions, either in the construction of deeds, wills or other writings.(*r*) Any other will would repeal the statute of wills, which requires them to be in writing; a will is, since the statute 34 and 35 Henry VIII, to be taken as a written declaration of the mind, will, or intention of the testator, as to what should become of his estate after his death. Before the statute, it might be by parol as a declaration of uses (Dy. 53, *b;* Sh. To. 399, 415 ; L. 111), where land was devisable by custom or tenure; but since then it must be by writing. So is the statute law of Illinois.(*s*)

26. One of the first and most sacred principles of the law is, that "the common law hath no controller in any part of it, but the high court of parliament; and, if it be not altered or abrogated by parliament, it remains still ; particular customs must be proved.(*t*) The same principle is the rule in Illinois and other States, in all cases to which the common law had been applied by adoption; and it remains now the law of descent of both real and personal estate, if the provisions of an act of assembly do not, in their words, embrace the very case in controversy.(*u*)

27. There is then, it seems, an HEIR AT COMMON LAW, distinct from the statutory heir, to whom the real estate of a person dying seized and intestate shall descend by the general course of the law in right of blood and inheritance. That the common law of both countries is the same, designating the same person, by the same rules and courses of descent, as the heir to an ancestor in all cases, and the heir to his estates of inheritance, unless, in the particular event which has happened, an act of assembly has substituted some other person or persons to take the place of the ancestor for its enjoyment.(*v*)

(*r*) Sh. To. 89, note; Gilb. Dev. 143.
(*s*) See pp. 33, 44, *supra*.
(*t*) L. 115, *b*. 33, *b*. 58, *b*. 113, *a. b. ;* Litt. § 169.
(*u*) *Johnson* v. *Haines*, 4 Dall . 64; *Cresoe* v. *Laidley*, 2 Binney, 279, 284.
(*v*) If the reader desire to pursue this subject further, he is referred to the learned opinion of Sir THOMAS PLUMMER. 2 Jac. & Walk. 65–132. A careful reading of this opinion will throw much light upon our statutes of wills, descent and conveyances.

28. DISTRIBUTION.* If, on the final settlement of the administrator's accounts, it appears he has satisfied all the claims allowed against the estate, and all charges and costs of administration, and that there remains in his hands a surplus, it shall be distributed according to the law of descent.

29. PROOF OF HEIRSHIP. Proof of heirship is required in case of an intestate estate before a distribution will be made to the heirs. This may be done on the petition of any one interested in the fund to be distributed, upon the testimony of two disinterested witnesses taken in open court, reduced to writing and filed in the case. No estate will be declared settled until the clerk's costs are paid.(*w*)

To those not conversant with the technicalities of law, our statutes may appear ambiguous on some questions that naturally arise in the distribution of property; for instance, the third rule makes no provisions for the distribution of the remaining estate, after giving the widow one-half of the real, and all the personal estate, including dower. This provision must be explained by the preceding one, both being intended to apply in case there should be no children or descendants of children of the intestate; the *third* rule applying when the intestate has left a widow, and the *second* when there is no widow, which distributes the estate equally among the parents, brothers and sisters of the intestate, in case there be no children or descendants of children. Hence, we must conclude, that after the widow has taken her one-half of the real, and all the personal estate, including dower, the residue is divided equally among the parents, brothers and sisters.

This question has not been settled by the supreme court; it has, however, frequently come up in practice in the circuit court, and has been decided as suggested above.

The fourth rule provides, that if there be no children, parents, brothers and sisters, and no widow, then the estate shall descend in equal parts to the next of kin, in equal degree, computing by the rules of the civil law, etc. The only question here presented is, what are the rules of the civil law? To explain the rules of descent of the civil law would extend this book far beyond its proper

(*w*) See Costs and fees, *infra*.

---

* DISTRIBUTION is, in practice, the division by order of the court having jurisdiction, among those entitled thereto, of the residue of the personal estate of an intestate after payment of the debts and charges.

The law of the domicile of the decedent governs in this distribution. See Hill's Chan. Pr., Domicile.

Proof of heirship.

limits, and we presume that there are few estates to which it will be necessary to apply these rules; therefore, none but the general rule for determining the next of kin will be given.

We must first take into consideration the distinction between *lineal* and *collateral* heirs. *Lineal* are such as are in a direct line from the intestate, either ascending, as the parents, grandparents, etc., or descending, as children, grandchildren, their children, and so on down in a direct line, always involving the relationship of parent and child; while *collateral* include all other heirs, however remote, as brother, sister, uncle, aunt, nephew, niece, cousin, etc., they not being related to each other in a direct line, but are relations merely because they have a common ancestor, by means of whom they determine that they are relatives.

The rule for determining the next of kin in the *lineal* line is to ascertain the number of degrees or generations between the intestate and the heir or person to whom the estate descends, as from the intestate to his son or father, one degree; grandfather or grandson, two degrees, etc.; but the rule is more complicated in collateral relationship: First ascertain the degrees between one of the persons related and the common ancestor; count, in like manner, the degrees down to the other, which number of degrees or generations will (according to the civil law) give the relationship existing between them; for instance, there are two degrees between brothers, counting one to the father or common ancestor in the ascending line, and one from the father to the other son in the descending line. From this example the number of degrees or generations will be easily determined, by searching out the common ancestor, and then ascertaining the number of degrees between him and the intestate, adding to that the degrees between the ancestor and heir. But, in applying these principles to this provision of the statute, we encounter a question which seems to have been left open by the statute. The great-grandparents, uncle and aunt, all being in the third degree from the intestate, shall the preference be given to the great-grandparents who are lineal heirs, or shall they share equally with the uncles and aunts of the intestate? The words of the statute seem to lean toward the latter conclusion, for it gives to the next of kin, in equal degree, an equal share of the estate, and perhaps this would be the construction given to the statute, and, in the absence of a legal construction to the contrary, this, no doubt, would be the proper course to pursue in all cases where the heirs are in equal degree, except in such cases as are definitely provided for in the statute.

There may other questions arise in distributing the estate, but we know of no way by which this subject can be explained better than by a practical illustration of all the leading principles relating to the subject. For this purpose, we will suppose that A died, leaving property (when the debts are paid) of the value of $30,000. This sum is divided equally between his two sons, B and C, or, if C has died, then one-half ($15,000) to B, to C's children, D and E, an equal portion each of C's share ($15,000), which would be $7,500 to each; and if both the sons (B and C) of the intestate have deceased, B leaving three sons, F, G and H, then B's share ($15,000) will be equally divided among his three sons, while C's share would go to his sons, in the same manner as in the other case. But if A leave no children or their descendants, then, if there be no widow, the parents, brother and sister, four in all, will each take one-fourth of the $30,000; but, if the widow is living, besides her dower, she is entitled to one-half of the real, and all the personal, estate, the residue being divided as in the other case. If there be none of the above-mentioned heirs, then we must proceed according to the rules of the civil law. The grandparents being in the next degree to the intestate, the estate will ascend to them in equal shares. Here, it will be remembered, that by our statute there is no representation among collaterals, except with the descendants of brothers and sisters of the intestate; hence, in default of these, we must ascertain who occupies the next degree (the third), which we find to be the great-grandparents, uncles and aunts, who are to divide the estate equally among them, and so on, according to the rules heretofore mentioned. We might go back from generation to generation, but it would be useless, for there are few estates that will require the application of all the rules laid down. We will, therefore, close this chapter by adding the table usually presented in kindred works in England, with a brief explanation, concluding this interesting subject of descent with a resume of some of the apposite decisions of the supreme court of Illinois, decisions which must ever command the admiration and respect of the well-read lawyer for their firm adherence to the ancient landmarks.

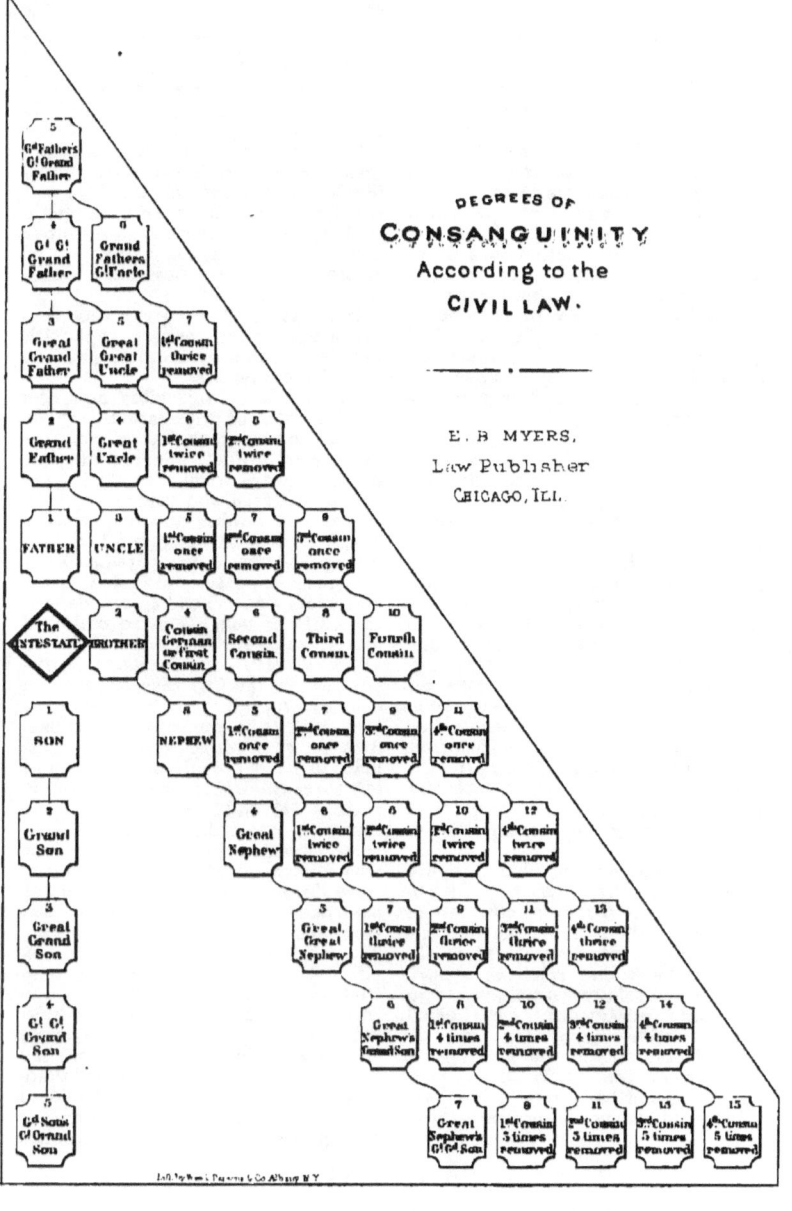

Explanation of the table.

EXPLANATION OF THE TABLE.

CONSANGUINITY, or kindred, is the connection or relation of persons descended from the same stock, or common, one and the same ancestor; it is either *lineal* or *collateral*. *Lineal* consanguinity is the relation in a direct line downward, as from the intestate to his son, grandson, great-grandson; or in a direct line upward, as from the intestate to his father, grandfather, great-grandfather, so that there are *lineals* in the *descending* line and also in the *ascending* line. Every generation, either way from the descent, constitutes a degree, *e. g.* The father is in the first degree in the *ascending* line, while the son is in the first degree in the descending line, so on, either up or down, as designated in the table.

Collateral kindred or *collaterals* (see sub. 5, § 1, act April 9, 1872) are such as lineally spring from one and the same ancestor, who is the *stirps* or root, the *stirpes*, trunk or common stock, whence these relations branch, *e. g.* I have two sons who have each a numerous progeny; the issues are cousins, collaterally related to each other, because they are all descended from me as the common ancestor; all have a portion of such a common ancestor's blood flowing in their veins, which gives them the name *consanguineos* or *consanguinity*.

Affinity, on the other hand, is relationship only by marriage. By the same father there may be children by different mothers, and from different fathers there may be children by the same mother; *i. e.*, relatives *a parte paterna* and relatives *a parte materna*, both called relatives of the half blood, while relatives descending from the same father and mother are termed relatives of the whole blood. Our statute prescribes that, in no case, shall there be any distinction between the kindred of the whole and the half blood. Sub. 5, § 1, act April 9, 1872.

The point was decided the same way in the absence of a statutory provision in the case of the Hartleys and the Harrisons who claimed under a will the one *a parte materna* the other *a parte paterna*, as the heir at law of Matthias Aspden. See Hill's Chancery Practice, 64–68.

Our statute (id.) prohibits representation among collaterals, except with the descendants of brothers and sisters of the intestate.

By the aid of this table now, the concise rules of the statute may be applied to every case that can possibly arise, *e. g.* First, suppose at your death you are unmarried, and have had no children, and you leave three sisters, one brother and a niece (the daughter of a deceased brother), surviving relatives, your parents being dead; or suppose you leave three daughters, one son and a granddaughter (child of your deceased child), in either case your estate would be divided into five equal parts, to be distributed, in the first case, one-fifth to each sister, or three-fifths to your sisters, one-fifth to your brother and one-fifth to your niece. Supposing this niece to have been dead, and to have left three children, then of your estate each of her children would take one third of one-fifth, together taking three-fifteenths, or the one-fifth that would have descended to their mother were she your survivor; in the second case, one-fifth would descend to each child and one-fifth to the grandchild. The other contingencies are quite specifically detailed, and to trace the cases that might arise would be but permutations of the numbers of the divisions and subdivisions of the statute. We leave further detail for the learned and curious, for whom there is ample scope to study either real or imaginary cases of distribution, or the application of the law of descent.

30. DECISIONS.

In the case of *Deltzer* v. *Scheuster*,(x) there was a deficiency of personal assets to pay the widow's allowance. She, as a creditor, applied to the court for sale of the real estate devised to the children

(x) 37 Ill. 301.

Decisions.

exclusive of that devised to herself. The supreme court, under *Cruce* v. *Cruce*,(*y*) held she was a creditor, but that the fund devised to her and the children, that is, the realty, was a common fund, and that that part devised to the widow should bear a proportion of the amount paid to her, and that for the residue the estate devised to the children should be sold. Equity is equality.

The presumption of our law is, that a person dying intestate has left heirs capable of succeeding to his estate ; and this presumption is so violent that it can only be repelled by proof.(*z*)

Prima facie, the term "children" means lawful children, and the statute of descents, by which property of an intestate is made to descend to and among children and their descendants, has reference to lawful children only.(*a*)

NEXT OF KIN. The computation of the civilians is adopted to ascertain who are next of kin to an intestate.(*b*)

Personal property of a minor vests immediately in the next of kin, no necessity existing of taking out letters of administration before instituting suit for the same.(*c*)

The title to the land of an intestate does not vest in his administrator as a trustee, but descends directly to the heirs. They hold the title in their own right, and only subject to the payment of the debts of their ancestor, in the modes prescribed by law, and not subject to any other control of the administrator.(*d*) Only, however, to the extent of the ancestor's estate which they inherit.

The heir is owner of the lands of an intestate, and the rents and profits derived therefrom, until divested by an order of sale or decree, for the purpose of paying debts.(*e*)

Where real estate is conveyed to an attorney, to save him harmless as against his liability as bail, without an intention to sell, an actual sale by the attorney will not change the character of the proceeds ; but these will descend to the heirs, and not go to the administrator.(*f*)

Rent, accruing after death of a decedent, goes to the heirs.(*g*)

(*y*) 21 Ill. 46.
(*z*) *Harvey* v. *Thornton*, 14 Ill. 217.
(*a*) *Blacklaws* v. *Milne*, 82 Ill. 503.
(*b*) *Hayes* v. *Thomas*, Breese, 136.
(*c*) *Lynch* v. *Rotan*, 39 Ill. 15.
(*d*) *Walbridge* v. *Day*, 31 Ill. 379.

(*e*) *Smith* v. *McConnell*, 17 Ill. 135.
(*f*) *Jennings* v. *McConnel*, 17 Ill. 148.
(*g*) *Green* v. *Massie*, 13 Ill. 363 ; *Foltz* v. *Prouse*, 17 id. 487 ; *Dixon* v. *Niccolls*, 39 id. 372.

Decisions.

Posthumous children take by descent with the antecedent children or with other heirs.(*h*)

A posthumous child will take directly from the parent, with the same effect as if it had been born at the time of the decease of the parent.(*i*)

A disclaimer by one or more of the heirs, in a chancery suit brought by the heirs, does not vest the interest so disclaimed in the remaining heirs.(*j*)

After the death of an heir, money, in which he was entitled to an equitable interest, while living, was used in the purchase of land after his death. Held, that the heir did not have an estate of inheritance in such purchase that could pass by descent to his heirs.(*j*)

Under the word "heirs" are comprehended the heirs of heirs *ad infinitum*. (*Merrill* v. *Atkin*, 59 Ill. 19.)

ORDER OF DESCENT. In this State, where a man dies intestate, leaving a widow, but no descendants, the widow inherits, as heir of the intestate, one-half of the real and all of the personal estate of which her husband died seized, which shall remain after the payment of his debts, and she is also entitled to her dower.(*k*)

In such case the property being all personal the widow takes the whole.(*l*)

The one-half of land in fee allowed the widow by statute under certain circumstances, in lieu of dower, embraces all classes of estates in which dower is demandable, equitable as well as legal estates of inheritance, limited, however, in this, that the husband must have died seized. Lands conveyed by him in his life-time without joinder by the wife are not embraced in the allowance.(*m*)

In such case she is entitled to the specific articles enumerated in the statute, but not to dower in the other half of the real estate, nor to the whole of the personal property.(*n*)

See distinction taken between widow of *testate* and widow of *intestate*.(*n*)

(*h*) *Smith* v. *McConnell*, 17 Ill. 135; *Botsford* v. *O'Conner*, 57 id. 72.
(*i*) *Detrick* v. *Migatt*, 19 Ill. 146; *McConnel* v. *Smith*, 23 id. 611.
(*j*) *Kane County* v. *Herrington*, 50 Ill. 232.

(*k*) *Tyson et ux.* v. *Postlethwaite*, 13 Ill. 728.
(*l*) *Rawson* v. *Rawson*, 52 Ill. 62.
(*m*) *Brown* v. *Pitney*, 30 Ill. 469, *Lessley* v. *Lessley*, 44 id. 527.
(*n*) *Lessley* v. *Lessley*, 44 Ill. 527 *McMurphy* v. *Boyles*, 49 id. 110.

CHAPTER XI.

APPEALS.*

1. Appeals when allowed in the cases in the administration of estates.
2. In guardianship.
3. Praying appeal.
4. How prayed.
5. Bond on appeal.
6. Security for costs by non-residents.
7. The requisites of the bond.
8. The bill of exceptions.
9. In cases of wills.

1. APPEALS shall be allowed from all judgments, orders or decrees of the county court in all matters arising under this act, to the circuit court, in favor of any person who may consider himself aggrieved by any judgment, order or decree of such court and from the circuit court to the supreme court, as in other cases, and bonds with security to be fixed by the county or circuit court, as the case may be.(a)

Appeals and writs of error may be taken and prosecuted from the final orders, judgments and decrees of the county court to the supreme [appellate] court in proceedings, * * on the application of executors, administrators, guardians and conservators for the sale of real estate. Such appeals and writs of error shall, when not otherwise provided, be taken and prosecuted in the same manner as appeals from and writs of error to circuit court.(b)

In all cases when an executor or administrator shall take an appeal from the judgment, decree or order of any court or justice of the peace to the county, circuit or supreme court, or when he may prosecute writs of error or *certiorari*, the appeal, *certiorari* or *supersedeas* bond shall be conditioned to pay the judgment or decree, with costs, in due course of administration; in all other respects such bonds shall be in the form prescribed by law in other cases.(c)

(a) Cothran's Stats.. 81, § 123; R. S. 1874, 126, § 123.
(b) Rev. Stats., 1874, 344, § 188.
(c) § 124, R. S. 1874, p. 126.

---

*This subject with the decisions may be found fully delineated and supported, with the authorities in our volumes on common law and chancery practice. 2 Hill's Common Law; Hill's Chan. Pr.

Guardianship, etc.

2. APPEALS shall be allowed to the circuit court from any order or judgment made or rendered under this act, upon the appellant giving such bond and security as shall be directed by the court; but no appeal from an order removing a guardian shall in anywise affect such order, until the same be reversed.(d)'

Appeals may be taken from the final orders, judgments and decrees of the probate courts to the circuit courts of their respective counties, in all matters, except in proceedings, on the application of executors, administrators, guardians and conservators, for the sale of real estate, upon the applicant giving bond and security in such amount and upon such condition as the court shall approve, and upon such appeal the case should be tried *de novo*. Appeals and writs of error may be taken and prosecuted from the final orders and decrees of the probate court to the supreme [appellate] court, in proceedings on the application of executors, administrators, guardians and conservators for the sale of real estate. Such appeals and writs of error, when not otherwise provided, shall be taken and prosecuted in the same manner as appeals from and writs of error to the circuit court.(e)

The conflicting statutes above exhibited have not yet been submitted to the supreme court in such manner that a decision has been rendered. As to county courts sitting in probate by the 68th section of the statute regulating the administration of estates, it is beyond doubt, the appeal will be taken to the circuit court, as from a justice of the peace; that is within twenty days from that on which the judgment is rendered. This, of course, excludes the day on which the judgment is rendered, and the bond must be filed in apt time.(f) It would seem that appeals from the probate courts must be perfected within the particular term of court at which judgment is rendered. This was the result arrived at both in the circuit court of Cook county (MCALLISTER, J.) and the appellate court of the first district, in *Falch* v. *Eigenmann, Adm'r, etc.*, unreported.

In *Fowler* v. *Perkins*, 77 Ill. 271, the supreme court has held that the statute of 1874, having relation to the perfecting of appeals

---

(d) An act in regard to guardians and wards. Cothran's Stats., 774, § 43.

(e) Act April 27, 1877; id. 426.

(f) *Darwin* v. *Jones*, 82 Ill. 107.

Guardianship, etc.

from final judgments of the county courts, in respect to taxes, is not imperative, that such appeals may still be carried to the circuit court. This ruling would seem also to include the judgments of such courts on the application of executors, administrators, guardians and conservators, for the sale of real estate. The language of the act is that they *may* be taken directly to the appellate court, so it does not repeal, by implication, the provisions of the original act. The appellant may elect the tribunal into which he will carry his cause.(g)

In regard to probate courts, however, a different rule applies. As to them it would seem, that the provision as to appeals must be strictly followed, the act being specific as to the practice in that court, and of a later date than any which have been referred to the appellate tribunals.

In taking appeals to the circuit court, the [practice is the same as that in perfecting appeals to the supreme court, hence exceptions must be taken and preserved by bill of exceptions and the record perfected as in trials in the circuit courts. (*Hulett* v. *Ames*, 74 Ill. 253.)

Where an appeal lies to the circuit court, a further appeal lies from its judgment to the appellate or supreme court, as the case may be. (*U. S. Express Co.* v. *Merrits*, 72 Ill. 293.)

An appeal may be taken from the court sitting in probate as to any one item allowed an administrator in his account. Such appeal does not bring before the appellate tribunal the whole account, but the trial, which is *de novo*, will be confined to the item appealed from. (*Morgan* v. *Morgan*, 83 Ill. 196.)

A judgment of the circuit court reversing a judgment rendered in the county court and remanding the cause is not a final judgment from which an appeal will lie. (*Phelps* v. *Dolan*, 75 Ill. 90; *Wright* v. *Smith*, 76 id. 216.)

3. THE APPEAL is prayed usually at the time of rendering the

(g) See *Ashford* v. *The People*, 82 Ill. 214.

In probate.

adverse judgment order or decree, but it may be prayed at any time during the term at which the judgment order or decree is rendered.(*d*)

4. How prayed. To pray an appeal, it is only necessary for the party aggrieved, or his counsel, to suggest that "we pray an appeal, if it please the court, from the (here specify the judgment order or decree appealed from), and ask your honor to fix the bond on appeal."

The court will then fix the amount of the bond and the time within which the appeal is to be perfected. At the same term, and within the time fixed, take the bond properly executed with the securities personally before the judge, or the court, if it be open, and they will be examined, and if approved the bond will be filed and the appeal perfected. The transcript from the record should be made and the case certified into the appellate court.(*e*)

5. Bond on appeal.

[*As in form, supra, page* 226, *to asterisk, then continue thus:*]

The condition of the above obligation is such, that whereas the said   , at the   term of the county court, in and for the county of   , to wit: on   day of   , A. D. 18   , being one of the days of said term, recovered an allowance against the estate of   , deceased, for the sum of   dollars, which allowance was ordered by the court to be paid, in due course of administration, from which allowance by an order of the court, the said   of the said estate has taken an appeal to the   . Now, therefore, if the said   , aforesaid, shall prosecute said appeal with effect, and shall comply with whatever judgment or order may be rendered by said appellate court, upon dismissal or trial of said appeal, then the above obligation to be void, otherwise to remain in full force and effect.

[SEAL.]
[SEAL.]
[SEAL.]

6. Non-resident executors, administrators, guardians and conservators or trustees, before commencing any proceedings in the courts in Illinois, are required to give security for costs.(*f*)

The first step for a non-resident is to file such security.(*g*)

An appeal bond by an executor, conditioned to pay the debt "in due course of administration," is good.(*h*)

Waiver. All irregularities in taking appeals from the county to

---

(*d*) *Ballance* v. *Frisby*, 1 Scam. 595; *McMillen* v. *Bethold*, 40 Ill. 34; *Illinois Central R. R. Co.* v. *Johnson*, 40 id. 35.
(*e*) See 2 Hill's Common Law, *Appeal*; Hill's Chan. Pr., *Appeal*.

(*f*) See chap. xiii. *infra*.
(*g*) 2 Hill's Com. Law, 625–637.
(*h*) *Mason* v. *John on*, 24 Ill. 159.

Guardianship, Wills, etc.

the circuit court are waived by the appearance of the appellees, without objection.(*i*)

Where a claim is filed in the probate court and carried up on appeal, the claimant, if he supports his claim, is entitled to the amount and interest, notwithstanding the judgment exceeds the amount of the original claim.

8. The appellant, from the probate court to the circuit court, who neglects to tender A BILL OF EXCEPTIONS, as required by law, cannot himself object, in the supreme court for the first time, to want of jurisdiction in the circuit court by reason of such neglect.(*j*)

Where a cause is appealed from the probate court to the circuit court, and the parties agree that the case be tried there on its merits, and it appears that the probate court had not jurisdiction of the cause, but the circuit court had, the circuit court may try the cause and render judgment as if the cause had been commenced there, but cannot direct the probate court to issue execution on the judgment.(*k*)

9. APPEAL IN PROBATE OF WILLS, AND MODE OF TRIAL. Appeals may be taken from the order of the county court, allowing or disallowing any will to probate, to the circuit court of the same county, by any person interested in such will, in the same time and manner as appeals may be taken from justices of the peace, except that the appeal bond and security may be approved by the clerk of the county court; and the trial of such appeals shall be *de novo*.(*l*)

PROOF OF WILL ON APPEAL TO CIRCUIT COURT. When the probate of any will and testament shall have been refused by any county court, and an appeal shall have been taken from the order or decision of such court refusing to admit such will to probate, into the circuit court of the proper county, as provided by law, it shall be lawful for the party seeking probate of such will to support the same on hearing in such circuit court, by any evidence competent to establish a will in chancery; and, in case probate of such will shall be allowed on such appeal, it shall be admitted to probate, liable, however, to be subsequently contested, as provided in the case of wills admitted to probate in the first instance.(*m*)

(*i*) *Mitchell* v. *Jacobs*, 17 Ill. 235.
(*j*) *Welch* v. *Wallace*, 3 Gilm. 490.
(*k*) *Allen* v. *Belcher*, 3 Gilm. 594.

See Hill's Com. Law, *Appeals;* Hill's Chan. Pr., *Appeals*.
(*l*) § 14, R. S. 1874, p. 1104.
(*m*) § 13, id.

CHAPTER XII.

MISCELLANEOUS MATTERS.

1. The executor or administrator, or his security, not chargeable beyond the assets of the testator or intestate.
2. Specific performance of the contracts made by decedent may be ordered.
3. The books of account of the decedent to be subject to the inspection of all concerned.
4. Estate, if found insolvent after two years from the grant of administration, to be so entered.
5. The executor or administrator may be coerced to apply for an order to sell real estate.
6. County courts to have power to enforce due observance of their process, judgments, orders and decrees, the same as the circuit courts.
7. The sheriff to serve and execute all process, papers, etc.
8. Executors and administrators to receive compensation not to exceed six per centum on amount of personal estate, nor more than three per centum on amount of proceeds of the real estate sold, with allowances for costs and charges in collecting the estate and defending claims.
9. Construction of the act relating to administration to be liberal, and to apply equally to executors and administrators, etc.
10. Repeal of former laws with saving clause.

1. MISCELLANEOUS PROVISIONS. No executor or administrator, or his security, shall be chargeable beyond the assets of the testator or intestate by reason of any omission or mistake in pleading, or by false pleading of such executor or administrator.(*a*)

2. All contracts made by the decedent may be performed by the executor or administrator when so directed by the county court.(*b*)

3. The books of account of any deceased person shall be subject to the inspection of all persons interested therein.(*c*)

4. If, after the expiration of two years from the time administration is granted on an estate, such estate is found to be insolvent, it shall be so entered of record by the county court, and such order made. No action shall be maintained against the executor or administrator of such estate except at the costs of the party suing; but persons entitled thereto shall receive their proportions of such estate as herein provided.(*d*)

5. Whenever real estate is required to be sold for the payment of

(*a*) § 125, R. S. 1874, p. 127.
(*b*) § 126, id.
(*c*) § 127, R. S. 1874, p. 127.
(*d*) § 128, id.

debts, the court may make all necessary orders to coerce the executor or administrator to make immediate application for an order to sell such real estate.(*e*)

6. County courts shall have power to enforce due observance of all orders, decisions, judgments and decrees made by them in discharge of their duties under this act; and they may issue attachments for contempt offered such courts or its process by any executor, administrator, witness or other person; and may fine and imprison, or either, all such offenders, in like manner as the circuit courts may do in similar cases.(*f*)

7. The sheriff shall, when required by the court, attend all sessions of said court, either by himself or deputy, and shall preserve good order in the court and execute all writs of attachment, summonses, subpœnas, citations, notices and other processes which may, at any time, be legally issued by such court, and make return thereof. And such sheriff shall be entitled to the same fees as he is allowed for similar services in the circuit court.(*g*)

8. Executors and administrators shall be allowed, as compensation for their services, a sum not exceeding six per centum on the amount of personal estate, and not exceeding three per centum on the money arising from the sale of real estate, with such additional allowances for costs and charges in collecting and defending the claims of the estate, and disposing of the same as shall be reasonable.(*h*)

9. All the provisions in this act relative to an executor or administrator shall apply and extend to an executrix or administratrix, or executors or administrators, and *vice versa*, unless otherwise expressly provided for; and whenever the singular number of the masculine gender is mentioned, the provisions shall apply to two or more, and to the feminine gender, as the case may require; and this act shall be liberally construed so that its true intent and meaning may be fully carried out.(*i*)

10. REPEAL OF FORMER LAWS. The following acts and parts of acts are hereby repealed: Chapter 109 of the Revised Statutes of 1845, entitled "Wills," except sections one, two, three, four, five, six, seven, eight, nine, ten, eleven, twelve, thirteen, fourteen, fifteen, sixteen, seventeen, eighteen, forty-six, forty-seven, fifty-one, fifty-two,

(*e*) § 129, R. S. 1874, p. 127.
(*f*) § 130, id.
(*g*) § 131, id.
(*h*) § 132, R. S. 1874, p. 127.
(*i*) § 133, id.

Repeal of former laws.

fifty-three, fifty-four and one hundred and twenty-eight; an act entitled "An act authorizing administrators and executors from other States to prosecute suits in this State," approved March 3, 1845; an act entitled "An act to amend an act relative to wills and testaments, executors and administrators, and the settlement of estates," approved February 21, 1845; an act entitled "An act further to define the duties of probate justices," approved February 19, 1847; an act entitled "An act to amend an act concerning wills," approved February 11, 1847; an act entitled "An act authorizing the resignation of certain officers," approved February 10, 1849; an act entitled "An act to amend the laws in relation to the settlement of estates," approved February 17, 1851; an act entitled "An act respecting executors, administrators, guardians and their securities," approved February 12, 1853; an act entitled "An act to regulate appeals in certain cases," approved February 8, 1853; an act entitled "An act conferring additional power upon administrators *de bonis non*, and for other purposes," approved February 14, 1855; an act entitled "An act to provide for the manner of selling real estate of deceased persons for the payment of debts," approved February 18, 1857; sections nine, ten and twelve of an act entitled "An act to reform the probate system," approved February 21, 1859; an act entitled "An act amending section four of the act entitled 'Wills,'" approved February 24, 1859; an act entitled "An act to amend chapter one hundred and ten, Revised Statutes, entitled 'Wills,'" approved March 7, 1867; an act entitled "An act to amend section one hundred and thirty-four of chapter one hundred and nine of the Revised Statutes of 1845," approved April 8, 1869; an act entitled "An act to facilitate the settlement of partnership interest of deceased persons' estates," approved March 26, 1869; an act entitled "An act to amend chapter one hundred and nine of the Revised Statutes, entitled 'Wills,'" approved March 31, 1869; and all other acts and parts of acts inconsistent with the provisions of this act: *Provided*, that this section shall not affect any suits that may be pending, or any rights that have accrued when this act shall take affect." (*j*)

(*j*) § 135, act April 1, 1872.

Miscellaneous provisions of the act of April 1, 1872.

MISCELLANEOUS PROVISIONS OF THE ACT OF APRIL 1, 1872.

1. Power of administrator to collect.
2. When his appointment shall cease.
3. General provisions as to bonds of executors and administrators.
4. Causes for revocation of letters testamentary and of administration.
5. Causes for removal.
6. Surety on bond may apply to be released.
7. New appointment to be made if executor or administrator fail to give new bond.
8. Letters *cum testamento annexo.*
9. Co-executor or co-administrator may be appointed.
10. Liability of administrator, who has been discharged, to his successor in trust.

1. POWER OF ADMINISTRATOR TO COLLECT. Every collector so appointed shall have the power to collect the goods, chattels and debts of the said deceased, according to the tenor of the said letters, and to secure the same at such reasonable and necessary expense as shall be allowed by the court; and the said court may authorize him, immediately after the inventory and appraisement of such estate, to sell such as are perishable or may depreciate by delay, and to account for the same; and for the whole trouble incurred by such collector the court may allow such commission on the amount of said personal estate as shall be actually collected and delivered to the proper executor or administrator, as aforesaid, as said court may deem just and reasonable. *Provided,* the same shall not exceed six per cent on the amount stated in such inventory or bill of appraisement.(*k*)

MAY SUE, ETC. Every such collector may commence suits for debts due to the decedent, and release the same on payment thereof; and no such suit shall abate by the revocation of his letters, but the same may be prosecuted to a final decision, in the name of and by the executor or administrator to whom letters testamentary or of administration may be granted.(*l*)

2. On the granting of letters testamentary or of administration, the power of any such collector, so appointed, shall cease, and it shall be his duty to deliver, on demand, all property and money of the deceased, which shall have come to his hands or possession

(*k*) § 15, R. S. 1874, p. 107.   (*l*) § 16, R. S. 1874, p. 107.

Miscellaneous provisions of the act of April 1, 1872.

(saving such commission as may be allowed by the court, as aforesaid), to the person or persons obtaining such letters; and, in case any such collector shall refuse or neglect to deliver over such property or money to his successor, when legal demand is made therefor, such person so neglecting or refusing shall be liable to pay twenty per cent over and above the amount of all such property or money as comes to his hands by virtue of his administration, and is not paid or delivered over as aforesaid, and shall forfeit all claim to any commission for collecting and preserving the estate, which said twenty per cent, together with all damages which may be sustained by reason of the breach of any bond, which may at any time be given by any such collector, may be sued for and recovered by the person or persons to whom letters testamentary or of administration may be granted, for the use of the estate of such decedent.(*m*)

3. GENERAL PROVISIONS IN REGARD TO BONDS OF EXECUTORS AND ADMINISTRATORS. When two or more persons are appointed executors or administrators of the same estate, the court may take a separate bond, with sureties, from each, or a joint bond, with sureties, from all.(*n*)

SUITS ON BONDS, ETC. All bonds which may at any time be given by any executor or administrator, either with or without the will annexed, or *de bonis non*, to collect, or public administrator, may be put in suit and prosecuted against all or any one or more of the obligors named therein, in the name of the people of the State of Illinois, for the use of any person who may have been injured by reason of the neglect or improper conduct of any such executor or administrator, and such bond shall not become void on the first recovery thereon, but may be sued upon, from time to time, until the whole penalty shall be recovered. *Provided*, that the person for whose use the same is prosecuted shall be liable for all costs which may accrue in the prosecution of the same, in case the plaintiffs fail in their suit; and certified copies of all such bonds, under the seal of the clerk of the county court, shall be received as evidence to authorize such recovery in any court of law or equity of competent jurisdiction.(*o*)

4. REVOKING LETTERS AND REQUIRING NEW BONDS. County courts shall revoke letters of administration in all cases where the

---

(*m*) § 17, R. S. 1874, p. 107. *Allen*, 86 Ill.166; *Tucker* v. *People*, 87
(*n*) § 24, R. S. 1874, p. 109. Ill. 76.
(*o*) § 25, R. S. 1874, p.109; *People* v.

Miscellaneous provisions of the act of April 1, 1872.

same were granted to any person upon the false and fraudulent pretense of being a creditor of the estate upon which administration is granted, or upon any other false pretense whatever. (*p*)

FRAUD, ETC. When it appears that such letters were fraudulently obtained by such administrator, the court revoking the same shall give judgment against the administrator for all costs of suit.(*q*)

DISCOVERY OF WILL TO REVOKE. If, at any time after letters of administration have been granted, a will of the deceased shall be produced and probate thereof granted according to law, such letters of administration shall be revoked. (*r*)

REVOCATION OF LETTERS TESTAMENTARY, ETC. In all cases where a will, testament or codicil shall have been proved and letters granted thereon, as aforesaid, and such will shall thereafter be set aside by due course of law, the letters granted thereon shall be revoked.(*s*)

INCAPACITY OF EXECUTOR OR ADMINISTRATOR; CAUSE FOR REVOCATION. The county court may revoke all letters testamentary, or of administration, granted to persons who become insane, lunatic or of unsound mind, habitual drunkards, are convicted of infamous crime, waste or mismanage the estate, or who conduct themselves in such manner as to endanger their co-executors, co-administrators or securities, in all which cases the court shall summon the person charged to be in default or disqualified, as aforesaid, to show cause why such revocation should not be made. When revocation is made, the reason therefor shall be stated at large upon the record. (*t*)

5. REMOVAL OF EXECUTOR OR ADMINISTRATOR, CAUSE FOR, ETC. When it shall come to the knowledge of the county court, by affidavit or otherwise, that any executor or administrator of an estate is about to remove or has removed beyond the limits of this State, it shall be the duty of such court to cause a notice to be published in some newspaper in the county where letters testamentary or of administration were granted, for four weeks successively; and if no newspaper is published in said county, then by posting up a notice at the court-house door, notifying the said executor or administrator to appear before him within thirty days after the date of such notice, and make a settlement of his accounts as required by law. If the executor or administrator neglects or refuses to make such set-

(*p*) § 26, R. S. 1874, p. 109.
(*q*) § 27, id.
(*r*) § 28, id.

(*s*) § 29, id.; see p. 99, *supra*.
(*t*) § 30, id.

Miscellaneous provisions of the act of April 1, 1872.

tlement, it shall be the duty of said county court to remove him from office.(*u*)

ADDITIONAL SECURITY REQUIRED; HOW AND WHEN. When any court grants letters testamentary or of administration, of the estate of any person deceased, without taking good security as aforesaid, or when any security heretofore or hereafter taken becomes insufficient, the court may, on the application of any person entitled to distribution, or otherwise interested in such estate, require such executor or administrator to give other and sufficient security; and in default thereof the letters testamentary or of administration shall be revoked, and administration *de bonis non* granted; but all acts done according to law by the executor or administrator so removed prior to such revocation shall be valid.(*v*)

SURETY, HOW RELIEVED. When a surety for an executor or an administrator, or his representatives, may conceive himself or themselves in danger of suffering by the mismanagement of such executor or administrator, and shall petition the county court for relief, in writing, setting forth the cause of such apprehension, the said court shall examine such petition, and, if the court shall deem the cause therein set forth sufficient to entitle such petitioner or petitioners to relief, if true, he shall summon such executor or administrator to show cause against such petition; and may dismiss the same, or direct such executor or administrator either to give good counter security to save such petitioner or petitioners harmless, or to give a new bond in the like penalty as the first; and, upon refusal or neglect to give such counter security or new bond, the letters granted to such executor or administrator may be revoked.(*w*)

6. SURETY MAY PETITION. Whenever any surety on the bond* of any executor or administrator desires to be released from further liability upon any such bond, he may petition the court in which said bond is filed for that purpose, and upon notice being given to the executors or administrators, as the court may direct, the court shall compel such executor or administrator, within a reasonable time, to be fixed by the court, to settle and adjust his accounts, and pay over whatever balance may be found in his hands, and file in such court a new bond in such penalty, and security, as may be ap-

(*u*) § 31, R. S. 1874, p. 110.   (*w*) § 33, id.
(*v*) § 32, id.

* The bond relates back to the grant of administration. § 34, R. S. 1874, p. 110.

Miscellaneous provisions of the act of April 1, 1872.

proved by the court, which being done, the surety may be discharged from all liability on such bond.(*x*)

7. NEW APPOINTMENT, REVOCATION, ETC. If such executor or administrator shall fail to comply with such order within the time fixed by the court, the court shall order that such executor or administrator be removed from his office, and shall appoint some other fit person as administrator, with the will annexed, or *de bonis non*, who shall give bond as required by law. And in case of the failure of the former executor or administrator to settle his accounts and to pay over to the person so appointed all moneys, effects or choses in action in his hands by reason of his said office, then such successor shall proceed to collect the same by suit against such executor or administrator, or by suit upon his bond; and upon collection thereof such surety shall be discharged.(*y*)

8. LETTERS *CUM TESTAMENTO ANNEXO*. When the sole or surviving executor or administrator dies without having fully administered the estate, if there is personal property not administered, or are debts due from the estate, or is any thing remaining to be performed in the execution of the will, the county court shall grant letters of administration, with the will annexed, or otherwise, as the case may require, to some suitable person, to administer the estate of the deceased not already administered. *Provided*, that when there is still a surviving executor or administrator, he may proceed to administer the estate, unless otherwise provided.(*z*)

9. CO-EXECUTORS OR CO-ADMINISTRATORS MAY BE APPOINTED. Where the letters of one of several executors or administrators are revoked, or one or more of the executors or administrators die or become disqualified, the court may join others in their place, and require additional bonds from the new administrator or administrators, or the survivor or survivors, or such as shall not have their powers revoked, shall proceed to manage the estate. When the letters of all of them are revoked, or all of such executors or administrators die before final settlement and distribution of the estate. administration, with the will annexed, or *de bonis non*, shall be granted to the persons next entitled thereto.(*a*)

10. In all cases where any such executor or administrator shall have his letters revoked, he shall be liable on his bond to such sub-

(*x*) § 35, R. S. 1874, p. 110. (*z*) § 37, id.
(*y*) § 36, R. S. 1874, p. 111. (*a*) § 38, id.

Miscellaneous statutes.

sequent administrator, or to any other person aggrieved, for any mismanagement of the estate committed to his care; and the subsequent administrator may have and maintain actions against such former executor or administrator for all such goods, chattels, debts and credits as shall have come to his possession, and which are withheld or have been wasted, embezzled or misapplied, and no satisfaction made for the same.(*b*)

MISCELLANEOUS STATUTES.

1. Specific performance of contract in case of vendor's death, etc., how enforced.
2. Executor or administrator may, of record, discharge a mortgage or trust deed.
3. Deposit of funds on final settlement belonging to unknown heirs or claimants and non-residents.
4. Foreclosure or *sci. fa.* necessary in case of death of mortgagee or debtor requisite.
5. When surety is released in case of death of the maker of a joint note.
6. Foreign guardian may receive the estate of his ward; procedure prescribed.
7. Competency of parties as witnesses.
8. The law of evidence in probate unchanged.
9. Miscellaneous decisions.
10. Proclamations by the sheriff in opening and closing, and at adjournment.
11. Oaths, witnesses, jurors, etc.

1. SPECIFIC PERFORMANCE OF CONTRACTS IN CASE OF VENDOR'S DEATH, ETC. By section 31 of Revised Statutes, 1845, chapter 24, "Conveyances," it was provided, that when any person or persons have entered into any contract, bond or memorandum in writing, to make a deed or title to land in this State, for a valuable consideration, and shall *depart this life*, or have *died heretofore without having executed or delivered said deed*, it shall and may be lawful for any court having chancery jurisdiction in the proper circuit in which such case shall arise, to make decree compelling the executors or administrators of such deceased person to execute and deliver such deed to the party having such equitable right as aforesaid to the same, or his heirs, according to the true intent and meaning of said contract, bond or memorandum of the deceased; and all such deeds shall be good and valid in law. Chapter 29, R. S. 1874, p. 270 gives a more comprehensive law.

(*b*) § 39, R. S. 1874, p. 111.

Miscellaneous statutes.

The courts are prohibited from making such decree, except upon the *petition* in writing of the person *entitled* to the benefit of same, or his heirs, setting forth the contract, etc., and fully describing the lands to be conveyed, nor until the parties so applying for such title shall have given reasonable notice of the time and place of such application to the executors, administrators and heirs of such decedent, and shall have fully paid, etc., the consideration of such contract, etc., according to the true intent, tenor and effect thereof. Where minor heirs are interested in such proceeding, reasonable notice of such application shall be given to the guardian or guardians of such minors, and if there be no guardian, then the said court (*of chancery*) shall appoint a guardian or guardians to litigate and act in such case.

The executors, administrators or heirs of such decedent, etc., who made such contract, etc., in his or her life-time, for such conveyance, for a valuable consideration, when such consideration has been paid, etc., to make application in writing (*by petition it is supposed*), to obtain such decree, upon giving notice to the party to whom such deed is intended to be made, and under the same condition as provided in this chapter (*by the sections above given; see act of* 1872, *as amended in* 1873).

Section 6 of the new act provides that, in all cases where such application shall be made, the court shall have power to continue the same from term to term, to obtain such evidence as the case requires; and no decree for such conveyance, upon such applications, shall be made unless the said court (*of chancery*) shall be satisfied that decree can be made without injustice to any heir or creditor of the deceased, and that the same is just and equitable, and section 7 directs that a complete record of such petition and proceedings thereon be made, and that the court shall decree payment of costs as shall appear right and equitable.(*c*)

There is little to be said under these statutes, except —

1. That a *petition in writing* must be presented to the proper chancery court in the proper circuit (this is, of course, the circuit court, unless some local court have jurisdiction in chancery of the matter). The proper circuit would be that of the county where the land lies, unless the defendants, or the major part, reside in another county.

(*c*) See Rev. Stat., 1845, ch. 24, "Conveyances," §§ 31 to 36 inclusive; Purple, pp. 160, 161; Scates, pp. 162, 163, Chancery Code; Laws 1872, 293; id. 277–279; Laws 1873, 70. R. S. 1874, p. 270.

Miscellaneous statutes.

Ordinarily, however, it is in the circuit court of the county where the decedent lived and died.

2. This petition must be in the ordinary chancery form. It may be presented by the party interested in getting the deed, or it may be presented by the executor, administrator or heir of the decedent.

3. The petition must set forth the contract, etc., sought to be enforced, must fully describe the lands, should name the executor, etc., and heirs, and ought to allege that the decree sought will work no injustice to any heir or creditor of decedent, and show that it is just and equitable. This, of course, will flow from the facts. It should show that the consideration, etc., has been fully paid.

4. The notice required by the statute should be given in this respect; where any of the parties are non-resident, the usual publication should be made. This notice is not the usual summons; it is distinct, and should be given, as directed by the statute, by the party interested, if petitioner, or by the executor, etc., if petitioner.

5. The court has power to appoint a guardian *ad litem*, or rather one *pendente lite*, where there is a minor, and no guardian appointed. It would seem that if the application be made by an heir, and he have a guardian, the proceeding can be had by such guardian in the name of the heir, but in no other case can the guardian institute such proceedings. He can unite with the other heirs.

6. As to costs, if the delay in making the deed was by the neglect of the decedent, his estate should pay the costs; if not, then the party benefited. But this is in the discretion of the court, so that it be equitable in view of the facts.

7. It would seem that full power is given the court to act as in other cases, by way of continuance, etc.(*d*)

3. A mortgage or trust deed of real or personal property may be released by the executor or administrator, heir or assignee of record of the mortgagee or trustee, and such instrument may be acknowledged or proved in the same manner as deeds of conveyance of lands.(*e*)

(*d*) See § 6, R. S. 1874, p. 270. (*e*) § 9, R. S. 1874, p. 712.

Miscellaneous statutes.

4. The law of 1869, in force March 30, 1869, "An act to protect widows and orphans from sacrifice of their property by sales upon mortgages and trust deeds," provides, that in case of the death of the grantor, in any mortgage or trust deed given for the security of money, no sale shall be made by virtue of any power or sale contained in such mortgage or trust deed, or given in relation thereto, but the same may be foreclosed as a mortgage not having such power may now be foreclosed at law, or in chancery (at law by *scire facias*, in chancery by bill of complaint).(*g*)

By act of May 7, 1879, like provision is made as to all real estate within this State, mortgaged or incumbered by trust deed or other conveyance in the matter of a mortgage, executed after July 1, 1879.

5. Whenever the principal maker of any note, bond, bill or other instrument in writing, shall die, if the creditor shall not, within two years after the granting of letters testamentary or of administration, present the same to the proper court for allowance, the sureties thereon shall be released from payment thereof to the extent that the same might have been collected of such estate if presented in proper time, but this section shall not be construed to prevent the holder from proceeding against the sureties within said two years.(*h*)

6. FOREIGN GUARDIAN. When there is no guardian in the State of a non-resident minor, his guardian, appointed and qualified according to the law of the place where the minor resides, having first obtained the authority of the county court of the county in this State where any of the personal estate of such minor may be, so to do, may collect, by suit or otherwise, receive and remove to such place of residence of the minor, any personal estate of such minor.(*i*)

When there is a guardian in this State of a non-resident minor, the court may authorize such guardian to pay over and transfer the whole or any part of the ward's property to the non-resident guardian of such ward, appointed and qualified according to the law of the

---

(*g*) § 13, R. S. 1874, p. 713.
(*h*) §§ 3, 4, R. S. 1874, p. 1049.

(*i*) § 44, R. S. 1874, p. 563: Cothran's Statutes, p. 774.

Miscellaneous statutes.

place where the ward resides, upon such terms as shall be proper in the premises, requiring receipts to be passed; and when the whole estate in the hands of the resident guardian shall be so transferred, may discharge him. (*j*)

But the court shall not grant the authority mentioned in sections 44 and 45, except upon petitition of such foreign guardian, signed by him and verified by his affidavit, and unless he shall file with the court properly authenticated copies of his letters of guardianship, and bond, with security in double the amount of the value of the property and estate sought, which shall have been executed and filed in the court which appointed such guardian. And unless it shall appear to the court that a removal of such estate will not conflict with the interest of the ward or the terms of limitation attending the right by which the ward owns the same, or the rights of creditors, the resident guardian shall have ten days' previous notice of such application. (*k*)

7. COMPETENCY OF PARTIES AS WITNESSES. No party to any civil action, suit or proceeding, or person directly interested in the event thereof, shall be allowed to testify therein of his own motion, or in his own behalf, by virtue of the foregoing section, when any adverse party sues or defends as the trustee or conservator of any idiot, habitual drunkard, lunatic or distracted person, or as the executor, administrator, heir, legatee or devisee of any deceased person, or as guardian or trustee of any such heir, legatee or devisee, unless when called as a witness by such adverse party so suing or defending, and also except in the following cases, namely: 1. In any such action, suit or proceeding, a party or interested person may testify to facts occurring after the death of such deceased person, or after the ward, heir, legatee or devisee shall have attained his or her majority.

2. When in such action, suit or proceeding, any agent of any deceased person shall, in behalf of any person or persons suing or being sued, in either of the capacities above named, testify to any conversation or transaction between such agent and the opposite party or party in interest, such opposite party or party in interest may testify concerning the same conversation or transaction.

3. Where, in any such action, suit or proceeding, any such party

(*j*) § 45, R. S. 1874, p. 563.   (*k*) § 46, id.

Miscellaneous statutes.

suing or defending as aforesaid, or any person having a direct interest in the event of such action, suit or proceeding, shall testify in behalf of such party so suing or defending, to any conversation or transaction with the opposite party or party in interest, then such opposite party or party in interest shall also be permitted to testify as to the same conversation or transaction.

4. Where, in any such action, suit or proceeding, any witness, not a party to the record, or not a party in interest, or not an agent of such deceased person, shall, in behalf of any party to such action, suit or proceeding, testify to any conversation or admission by any adverse party or party in interest, occurring before the death and in the absence of such deceased person, such adverse party or party in interest may also testify as to the same admission or conversation.

5. When in any such action, suit or proceeding, the deposition of such deceased person shall be read in evidence at the trial, any adverse party or party in interest may testify as to all matters and things testified to in such deposition by such deceased person, and not excluded for irrelevancy or incompetency.(*l*)

8. The act relating to evidence (R. S. 1874, pp. 488–496) contains this exception, "Nothing in this act (act of 1867, R. S. 1874, p. 490. § 8) contained shall in any manner affect the laws relating to the settlement of the estates of deceased persons, infants, idiots, lunatics, distracted persons, or habitual drunkards having conservators, or to the acknowledgment or proof of deeds and other conveyances relating to real estate to entitle the same to be recorded, or to the attestation of the execution of last wills and testaments, or of any other instrument required by law to be attested," which leaves the law of evidence in probate matters where it stood in 1867.(*m*)

The repealing section of the revised act in relation to guardian and ward is a resumé of the former laws on that subject.(*n*)

(*l*) See 2 Hill's C. L., Evidence.
(*m*) Cothran's Statutes, § 8, p. 665.
(*n*) § 51, act April 10, 1872. See p. 7, *supra;* appendix.

Miscellaneous statutes.

9. MISCELLANEOUS DECISIONS. Under the Revised Statutes, an administrator cannot, by his admissions, bind the estate of his intestate.(*n*)

In an action in the name of the people for the use of an administrator upon the official bond of another administrator, upon a dismissal of the cause, judgment was entered against the plaintiff for costs. This was erroneous, for if the people were plaintiffs, no judgment of costs could be given against them; if the administrator for whose use the suit was brought, then the judgment should not have been against him personally, but to be paid in due course of administration.(*o*)

Executors or administrators must all join, and cannot sue separately,(*p*) even though some of them have renounced.(*q*) But any defect of parties on this account would be waived, if not pleaded, in abatement.(*q*) The statute also authorizes executors or administrators to maintain actions for wrongs committed to the property, rights or interests of their testator or intestate, against the wrongdoer, and after his death, against his executors or administrators. The provision, however, does not extend to actions for slander and libel; assault and battery, false imprisonment, and actions on the case for injuries to the person of the plaintiff and to the person of the testator or intestate are included.(*r*)

The proceedings of a court of competent jurisdiction upon a petition of an administrator to sell lands of his intestate for the payment of debts, cannot be attacked collaterally.(*s*)

The judgment of a county court against an administrator is only *prima facie* evidence as against the heir of the existence of a debt of the estate; but when the administrator applies for leave to sell real estate to pay such judgment, the heir, being neither a party nor a privy to it, is not concluded from contesting such application; if he has joined in taking an appeal from such judgment, he would be bound by the judgment on the appeal.(*t*)

(*n*) *Marshall* v. *Adams*, 11 Ill. 37.
(*o*) *The People* v. *Cloud*, 50 Ill. 439.
(*p*) *Smith* v. *Archer*, 53 Ill. 241; § 122, R. S. 1874, p. 126.
(*q*) 5 Wend. 313.
(*r*) 2 R. S., N. Y., 365, §§ 1, 2; see *Reed* v. *Railroad Co.*, 18 Ill. 403.
(*s*) *Wimberly* v. *Hurst*, 33 Ill. 166.
(*t*) *Stone* v. *Wood*, 16 Ill. 177; see, also, *Hopkins* v. *McCann*, 19 id. 113.

Miscellaneous statutes.

In an action to set aside an administrator's sale of land for a defect in the certificate of publication of the notice of application for leave to sell, in not stating the first and last days of publication, the court will presume, from the recital in the decree of the probate court, that due "notice was given according to law," that the probate court received other and sufficient evidence of the dates of publication.(*u*)

No particular form is required in the proceedings of an inferior court to render its order a judgment. It is sufficient if it be final, and the party may be injured. (*v*)

So where the order of a county court in respect to a claim presented against an estate was, after having taken the matter under advisement, "the court this day after due deliberation rejects the claim," this was held to be a sufficiently formal judgment from which an appeal or *certiorari* would lie.(*v*)

A person, just before his death, delivered his money to be paid over to his family, and the person who received the money was afterward sued by the administrator of the deceased, on the ground that he had not accounted for all the money so received. *Held*, that it was erroneous in the court to instruct the jury that "it was not incumbent on the defendant to account for what the deceased did with his money;" that it was for the jury to determine whether the facts and circumstances in the case satisfied them that the deceased had, at the time of his death, more money in his possession than had been accounted for by the defendant, and whether or not there was sufficient *prima facie* evidence in the case against the defendant, to call upon him to explain how it was that he received no more money from the deceased.(*w*)

An executor or administrator could in no case at common law bring an action for a wrong done, either to the person or property of his testator or intestate in his life-time. An action of trespass or trover will, however, lie for an injury to, or the conversion of, the personal property of such testator or intestate in the name of his executor or administrator as plaintiff, though the injury was committed in the life-time of such testator or intestate. This is by a particular statute giving in terms an action of trespass only to an executor, etc., in such case.(*x*) But the construction given to the

(*u*) *Moore* v. *Neil*, 39 Ill. 256.
(*v*) *Johnson* v. *Gillett*, 52 Ill. 358 ; see Jones' Forms, 395–402.
(*w*) *Eames* v. *Blackhart*, 12 Ill. 195.
(*x*) 1 Ch. Pl. 67.

provisions of this statute has been very liberal, and its equity is now understood to reach every injury to the personal property of the deceased. Trover, replevin, case or debt, for an escape, or case for removing goods under execution, without paying the year's rent, etc., are accordingly held to lie in the right of the deceased.(*y*)

In all other cases, however, the action for a wrong dies with the person.

10. Proclamation by Sheriff or Deputy.

OPENING AT THE BEGINNING OF THE TERM.

Hear ye! Hear ye!! Hear ye!!! the honorable the county court of the county of   , and State of Illinois, is now opened and in session in course for the term.

ADJOURNMENT.

Hear ye! Hear ye!! Hear ye!!! the honorable the county court of the county of   , and State of Illinois, is now adjourned, and will stand adjourned until   o'clock to-morrow morning (*or as the case may be*).

OPENING AFTER ADJOURNMENT.

Hear ye! Hear ye!! Hear ye!!! the honorable the county court of the county of   , and State of Illinois, is now open and in session pursuant to adjournment.

CLOSING AT THE END OF THE TERM.

Hear ye! Hear ye!! the honorable the county court of the county of   , and State of Illinois, having closed its session in course for the present term, is now adjourned, and from henceforth stands adjourned without day.

If the sheriff, or one of his deputies, be present, the court may be opened and adjourned by proclamation, if not, the court opens or adjourns by order, entered on the minutes of the clerk. It is more formal and business like to open and close by proclamation all the sessions of the court day by day, both forenoon and afternoon, and at the beginning and close of the term. The sheriff or deputy should always be in attendance, keep order and perform the duty of making proclamation of opening and closing.

11. Oaths.

INTERPRETER'S OATH.

You do solemnly swear, by the ever-living God (*or, you do solemnly, sincerely and truly declare and affirm*), that you will well and truly interpret and trans-

(*y*) 1 Ch. Pl. 67, 68; 2 Johns. 227.

Oaths.

late the English language into (German) and the (German) into English, between the counsel, the witness, the court and the jury, relating to (*the proceedings now before this court*) (or *the issue joined between A B, plaintiff, and C D, defendant*) to the best of your ability. So help you God.

WITNESS' OATH.[*]

You do solemnly swear, by the ever-living God, that the testimony you shall give in the *matter now on hearing* (or the cause now on trial) shall be the truth, the whole truth and nothing but the truth. So help you God.

AFFIANT'S OATH.

You do solemnly swear, by the ever-living God, that this affidavit, by you subscribed, is true. So help you God.

JURORS' OATHS.

Preliminary Oath.

You and each of you do solemnly swear, by the ever-living God, that you will true answers make to all questions that shall be put to you, either by court or counsel, touching your competency to sit as jurors in this cause. So help you God.

TO TRY THE ISSUES.

You and each of you do solemnly swear, by the ever-living God, that you will truly try the issues joined in this cause, now on hearing before the court, wherein A B is plaintiff and C D is defendant, and a true verdict render according to evidence.

TO TRY THE ISSUES AND ASSESS DAMAGES.

You and each of you do solemnly swear, by the ever-living God, that you will well and truly try the issues joined in the cause now on hearing before the court, between A B, plaintiff, and C D, defendant, and also well and truly assess the damages of the said plaintiff against said defendant, and a true verdict and assessment render according to evidence. So help you God.

JURY POLLED.

Question to be asked of the jurors severally. Was this, and is this now, your verdict?

OATH TO QUALIFY.

You do solemnly swear, by the ever-living God, that you will true answers make to all questions put to you touching your qualifications as *security on the bond of A B, administrator of the estate of C D, deceased.* So help you God.

OATH ON APPLICATION OF A JUROR TO BE EXCUSED.

You do solemnly swear, by the ever-living God, that you will true answers make to such questions as shall be put to you touching your application to be excused from serving as a petit juror at this court. So help you God.

---

[*] See chapter 76, R. S. 1845; chap. 101, R. S. 1874, p. 725.

Miscellaneous statutes.

OATH OF A PARTY OF THE LOSS OR DESTRUCTION OF A PAPER.

You do solemnly swear, by the ever-living God, that you will true answers make to such questions as shall be put to you touching the loss or destruction of any paper which would be proper evidence in this cause. So help you God.

OATH OF TRIERS UPON A CHALLENGE FOR FAVOR.

You do solemnly swear, by the ever-living God, that you will well and truly try and find whether A B, the juror challenged, stands indifferent between E F, plaintiff, and C D, defendant, in the issue now about to be tried. So help you God.

OATH OF A WITNESS ON A CHALLENGE.

You do solemnly swear, by the ever-living God, that you will true answers make to such questions as shall be put to you touching the challenge of A B, a juror, called in this cause, etc.

OATH OF OFFICER ATTENDING A JURY ON THEIR RETIREMENT.

You do solemnly swear, by the ever-living God, that you will, to the utmost of your ability, keep the persons sworn as jurors on this trial in some private and convenient place, without meat or drink, except water, unless ordered by the court; that you will not suffer any communication with them, orally or otherwise, unless by order of the court, or to ask them if they have agreed upon a verdict, until they shall be discharged, and that you will not, before they render their verdict, communicate to any one the state of their deliberations or the verdict they have agreed upon. So help you God.

OATH OF A PARTY TOUCHING HIS ABILITY TO PROCURE THE ATTENDANCE OF A SUBSCRIBING WITNESS.

You do solemnly swear, by the ever-living God,* that you will true answers make to such questions as shall be put to you touching your ability to procure the attendance of X Y, a subscribing witness to the paper-writing now here in question. So help you God.

Other oaths may be framed to suit the various occasions in practice. The form is prescribed.(z)

IN CASE THE WITNESS OR PARTY TO BE SWORN WISHES TO *affirm*, COMMENCE THE *affirmation*.

You do solemnly, sincerely and truly declare and affirm (concluding as in the oath above, after the *).(a)

(z) Ch. 76, R. S. 1845, §§ 1, 2, 3, 4; R. S. 1874, 725.   (a) § 2, id.

In case of appeal costs discretionary.

CHAPTER XIII.

COSTS AND FEES.

1. The statute of costs and fees applies in probate matters.
2. In case of appeal in such matters, costs discretionary.
3. Actions and proceedings by non-residents and on office bonds; security in the first instance must be given, or suit on motion must be dismissed.
4. Form of preliminary security.
5. The motion to dismiss must, however, be made in apt time.
6. Security after suit brought.
7. Affidavits of parties.
8. Form of security to be given, when required after suit brought.
9. Non-residents cannot be executors or administrators, guardians or conservators; foreign executors or administrators, guardians or conservators, however, may be empowered, but must always, before instituting proceedings, file security for costs.
10. Non-resident creditors of an estate in probate must file preliminary security, *quære*.
11. Appraisers' fees $2 *per diem*.
12. Fees of the officers of court.
13. Compensation of executors, etc.
14. Allowances to, for costs and disbursements.
15. After expiration of two years, claimants to pay costs in certain cases.
16. The applicant to be discharged on resignation as executor or administrator must pay the costs of the application.
17. Suits on bonds; the party for whose use suit is brought must give preliminary security, and is liable to pay costs on failure to maintain his suit.
18. Delinquent executors and administrators cited or attached, must pay costs.
19. In probate, as in chancery, costs are usually discretionary.
20. Witness' fees.
21. Commissioners' fees, etc.

1. The statute of costs and fees applies to all actions commenced in the probate court on official bonds, for the use of any person; but when the opposite party omits to make a motion to dismiss the action for that cause in the inferior court, he waives the objection and cannot make it in the circuit court.(*a*)

2. IN ALL CASES OF APPEAL from the decision of a court of probate, the costs shall be in the discretion of the circuit court.(*b*)

(*a*) *Robertson* v. *Co. Coms.*, 5 Gilm. 559; *Yocum* v. *Waynesville*, 39 Ill. 220.
(*b*) § 18, ch. 26, R. S. 1845; the statute and decisions are given in full in 2 Hill's Common Law, at pp. 625–637; see, also, Hill's Ch. Pr., *Costs*; § 21, R. S. 1874, p. 300.

Security after suit brought.

3. IN ALL ACTIONS ON OFFICE BONDS for the use of any person; actions on the bonds of executors, administrators or guardians; *qui tam* actions; actions on any penal statute; and in all cases in law or equity, where the plaintiff, or person for whose use an action is to be commenced, shall NOT BE A RESIDENT OF THIS STATE, the plaintiff or person for whose use the action is to be commenced, shall, before he institutes such suit, file, or cause to be filed with the clerk of the circuit or supreme court, in which the action is to be commenced, an instrument in writing, of some responsible person, being a resident of this State, to be approved by the clerk, whereby such person shall acknowledge himself bound to pay, or cause to be paid, all costs which may accrue in such action, either to the opposite party, or to any of the officers of such courts:

4. Which INSTRUMENT IN WRITING may be in THE FORM and purport following, to wit:

A. B.
 v.   } *Court.*
C. D.

I do hereby enter myself security for all costs which may accrue in the above cause.

Dated this   day of   , A. D. 18 .

(Signed.)

E. F.

Before commencing proceedings for a non-resident party in any court in Illinois, this statutory bond must be filed and approved by the clerk.

5. It cannot be dispensed with. It may be waived, by steps taken on the part of the adverse party, but if a motion to dismiss the proceeding for the want of preliminary security, where it is required, be aptly made, the proceeding must be dismissed. The statute is peremptory, viz.: If any such action shall be commenced without filing such instrument, the court, on motion, shall dismiss the same, and the attorney of the plaintiff shall pay all costs accruing thereon. (*c*)

6. SECURITY AFTER SUIT BROUGHT. Again, if in any case the court shall be satisfied that any plaintiff is unable to pay the costs of suit, or that he is so unsettled as to endanger the officers of the

---

(*c*) *People* v. *Cloud*, 50 Ill. 439; § 3, R. S. 1874, p. 297.

Non-resident creditors must file preliminary security.

court, with respect to their legal demands, it shall be the duty of the court, on motion of the defendant, or any officer of the court, to rule the plaintiff on or before a day in such rule named, to give security for the payment of costs in such suit; if such plaintiff shall neglect or refuse, on or before the day in such rule named, to file an instrument of writing of some responsible person being a resident of this State, whereby he shall bind himself to pay all costs which have accrued, or may accrue in such action, the court shall, on motion, dismiss the suit.(*d*)

7. On application for security, under this section, the affidavits of the parties may have equal weight.(*e*) The motion is addressed to the discretion of the court; its decision cannot be assigned for error.(*f*) If the affidavit be insufficient, however, and the motion be granted, the decision will, on error, be reviewed.(*g*)

8. When required, the instrument to be filed under section 2 may be as follows:

(*Title of suit.*)

I do hereby enter myself security for costs in this cause, and hereby bind myself to pay all costs which have accrued or may accrue in such action, either to the opposite party or to any of the officers of this court, in pursuance of the laws of this State.   E F.

Dated this   day of   , 18 .

9. No non-resident of this State can be appointed or allowed to act as administrator.(*h*) But executors and administrators appointed in any other State or territory of the United States may, under certain restrictions, act.(*i*) And foreign executors or administrators must give the preliminary bond for costs, as in case of non-residents.(*j*) So with foreign guardians,(*k*) and so with foreign conservators or trustees. (*l*) This security must be given to begin with by such non-residents.(*m*)

10. Non-resident creditors of an estate of a decedent testate or intestate who inaugurate proceedings against an executor or administrator under section 61, act of April 1, 1872, must file preliminary security under section 1, chapter 26, Revised Statutes, it would seem.

(*d*) § 4, R. S. 1874, p. 297.
(*e*) *Hamilton* v. *Dunn*, 22 Ill. 259.
(*f*) *Selby* v. *Hutchinson*, 4 Gilm. 319; *Gesford* v. *Critzer*, 2 Gilm. 698.
(*g*) *Ball* v. *Bruce*, 27 Ill. 332.
(*h*) § 18, R. S. 1874, p. 107.
(*i*) §§ 42, 43, R. S. 1874, p. 112.

(*j*) § 42, id.
(*k*) § 50, act of April 10, 1872. See p. 68, *supra*.
(*l*) § 7, act of February 12, 1853; G. 333; P. 612; S. 828.
(*m*) C. 33, R. S. 1874, p. 297, p. 295, *supra*.

Fees of the officers of court.

On appeal by a non-resident from any order, decree or judgment of the county court, security for costs must be filed in the first instance.

Where appeal is prayed for, however, the bond for costs is given by all, whether resident or non-resident, in order to perfect the appeal.(*n*)

11. Appraisers are allowed two dollars per day each for actual time spent in attendance upon and in the performance of their duties.(*o*)

12. The fees of the officers of court are to be paid, from time to time, as the services are rendered.

13. Executors and administrators are allowed, as compensation for their services, to be fixed by the court, a sum not exceeding six per centum on the amount of personal estate, and not exceeding three per centum on the money arising from the sale of real estate.

There are two grounds upon which an executor or administrator may be charged with interest. 1st. When he has been guilty of negligence in laying out the money for the benefit of the estate. 2d. When he has made use of the money to his own profit and advantage, or has committed some other malfeasance.(*p*)

As against administrators, the general rule is that he is chargeable with interest whenever he receives interest, uses the money, or retains it unreasonably.(*q*)

14. Additional allowances are to be made for costs and charges in collecting and defending the claims of the estate, and disposing of the same, as may be reasonable.(*r*) As an executor is a trustee for the estate he represents, he can receive no compensation for his time and services expended in preparing the defense to a suit against the estate, or a claim for dower, nor can he receive compensation for professional services rendered, by him, as an attorney at law, in defending such suit, for a trustee can make no profit out of his office. The statute which provides that executors and administrators may receive "such additional allowances for costs and charges in collecting and defending the claims of the estate, and

---

(*n*) See Appeal, p. 272, *supra*.
(*o*) § 59. R. S. 1874, p. 114; Cothran's Statutes, p. 63.
(*p*) *Rowan* v. *Kirkpatrick*, 14 Ill. 10.
(*q*) Id.; conservators' fees, see p. 141, *supra*.
(*r*) § 133, R. S. 1874, p. 127. The amount must be governed by the circumstances of each particular case. A reasonable compensation is all that the law provides for. It is not expected he will speculate off the estate. And see *Bassett, Adm'r,* v. *Willard, Adm'r,* 27 Ill. 38, 39.

Delinquent executors and administrators.

disposing of the same, as shall be reasonable," does not proceed further than to give such officers "money out of pocket," that is, money actually paid by them to others in the discharge of their duty. It is no warrant for an allowance for their own services, as agent or attorney of the estate.(s)

15. The party suing after the expiration of two years from the time of the grant of letters, and after the estate is found to be and recorded as insolvent, must pay all costs.(t)

Guardians, on settlement, shall be allowed such fees and compensation for their services as shall seem reasonable and just to the court.(u)

An attorney employed by an executor may enforce the payment of his fee against an administrator *de bonis non* of the same estate.(v)

16. RESIGNATION. An executor or administrator on resigning must pay all costs incurred on the application for his discharge; a judgment may be entered therefor and collected on execution.(w)

17. SUITS ON BONDS. The party for whose use a suit may be instituted on executor's, administrator's, guardian's or conservator's bonds must give security for costs, and in the first instance is made liable therefor in case he fail in his suit.(x)

18. DELINQUENCY. An executor, or administrator, or guardian, or conservator delinquent in his inventory or account, or in other matters, is liable and must pay the costs of citation and attachment when such proceedings become necessary.(y)

19. Inasmuch as the clerks of the several courts of record are of their own motion to tax and enter the costs and fees in the proceedings which we are now considering, it is unnecessary to pursue the subject further here. If the reader desire full information in the matter of costs and fees, he would do well to read the chapters on COSTS AND FEES in Hill's Chancery Practice, 2 Hill's Common Law, and in the Municipal Officer.

When the fee bill is made up by the clerk, it will be regarded as *prima facie* correct, and the debtor of costs can challenge it only

---

(s) *Hough* v. *Harvey*, 71 Ill. 72.
(t) § 129, R. S. 1874, p. 127.
(u) § 42, R. S. 1874, p. 56.
(v) *Green* v. *Grimshaw*, 11 Ill. 389.
(w) § 40, R. S. 1874, p. 111.

(x) § 1, ch. 26, R. S. 1845; § 25, act April 1, 1872; R. S. 1874, p. 109; Cothran's Statutes, p. 54.
(y) § 114, R. S. 1874, p. 125; see pp.239, 240, *supra;* Cothran's Statutes, 1880, p. 78.

Commissioner's fees, etc.

in a direct proceeding, either by replevying the fee bill under the 26th section of the statute of costs (Cothran's Annotated Statutes, 354), or by a motion to re-tax costs.(z)

20. WITNESS FEE. The act of March 29, 1872 (§ 49) fixes the fees for each witness in probate matters at one dollar per day, if the fee be claimed at the trial, which the clerk is to tax as costs, when the fee is claimed, by affidavit of attendance filed.

21. DEPOSITIONS of resident witnesses may be taken before any judge, justice of the peace, clerk of a court, master in chancery or notary public, without a commission or filing interrogatories, on giving ten days' notice of the time and place of taking the same, and one day in addition thereto, Sundays inclusive, for every fifty miles travel from the place of holding court to the place where the deposition is to be taken. If the party entitled to notice and his attorney reside in the county where the deposition is to be taken, five days' notice will be sufficient. The depositions of non-resident witnesses are to be taken upon commission directed to any competent and disinterested person, or any judge, master in chancery, notary public or justice of the peace of the county or city in which the witness resides, or if the witness be in military or naval service of the United States, to any commissioned officer in such service. In both cases a commissioner of deeds appointed for the State may act to take the deposition.

In making return of a deposition, great care should be exercised. Every provision of the statute regulating the mode of procedure must be substantially complied with. It has been held that where a note, professedly an exhibit referred to in a deposition, was not attached or inclosed with the commission and interrogatories sealed and sent to the clerk, but a part only of the papers were so sent by the commissioner, but the note, interrogatories and commission and other papers were sent by him to the party's attorneys, the deposition should have been suppressed on motion.(a)

(z) *Parisher* v. *Waldo*, 72 Ill. 71.
(a) *Edleman* v. *Byers & Gilmore*, 75 Ill. 367; See act March 29, 1872. Ch. 51, R. S. 1874, p. 488; Cothran's Statutes, p. 662.

CHAPTER XIV.

THE PROBATE RECORD.

The probate record, as a whole, comes now for examination before us. The clerk keeps this record, but the litigants and the court do each a share in making and perfecting the record in civil procedure, either in probate, at common law, or in chancery. The integrity of the record and its completion and perfection is, or should be closely watched and firmly insisted on by the court, and constantly aimed at by all the parties in a cause.

Having quite fully suggested the forms* of procedure, mainly as we find them stereotyped on the records in the county courts of Illinois, modeled after the forms of the civil law from point to point, in developing the subject, so interesting, yet so delicate and important, it is unnecessary now to do more than to indicate the stages of the growth and development of THE RECORD in this jurisdiction. Uniformity and systematic care in all the forms, simple and plain though they be, are desirable, especially in matters pertaining to landed property — real estate. Much depends upon the competency and fidelity of the clerk, the custodian of the records, for their neatness, style and system; more, upon the careful supervision of the county judge. Passing, generation after generation, in one form or another through the probate jurisdiction, as one by one their proprietors leave "this bank and shoal of time," estates should be carefully administered and faithfully transmitted, unimpaired, either

---

*ALPHABETICAL LIST OF FORMS IN THE PRECEDING PAGES:

Acceptance of appointment of guardian and guardian *ad litem*, 117	Administrator's notice of settlement of claims................ 225
Acceptance of resignation of executor or administrator.......... 98	Administrator's sale of personal estate........................ 181
Acceptance of resignation of a guardian................... 124	Administration, letters of........ 79
Account, administrator's......240, 242	Administration, petition for revocation of letters of..........99, 100
Account of personal estate and debts preliminary to sale of real estate....... 202	Administration, decree revoking letters of...................... 101
Absence, affidavit of............. 130	Advertisement, certificate of..... 51
Administration, petition for letters of............................ 77	Advertisement, notice to guardian........................... 131
Administrator, oath of........... 79	Affidavit of death and intestacy.. 77
Administrator with the will annexed, oath of................ 80	Affidavit of infancy............. 117
	Affidavit of absence............. 130
Administrator's account......240, 242	Affidavit of concealment......... 130
	Affidavit of non-residence........ 129

The forms.

according to the law of descent or the will of their late owners, to their kinsmen and beneficiaries. Whether, in a given cause, this has been done is to be determined by the record. Although this cannot be impeached if the court acquires jurisdiction, except on appeal or in error, yet it is requisite that a high degree of care be exercised in all matters in probate, that true and perfect records be made. The integrity and honor of the trustees, whose functions and powers it has been our province to consider, are involved in their records here. Theirs are the most important and sacred trusts known to the law, and can only be discharged through a perfect and complete record in the probate court from which they derive their authority.

Affidavit of posting notices...... 182
Affidavit for a *dedimus*.......... 37
Allowance to the widow and children........................ 221
Appointment of guardian *ad litem*, 117
Appraisement, warrant for...... 171
Appraisement bill 173
Assent to resignation of executor or administrator 99
Attachment to compel the production of a will................. 16
Attachment to compel the attendance of witnesses............. 32
Award, widow's 221

Bond of administrator 78
Bond of administrator, with the will annexed 80
Bond of executor 30
Bond of guardian.. 113
Bond by legatee or distributee ... 234
Bill, the appraisement 178
Bill of sale.... 183

Certificate to appraisement bill .. 173
Certificate of publication, printer's 51
Certificate of the clerk to letters testamentary 50
Certificates of proof under a *dedimus*......................... 38
Certificate of insanity........... 156
Citation to a minor.............. 112
Citation notice and proof, of a nuncupative will 51
Claims, notice of settlement of... 225
Codicil........ 12
Concealment, affidavit of 130
Conservator, petition for 154
Conservator's inventory 185

Death, affidavit of 77

Debts, desperate............ 176–179
Decree for removal of guardian.. 133
Decree removing an executor or administrator....... 101
Dedimus.................... 33, 34
Dedimus (short form) 38
Dedimus, affidavit for 37
Desperate debts, suggestion of... 177
Desperate debts, application to sell and compound.............. 177
Distributee, bond by ....,.. 224

Entry of an order to compel the production of a will 15
Executor's bond 30
Executor's oath................ 29
Executor, petition to remove an.. 59
Executorship, renunciation of.... 16

Guardian's bond 113
Guardian's inventory............ 185
Guardian, petition of, for permission to resign............ 123, 124
Guardian, petition for the removal of a. 124, 125
Guardian, summons to a 125
Guardian, decree of removal of .. 133
Guardian (see constructive service).
Guardian *ad litem*, order appointing a 117
Guardianship, petition for....... 111
Guardianship, letters of 116

Infancy, affidavit of 117
Inquisition as to insanity........ 155
Insane, record of proceeding in case of the 156
Insanity, inquisition as to........ 155
Insanity, statement of (petition)........................ 154

CH. XIV.] THE PROBATE RECORD. 303

The fiduciary relation.

The jealousy with which these trustees are watched by the courts, in the discharge of their trusts, is, perhaps, nowhere more fully illustrated than in the cases where they have attempted to so administer the estates committed to their charge as to make gain for themselves, beyond the compensation which the law gives them. The fiduciary relation, especially in sales by agents and trustees, seems to have been made use of more frequently for this purpose. But equity has established an unbending rule to meet every exigency — a rule of disability. The rule involved is not only: (1.) That an agent intrusted to sell property, or a trustee cannot purchase at his own

Instructions for taking a deposition	34, 35	Oath of administrator with the will annexed	80
Intestacy, affidavit of	77		
Inventory of the estates of the deceased	170	Pendency of suit to sell real estate,	206
		Petition for guardianship	111
Inventory by the guardian and conservator	185	Petition for a guardian by minors,	112, 113
		Petition for a guardian by a third party	114, 115
Legatee, bond by	224		
Letters of administration	79	Petition of guardian for permission to resign	123, 124
Letters of administration, petition for	77	Petition for the removal of a guardian	124, 125
Letters of guardianship	116		
Letters testamentary, petition for,	29	Petition for process to compel the production of a will	15
Letters testamentary	49, 50		
Letters testamentary and letters of administration, petition for revocation of	99, 100	Petition for letters of administration	77
		Petition for letters testamentary	29
Lunatico de inquirendo, writ of	155	Petition to supersede the appointment of an executor	59
		Petition for revocation of letters testamentary or of administration	99, 100
Minor, citation to a	112		
Non-residence, affidavit of	129	Petition for conservator of an insane person	154
Notice and citation to heirs, etc., of probate of nuncupative will,	51	Petition for the sale of real estate,	204
Notice, publication, to guardian	131	Posting, affidavit of	182
Notice, administrator's sale of desperate claims	176, 177	Printer's certificate	51
		Production of a will, petition for process to compel	15
Notice of administrator's sale of personal estate	181	Production of a will, order of entry,	15
Notice, affidavit of posting	182	Production of a will, attachment,	16
Notice, administrator's, of the settlement of claims	225	Proof of will (common form)	46
		Proof of execution of a will, with the record	48, 49
Notice of petition to sell real estate,	206	Publication notice to guardian	131
Nuncupative will	13	Publication, printer's certificate of,	51
		Publisher's certificate	51
Order on granting a petition to compel the production of a will,	15		
Order appointing a guardian *ad litem*	117	Real estate, notice of application to sell	206
Oath of executor	29	Real estate, sale of, petition for,	194, 205
Oath of administrator	79	account preliminary to sale,	202

The fiduciary relation.

sale; but,(a) (2.) That he cannot purchase surreptitiously by interposing a third party, or by connivance with another(b) at the time of or during the very transaction for which his agency or trust was established, or while his trust relation continues; and, (3.) It is a rule of *disability*, up to the close of the sale, the conveyance and the payment of the purchase-money;(c) (4.) But an executor or administrator or guardian or conservator cannot renounce his trust, shake off his fiduciary relation, and purchase.(d)

And further, the wrongful receipt and conversion of trust property place the receiver in the same situation as the trustee from whom he received it, and he is subject to the same liability as the trustee himself.(e)

In such cases a court of equity, with a broader jurisdiction, brand-

(a) *Currier* v. *Green*, 2 N. H. 225.
(b) *Kruse* v. *Steffens*, 47 Ill. 112; *Kerfoot* v. *Hyman*, 52 id. 512; *Robbins* v. *Butler*, 24 id. 432; *Lewis* v. *Hillman*, 3 H. L. 607; *Oliver* v. *Court* 8, Price, 127, 164.
(c) *Rosenberger's Appeal*, 26 Penn. St. 67; *Miles* v. *Wheeler*, 43 Ill. 123; *Charter* v. *Trevelyan*, 11 Cl. & F. 714.
(d) *Despard* v. *Ormsby*, Colles' P. C. 459; *Shelton* v. *Homer*, 5 Metc. 468; *Thorp* v. *McCullum*, 1 Gilm. 614, Underwood's Notes and cases cited; see HILL'S CHAN. PR. 394–402.
(e) *Rolfe* v. *Gregory*, 34 L. J. Ch. 274; *Moloney* v. *Kernan*, 2 Dr. & W. 31; *Cumberland Coal Co.* v. *Sherman*, 16 and 20 Md.; *Tyrrell* v. *Bank of London*, 10 H. L. 26; *Rosenberger's Appeal*, 26 Penn. St. 67.

Relinquishment of specific articles by the widow or children...... 220	Statement of insanity.......... 154
Removal of guardian, decree for.. 133	Subpœna for subscribing witnesses to a will................. 31, 32
Renunciation of executorship.... 16	Summons to a guardian......... 125
Resignation, acceptance of a guardian's...................... 124	Testamentary, petition for letters, 29
Resignation of executor or administrator................... 97, 98	Testamentary letters........ 49, 50
Resignation of executor or administrator, notice of............. 97	Testamentary, petition for revocation of letters............. 99, 100
Resignation of executor or administrator, acceptance of...... 98	Testamentary letters, decree of revocation of................. 101
Resignation of executor or administrator, assent to............ 99	
Residence unknown, affidavit of.. 130	Unknown residence, affidavit of.. 130
Return of *cepi corpus* on an attachment.... 32	Venire for a jury on a writ *de lunatico inquirendo*............... 156
Revocation of letters testamentary, etc...................... 101	Warrant for appraisement....... 171
	Widow's award................. 221
Sale, administrator's sale of personal estate 181	Widow's relinquishment of specific articles........ 220
Sale, bill of 183	Will 11, 12
Sale of desperate debts..... 176–179	Will, nuncupative.............. 13
Sale of real estate, preliminary account 202	Will, petition to compel the production of a.................. 15
Sale of real estate, petition for, 204, 205	Will, proof of (common form).... 46
Service of a subpœna, proof of... 32	Witnesses, subpœna for...... 31, 32

The forms.

ing the transactions as fraudulent, at once goes behind the record, and with care and firmness compels an honest and faithful administration; and nowhere else than in Illinois has the rule been more promptly or persistently applied, as the cases already cited abundantly attest. We now turn to the record.

At common law the making of the record, as well as in chancery, has acquired the name of pleading. (*f*)

In probate, matters of guardianship and conservation, the general rules of pleading are applicable to a certain extent.

The petition is the usual mode of making application in these matters for the process, and the orders, judgments and decrees of the court.

The summons, the citation and the attachment, the notice and proofs of service by publication, and by the sheriff and his deputies, are common to all these courts, at common law, in chancery as well as in probate.

The chancery practice is prescribed in matters pertaining to the exercise of this jurisdiction over real property. (*g*)

Facts are to be presented and embodied in the record. An applicant may, of his own knowledge, be cognizant of facts, or he may be morally certain of their existence upon information, and from circumstances known to him which afford him conclusive proofs. But in presenting such facts, he must be exceedingly careful to give the court the same kind of information that he has, for the court, and not the applicant or witness, is the arbiter. Facts of a certain kind, like the days of the week, month or year, the times of holding court, the incumbents of the county offices, are known to the court; no allegation, no proof, is essential in such matters. But where a witness was present and saw another die; saw a contract made; a will executed, he knows he can speak of his own knowledge. The rules of evidence are of equal force in all courts. (*h*)

Allegations or statements of facts, in a verified petition or affidavit, must be made in such a manner as to apprise the court upon what evidence the petitioner or affiant speaks.

The solemnity and binding force of an oath are great, and require that care should be exercised and discrimination used in detailing facts for the purposes of judicial procedure.

(*f*) See 2 Hill's C. L. Pr., Pleading; Hill's Chan. Pr., Pleading.
(*g*) See p. 206, *supra*.
(*h*) 2 Hill's C. L., Evidence; Greenleaf on Ev., etc.

The forms.

The test of an affidavit is, that its statements are to be made in such a positive and pointed manner that, if untrue in point of fact, perjury may be predicated upon it.

The petition differs somewhat from an affidavit; it partakes of the nature of a pleading, and oftentimes contains allegations of facts, which are to be supported by proofs to be adduced on the hearing.

The affidavit is the evidence adduced in writing, and the basis of the application. When verified, the petition oftentimes, however, performs the office of the affidavit. So that, in putting statements of facts material to any step in judicial proceedings into writing, care must be used not to involve a petitioner, a pleader, an affiant, a deponent or a witness in the crime of perjury.

Every person having taken a lawful oath, or made affirmation, in any judicial proceeding, or in any other matter where by law an oath or affirmation is required, who shall swear or affirm willfully, corruptly and falsely, in any matter material to the issue or point in question, or shall suborn any other person to swear or affirm as aforesaid, shall be deemed guilty of perjury or subornation of perjury (as the case may be), and, upon conviction thereof, shall be punished by confinement in the penitentiary for a term not less than one year nor more than fourteen years. (*i*)

Truth is the basis of all judicial procedure, and to find the facts and act upon them, as occasion requires, constitutes the business of courts of judicature.

The affidavit, wherever used, is to be of one general form, and tested by this general rule:

An affidavit should be entitled of the cause or proceeding; begin with the venue, introduce the affiant, state the subject-matter known positively to the affiant in direct and pointed language, and the subject-matter which affiant believes, or has reason to believe, as true upon information and belief, detailing the circumstances so as to show that the belief is well founded, and conclude with the jurat and signature.

A petition should be entitled of the cause; begin with the address to the court, introduce the petitioner, and in like manner state the subject-matter. It should, if verified, conclude with an affidavit that it is true of the knowledge, or information, and belief of the petitioner.

(*i*) R. S. 1874, p. 387.

The forms.

Before proceeding with the evolution of the probate record, it may be well to consider the requisites of affidavits and verified pleadings generally in the light of the authorities.

The petition is filed, and entered either in part or at large, upon the record by the clerk; so with the other papers, such as process, the affidavits, certificates and the like. The orders, decrees, and judgments are recorded at full length upon the records of the court. In every proceeding there are the *files*, and the *entries*, and the *records*, but taken together they are usually called, in speaking of any proceeding, THE RECORD.

The importance of recording in full all the papers which make up this record, as well as the orders, decrees and judgments of the county court, in probate and other matters involving titles to real estate and the rights of the absent, the incapacitated, the widow and the orphan, cannot be too strongly urged upon the clerks of these courts.

One generation passeth away and another generation cometh, so that every thirty years nearly all the real and personal property of the county passes, in one form or another, under the administration in probate. Uniformity in these records throughout the State is also desirable. To attain this uniformity, very many of the forms are prescribed as we have seen by the statute, while in matters touching real estate, the well-known forms which have been so long stereotyped, and so continually repeated, and so well settled by the profession and the courts in Illinois as to make perhaps the most admirable system to be found anywhere in civil procedure, are made the means, the models, the practice in this jurisdiction.

Coming directly from the exalted jurisdiction of the chancellor,(*j*) we naturally feel a degree of pride in these ample forms, and shall endeavor to delineate them for use in this equally important department of our jurisprudence, and, if possible, with a higher degree of care through this chapter of our undertaking.

In the former chapters we have considered the prescribed occasions for the exercise of the administrative jurisdiction of what in some States is called the orphan's court,(*k*) and carefully and critically examined the successive steps necessary to be taken in caring for the person and the estates of those who, in the law, are incapacitated, incapable of caring for themselves, and in protecting the rights of

---

(*j*) See Hill's Chan. Pr.   (*k*) *e. g.* Pennsylvania.

creditors and the heirs of the deceased, according to the law of descent and the executive powers of the county judge in supervising the transmission of property according to this law, or the law of wills from the dead to the living. We now come to the making of the records for these several occasions, for the exercise of such important functions by these lesser but not inferior courts, through well-settled forms.

The placita, or convening order of the court, is an essential recital to the record, and first comes into view.(*l*)

It should disclose (1) the venue, (2) the court, (3) the term of the culmination of the record into an order, or judgment, or decree, and (4) the names of the officers, the judge, the clerk and the sheriff concerned in the production of the several parts of which the record is made up. One general form may be given, so that by filling the blanks in a given cause no error in this, the beginning of the record, may be made.

THE PLACITA.

United States of America.

STATE OF ILLINOIS, } ss
County of   . }

Pleas(*m*) before the honorable   , judge of the county court of   county, in the State of Illinois, and sole presiding judge of said court, and at a regular term thereof, begun and held at the court-house in the   of   , in the year of our Lord one thousand eight hundred and   , and of the independence of the United States the ninety   . Present, the honorable   , county judge of   county, in the State of Illinois.

Attest: , *Clerk.*   , *Sheriff said County.*
        , *State's Attorney.*

The placita should always be the beginning of a transcript of the record in any of the proceedings for use in other courts and places, for the reasons so clearly stated by Judge MCALLISTER.(*n*) His language is applied to the record at common law, but, if we mistake not, it applies with equal force to the chancery or the probate record. He says: "The experience and wisdom of ages have taught that these forms are necessary to prevent legal proceedings from degenerating into such looseness and confusion as to render rights acquired under them insecure."

Other forms are used frequently, but the above has long been the accepted form at common law and in chancery, and we know of no

---

(*l*) 2 Hill's C. L. 18.   (*n*) 2 Hill's C. L. 18–20.
(*m*) The record ; 2 C. L. 15.

The forms

reason why it should not be used here. It would be difficult to make it less formal, or to abridge it.

Next comes the

PREAMBLE AND RECITAL.

Be it remembered that heretofore, to wit, on the   day of   , in the year of our Lord one thousand eight hundred and seventy   (or A. D. 187 –), A B (if by attorney, by C D, his attorney,) and filed in the office of the clerk of this court, his certain petition, in writing, which is in words and figures following:

(Here copy at length the petition, as at page 94, *supra*.)

Together with the following exhibit thereto attached, which is in words and figures following:

Here copy the will filed with the petition, and then complete the record, as at page 48, *supra*, concluding with the record of the letters testamentary, and of the bond and oath of the executor. (*o*)

For entries, the clerk may conveniently use the following:

PLACITA.

(*To be used in Counties under Township Organization.*)

STATE OF ILLINOIS,
County of   . } *ss* :   Term, A. D. 18 .

The county court of   county,   term, began and held at the courthouse, in the   of   , in said county, on Monday,   day of   , A. D. 18 . Present, Hon.   , Judge ;   , Clerk ;   , Sheriff. Court opened by proclamation.

PLACITA.

(*To be used in Counties not under Township Organization.*)

STATE OF ILLINOIS,
County of   . } *ss* :   Term, A. D. 18 .

The county court of   county, sitting for the transaction of judicial business, began and held at the court-house in the   of   , in said county, on Monday, the   day of   , A. D. 18 . Present, Hon.   , Judge ;   , Clerk ; and   , Sheriff. Court opened by proclamation.*

PLACITA.

(*For any day of the term after its commencement.*)

STATE OF ILLINOIS,
County of   . } *ss* :   Term, A. D. 18 .

The county court of   county, sitting for the transaction of official business, Tuesday,   the   , A. D. 18 . Court opened pursuant to adjournment. Present, same as yesterday.

(*o*) See pp. 48, 50, *supra*.

---

* It is not necessary that the sheriff should open the court.

The forms.

ENTRY OF GRANT OF ADMINISTRATION.

In the matter of the estate of , deceased. } *Appointment of Administrator.*

This day appeared in open court, , and applied to the court for letters of administration on the estate of , deceased, to issue to her and . And it appearing to the court by satisfactory evidence that the said . , late of county, in the State of Illinois, died in the said county on or about the day of , A. D. 18 , leaving at the time of his decease property and effects in this State, which may be lost, destroyed, or diminished in value if administration be not granted thereon; but leaving no will and testament; and it further appearing to the court that said is the widow (*or, as the case may be*) of said intestate, and is competent, and by law entitled, to administer upon the estate of which the said died seized, and she desiring that the said be associated with her in such administration; and it further appearing to the court that the value of the estate of which the said died seized is about dollars; it is thereupon

ORDERED and adjudged by the court, That administration on the estate, goods, chattels and effects of the said , deceased, be granted to the said and , upon their entering into bond in the penal sum of (*here insert double the value of the estate*) dollars, conditioned and payable according to the statute in such cases made and provided.

And now again come the said and , and present to the court for approval their bond, in form as before by this court required, with A B and C D as their securities thereon, and the court being now sufficiently advised concerning the said bond and said security, it is

ORDERED and adjudged by the court, That the said bond be approved and recorded.

And the said and , having respectively taken the oath required of them by law, as such administratrix and administrator, it is

ORDERED, That letters of administration on said estate be issued to the said and .

If the person entitled to administer renounce, that fact should be stated on the records. In short, in all cases the material facts, upon which is founded any order of the court, should appear upon the face of the records, so as to make the legality of the proceedings of the court apparent.

ORDER APPOINTING APPRAISERS.

In the matter of the estate of , deceased. } *Appointment of Appraisers.*

It is ORDERED by the court, That C D, E F and G H be authorized and appointed to appraise the goods, chattels and personal estate of the said deceased, and that a warrant therefor be issued to them.

The forms.

WHERE APPRAISERS DIE, NEGLECT OR REFUSE TO ACT.

In the matter of the estate of _____, deceased. } *Appointment of Appraisers.*

It appearing to the court that C D, one of the appraisers heretofore appointed to appraise the goods, chattels and personal estate of the said _____, deceased, refuses to act (*or as the case may be*), as such appraiser, it is, therefore,

ORDERED, That J K be appointed in his place, to act in conjunction with E F and G H, heretofore appointed appraisers of said estate.

ORDER ON THE RETURN OF THE INVENTORY.

In the matter of the estate of _____, deceased. } *Order on Inventory.*

On this day comes _____, administratrix of the said estate, and presents to the court the inventory of the real and personal estate, and the proceeds thereof, of the said _____, deceased, so far as the same have come to the possession or knowledge of the said administratrix; and now, the court having inspected said inventory, and being sufficiently advised concerning the same, it is

ORDERED, That the said inventory be approved and filed.

It is a good practice observed in some counties to record the inventory, whether the law requires it or not.

ORDER FOR A CITATION AGAINST AN ADMINISTRATOR OR EXECUTOR, TO COMPEL AN INVENTORY.

In the matter of the estate of _____, deceased. } *Order for Citation.*

On this day comes C D, security on the bond of J K, executor (*or* administrator) of the estate of the said _____, deceased, and presents to the court his petition for a citation to issue out of this court, against the said executor, to show cause why he should not file in this court an inventory of the estate of the said _____, deceased, and the court being now sufficiently advised concerning the said petition, and the matters and things therein contained, it is

ORDERED and adjudged, That a citation issue in accordance with the prayer of said petition, returnable to the next term of this court, to which time it is

ORDERED, That the hearing of the said petition be continued.

ORDER TO FILE AN INVENTORY.

C D *v.* J K, executor of the estate of _____, deceased. } *Order to File Inventory.*

And now on this day again comes the said C D, as also the said J K, executor of the said estate; and the said petition heretofore filed by the said C D, requiring the said J K to file an inventory of the said estate, coming on to

The forms.

be heard, and the court being now advised touching the matters in said petition alleged against the said J K, and it appearing to the court that the said J K has failed to file such inventory within three months from the date of his letters testamentary, it is

ORDERED and adjudged, That the said J K make out and file in this court, on or before the first day of the next regular term hereof, a full and perfect inventory of the real and personal estate of the said   , deceased, to which time it is

ORDERED, That these proceedings stand continued.

If the executor or administrator do not appear at the return of the citation, the order should be varied.

In the place of the words, "as also the said J K," insert "and the said J K, though called, came not. And it appearing to the court that the citation herein has been duly served upon the said J K."

In case the executor does not appear, add "and that a copy of this order be served on the said executor."

REVOCATION OF LETTERS TESTAMENTARY, OR OF ADMINISTRATION, OR OF GUARDIANSHIP.

In the matter of the ⎫
  estate of   , ⎬   *Order of Revocation of Letters.*
  deceased.   ⎭

And now on this day comes   , who heretofore filed his petition in this court, praying that the letters of administration granted to A B, administrator of the said estate, be revoked and repealed for the causes in such petition set forth, and the said A B also comes, as well in person as by G L, his solicitor. And now the said petition coming on to be heard, and it appearing to the court that (*here state the particular ground upon which revocation is to be ordered*), and the court being now sufficiently advised touching the premises, it is

ORDERED and adjudged, That the letters of administration (testamentary *or* guardianship, *as the case may be*), granted to the said A B, by this court, on the   day of   , A. D. 18 , be and the same are forever revoked and repealed, and the said A B removed from his office as   of the said   . And it is further

ORDERED, That he pay the costs by the said   in and about his petition expended, which are taxed at   dollars, and that execution issue therefor. (*p*)

ORDER APPOINTING AN ADMINISTRATOR OR GUARDIAN, WHERE THE OFFICE HAS BECOME VACANT.

In the matter of the ⎫
  estate of   , ⎬   *Order Appointing Administrator.*
  deceased.   ⎭

And now on this day comes   , and applies to the court for letters of

---

(*p*) See p. 299, *supra*.

The forms.

administration on the estate of the said   , deceased, to issue to him, appointing him administrator in place of   , late administratrix of said   , deceased, who was at the last term of this court removed, and the letters granted to her repealed (*or* who resigned, *or* died, *as the case may be*). And it appearing to the court that the said   , late administratrix of the estate of the said   , deceased, was removed by this court on the   day of   , A. D. 18   (*or* has resigned, *as the case may be*), not having fully completed the administration of the said estate, and it also appearing that the said   is competent, and by law entitled, to administer upon said estate; it is, therefore,

ORDERED and adjudged, That letters of administration of the goods and chattels, rights and credits which were of the said   , deceased, at the time of his decease, not administered by the said   , be granted to the said   , upon his entering into bond in the penal sum of   dollars, conditioned and payable as the law requires.

And now again comes the said   , and presents to the court here, for its approval, his bond as administrator of the estate of the said   , deceased, executed by said   as principal, and   as security, in form and substance as by law and the order of this court required; and the court being now sufficiently advised touching the said bond and the said security, it is

ORDERED and adjudged, That said bond and security be approved; and it is further

ORDERED, That the said bond be filed and recorded in this court.

Slight verbal alterations would readily adapt the form to the office of guardian.

The letters issued in such cases are to be varied from the original to suit the facts of each particular case. (*q*)

ORDER ON RETURN OF THE APPRAISEMENT BILL.

In the matter of the estate of   ,   deceased.   } *Order on Appraisement Bill.*

On this day comes   , administrator of said estate, and presents to the court the bill of the appraisement of the goods, chattels and personal estate, which were of the said   , deceased, at the time of his death, and the court having examined the same, and being sufficiently advised concerning said appraisement, it is

ORDERED by the court, That the said appraisement be approved; and it is further

ORDERED by the court, That the said bill of appraisement be filed (and recorded).

(*q*) See p. 79, *supra;* § 21, R. S. 1874, p. 108.

The forms.

ENTRY ON ADJUSTMENT OF CLAIMS.

In the matter of the estate of   , deceased. }   *Adjustment of Claims.*

On this day comes   , administrator of said estate (*or* executor of the last will and testament, etc.), and files in court proof of the publication of notice given by said administrator, appointing this day for the settlement and adjustment of claims against said estate, whereupon the following described claims were presented, and the court being advised by evidence that the same are respectively just and unpaid, it is

ORDERED, That the said claims be severally allowed, classified and paid, as follows:

NAMES.	CLASS.	AMOUNT.
A B................................	First...............	$60 00
C D................................	Fourth.............	19 00

ENTRY WHEN ESTATE IS FOUND TO BE INSOLVENT.

In the matter of the estate of   , deceased. }   *Insolvency.*

And now on this day comes   , administrator of said estate, and files in court a statement, from which it appears that the claims allowed against said estate and unpaid, amount to the sum of   dollars, and that the whole amount of property, rights and credits belonging to said estate is   dollars, and the court being now sufficiently advised concerning the condition of said estate, and it appearing that the same is not solvent, and that there are not sufficient assets with which to pay the just indebtedness thereof, it is

ORDERED, That the said estate be declared insolvent, and be so entered of record.

ORDER TO COMPEL EXECUTOR OR ADMINISTRATOR TO SELL REAL ESTATE.

In the matter of the estate of   , deceased. }   *Order to Compel the Sale of Real Estate.*

On this day comes   , a creditor of said estate, and moves the court for an order that   , the administrator of said estate, make immediate application to the circuit or county court, for the sale of the real estate of which the said   died seized, or so much thereof as will be sufficient to pay the just debts of the said estate, and the court being now sufficiently advised concerning said motion, and it appearing to the court that the personal property belonging to said estate is insufficient to pay the debts thereof, it is

ORDERED, That the said administrator make immediate application to the court for license to sell so much of the real estate of which said   died seized, as will be sufficient to pay the debts of said estate.

The forms.

DECREE FOR THE SALE OF REAL ESTATE.

A. B., Administrator of the estate of C. D.,   ⎫   In the County Court of   County.
                   vs.   ⎬
M. B., W. B., C. B., and D. B.   ⎭   Term, A.D. 18   .

This cause coming on to be heard upon the petition of A. B., administrator of the estate of C. D., asking for leave to sell the real estate of said decedent described therein, or such portion thereof as may be necessary to satisfy the indebtedness of said decedent and the expenses of administration, as well as upon the answers of M. B., and W. B., and the replication of A. B., administrator as aforesaid, thereto. [*If the facts require it, add the recitals somewhat as follows:* And it now appearing to the court that C. B. has been summoned and failed to appear, and that D. B. is a non-resident of this State, and that publication has been made in the   , a newspaper published in said county, once in each week for four successive weeks, containing a notice* of the filing of the petition, the names of the parties thereto, the title of the court, and the time and place of the return of the summons in the case, and a description of the premises described in said petition, the first publication having been made in the paper dated the   day of   , A.D. 18 , and the last publication in the paper dated the   day of   , A.D. 18 , and that a copy of said notice was, within ten days of the first publication of said notice, and on the   day of   , A.D. 18 , sent by mail, addressed to the said D. B., at   , his place of residence; and the said C. B. and D. B. having failed to appear, and forty days having already intervened between the first publication as aforesaid and the first day of the   term, A.D. 18 , of this court, and defaults having at said term been taken against the said C. B. and D. B., and decree *pro confesso* ordered against them herein respectively.] And upon the issues formed or taken, the court having heard and examined the allegations and proofs of the parties herein (and after argument by counsel for the respective parties) it further appearing to the satisfaction of the court, upon due examination as aforesaid, that the said A. B., administrator as aforesaid, has made a just and true account of the condition of the estate, and that the personal estate of the decedent is not sufficient, as it now appears, by the sum of   dollars, to pay the debts against such estate; and it further appearing that all the allegations of said petition are true in fact; now, therefore, it is hereby

DECREED, ORDERED and adjudged by the court, That the said administrator have leave, and be authorized to sell the following described real estate, situate in the said county of   , and State of Illinois, to wit: , or so much thereof as may be necessary to pay the debts of the said estate; and it is further

ORDERED and adjudged by the court, That the said administrator sell the said land on the   day of   next, at the hour of   o'clock P. M. of said day, on the premises. the said administrator having first given notice of such intended sale according to the requirements of the law, and that in case the said administrator should deem it best for the interest of said estate, he may postpone the said sale to such other day as he may appoint, always giving notice of such postponed sale the same as in the first instance ; and it is further

ORDERED, That said land be sold on the following terms :   cash in hand, in   months, and the balance in   months, each with interest, the purchaser to give a mortgage on the premises, with approved personal security; and that said administrator report his acts and doings herein to this court, and that this application be, for that purpose, continued to the next   term of this court.

ADMINISTRATOR'S SALE.

In the estate of   , deceased. By virtue of a decretal order of the county court of   county, Illinois, entered of record on the   day of   , 18 ,

---

* This notice being jurisdictional, it is of the greatest importance that it be properly given and accurately recited. *Botsford* v. *O'Conner*, 57 Ill. 72. *Donlin* v. *Hettinger*, id. 348. See pp. 62, 63, 193–207, *supra*.

The forms.

we will sell at public auction to the highest and best bidder, on the   day of   , 18 , at the hour of   o'clock A. M., on the premises designated as, in the   of   , in said State, the following described real estate of said deceased, to wit: , in the county of   , and State of Illinois. Subject to a mortgage of $. Terms of sale, half cash, and half in   months, with approved security, with interest at 8 per cent per annum.

, *Administratrix*, and
, *Administrator of deceased's estate.*

Dated,   18 .

ORDER CONFIRMING SALE OF REAL ESTATE.

Title as in the decree, p. 307, *supra*.   *Order Confirming Sale of Real Estate.*

And now on this day comes   , administrator of the said estate, and presents to the court a report of his acts and doings under the leave of this court, to sell the real estate of which said   died seized, and the court having examined said report, and it appearing that said administrator caused proper notice of the time and place of said sale to be published and posted, as by law and the order of this court required; that, in pursuance of said order and notices he did, on the   day of   , A. D. 18   , at   o'clock in the afternoon of said day, on the premises, sell said real estate, in said order described, at public sale to one C D, for the sum of   dollars, and that said C D did thereupon comply with the terms of said sale, and the said administrator having thereupon made a deed of conveyance of the said land to the said C D, which is now shown to the court for approval, and the court being now fully advised touching said sale, it is

ORDERED and adjudged by the court, That the said acts and doings of the said administrator, in and about said sale be approved, and said sale confirmed, and that the deed so made by him be approved, and that he deliver the same to the said C D.

ORDER APPOINTING A GUARDIAN.

In the matter of the guardianship of   .   *Appointment of Guardian.*

On this day comes   , and represents to the court that   , of the said county of   , is an orphan minor, of the age of   years, has no father living, and is without a guardian in this State; and prays the court that he be appointed guardian of the said minor; and it appearing to the court that said   is an orphan minor, as represented, and that said   is the   of said minor, and a suitable person to have the custody, education and maintenance of said minor, it is

. ORDERED, That said   be appointed guardian of the person and estate of the said   , upon his entering into bond, with security, as the law directs, in the penal sum of   dollars.

And now again comes the said   , and presents to the court his bond

The forms.

as guardian of said   , with A B and C D as his securities thereon; and the court being now sufficiently advised concerning said bond and the said securities, it is

ORDERED, That the same be approved and filed; and it is further

ORDERED, That letters of guardianship issue to said   .

Where the minor is fourteen years of age, or upward, omit "prays the court that he may be appointed guardian," etc., and insert, "and it appearing to the court that the said   is of the age of fourteen years and upward, and the said minor being present in open court, chooses for his guardian the said   ."

These forms and entries might be indefinitely extended, so as to embrace the almost endless variety of cases that come before the probate courts, but those already given will abundantly show the manner in which such papers should be drawn, and how the record is to be made.

PROOF OF DEATH OF TESTATOR.

STATE OF ILLINOIS,
County.   } ss.:

        , of said county, being first duly sworn, says that   , late of said county, died on or about the   day of   , A. D. 18 , at the said county, leaving, at the time of his decease, property and effects therein, and also an instrument in writing which affiant believes to be his last will and testament, which paper writing he now produces to the court for probate.

        , County Clerk.

Subscribed and sworn to before me,
this   day of   , A. D. 18   .

SUBPŒNA TO WITNESSES TO PROVE EXECUTION OF A WILL.

STATE OF ILLINOIS,
County.   } ss.:

The People of the State of Illinois to the Sheriff of said County, greeting:

You are hereby commanded to summon E F and G H, if to be found in your county, to be and appear before the county court of   county, on the   Monday in the month of   next, at   o'clock A. M., of said day, to testify the truth in a certain matter depending before the said court, touching the proof, execution and validity of the last will and testament of   , late of said county, deceased, and such other matters as shall then and there be required of them, relating to the same; and this they are not to omit under penalty. And then and there return this writ.

[SEAL.]   Witness   , clerk of said court, and the seal thereof, at   , this   day of   , A. D. 18   .

        , County Clerk.

The forms.

CLERK'S CERTIFICATE TO COPY OF WILL, LETTERS, ETC.

STATE OF ILLINOIS,} ss.:
     County.

I,   , clerk of the county court of said county, the same being a court of record, and having an official seal, and having exclusive original jurisdiction of all matters, probate and testamentary, in said county, do hereby certify that the foregoing annexed papers are a true, full and correct copy of the original last will and testament of   , late of said county, deceased, as the same was admitted to probate by and recorded in said county court, and of the letters testamentary issued thereon; that the said will was duly proved and letters thereon granted, in accordance with the laws of the State of Illinois, and that said letters remain in full force.

[SEAL.]   In testimony whereof, etc.

CITATION FOR ADMINISTRATORS, EXECUTORS AND GUARDIANS.

STATE OF ILLINOIS,} ss.:
     County.

The People of the State of Illinois, to the Sheriff of said County, greeting:

WHEREAS (*here insert the particular state of facts upon which the citation was awarded*).

You are therefore hereby commanded that you cite and give notice to the said   , as aforesaid, that he be and appear before our county court of   county, at a special term thereof, to be holden at the court-house, or usual place of holding courts, in   , on the   day of   , A. D. 18   , then and there to answer as such   in the premises; and further to do and perform what shall then by our said court be required and adjudged.

And hereof make due service and return as the law directs.

          Witness,   , clerk of said county court for the county
[SEAL.]   of   , at his office in   , this   day of   ,
          A. D. 18 .

                                            County Clerk.

CITATION TO ADMINISTRATOR OR EXECUTOR.

STATE OF ILLINOIS,} ss.:
     County.

The People of the State of Illinois, to   , administrator of   , deceased.

WHEREAS, complaint has been made to the county court of said county, by one A B, because you have [failed to file an inventory of the estate of said   , deceased, within three months from the date of your letters of administration]: You, the said administrator, are hereby cited to appear before the said county court of   county, at the next regular term thereof, to be holden at the court-house in the city of   in said county, on the   Monday of   , A. D. 18 [to show cause why you should not file such inventory.]

    [SEAL.]   In witness whereof, etc.

The forms.

A variety of citations may be constructed by omitting what is in brackets and inserting in lieu thereof whatever may be required for any different state of facts.

WAIVER OF DOWER BY A WIDOW ACCEPTING A PROVISION IN THE WILL IN HER BEHALF.

KNOW ALL MEN BY THESE PRESENTS, That whereas, my late husband,   , deceased, late of the county of   , in the State of Illinois, in and by his last will and testament probated in said county, provided as follows: (*Here insert a copy of the provision made in the will, which the widow may accept in lieu of dower.*) I, the said   , in consideration thereof, accept the said provision, so made and expressed, to be in lieu of my dower in the real estate of which the said   died seized, and acknowledge the same now paid to me by   executor of the said last will and testament of said   , deceased, to be in full satisfaction of all my right and claim of dower, which I might otherwise have been entitled to, in the real estate which was of the said   , deceased, during our coverture, and by these presents do release, renounce and discharge all my right and claim of dower, of, in and to all such estate.

In witness whereof, I have hereunto set my hand and seal, this   day of   , A. D. 18   .   . [SEAL.]

RENUNCIATION OF PROVISION IN A WILL IN LIEU OF DOWER.

WHEREAS,   , late of the county of   , in the State of Illinois, in and by his last will and testament, proved in the county court of said county, made the following provision for the undersigned in lieu of dower, to wit: (*Here insert copy of such provision*,) which said provision so made, I,   , widow of the said   , deceased, of said county, do not accept in lieu of my dower interest in the estate left by said   , but hereby renounce the said provision, and shall and do insist upon my right and claim of dower, in the estate of the said   , deceased, to which I may be legally and justly entitled, notwithstanding any provision in the said will to the contrary; and I desire that this my renunciation be entered of record.

In witness whereof, I have hereunto set my hand and seal, this   day of   , A. D.   .

                                    . [SEAL.]

FORM OF APPRENTICE'S INDENTURE.

THIS INDENTURE, made this   day of   , A. D. 18   , WITNESSETH, That   , now of the age of   , on the   day of   , A. D. 18   , hath put himself, and by these presents, by and with the approbation of the judge of the county court of   county, Illinois, doth voluntarily, and of his own free will and accord, put himself apprentice to   of the county of   , and after the manner of an apprentice to serve from the day of the date hereof, for and during and until the end and term of   years, or until the   day of   , A. D. 18   .

During all of which time the said   his master shall faithfully serve, his secrets keep, and his lawful commands everywhere obey. He shall do no

The forms.

damage to his said master, nor see it done by others without giving notice thereof to his said master; he must not contract matrimony within the said term; he shall not waste his master's goods, nor lend them unlawfully to any; at cards, dice, or any unlawful game he shall not play, whereby his said master shall have damage; he shall not absent himself night or day without his leave, but in all things behave himself as a faithful apprentice ought to do.

And the said master agrees, to the utmost of his power, to procure and provide for the said apprentice during said term of   years, or until the said   shall attain the age of   years. And shall cause said   to be taught to read and write, and the ground rules of arithmetic; and shall also, at the expiration of said term of service, give to said   a new bible and two new suits of complete wearing apparel, suitable to his condition in life; and shall also, during the continuance of said term of service, according to the best of his endeavors, find his said apprentice with sufficient wearing apparel, washing and mending, suitable and fit for an apprentice to wear.

And for the true performance of all and singular the covenants and agreements aforesaid, the said   binds himself unto the said   firmly by these presents.

In witness whereof, the said parties have hereunto set their hands and seals, the day and year first above written.

Witness,   , [SEAL.]
                                                                         , [SEAL.]

LETTERS OF GUARDIANSHIP.

STATE OF ILLINOIS, }
        County.   } *ss.:*

The People of the State of Illinois, to   , greeting:

WHEREAS, At the county court, holden in and for said county, at   , on the   day of   , A. D. 18   , you were duly appointed by said court guardian for   , minor , aged as follows : (*Here insert ages.*)

Trusting in your fidelity, therefore, the said court do by these presents allow, constitute and appoint you, the said   , to be guardian unto said minor , and authorize and empower you to take and have the care of   person, and the custody and management of   property, frugally, and without waste or destruction, to improve and account for the same in all things according to law.

In witness whereof, I have hereunto set my hand and affixed [SEAL.] the seal of said county court, at my office in   , this   day of   , A. D. 18   .

                                                                 , *County Clerk* .

EXECUTION FOR COSTS.*

B A   }
  v. }   *Defendant's Costs.*
C D.   }

To amount of clerk's fees, as follows : (*Here insert copy from fee book.*)

I, A B, clerk of the county court of said county, do hereby certify that the above is a true copy of defendant's costs, as appears on my fee book.

                                                    A B, *County Clerk.*

---

* See *Whitehurst* v. *Coleen*, 53 Ill. 247; 2 Hill's C. L. 635; *Rowan* v. *Kirkpatrick*, 14 Ill. 1; pp. 294–300, *supra*.

The forms.

STATE OF ILLINOIS, } *ss*:
County.

The People of the State of Illinois to the Sheriff of said County, greeting:

We command you that, if the above fee bill, amounting to   dollars, shall not be paid within thirty days after being by you demanded, you cause the same to be made of the goods and chattels, lands and tenements of the said   , in your county, according to the statute in such case made and provided, and make return hereof within ninety days, in what manner you shall have executed the same.

[SEAL.]   Witness, A B, clerk of the county court of said county, and the seal thereof, at   , this   day of   , 18 .

A B, *Clerk.*

COMMISSION TO TAKE DEPOSITION OF NON-RESIDENT WITNESS.

STATE OF ILLINOIS, } *ss.*:
County.

The People of the State of Illinois to (here insert the name of person who is to take the deposition).

WHEREAS, It has been represented to us that *(here insert the names of the witnesses)* — material witnesses in a certain cause now depending in our county court, in and for the county of   aforesaid, between   , plaintiff, and   , defendant, (*or* touching the proof of the execution and validity of the will of   (*as the case may be*), and that the said witnesses reside at   aforesaid, without the said State of Illinois, and that   personal attendance cannot be procured at the trial of the said cause. Now, know ye, that we, in confidence of your prudence and fidelity, have appointed you commissioner to examine the said witnesses, and do, therefore, authorize and require you to cause the said witnesses to come before you, at such time and place as you may therefor designate and appoint, and diligently to examine the said witnesses, on the oath or affirmation of the said witnesses, by you first duly in that behalf administered, and faithfully to take the deposition of the said witnesses upon all interrogatories inclosed with or attached to these presents, both on the part of the said plaintiff and of the said defendant, and none others; and the same, when thus taken, together with this commission, and the said interrogatories, to certify into our said county court with the least possible delay.

[SEAL.]   Witness,   , clerk of our said court, and seal thereof, at   , in said county, this   day of   , A. D. 18 .

, *Clerk.*

Attach to the *dedimus potestatum* instructions as to the manner of taking and returning depositions. (*r*)

When the sale is made, the purchaser is entitled to a deed from the administrator; and, if the land be sold on a credit, the pur-

(*r*) See p. 34, *supra.*

chaser is required to give bond (or note), with good security, and a mortgage on the premises sold. By "good security" is meant such personal security as the administrator may, in a reasonable exercise of his judgment, approve. If a person whose bid has been received tender unquestionable security, and a proper mortgage on the premises, the administrator has no right to refuse it, out of mere caprice. The deed may be as follows:

DEED BY AN ADMINISTRATOR, UNDER A DECREE OF COURT.

To All to whom these Presents shall come:

A B, of   , in the county of   , and State of Illinois, administrator of the goods and estate which were of C D, late of the said county, deceased, intestate, sends greeting:

WHEREAS, at the   term of the circuit court of the said county of   and State aforesaid, in the year of our Lord one thousand eight hundred and   , in the matter of the petition of A B, administrator as aforesaid, for leave to sell the following described real estate, situated in the county of   and State of Illinois, to wit: (*here describe the land*), it was ordered and decreed by said court, in chancery sitting, in the words following, to wit: (*here set forth the order and decree at large*); and whereas, in pursuance of said order and decree, I did proceed to sell the premises aforesaid, after having given the notice aforesaid, on the day and between the hours aforesaid, at the place aforesaid, at public vendue, and the said premises were struck off to E F, of said   , he being the highest and best bidder therefor, for the sum of   dollars:

Now, therefore, know ye that I, the said A B, administrator as aforesaid, by virtue of the order and decree aforesaid, and in consideration of the sum of   dollars, to me paid by the said E F, the receipt whereof I do hereby acknowledge, do hereby grant, sell and convey unto the said E F, his heirs and assigns, all that tract and parcel of land situated in the county of   , to wit: (*here describe the land*): To have and to hold the said premises unto the said E F, his heirs and assigns, to his and their behoof forever. And I, the said A B, administrator as aforesaid, do hereby covenant with the said E F, his heirs and assigns, that I have in all respects complied with the order and decree of said circuit court, and with the directions of the law generally, in such case made and provided.

In witness whereof, I, the said A B, in my said capacity of administrator, have hereunto set my hand and seal, this first day of   , A. D. 18   .

A B. [L. S.]

Signed, sealed and delivered in }
   presence of   }

After completing the sale, the administrator should report to the court and obtain a confirmation thereof.

The forms.

REPORT.

State of Illinois, } ss.:   County Court of   County,
  County.   Term, 18   .

To Hon.   , Judge of said Court :

In the matter of the application of   , administrator of   , deceased, to sell real estate.

The said administrator, charged with the execution of the order of sale entered in said cause at the last   term of this court, would respectfully submit the following report of his acts and doings under said order:

That in pursuance of said order of sale, he did, on the   day of   , A. D. 18   , put up notices of the sale of said real estate, in said order directed to be sold, in four of the most public places in the said county of   , to wit: one at the court-house, one at the post-office in   , etc., a copy of which notice, with proof of such posting, is hereto attached; that he caused a similar notice to be published in the   , a weekly paper, published at   , in said county, for four successive weeks prior to said sale, a copy of which advertisement, with the publisher's certificate of the due publication thereof, is also hereto attached.

That in pursuance of said order of sale, and the said notice, he did, at the time and place mentioned in such notice, sell at public sale the said real estate in the said order directed to be sold, to C D, of   , aforesaid, for the sum of four thousand dollars, his being the highest and best bid therefor, on a credit of   months. That thereupon the said C D having complied with the terms of said sale, by giving his note, with good approved personal security, and a mortgage upon the said premises, the undersigned executed to said C D a deed of the said premises, and delivered the same to him.

All of which is respectfully submitted, and an order confirming all the said acts and doings is hereby prayed for.

                  , Administrator of   , deceased.

The lands affected are to be described in the notices with legal certainty.

Notices should be posted up at least four weeks before the time of sale, and a similar notice published in such newspapers four weeks successively. Copies of the notices should be preserved by the person posting them, and his affidavit of the time when and the places where he posted them, indorsed upon each, and filed in the court making the order. A copy of the newspaper notice, with the publisher's certificate of publication, should likewise be filed, and both attached to and returned to court with the report of the sale made by the administrator for an order confirming the sale.*

NOTICE OF SALE.
Notice of Administrator's Sale.

By virtue of an order and decree of the   court of   county, Illinois,

---

* See page 200, *supra*. Also ch. 3, § 109, R. S., as amended April 7, 1875, Laws of 1875, p. 1. Cothran's Stats., p. 76; *Marshall* v. *Rose, Adm'x.*, 86 Ill. 374; *Allen* v. *Shepard*, 87 Ill. 314; *Kellogg* v. *Wilson*, 89 Ill. 357.

The forms.

made on the petition of the undersigned, administrator of the estate of   ,
deceased, for leave to sell the real estate of said deceased, at the last December
term of said court, to wit, on the 3d day of December, 18 , I shall, on the 2d
day of April next, between the hours of 10 o'clock, A. M., and 4 o'clock, P. M.,
of said day, sell at public sale, on the premises, the following described real
estate, situate in the county of   , and State of Illinois, to wit: , more
or less, on a ˙ of   months, the purchaser to give approved personal security,
and a mortgage on the premises sold, to secure the payment of the purchase-
money.

             , Administrator of   , deceased.
 Dated   , 18 .

The sale is to be public, *i. e.*, at auction. If there are several tracts of land to be sold, each is to be put up separately; a sale *en masse* would not be authorized. A sale made before 10 o'clock, A. M., or after 5 o'clock, P. M., of the day, would be void.*

The order should generally provide for, and the mode of, a postponement of the sale; where it fails to do so, and fixes the day of sale, if there be no bidders, or the administrator deem it best for the interest of the estate, he may refuse to put it up, but cannot continue it. He must again apply to the court for a new order, fixing another day of sale. If an administrator sell the land contrary to the provisions of the law, he is liable to forfeit and pay five hundred dollars, for the use of any person interested.

RENUNCIATION

STATE OF ILLINOIS, } *ss.:* *In the County Court of County,*
  County.   }   *of the term, A. D.* 18 .

In the matter of the estate of)
A B, deceased, leaving a last }
will and testament.   )

WHEREAS, A B, late of   , deceased, died on the   day of   ,
18 , at   , having made and duly executed his last will and testament,
being the   day of   18 , and thereof appointed me the undersigned sole executor.

Now I, the said C D, do hereby declare that I have not intermeddled in the personal estate and effects of the said testator, and will not hereafter intermeddle therein, and I do hereby renounce all my right and title to the probate and execution of the said will.   C D.

Signed by the said C D, this   day of)
  , 18 , in the presence of   }
    (Signed.)

RENUNCIATION OF THE RIGHT TO ADMINISTER.

STATE OF ILLINOIS, } · *In the County Court of County,*
  County.   }   *of the term, A. D.* 18 .

In the matter of the estate of (
A B, deceased, intestate.   )

WHEREAS, A B, late of   in the county of   , deceased, died on the

---

* See page 200, *supra.* Also Cothran's Stats., p. 76, and cases cited.

The forms.

    day of   , 18 , at   , intestate, a widower; and whereas, I, C D, am his natural and lawful and only child.

    Now, I, the said C D, do hereby renounce all my right and title to the letters of administration of the personal estate and effects of the said A B, deceased.

Signed by the said C D, this   day of }   C D.
    , A. D., in the presence of   .}
        (Signed.)

The foregoing form, at page 226, *supra*, may be used by a distributee by a slight alteration, substituting "administrator," etc., for "executor," etc., and "distributee" for "legatee."

When a legacy is given to a married woman, the husband should execute the bond for her, or with her, in addition to the security. In case the legatee, after being ordered to refund, shall neglect to do so within sixty days thereafter, it works a breach of the bond. In case there is no bond taken, an action of debt may be maintained against such legatee or distributee, for his share ordered to be refunded.

DEED BY AN EXECUTOR UNDER AN AUTHORITY IN A WILL.

To all persons to whom these presents shall come:

A B, of the county of   , and State of Illinois, executor of the last will and testament of C D, late of said county, deceased, testate, sends greeting:

WHEREAS the said C D, in order to enable his said executor fully to carry into effect his intentions, did, in and by his last will and testament, authorize and empower his said executor (*here set out the power, in the language of the will*).

Now, THEREFORE, KNOW YE, That I, the said A B, executor as aforesaid, by virtue of the authority to me given by the said C D in the said last will and testament, and in consideration of   dollars, to me paid by E F, of the said county of   , the receipt whereof I do hereby acknowledge, do hereby grant, bargain, sell, and convey to the said E F, his heirs and assigns, all that tract or parcel of land situate in the county of   , and known and described as follows, to wit: , containing   acres of land, be the same more or less.

To have and to hold the said premises, to him the said E F, his heirs and assigns, to his and their use and behoof forever. And I, the said A B, covenant with the said E F, his heirs and assigns, that I am lawfully the executor of said last will and testament, and that I have not made or suffered any incumbrance in said premises, since I was appointed executor of the said C D; and that I have, in all respects, in making this conveyance, acted in strict pursuance of the authority granted to me in and by said last will and testament of the said C D.

In witness whereof, I, the said A B, in my said capacity of executor of the

The forms.

said C D, have hereunto set my hand and seal, this   day of   , A. D 18 .

A B. [SEAL.]

Signed, sealed, and delivered }
 in presence of   }

Upon discovering the insolvency of the estate it is the duty of the administrator to take immediate steps to convert the real property into assets for the benefit of the creditors. Should he neglect to do so, the county court may coerce him to make such application.

The statute does not prescribe the mode of such coercion. The usual practice in such cases is, a motion to the court, setting forth the interest of the party applying to the court, the fact of insolvency, and that there is real estate of the intestate, the neglect of the administrator to take steps under the statute to have the real estate sold, and reduced to assets for the payment of the debts. An affidavit is not required as the foundation of such motion, the facts are matter of record in the court; yet if put in, it would present all the necessary facts in a more tangible form.

The order of the court, compelling the executor or administrator to sell real estate, has been given.(s) After the order is made, the proceedings for sale by the executor or administrator are as already given, in the case of his voluntary application to sell.

The court, by the "account and report," is advised of the extent of the deficiency; it should also be advised of the value of the land sought to be converted into assets to meet such deficit, so as to determine whether it is necessary to sell the whole, or only a part of it; the situation of the estate should also be shown, that the court may know whether it would be prejudicial to the interest of the heirs to sell a part instead of the whole. This evidence is generally the testimony of witnesses acquainted with the property. The administrator may himself be a witness.

PROCEEDINGS SUBSEQUENT TO THE ORDER. After the order has been obtained by the administrator to sell the real estate of the deceased, he is first to give notice of the time and place of the sale. The notice is to be "published for the space of six weeks successively, by putting up notices in at least four of the most public places in the county where such real estate is to be sold; and also by causing a similar notice thereof to be published in the nearest newspaper in this State."

(s) See p. 314, also amended act as to sale, etc., Cothran's Stats., p. 76; cases cited.

The forms.

The statute provides that whenever it shall be represented to the court that any orphan minor above the age of fourteen years has not a guardian, it shall be the duty of the court to issue a notification to such minor to appear before the said court and choose a guardian.

This representation made to the court may or may not be in writing; but the best practice is to require it in writing.

The following short form may be used:

REPRESENTATION.

STATE OF ILLINOIS, } ss: County Court of   County,
County.   term, A. D. 18   .

To Hon. E F, Judge of said Court:

The undersigned respectively represents and shows to your honor, that one A B, resident of said county, is an orphan minor above the age of fourteen years, to wit, of the age of sixteen years, and has no guardian; that the undersigned verily believes that the interest and welfare of the said A B requires the appointment of a guardian for him; wherefore, the undersigned prays the court to notify the said A B to appear in said court, at the next   term thereof, and choose a guardian; and if he neglect so to do, that the court will appoint a guardian for him.

Dated   , 18 .   C D.

NOTICE OF APPLICATION TO SELL REAL ESTATE.

Guardian's Notice.

STATE OF ILLINOIS, } ss: In the County Court of   County,
County.   term, A. D. 18   .

To all persons concerned:

Take Notice, That the undersigned, guardian of E F, a minor, will apply to the circuit court of said county, at the next   term thereof, to be holden at the court-house in said county on the   Monday in   next, for an order to sell the following described real estate, belonging to said minor, and situate in the county of   , and State of Illinois, to wit: (*here describe the land*), and that the petition therefor is now on file in the office of the clerk of said court.

A B, *Guardian of E F.*

Dated   , 18 .

The statute may not require the petition to be on file before the sitting of the court, but such is a just practice, as it will afford those interested an opportunity, which is due them, to examine the grounds upon which the application is based.

The proof of publishing the notice is to be made as in other cases.

FORM OF PETITION FOR SALE OF REAL ESTATE BY GUARDIAN.

STATE OF ILLINOIS, } ss: In the County Court of   County
County.   term, A. D. 18   .

To the Hon. B C, Judge of said Court:

The petition of A B, of the county of   , and State of Illinois, guardian

The forms.

of E F, a minor, respectfully represents and shows to your honor: That your petitioner was, on the   day of   , A. D. 18 , appointed guardian of the said E F, by the county court of   county, as will appear on the hearing hereof, by the production of his letters of guardianship in evidence.

And your petitioner further shows, that as such guardian he has faithfully applied all the personal estate belonging to said minor, and has fully exhausted the same, as will appear on the hearing hereof, by a certified copy of his account rendered to the county court of   county, aforesaid, at the last term thereof, and the order of said court approving the same, which is hereto attached, marked "Exhibit A."

And your petitioner further represents, that the said E F is the owner in fee of the following described real estate, situate in the county of   , and State of Illinois, to wit: (*here insert description of the land*); that said land is improved, and has upon it a dwelling-house and out-buildings; that the said buildings and the improvements on the said land are in a dilapidated condition, and rapidly decaying; that the dwelling-house is becoming untenantable, and the fence insufficient to protect the fields; that petitioner has no funds belonging to said minor to put the said property in tenantable repair; that said real estate is deteriorating in value for the reasons aforesaid.

And your petitioner further shows, that funds are needed to maintain and educate said minor in a proper manner.

And your petitioner further states, that said real estate is now worth   dollars, and that the interest of his said ward would be greatly promoted by a sale of the said property, and an investment of the funds arising from the sale thereof in wild land, after deducting such an amount as will be necessary for the maintenance and education of said minor.

Wherefore, in consideration of the premises, your petitioner prays leave to sell the said real estate, according to the statute in such case made and provided.

And your petitioner will ever pray, etc.   A B,
Dated   , 18 .   *Guardian of E F.*

In the petition by a resident guardian for the sale of real estate, it must appear that he has faithfully applied all the personal estate, or if there was no personal estate, that fact must be distinctly set out, to give the court jurisdiction. The court is authorized to order the sale for two purposes, either for the support and education of the ward, or that the proceeds may be invested in other real estate.(*t*)

The law in regard to non-resident guardians of infants, who own real estate in Illinois, appears to dispense with the foregoing requisition in regard to the application of all the personal estate. Non-resident guardians are entitled to an order for the sale of the real estate of their wards, without other limitations than the filing with the petition authenticated copies of their letters of guardianship,

(*t*) *Young* v. *Lorain*, 11 Ill. 638.

and the bond required by such act for the faithful application of the proceeds of such sale, in such manner as the court appointing the guardian may direct, and the approval thereof. The sale in such a case is to be for the purpose of educating and supporting the ward, or of investing the proceeds of the sale in such real estate as the court appointing the guardian may direct.

In all other respects the proceedings on applications to sell real estate by non-resident and resident guardians are the same.

The order will direct the terms, time and place of sale, and the notice thereof to be given, which order must be strictly followed, to render the sale legal.

NOTICE OF GUARDIAN'S SALE.

Guardian's Sale.

STATE OF ILLINOIS, } *ss*:
    County.   }

By virtue of a decretal order of the county court of said county, entered at the last   term of said court, on the application of the undersigned, guardian of E F, a minor, to sell the following described real estate belonging to said minor, situate in the county of   , and State of Illinois, to wit: (*here insert description of the land*), I shall, on the   day of   next, between the hours of 10 o'clock A. M., and 4 o'clock P. M., of said day, sell the said real estate at public sale, on the premises, to the highest and best bidder. Terms of sale as follows: one-half cash in hand, one-fourth in one year, and the balance in two years, with six per cent interest. Approved personal security, and a mortgage on the premises for the payment of the unpaid purchase-money, will be required of the purchaser. Deed made to the purchaser on the day of sale.

No bid will be received under   dollars per acre.

A B,
Guardian of E. F.

Dated   , 18 .

The notice should follow the order of court, and be posted or published in the manner required by the order.

After the sale, the guardian is required to report it and the conveyance to the county court, for its approval.

The following decisions have been made by the supreme court upon this point. In case of *Rawlings* v. *Bailey*, 15 Ill. 178, the court say: A guardian's deed is inoperative, unless the sale and conveyance have been reported to, and approved by the circuit court. The same principle is also laid down in 15 Ill. 433, 444, 481; 11 id. 642.

Where a statute provides that title to land may be transferred in

The forms.

a particular way, it must be done in the way prescribed, or it receives no sanction from the statute, and is void. 15 Ill. 481.

REPORT OF GUARDIANS' SALE.

STATE OF ILLINOIS, } ss.: *In the County Circuit Court of   County,*
County.   *term, A. D. 18 .*

In the matter of the application of }
A B, guardian of E F, to sell real } *Report of Guardian's Sale.*
estate.   }

The undersigned, guardian of E F, would respectfully submit the following report of his acts and doings, under the decretal order of this court, entered in said cause at the last   term thereof, for the sale of the real estate in said order described.

That in pursuance of said order and decree, the undersigned did, on the   day of   , 18 , put up notices of the sale of said land in three of the most public places in said county, to wit: (*here name the places where posted*) a copy of which said notices is hereto attached and made a part of this report, marked "Exhibit A." That said notices were posted more than   weeks before the sale of said land hereinafter mentioned.

I do further report, that on the said   day of   , A. D. 18 , and at the hour of 12 o'clock meridian, I did expose and offer at public sale, on the premises, the said tract of land, in said decree described, in pursuance of the said decree and the said notice, when   bid for the same the sum of   dollars, and he being the highest and best bidder for the said tract of land, it was sold to him for the sum of   dollars. And the said   then and there paid to me the sum of   dollars in hand, and executed to me, as such guardian, his promissory notes for the balance of said purchase-money; one for the sum of   dollars, payable six months after date, and the other for the sum of   dollars, payable twelve months after date, each with interest. Said   also executed to the undersigned a mortgage on the premises, to secure the payment of the said unpaid purchase-money, whereupon I, the said A B, as such guardian, executed to the said   , a deed of conveyance in fee of the said tract of land so sold, which said deed is here shown to the court for approval.

All of which is respectfully submitted, and an approval and confirmation of said acts and doings prayed for.

                                                A B,
                                        Guardian of E F.

ADVERTISEMENT OR NOTICE TO BE GIVEN BY EXECUTORS OR ADMINISTRATORS, SO SOON AS THEY ARE QUALIFIED AS SUCH.

Public notice is hereby given, that the undersigned has taken out letters testamentary of the last will and testament (*or* of administration of the goods

The forms.

and chattels, rights and credits, as the case may be) of A B, deceased, and qualified as such executor (*or* administrator). All persons having claims against the estate of the deceased are hereby notified and required to exhibit the same to me, or to the county court of the county of   , for settlement, within   months from the date hereof. Dated at   , this   day of   , A. D. 18   .

C D, Executor, etc.

CITATION TO RETURN INVENTORY AND APPRAISEMENT.

STATE OF ILLINOIS,   } ss:
County of   .

The People of the State of Illinois, to the Sheriff of said county, greeting:

WHEREAS, it appears to our county court of   county, upon an inspection of the records thereof, that more than three months have elapsed since the grant of letters to   , as administrator of the estate of   , deceased, and that the said   , administrator, ha   not returned an inventory and appraisement of said estate, as required by statute, but fails and neglects so to do.

We do, therefore, hereby command you to cite the said   , administrator as aforesaid, to be and appear before our county court of   county, at the court-house in   , in said county, on the   day of   , A. D. 18   , at   o'clock   M., then and there to answer for such   neglect, and show cause why   he ha   not exhibited an inventory and appraisement of the estate of said decedent, and why he should not be removed for such neglect; and further to do and receive in this behalf as unto law and justice shall appertain under pain of the law and contempt thereof.

And hereof make due service and return as the law directs.

Witness,   , clerk of the county court of   county, and the seal of said court, at   , in said county, this   day of   , A. D. 18   .

, Clerk.

AFFIDAVIT OF CLAIM AGAINST ESTATE OF DECEASED.

STATE OF ILLINOIS, } ss.   *In the County Court of   County.*
County of   .

        , being duly sworn, deposes and says, that the annexed account against the estate of   , deceased, is just and   unpaid, and this deponent verily believes that all credits and offsets thereto have been allowed, and that he has no other claim against said estate.

Sworn to and subscribed before me, }
this   day of   , A. D. 18   .

        , *Clerk of the County Court.*

        claim of the estate   , deceased, as the amount due on   , hereto annexed, over and above all credits and offsets, the sum of   dollars and   cents, and interest on   from   , A. D. 18   , at   per cent per annum.

, Plaintiff.

The forms.

CITATION TO ADJUDICATE.

STATE OF ILLINOIS, } ss.:
County of   . }

The People of the State of Illinois, to the sheriff of said county, greeting:

WHEREAS, it appears to our county court of   county, upon an inspection of the records thereof, that more than six months have elapsed since the grant of letters   , and that the said   ha   not fixed upon a term of said court for the settling and adjusting all claims against said decedent as required by law, but fails and neglects so to do.

We do, therefore, hereby command you to cite the said   , as aforesaid, to be and appear before our county court of   county, at the court-house in   , in said county, on the   day of   , A. D. 18   , at   o'clock, M., then and there to answer for such neglect, and show cause why he should not be removed; and further to do and receive in this behalf as unto law and justice shall appertain, under pain of the law and contempt thereof.

And hereof make due service and return as the law directs.

Witness,   , clerk of the county court of   county, and the seal of said court, at   , in said county, this   day of   , A. D. 18   .

, *Clerk.*

INDENTURE OF APPRENTICESHIP OF A MINOR, WITH THE CONSENT OF FATHER, MOTHER OR GUARDIAN.

This indenture, made and entered into this   day of   , A. D. 18   , between A B, a minor, of his own free will and accord, and by and with the consent and approbation of E F, his father, of the county of   , and State of Illinois (*or* mother or guardian, as the case may be), of the one part, and G H, of the same county and State, of the other part, witnesseth: That the said A B does, by these presents, of his own free will and accord, and by and with the consent of E F, his father (*or* mother or guardian), bind himself to the said G H, as an apprentice, to learn the art (trade or mystery of merchant, hatter, tanner or carpenter, or as the case may be), to dwell with and serve the said G H, from the day of the date hereof until the   day of   , in the year 18   , at which time the said A B will be twenty-one years of age. During all of which time, or term, the said apprentice his said master well and faithfully shall serve, his secrets keep, and his lawful commands everywhere, at all times, readily obey; he shall do no damage to his said master, nor knowingly suffer any to be done by others; he shall not waste the goods of his said master, nor lend them unlawfully to any; at cards, dice, or any other unlawful game, he shall not play; matrimony he shall not contract during the said term; taverns, ale-houses, and places of gaming he shall not frequent or resort; from the service of his said master he shall not absent himself; but in all things, and at all times, he shall demean and conduct himself as a good apprentice ought, during the whole term aforesaid.

And the said G H. on his part, does hereby covenant and agree to furnish the said apprentice good and sufficient diet, clothing, lodging and other necessaries convenient and useful for said apprentice during the term aforesaid, and also

The forms.

shall cause said apprentice to be taught to read and write, and the ground rules of arithmetic; and shall also give unto said apprentice a new Bible and two new suits of clothes, suitable to his condition, at the expiration of his term of service.

In testimony whereof, etc.

A B. [L. S.]
E F. [L. S.]
G H. [L. S.]

INDENTURE OF APPRENTICESHIP, BY COUNTY JUDGE, TWO JUSTICES OF THE PEACE, OR TWO OVERSEERS OF THE POOR.

This indenture, made and entered into this day   of   , A. D.   , between A B and C D, overseers of the poor (*or* justices of the peace, or county judge), in and for the county of   , and State of Illinois, of the one part, and E F, of the same county and State, of the other part, witnesseth: That the said overseers of the poor, by virtue of the law of the State of Illinois in such cases made and provided, have placed, and by these presents do place and bind out, as an apprentice, a poor child, named   , son of   , of said county of   , who is legally settled in and become chargeable to said county, and who is proven to said overseers to be unable to maintain him, the said child, who is now of the age of   years, to said E F, to learn the art, trade or mystery of   , of the said E F, after the manner of an apprentice, to dwell with, and serve the said E F, from the day of the date hereof, until the   day of   , A. D.   ; at which time the said apprentice will be twenty-one years of age. During all of which time or term, the said apprentice his master well and faithfully shall serve, his secrets keep, and his lawful commands, everywhere and at all times, readily obey; he shall do no damage to his said master, nor knowingly suffer any to be done by others; he shall not waste the goods of his said master, nor lend them unlawfully to any; at cards, dice or any other unlawful games, he shall not play; matrimony he shall not contract during the said term; taverns, ale-houses, or places of gaming he shall not frequent or resort; from the service of his said master he shall not absent himself; but in all things, and at all times, he shall demean and behave himself as a good and faithful apprentice ought, during the whole term aforesaid.

And the said E F binds himself to cause said apprentice to be taught to read and write, and the ground rules of arithmetic; and shall also give unto said apprentice a new Bible, and two suits of clothes, suitable to his condition, at the expiration of his said term of service.

In testimony, etc.*

A B. [L. S.]
C D. [L. S.]
E F. [L. S.]

---

*The above indenture, by the overseers of the poor, must be executed with the consent of the county judge. It will be sufficient for him to indorse such consent on the back of said indenture. In every case of binding a poor or orphan child, by any of the authorized officers, a copy of the indenture must be filed with the county judge for safe-keeping. R. S. 1874, p. 146.

The forms.

. NOTICE TO MINORS.

WHEREAS, it is represented to the court of probate, that you, the said A B, are an orphan minor, above the age of fourteen years, and entitled to some estate (real or personal, as the case may be) of your deceased father, and that you have no guardian; you are, therefore, hereby notified to appear before the court of probate, on the   day of   next, and choose a guardian; and if you shall neglect or refuse to appear and choose a guardian, the said court will proceed to appoint one for you.

(*Teste.*)

The Chicago fire (October 8, 9, 1871), necessitated the Burnt Records Bill.* The following section pertains to the probate jurisdiction:

"In case of the destruction by fire or otherwise of the records, or any part thereof, of any county court having probate jurisdiction, the judge of any such court may proceed, upon his own motion, or upon the application, in writing, of any party in interest, to restore the records, papers and proceedings of his court relating to the estates of deceased persons, including recorded wills and wills probated or filed for probate in said court; and for the purpose of restoring said records, wills, papers or proceedings, or any part thereof, may cause citations to be issued to any and all parties to be designated by him, and may compel the attendance in court of any and all witnesses whose testimony may be necessary to the establishment of any such record or part thereof, and the production of any and all written or documentary evidence which may be by him deemed necessary in determining the true import and effect of the original record, will, paper or other document belonging to the files of said court; and may make such orders and decrees establishing said original record, will, paper, document or proceeding, or the substance thereof, as to him shall seem just and proper; and such judge may make all such rules and regulations governing the said proceedings for the restoration of the record, will, paper, document and proceeding pertaining to said court, as in his judgment will best secure the rights and protect the interests of all parties concerned."

---

* § 3, act to provide for the restoration of court records which have been lost or destroyed. March 19, 1872. R. S. 1874, p. 838.

The forms.

PETITION FOR THE RESTORATION OF A PROBATE RECORD.

STATE OF ILLINOIS,⎱ ⎰ *In the County Court of   County,*
      County.   ⎰ *ss :*   *term,* 18   .

In the matter of the restoration⎫
of the files and records in the ⎬
estate of   , deceased.   ⎭

To the Honorable   , Judge of said Court :

Your petitioner   , respectfully showeth unto your honor :

GRANT OF ADMINISTRATION. That on the   day of   , 18 ,   filed h petition for administration upon the estate of the said deceased in said court, a   copy of which petition is herewith presented, marked " Exhibit   ,"   That on said day last named said   also filed in said court h   bond as such administrat   in the penal sum of $, with   as sureties, which bond was then and there approved by said court, a   copy of which is herewith presented, marked " Exhibit   ," certified by said sureties to be a true copy of the original bond ; that thereupon said court, on the day last named, made the usual order granting letters of administration according to the prayer of said petition, a   copy of said letters of administration is herewith presented, marked " Exhibit   ."

That before receiving said letters, and on the day last named, said administrat   in open court subscribed and swore to the usual administrator's oath, a   copy of which is herewith presented, marked " Exhibit   ."

INVENTORY. That on said day last named said administrat   caused to be filed in said court an inventory of the estate of said deceased, which was then approved by said court, a   copy of which is herewith presented, marked " Exhibit   ."

APPRAISEMENT. That   were on said day last named appointed appraisers of said estate, and a warrant was then issued to them, a   copy of which is herewith presented, marked " Exhibit   ," to which is also appended a   copy of the oath taken by the appraisers ; the said appraisers, after taking and signing the oath of office, made an appraisement of the personal estate of said deceased, subject to appraisement, which was approved by said court on the   day of   , 18 , a   copy of which is herewith presented, marked " Exhibit   ."

WIDOW'S AWARD. That said appraisers made out and appraised the widow's award, amounting to $, which award was on the day last named approved by said court, a   copy of which is herewith presented, marked " Exhibit   ."

WIDOW'S SELECTION. That on the   day of   18 ,   widow of said deceased, filed her selection, amounting to $, a   copy of which is herewith presented, marked " Exhibit   ."

SALE OF PERSONAL PROPERTY. That said administrat   on the   day of   , 18 , sold the personal property of said deceased at public vendue, and returned a sale's bill thereof amounting to $ to said court, which was

The forms.

approved on the   day of   , 18 , a   copy of the notices posted for such sale, the affidavit of posting, and the sale's bill, are hereto attached, marked "Exhibit   ."

ADJUDICATION OF CLAIMS. That the administrat   fixed upon the   term, 18 , of said court for the adjustment of all claims against the estate of said deceased, and posted and published the notice for such adjudication as required by the statute, a   copy of such notice, together with the proof of posting and certificate of publication, are herewith presented, marked "Exhibit   ." That on the   day of   , 18 , the said court entered the usual order of adjudication in said estate, and that the following is a true statement of all claims allowed against said estate up to the   day of   , 18 , with the amount and date of allowance:

Class	allowed on the	day of	, 18	, for $
Class	allowed on the	day of	, 18	, for $
Class	allowed on the	day of	, 18	, for $
Class	allowed on the	day of	, 18	, for $

ACCOUNTS. *First Annual.* — That on the   day of   , 18 , said administrat   presented h   first annual account, showing receipts amounting to $, and disbursements amounting to $, for approval, which on said day last named was approved by said court, a   copy of which is herewith presented, marked "Exhibit   ."

Second Annual. — That on the   day of   , 18 , said administrat   presented h   second annual account, showing receipts amounting to $, and disbursements amounting to   , for approval, which, on the day last named, was approved by said court, a.   copy of which is herewith presented, marked "Exhibit   ."

Final. — That on the   day of   , 18 , the said administrat   presented to said court h   final account, showing receipts amounting to $ and disbursements amounting to $, which, on said day last named, was approved by said court, a   copy of which is herewith presented, marked "Exhibit   ."

PROOF OF HEIRSHIP AND DISCHARGE. That on said day last named proof of heirship was taken in open court and   were found to be the only heirs of said deceased, and the said administrat   then producing the receipts of all of said heirs for their distributive shares of the estate of said deceased, the court then found that all the assets of said estate had been collected ; that all claims against the same had been paid ; that more than two years had elapsed since the appointment of said administrat   , and ordered h   discharge and declared said estate settled, a   copy of which order, together with a copy of the testimony upon which it was founded, is herewith presented, marked "Exhibit   ."

The forms.

That your petitioner believes the above to set forth substantially all the orders of court made in the matter of the administration of the estate of said deceased, and the files upon which said orders were based; that petitioner is interested in said estate as   . That the records of said court, and the files relating to said estate were all destroyed by fire on the 9th of October, 1871, wherefore your petitioner prays that your honor will find the copies herewith presented, as Exhibits, to be true copies of the originals so destroyed as aforesaid, and order them to be entered and recorded as such, and restore all orders that have been made in the administration of said estate, and that all further orders necessary may be entered.

                    , *Attorney for Petitioner.*

STATE OF ILLINOIS, } ss:
    County. }

            being duly sworn, doth depose and say that h   has read the above petition by h   subscribed, and know   the contents thereof, and that the same is true of h   own knowledge, except as to matters stated upon information and belief, and as to these matters h   believes it to be true.

Subscribed and sworn before me }
this   day of   , 18 .   }
            , *Clerk.*

INDORSEMENT.

County Court of   County. Estate of   , deceased. Petition of   , for the restoration of the files and records of an intestate estate.

Filed this   day of   , 18 .
                                , *Clerk.*

APPENDIX.

The act of April 1, 1872, entitled "An act in regard to the administration of estates," is to be thoroughly understood by all who would successfully and satisfactorily administer upon the estates of decedents in Illinois. Although the several sections of this act are embodied (exactly as we find them on the statute book) in the foregoing pages, to the proper exposition of the law, we here add a logical summary, and in the index give an alphabetical synopsis of the act. The other acts referred to at page 7 *supra* are sufficiently delineated throughout the preceding pages and in the index. Consult STATUTES in the index, *infra*.

LOGICAL SUMMARY OF THE ACT IN REGARD TO THE ADMINISTRATION OF ESTATES.

TESTAMENTARY LETTERS may issue on probate of will, accepting the trust, and giving bonds. § 1, act April 1, Laws 1872, 77. See pp. 49, 53, 54, *supra*.

ADMINISTRATOR DE BONIS NON, if no executor be named in the will, if the executor die, refuse to act, or become incapacitated or disqualified, may be appointed as if for an intestate estate. Id.

EXECUTOR, IF NOT NAMED IN THE WILL, if he dies, refuses to act, or is otherwise disqualified to act, administration *cum testamento annexo* to take place as if testate had died intestate. Id.

LETTERS TESTAMENTARY may issue on probate of will, accepting the trust, and giving bonds. Id.

WILL, COPY OF, in all cases must go out with the letters. Id.

APPEARANCE OF WIDOW OR NEXT OF KIN, or creditor of decedent. It becomes the duty of the court to revoke the letters given to the public administrator and grant the same to those entitled. § 48, act April 1, Laws 1872, p. 89. See p. 71, *supra*.

Two or more appointed executors, if one or more die, refuse to act, or become disqualified, the survivor or survivors may take the trust. § 5, Laws 1872, p 78. See p. 282, *supra*.

Form of oath of executor or administrator *cum testamento annexo*. § 6, id See pp. 28, 29, 80, *supra*.

Oath to be attached to and form a part of the record. Id.

Oath of executor or administrator *cum testamento annexo*. Id.

EXECUTOR'S BOND. Form of, must be filed and recorded. § 7, id. See pp. 28, 30, *supra*.

Bond, in case of estate more than enough to pay debts, may direct that no security be required, but the court may, in its discretion, even then require security. § 8, id. See p. 56, *supra.*

REMOVAL OF EXECUTOR OR ADMINISTRATOR not to affect the jurisdiction or power of the court first taking probate of the will. § 9, id.

DIVISION OF A COUNTY, on, if letters have been granted to proceed notwithstanding, or in removal of executor or administrator to another county. Id.

LETTERS TESTAMENTARY, FORM OF. § 10, id. See p. 49, *supra.*

ADMINISTRATOR TO COLLECT. In case of any contingency causing great delay in proof of will or granting letters, may be appointed. § 11, id. See pp. 67, 72, *supra.* Letters to, § 12, id. See p. 72, *supra.* Bond of, § 13, id. See p. 77, *supra.* Oath of, § 14, id. See p. 73, *supra.* Power of, §§ 15, 16, id. See p. 278, *supra.* Revocation of, § 17, id. See p. 279, *supra.*

DEATH. Proof of death must be made before administration can be granted. § 18, id. See pp. 64, 67, 77, *supra.*

INTESTACY. Proof of, must be made before granting administration. §§ 18, 20, id.

LETTERS OF ADMINISTRATION to widow or widower, next of kin, creditors or discretionary. Widow or next of kin must apply within sixty days after death of decedent, creditors within the next fifteen days, then the court may exercise its discretion. Id.

PROOFS of death and intestacy must be made to obtain administration. §§ 18, 20, id.

RELINQUISHMENT. Administration not to be granted within seventy-five days after death of decedent, unless relinquishment be made by all those entitled; after seventy-five days, the court may act at its discretion. § 19, id. See pp. 64, 75, *supra.*

APPLICANT FOR LETTERS must file an affidavit, showing date of death and probable amount of personal estate, and the names of heirs and widow or widower, if known. § 20, id.

LETTERS OF ADMINISTRATION. Form of, to be changed and applied *mutatis mutandis* to all cases of administration. § 21, id. See p. 79, *supra.*

OATH OF ADMINISTRATOR. Form of, to be made and filed. § 22, id. See p. 79, *supra.*

BOND OF ADMINISTRATOR. Form of, to be changed and applied to all cases of administration *mutatis mutandis.* § 23, id. See pp. 79, 80, *supra.*

TWO OR MORE EXECUTORS may give joint or several bonds, as the court may direct. § 24, id. See p. 279, *supra.*

SUITS ON BONDS may be had in the name of the people of the State of Illinois, for the use and at the cost of whom it may concern. § 25, id. See p. 279 *supra.*

REVOKING LETTERS. If letters be obtained upon false or fraudulent representations or pretense, the court must revoke them. § 26, id.* See p. 280, *supra.*

COSTS TO BE PAID by party obtaining letters fraudulently, and on their revocation. § 27, id. See p. 280, *supra.*

WILL, DISCOVERY AND PROBATE OF, to revoke letters of administration. § 28, id. See p. 280, *supra*.

CANCELLATION OF A WILL in due course of law to revoke the letters testamentary thereon. § 29, id. See p. 280, *supra*.

ADMINISTRATOR *de bonis non* may be appointed. § 37, id. See p. 282, *supra*.

ADDITIONAL BONDS, executors or administrators, etc., may be required to give, or others appointed and empowered. § 38, id. See p. 282, *supra*.

FORMER ADMINISTRATOR shall be liable for *devastavit*, etc. § 39, id. See p. 283, *supra*.

RESIGNATION may be made by either executor or administrator, in the discretion of the court, on full settlement of accounts and surrendering estate. § 40, id. See p. 96, *supra*.

FOREIGN EXECUTOR OR ADMINISTRATOR may file duly authenticated copy of his letters in any court in this State and enforce claims and sell land to pay debts (§ 42, id.), if there be no executor or administrator in this State. § 43, id. See pp. 82, 96, *supra*.

FOREIGN ADMINISTRATOR'S OR EXECUTOR'S SUIT to inure to benefit of domestic executor or administrator if one be appointed *pendente lite*. § 43, id. See p. 82, *supra*.

PUBLIC ADMINISTRATORS are to be appointed by the governor by and with the advice and consent of the senate, one for each county whenever vacancy may occur, who must take the oath prescribed. § 44, id. See pp. 70, 71, *supra*.

INTESTATES LEAVING NO RELATIVES OR CREDITORS, possessed of real estate, the same is to be, on the application of any person interested therein, committed to the public administrator. § 46, id. See p. 71, *supra*.

COMMISSIONS AND EXPENSES EARNED AND INCURRED BY A PUBLIC ADMINISTRATOR are not affected by a re-grant of administration to those entitled. § 47, id. See p. 71, *supra*.

BOND OF PUBLIC ADMINISTRATOR to be required as in the other cases, failure to give, for sixty days, a *vacatur* of his office, and upon certificate of the fact from the county judge, the governor is to fill the vacancy. § 47, id. See p. 71, *supra*.

CARE, CUSTODY AND MANAGEMENT of the estate of intestates committed to the public administrator. § 49, id. See p. 71, *supra*.

DUTY OF PUBLIC ADMINISTRATOR to protect estates generally until administration. § 50, id. See p. 71, *supra*.

INVENTORY TO BE RETURNED within three months after letters are granted, containing: 1. Description of quantity, situation and title of the real estate. 2. Specifying the nature and amount of all annuities, rents, goods, chattels, rights, and credits, and money on hand, and whether the credits are good, doubtful or desperate. § 51, id. See p. 167, *supra*.

ADDITIONAL INVENTORY is to be returned whenever any other real or personal property becomes known to the administrator. § 52, id. See p. 167, *supra*.

APPRAISERS, to be three disinterested persons, their warrant to issue with the letters, their powers and duties, form of warrant, vacancy in number may be filled. § 53, id. See p. 171, *supra*.

APPRAISERS TO TAKE AND SUBSCRIBE AN OATH to be indorsed upon or annexed to the warrant; form of oath. § 54, id. See p. 172, *supra*.

METHOD OF MAKING APPRAISEMENT. To set down each article with the value thereof in dollars and cents, in columns, as prescribed. Id.

BILL OF APPRAISEMENT to be certified by the appraisers, under their hands and seals, to the executor or administrator, and by him to be returned within three months after grant of letters. § 55, id. See p. 172, *supra*.

INVENTORIES AND APPRAISEMENT bills, and authenticated copies thereof, *prima facie* evidence only of their contents respectively. § 56, id. See p. 173, *supra*.

ADDITIONAL APPRAISEMENT to be made if other property be discovered, and within three months after discovery. § 57, id. See pp. 173, 174, *supra*.

EXECUTORS AND ADMINISTRATORS chargeable for all estate which may or might after due and proper diligence be recovered. § 58, id. See p. 174, *supra*. Johnson v. Maples, 49 Ill. 101 ; Neubrecht v. Santmeyer, 50 id. 74.

APPRAISERS' FEES FIXED at two dollars per day for necessary attendance, to be allowed by the court. § 59, id. See p. 174, *supra*.

ASSETS. If, after appraisement, the assets do not exceed the widow's allowance, the executor or administrator is to report, and the court, if it finds the facts true, is to order the same transferred to her and close the administration. Id.

DISCOVERY OF NEW ASSETS. In such cases administration may be granted *de novo*. Id.

ATTACHMENT, CITATION. And on failure of executor or administrator to report deficiency of assets, etc., for widows' allowance. Id.

CLAIMS against estates. §§ 60–73, id. See pp. 215, 217, 222–225, *supra*.

Widows' award. §§ 74–77. See pp. 209–212, *supra*. Renunciation. §§ 78, 80, id. See pp. 219, 220, *supra*. Collection and disposition of assets. §§ 81–96, id. See pp. 174–183, *supra*. Sale of real estate. §§ 97–111, id. See pp. 186–201, *supra*. Settlement by administrators and executors. §§ 112–119. See pp. 190, 233, 239, 240, *supra*. Mortgage of real estate. §§ 120, 122, id. See pp. 191, 192, *supra*. Actions. § 123, id. See pp. 83, 192, *supra*. Appeals. §§ 124, 125, id. See pp. 272, 273, *supra*.

DISQUALIFICATION OF COUNTY JUDGE, as a material or necessary witness, or a party interested, transfers the case to the circuit court of the county ; case to be certified to circuit court. § 69, id. See pp. 224, 225, *supra*.

NONFEASANCE, MISFEASANCE OR MALFEASANCE of executor or administrator not to create liability in certain cases, beyond assets of testate or intestate. § 126, id. See p. 275, *supra*.

CONTRACTS OF DECEDENT may be performed by the executor or administrator under the directions of the county court. § 127, id. See p. 275, *supra*.

INSOLVENT ESTATES, after the expiration of two years from grant of administration to be so reported and entered of record; persons entitled to be paid *pro rata* ; costs then to be paid by parties serving. § 129, id. See p. 275, *supra*.

JUDGMENTS, DECREES AND ORDERS may be enforced. County courts shall have power to enforce due observance of all orders, decisions, judgments and decrees made by them in matters of administration, by process for contempt, and may fine and imprison offenders as fully as the circuit court may do in similar cases. § 131, id. See p. 276, *supra*.

SERVICE, SHERIFF; SUBPŒNAS, citations, notices and other process to be served and returned by the sheriff or his deputies. § 132, id. See p. 276, *supra*.

FEES OF SHERIFF to be the same as for similar services in the circuit court. § 132, id. See p. 276, *supra*.

FEES OF EXECUTORS AND ADMINISTRATORS to be not exceeding *six per centum* on proceeds of real estate, and *three per centum* on proceeds of personal estate with reasonable allowances for collection and enforcing claims. § 133, id. See p. 276, *supra*.

CONSTRUCTION OF THE STATUTE. Executor to mean administrator and administrator to mean executor, *his* to mean *her*, *one* to mean *two* or *more*, etc., whenever the same requires it in applying the law liberally. § 134, id. See p. 276, *supra*.

REPEALED ACTS, ENUMERATED. § 135, id. See pp. 7, 277, *supra*.

SAVING CLAUSE of repealing act, suits pending and rights accrued, not affected by the repeal. Id.

An alphabetical synopsis of the act* in regard to the administration of estates, will be found under STATUTES in the index.

LOGICAL SUMMARY of the "Act in regard to wills," or the "Act of March 20, 1872." See p. 7, *supra*, Laws 1872, pp. 775–781.

Persons competent to dispose of property by will enumerated. § 1. See pp. 11, 44, *supra*.

Requisites of a will. § 2. See pp. 11, 44, 46, 47, *supra*.

Subscribing witnesses, their duty to appear and testify. § 3. See pp. 38, 39, *supra*.

Testimony of non-resident witnesses; dedimus. § 4. See pp. 36, 37, *supra*.

County judge a witness, procedure in the circuit court. § 5. See pp. 45, 46, *supra*.

Death or absence of a witness. § 6. See pp. 30, 39, *supra*.

Probate of wills; remedies. § 7. See pp. 16, 43, *supra*.

Interested witnesses, how far excluded. § 8. See pp. 38, 42, *supra*.

Executing wills without the State. § 9. See p. 52, *supra*.

They are admissible to probate. § 10. See p. 52, *supra*.

Venue or proper county to probate the will. § 11. See p. 14, *supra*.

Custodian of the will to produce it; penalty. § 12. See pp. 14, 16, *supra*.

Appeals, procedure. §§ 13, 14. See p. 274, *supra*.

Nuncupative wills, procedure. §§ 15, 16. See pp. 11, 50, 51, *supra*.

Probate of nuncupative will. § 16. See pp. 50, 51, *supra*.

Revocation of a will. § 17. See p. 11, *supra*.

Record and preservation of wills. § 18. See p. 17, *supra*.

---

* Act of April 1, 1872, Laws 1872.

Debtor as executor. § 19. See p. 54, *supra*.

Attesting creditor competent. § 20. See p. 46, *supra*.

REPEALING SECTION. The following acts and parts of acts are hereby repealed:

"Sections one, two, three, four, five, six, seven, eight, nine, ten, eleven, twelve, fifteen, sixteen, seventeen and eighteen, of chapter one hundred and nine, of the Revised Statutes of 1845, entitled 'Wills.'"

"An act entitled 'An act respecting the Probate of Wills,' approved February 25, 1845."

"An act entitled 'An act to amend the one hundred and ninth chapter of the Revised Statutes, entitled 'Wills,'' approved February 14, 1855," and all other acts inconsistent with the provisions of this act. *Provided*, that nothing contained in this section shall be so construed as to affect any suits that may be pending, or any wills that may be existing, or any rights that may have accrued when this act shall take effect. § 21. See p. 7, *supra*. See STATUTES in the index, *infra*.

The other acts mentioned at p. 7, *supra*, are given in full in the foregoing pages. Id.

PERSONAL REPRESENTATIVES. The terms "personal representatives" and "legal representatives" have given rise to considerable discussion, especially in the construction of wills and statutes.

A careful examination of the decisions will, we think, show that these terms are, if not quite, almost synonymous. 6 Madd. Ch. 159; 5 Ves. Ch. 402; 1 Madd. Ch. 108; 2 Jarm. on Wills, 28; 1 Beav. Rolls, 46; 1 Russ. & M. Ch. 587; 3 Vesey's Ch. 486; 3 Brown's Ch. 224; 1 Yeates, 213; 2 id. 585; 2 Dall. 205; 6 Serg. & R. 83; 3 Bradf. 45; 1 Anst. Exch. 128; 6 Eng. L. & E. 99.

The English cases are collated and commented upon, 2 Williams on Executors, 1049-1061.

In *Cotton* v. *Cotton*, 2 Beav. 67, the term "legal representatives" was held to mean *next of kin*.

Chapter 93 of the 9th and 10th Victoria gives an action to "the executor or administrator of the person deceased" in case of death caused by the wrongful act, neglect or default of another. 1 Gross, 60; Laws 1853, 97; *Chicago* v. *Major*, 18 Ill. 349; *Railroad Co.* v. *Morris*, 26 id. 400.

The learned judge who gave the opinion in 18 Ill. 349, at p. 358, says of the term "personal representatives," as used in § 2 of the act of 1853, "that is," the suit must be brought "by the executors or administrators."

No point was made upon the construction of the term. It was there held that the father of a minor might take out letters of administration upon the deceased minor's estate, and, as administrator, proceed under the statute. *Railroad Co.* v. *Morris*, 26 Ill. 400; *Railroad Co.* v. *Shannon*, 43 id. 338. But was administration necessary for the purpose?

In *Lynch* v. *Rotan*, 39 Ill. 15, pp. 75, 270, *supra*, it was held that the personal property of a minor vests immediately in the next of kin, and there is no necessity of taking out letters of administration before instituting suit in equity against the sureties of a guardian for a discovery and an account on the ground of maladministration. If not in equity, why at law?

Is it, then, necessary for the next of kin to take out letters of administration on a minor's estate in order to sue as in Major's case? Does not the term *personal representatives*, in the second section of the act of 1853 (1 Gross, 60), also include in such cases the *next of kin?*

In *Chicago* v. *Major*, it was held that the object of section 2 of this statute is to exclude creditors from the benefit of the damages recovered under it, and to prevent the same from becoming a part of the estate of the deceased, and that the act is not limited to the case of those leaving widows.

In *Railroad Co.* v. *Morris*, it was established that there must be those for whose benefit the action is brought, and that the existence of such persons must be averred and proved. 1 Hill's C. L. 78.

It is difficult to see why the term "personal representatives" does not include the *next of kin* in cases where there is no necessity for administration for other purposes, as in the case of a minor.

The cases brought under this statute rest exclusively upon its provisions. 26 Ill. 400.

The rule of damages in these actions is very close. 2 Hill's C. L. 498.

The amount recovered under this statute is not assets in the proper acceptation of that term. See note *u*, p. 92, *supra*.

The law requires no idle ceremonies; then, was not the term *personal representatives* inserted in this statute to cover just such cases including *next of kin?* Why the difference in this respect between our statute and chapter 93, 9th and 10th Victoria? 1 Gross, 60.

We add the following cases, which are not inserted in the body of the work:

THE STATE AS A CREDITOR OF ESTATES OF DECEDENTS. The State is not bound to wait until the estate of a deceased is administered, and then participate with other creditors in the proceeds, but may enforce payment, to the exclusion of all other creditors. So of an insolvent estate in the hands of trustees. *Dunlap* v. *Gallatin Co.*, 15 Ill. 7.

VENDOR AND VENDEE. A purchaser of land gave his promissory note for an unpaid balance of the purchase-money, the vendor covenanting "that, upon the payment of said sum being made at the time and in the manner aforesaid," he would convey. The vendor died without having made a conveyance. In an action by his administrator upon the note, it was *held* that, as the title to the land was the only consideration for the note, until that title was made, which the administrator could not make without the aid of chancery, no right of action accrued on the note. *Hulshizer* v. *Lamoreux, Adm'x*, 58 Ill. 72.

ADVANCEMENTS. Where the heir of an intestate has received property from such intestate, in his life-time, and by an instrument in writing, whether under seal or not, acknowledged the receipt thereof as his full share of the estate, the property so received, not having been charged to him, and the transaction being untainted with fraud, must be held to be in full payment and satisfaction of his share of the estate, by express agreement.

The provisions of sections 63 and 164 of the statute of wills, bearing upon the subject of advancements, have no application to a case of this character. *Bishop* v. *Davenport*, 58 Ill. 105.

But in such case, if, at the time of the execution of the release, the person giving it was a *femme couverte*, such agreement is void, or, if a minor, it is not

44

binding upon him. Nor will it avail anything that such release was executed by a married woman, jointly with her husband. The husband has no authority to make an agreement of that character, which will bind his wife. *Bishop v. Davenport*, 58 Ill. 105.

ATTESTATION OF WILLS. The statute does not require that the attesting witnesses to a will should be in the presence of each other when they sign it. *Flinn v. Owen*, 58 Ill. 111.

CONSTRUCTION OF A PARTICULAR INSTRUMENT. B and H were partners in business. H was taken sick, and made his will, by the terms of which it was provided, that if B would deliver over to W, the executor named in the will, certain notes which were held by the firm, for the benefit of H's daughter, and would pay H's debts after his decease, B should have all the remainder of H's estate, including the firm property. Before signing the will, H caused it to be read to B, who thereupon verbally accepted the terms proposed, and it was then executed. After H's decease, B demanded an appraisement of the property, to see if he would accept of it under the terms proposed, which was had, and he again accepted, and delivered over the notes to W, and retained the remainder of the property belonging to the estate. B failed to pay the debts, and they were proved up against the estate of H, and paid by W, the executor. Afterward B and W died, and the administrator of W's estate filed this claim against the estate of B, to which was pleaded the statute of limitations and the statute of frauds. *Held*, that the statute of limitations constituted no bar to the act; that a direct trust was created by the express terms of the will, and that B received the property under the conditions imposed, and entered upon the discharge of his duties, and that the relation of trustee and *cestui que trust* was thereby created between the parties, and not that of debtor and creditor. *Albretch v. Wolf*, 58 Ill. 186.

RULES OF PRACTICE

OF THE

PROBATE COURT OF COOK COUNTY.

Ordered, That the following rules of practice be, and they are, hereby adopted in this court:

ADMINISTRATION.

PROOF OF WILL.

RULE 1. The testimony taken in the matter of the proof of any last will and testament shall be reduced to writing, and filed with the clerk of the court.

ORDER OF INVENTORY — WIDOW'S SELECTION AND SALES BILL.

RULE 2. The inventory widow's selection and sales bill shall follow the order in which the articles are set down in the bill of appraisement.

ADJUSTMENT OF CLAIMS.

RULE 3. The proof of posting and publishing notices for the adjustment of claims shall be filed with the clerk, on or before the first day of the term to which claimants are notified and requested to appear. The clerk shall keep a list of all such proofs of posting and publishing adjustment notices each term, in the order filed, and the court will take up and dispose of the same in the order of such list.

MANNER OF PRESENTING CLAIMS.

RULE 4. Claims against estates shall be presented as follows: If at or before the regular adjustment, by filing a bill of items of the claim with the clerk. If after the adjustment term, by filing a copy of the claim, together with a præcipe for a summons to the executor or administrator, or by filing with such claim the appearance, in writing, of the executor or administrator.

The heir, or any other person interested in the estate, wishing to contest any claim filed, must enter an appearance, in writing, in the matter of such claim.

CLAIM DOCKET AND TRIAL OF CLAIMS.

RULE 5. The clerk shall prepare a claim docket each term, and the court will commence the call of such docket for the trial of claims, on the fourth Monday of each term, and continue such call, from day to day, until concluded.

DEFAULT OR NEGLECT OF EXECUTOR OR ADMINISTRATOR.

RULE 6. Upon the failure of any executor or administrator to present his inventory and appraisement to the court within three months, or cause an order of adjustment of claims to be entered within six months, or to present his account within thirteen months from the date of his letters, and every year thereafter, until the estate of his decedent is fully administered and settled, the court will order a citation to issue, and if the executor or administrator fail to appear as required by the citation, the court will order an attachment against the executor or administrator, and enforce the performance of such neglected duty.

NOTICE TO HEIRS OF FINAL ACCOUNT.

RULE 7. No executor or administrator shall be discharged from the duties and responsibilities of his appointment, or have his final account approved (where the heirs at law, residuary and unpaid legatees, if any, do not enter their appearance in writing in such final accounting), unless he shall give notice to the heirs at law, residuary and unpaid legatees, if any, of the decedent, of the time of his intended application to the court for the approval of such final account, as follows :

When the heirs at law, residuary or unpaid legatees, if any, are residents of Cook county, personal service of a copy of such notice shall be made, and in the event of the temporary absence from Cook county of such resident heirs at law, residuary or unpaid legatees, if any, a copy of such notice shall be left at the usual place of abode of such heirs, residuary or unpaid legatees, if any, with some person of the family of the age of ten years or upwards, and informing such person of the contents thereof, such service to be at least ten days before such application.

When such heirs at law, residuary or unpaid legatees, if any, reside without the limits of Cook county, and in any of the United States or Territories, a copy of such notice shall be published at least once in some newspaper published in the city of Chicago, at least thirty days before such application. When such heirs at law, residuary or unpaid legatees, if any, reside without the limits of the United States and Territories, or whose names and places of residence, either or both, are unknown to such executor or administrator, such notice shall be published at least once in some newspaper published in the city of Chicago, at least sixty days before such application; and where the heirs at law, residuary or unpaid legatees, if any, or any of them, are not residents of Cook county, such executor or administrator shall make and file with the clerk of the court his, her or their affidavit, or the affidavit of some one of them, setting forth the names and post-office address of such heirs at law, residury or unpaid legatees, if any, or if the same be unknown, thus stating the fact; and where the names and post-office address are set forth in such affidavit, such executor or administrator shall cause a copy of such notice to be mailed, postage paid, to such heirs at law, residuary or unpaid legatees, to such address by the clerk of this court within five days after such publication, and a certificate of such mailing to be made by the clerk and filed in the proper estate.

NOTICE OF RESIGNATION OF EXECUTOR OR ADMINISTRATOR.

RULE 8. Upon the petition of any executor or administrator to resign his trust, notice thereof, and of the time of hearing, shall be given to the legatees, devisees or distributees, and to his co-executor or co-administrator, and the sureties on his bond, if any, in the same manner as notice is required to be given to the heirs at law, residuary and unpaid legatees, in case of final account, as provided by rule seven, unless such legatees, devisees or distributees, and co-executor or co-administrator, and the sureties on his bond enter their appearance in writing in such matter.

PROOF OF HEIRSHIP.

RULE 9. Proof of heirship for the purpose of distribution and final settlement of an estate shall be made by the testimony of witnesses examined in open court, reduced to writing and filed, or by testimony taken in pursuance of a *dedimus potestatem*, issued for that purpose, or by a certified copy of a decree of a court of record, finding the heirs at law of the decedent.

EXECUTOR AND ADMINISTRATOR'S REPORT.

Rule 10. Every executor and administrator's account shall be accompanied with a written report, under oath, briefly stating the condition of the estate, the amount of receipts and expenditures and the balance, if any, and the present responsibility and sufficiency of the sureties on the bond of such executor or administrator.

GUARDIANSHIP.

APPOINTMENT OF GUARDIAN.

Rule 11. No application for the appointment of a guardian (other than applications by the father, or by the mother, if he be dead) will be entertained when the infant has a father or mother living in this State, unless upon written notice of such intended application to the father, or if the father be dead, to the mother, and to both if they be living apart in this State, setting forth the time when the same will be heard, which notice shall be given not less than three days prior to such application, if the parent or parents reside in Cook county, and not less than ten days if non-residents of Cook county, provided that no such notice shall be required when such parent or parents enter their appearance and consent to an immediate hearing.

GUARDIAN'S INVENTORIES AND ACCOUNTS.

Rule 12. Upon the failure of any guardian to return to the court, verified by the affidavit of the guardian, a true and perfect inventory of the real and personal estate of the ward, including therein a description of the real estate, its probable value and rental, and whether incumbered, and, if so incumbered, how and for how much; what amount of money is on hand, all personal property, including annuities and credits of the ward, designating them as good, doubtful or desperate, as the case may be, within sixty days after appointment, or at the expiration of one year from his or her appointment, and at least once every three years thereafter, and as much oftener as the court may require, settle his or her accounts with the court, such guardian will be cited by the court, and the performance of such delinquent duty enforced.

LEASING WARD'S REAL ESTATE.

RULE 13. The court will, upon petition of the guardian, order that the guardian lease all the ward's real estate; but before delivering any lease or possession to the lessee, that the guardian obtain the written approval of the judge of this court indorsed on the lease; but no such approval will be given until testimony has been taken in open court, showing the rental value of the real estate.

FINAL SETTLEMENT OF GUARDIAN WITH WARD.

RULE 14. No guardian shall be discharged from the duties of his appointment on final settlement with his ward, unless such ward appears before the court and acknowledges such settlement in full in open court; provided, where such facts are disclosed, by affidavit filed with the clerk, as render the personal attendance of the ward impracticable, and the court shall be satisfied, from evidence produced in open court, that such final settlement is just and equitable, and that the ward is in possession of all his or her estate, such personal attendance of the ward may be waived by the court.

GUARDIAN'S REPORT.

RULE 15. Every guardian's account shall be accompanied with a written report of the guardian, verified with his affidavit, setting forth the manner in which any funds under his control belonging to his ward are invested, the debts, credits, and effects of the ward's estate, so far as the same have come to his knowledge, and the present responsibility and sufficiency of the sureties on his bond, and if the guardianship be of the custody and tuition of the minor, shall state the length of time the ward has attended school, and where, since his appointment, or last report.

CONSERVATORS.

DEFAULT OR NEGLECT OF CONSERVATORS.

RULE 16. Upon the failure of any conservator to return to the court, verified by the affidavit of such conservator, a true and perfect inventory of the real and personal estate of his ward, with a description of the real estate, its probable value and rental, and stating whether the same is incumbered, and if incumbered, how and for how much, what amount of money is on hand, and also containing a list of all personal property, including annuities and credits of the ward, designating them as good, doubtful or desperate, as the case may be, within sixty days after his appointment, or at the expiration of one year from his appointment, and at least once each year thereafter, and as much oftener as the court may require, to settle his accounts as conservator with the court, will be cited by the court, and the performance of such delinquent duty enforced.

LEASING BY CONSERVATOR.

RULE 17. The court will, upon the petition of the conservator, order that the conservator lease all his ward's real estate, but before delivering any lease or possession to the lessee, that the conservator obtain the written approval of the judge of this court, indorsed on the lease, but no such appoval will be given until testimony has been taken in open court, showing the rental value of the real estate.

MISCELLANEOUS.

PETITIONS AND MOTIONS.

RULE 18. Petitions and motions will be heard upon the coming in of the court in the morning and afternoon, and all motions and other applications to the court shall be made in writing and filed with the clerk, and when not based on matters which appear of record, the facts must be supported by affidavit.

APPEARANCE.

RULE 19. Whenever any heir at law, legatee, creditor, or other person not a party to the record, desires to contest or be heard in any matter before the court, such heir at law, legatee, creditor, or other person, shall first enter an appearance in writing in such matter, and file the same with the clerk.

RULE TO PLEAD.

RULE 20. In all cases (except citations and adjustment of claims) commenced by summons, the defendant, if served ten days before the return day of such summons, shall plead on or before the opening of court, on the third day of the term to which such summons is made returnable.

RULE 21. The clerk shall have the foregoing rules, and all rules of this court, hereafter entered, carefully transcribed in a book to be kept for that purpose, in the order of date in which they shall be respectively entered.

INDEX.

A.

ABATEMENT AND REVIVAL,
    administrator how made a party, 87, 289, 290.

ACCEPTANCE,
    of trust by the executor, 49.
    of resignation, equivalent to revocation of letters, 100.

ACCOUNT,
    the books of, by the decedent, 275.

ACCOUNTS, 230.
    I. By the executor or administrator, 238, 242.
    II. By the guardian and conservator, 243, 250.

        I. — BY THE EXECUTOR OR ADMINISTRATOR, 238, 242
        1. General instructions to the executor or administrator, 238.
        2. Settlements to be made annually at least, 238, 239.
        3. Apportionments to be made, 239.
        4. Settlement may be enforced, 239, 240.
        5. *Devastavit*, etc., 240.
        6. Administrator's account, 240, 241.
        7. Procedure for administrator or executor when cited to account, 241, 242.
        8. Form of account, 242.

        II. — BY GUARDIAN AND CONSERVATOR, 243–250.
        1. Guardian must account, 243.
        2. He must pay over to those entitled at the expiration of his trust, 243.
        3. Accounts must be filed, 243.
        4. Instructions in general to guardians and conservators, 243, 244.
        5. Accounts, how kept, 244, 245.
        6. Form of report to the court in accounting, 245.
        7. Another form, 245.

ACQUIESCENCE,
    infants not affected by, 103.
    See *Laches*.

ACQUISITION OF LANDS,
    subsequently to the making of a will, effect of, 42.

ACT,
    April 1, 1872, and other acts, 7.
    See *Appendix; Statutes*.

ACTION,
  right of, in cases of death caused by negligence, etc., 344.
  See *Appendix*.

ACTIONS,
  by executors and administrators, 275, 281, 283, 289.
  by conservators, 141.
  on administrators' bonds, 81, 289.
  by and against minors, 104–107.
  which survive (§ 123, act of April 1, 1872), 192, 281, 282, 289, 290.
  See *Claims*.

AD LITEM, GUARDIAN,
  appointment, powers and duties of, 116, 117, 133, 134.

ADMINISTRATION,
  not always necessary, 75, 76, 344.
  the regular grant of, 68, 69.
  grant of, to be preceded by proof of death and intestacy, 67, 68.

ADMINISTRATOR,
  the term defined, 65.
  the personal representative of the deceased, 83, 162.
    See *Appendix*.
  how to be appointed, 76, 77.
  de facto, the acts of, cannot be collaterally questioned, 76.
  de bonis non, 84, 282, 283.
  to collect, 71.
  appointment and powers of, 71, 278.
  the public, 70–72.
  with the will annexed, 17.

ADMINISTRATOR'S BONDS,
  actions on, 81.
  See *Forms*.

ADMINISTRATORS,
  purchasing at their own sale. guilty of fraud, *per se*, 96, 296, 303, 304.
  appointment of, 64–82.
    1. Administrators virtually executors, 65, 66.
    2. Of several kinds, general and special, 66.
    3. An intestate, 66.
    4. Special administrators, 67.
    5. Administrator *de bonis non*, 67.
    6. Administrator *pendente lite*, 67.
    7. Letters of administration are a grant of power, 67.
    8. Intestacy and death of decedent must be proved, 67, 68.
    9. How proved, 68.
    10. The English Statutes and, 68, 69.
    11. Our statute compared, 68, 69.

ADMINISTRATORS — *Continued*.
- 12. The *jus representationis*, 69.
- 13. Degrees of consanguinity according to the civil law, 70, 268.
- 14. The public administrator appointed by the governor, by and with the consent of the senate, 70.
- 15. When the estate may be committed to the public administrator, 70, 71.
- 16. His duties in general, 71.
- 17. His expenses preferred, 71.
- 18. Removal in special cases, on appearance of parties entitled, within six months after his appointment 71.
- 19. To advertise on settlement, etc., 71.
- 20. Administrator to collect, 71, 72.
- 21. Letters to collect, 72.
- 22. Bond of administrator to collect, 72, 73.
- 23. His oath, 73.
- 24. Who may be administrators generally, 73–76.
    - 1. They should be of lawful age and legally competent, 73.
    - 2. The preference conferred by statute, 74.
    - 3. Waiver of *juris representationis*, 74.
    - 4. Who to administer, on the death of the surviving husband, as administrator *de bonis non* of his deceased wife's estate, *quære?* 74, 75.
    - 5. Next to kin, the relatives generally, 75.
    - 6. Renunciation or relinquishment, 75, 76.
- 25. Venue, the proper county, 76.
- 26. Practice — how to be appointed administrator, 76, 77.
- 27. Petition for letters of administration, 77.
- 28. Affidavit of death, intestacy, etc., 77.
- 29. The administrator's bond, 77, 78, 79.
- 30. And letters of administration, 79.
- 31. The oath, 79.
- 32. Form of bond by administrator with the will annexed, 80.
- 33. Oath of, 80.
- 34. Additional bond, 80, 81.
- 35. Decisions in Illinois, 81.
- 36. Foreign executors and administrators, how, where and when they may act, limitations and restrictions, 82.

the powers, duties, rights and liabilities of, 83–96.
- 1. The scope of the office of administrator, 83.
- 2. Administrators are personal representatives of their intestates, 83.
- 3. Decisions of the supreme court of the State of Illinois, 84–96.

See *Resignation*.

ADVANCEMENTS, 103, 345.

See *Descent*.

ADVERTISEMENT, 51, 290.
  See *Constructive Service; Personal Estate; Notice.*
AFFIANT'S OATH, 292.
AFFIDAVIT,
  for a dedimus, 37.
  requisites of, 297.
    See *Probate Record; Forms.*
AFFIRMATION,
  form of, 293.
AGE,
  males, at 21, females at 18, are of lawful, **102.**
AGREEMENTS, 160, 161.
    See *Contracts.*
ALLEGATIONS,
  of fact, how to be made, 305.
ALPHABETICAL LIST OF FORMS, 301.
    See *Forms.*
APPEARANCE,
  by heirs to contest claims should be in the name of the administrator, 88.
APPEAL,
  may be taken from the order admitting a will to probate, 30.
APPEALS, 271, 273.
  1. Appeals when allowed in cases in the administration of estates, 224, 271.
  2. In guardianship, 271.
  3. Praying appeal, 271, 272.
  4. How prayed, 272.
  5. Bond on appeal, 272.
  6. Security for costs by non-residents, 272.
  7. The requisites of the bond, 272, 273.
  8. The bill of exceptions, 273.
  9. In cases of wills, 273.
APPENDIX, 339.
APPOINTMENT,
  of an attorney by an infant absolutely void, 102.
  letters testamentary as evidence of the, of the executor, **50.**
    See *Petition.*
APPRAISEMENT, THE, 172-174.
ARBITRATION,
  administrator cannot submit a claim to, 89.
ASSETS,
  what are, 92, 93, 94, 275.

ASSETS — *Continued.*
> See 53 *Ill.* 224.
> See *Personal Estate; Real Estate.*
> personal property, 157–185.
>> 1. Things personal, 158.
>> 2. Mercantile transactions, 158.
>> 3. Insufficiency of assets, 158.
>> 4. Distinctions between *things personal* and *things real*, 158, 159.
>> 5. Conversion of real property; special proceedings necessary for the purpose against the property and also against the heir, 158, 159.
>> 6. The practice in such cases governed by the superior courts, through the right of appeal, 159.
>> 7. The absolute title and qualified right of the administrator or executor to the assets of the decedent, 159.
>> 8. The assets considered, 159.
>> 9. Contract in general, 159, 160, 161.
>> 10. Contracts defined, 160, 161.
>> 11. Consideration essential to, 160.
>> 12. Sale or exchange, 161, 162.
>> 13. Fraud annuls all contracts which it infects, 162.
>> 14. Warranty, 162.
>> 15. *Caveat emptor,* 162.
>> 16. Guaranty, statute of frauds, 162, 163.
>> 17. Bailment, pawn, 163.
>> 18. Lien, 163.
>> 19. Hiring and borrowing, 164.
>> 20. Debts, 164.
>> 21. Bonds, 164.
>> 22. Bills of exchange, 164, 165.
>> 23. Cheques, 165, 166.
>> 24. Promissory notes, 166.
>> 25. Insurance policies, 166, 167.
>> 26. Bottomry, 167.
>> 27. The care and judgment required in the **management of the** assets, 167.
> insufficiency of, 158, 159–165.

ASTOR, GRIGNON v., 2 *How.* 193.
> discussed, 6, 62, 63.

ATTACHMENT, 32.

ATTENDANCE,
> of the sheriff, 274.
> to compel the production of a will, 16.
> for a witness, 32.
> for contempt, when the remedy to compel distribution, **87, 88.**

ATTESTED,
  a will must be, 40, 47, 346.

ATTESTING,
  creditor may be a competent witness, 46.

ATTORNEY,
  a minor cannot appoint an, 102.
  rendering services for an executor acquires claim against the estate, 88.

AWARD, WIDOWS', 217, 218.

B.

BAILEES,
  lien of, 163.

BAILMENT, 163.

BANK NOTE, 166.

BARGAIN,
  when complete, 162.

BILL, BURNT RECORDS', 334.

BILL OF EXCEPTIONS, 334.

BILL OF EXCHANGE, 164.

BILL OF SALE, 183.

BOND, 164.
  an infant connot bind himself by, 102.
  executor's, how approved, 30.
  to be filed and recorded, 30.
  of the executor, the form prescribed, 30.
  joint and several, 279.
    See *Forms*.

BOOKS OF ACCOUNT, 275.

BORROWING, HIRING AND, 164.

BOTTOMRY, 167.

BREACH,
  of administrator's bond, joint or several action will lie on, 81.

BUILDINGS,
  when personal estate, 189.

BURIALS,
  the law of, 190.

BURNT RECORDS' BILL, 334.

C.

CARE,
  and judgment of the prudent and discreet, essential in administration, 167.

CAPACITY, TESTAMENTARY,
  must be shown, 43, 44, 45, 47.

CAVEAT EMPTOR, 162.

CERTIFICATE
    of proof of a will, 46.
    of the execution of a dedimus, 35–38.
    to be indorsed on a deposition, 48.
    of oaths of attesting witnesses, effect as evidence, 43.
    of the clerk attached to letters testamentary, 49, 50.
    of foreign will, as evidence, 42.
    of publication, 51, 290.
        See *Forms*.

CHAMBER
    in a house may be separate real estate, 189.

CHANCERY,
    the probate of the will may be contested by bill in, 30.
    heirs should proceed by bill in, if dissatisfied with the settlement of estate by the administrator, 88.

CHANCERY JURISDICTION, 94, 95, 96.
    § 34 of the conveyance act, construed, 94.
    specific performance, etc., 94, 95.
        See *Hill's Chancery*, p. 283–286.

CHANGE OF VENUE, 224, 225.

CHATTELS, GOODS AND, 159.
    defined, 83, 160, 161.
        See *Personal Estate*.

CHATTELS REAL, 165, 191.

CHECK OR CHEQUE, 165, 166.

CIRCUIT COURT,
    creditors of an intestate may sue in the, in the first instance, 88.
    See *Appeals*.

CITIZEN,
    of another State may come in and cause administration to be granted, when and how, 82.
    See *Foreign Executor, etc.*

CITATION,
    and notice to heirs and legal representatives, 50, 51.
    See *Forms*.

CIVIL LAW,
    degrees of consanguinity by the, 70, 257, 278.
    See *Descent*.

CLAIMS,
    practice in presenting, 87.
    heirs may appear in name of administrator and contest, 88.

CLAIMS — *Continued.*
   defenses to, may be defenses to application to sell real estate, 88.
   desperate, 176, 177, 178, 179.
   against estates, 222–232.
      1. Notice of term fixed by executor or administrator for adjustment of; procedure prescribed; jury trial, etc., 222, 223.
      2. When a creditor may file his claim, summons to issue to the executor or administrator, 223.
      3. Return terms, cause to be continued if summons be not served ten days before, 223.
      4. Procedure prescribed, 223, 224.
      5. Claimant may be compelled to make oath that his "claim is just and unpaid," 224.
      6. Evidence, 224.
      7. Counter-claim, 224, 236.
      8. Claims not yet due may be proven, 224, 236.
      9. Appeal may be taken by either party to the circuit court, 224.
      10. Change of venue to circuit court if county judge be interested, or a witness in any case or matter pending in his court, 224, 225.
      11. Adjudication of claims, instructions to executors or administrators, 225.
      12. Administrator's notice, 225–228.
      13. Creditor's rights, how enforced, 228, 229.
      14. Time in which claims are to be presented, 229.
      15. The decision collated, 229–232.

CLERK'S ENTRIES,
   in probating a will, 48.
   See *Forms.*

CLOSING, OPENING AND,
   of terms and sessions of court, 291.

CO-EXECUTORS OR ADMINISTRATORS,
   several may be appointed, 282.

COMMON LAW,
   the, deeply rooted in our usages and institutions, 186.
   See *Descent*.

COMPETENCY,
   of attesting creditor, 46.
   See *Witnesses*, 287, 288.

COMPROMISE,
   of debts, administrator may make, 86.

CONSANGUINITY,
   degrees of, as affecting the *jus representationis*, 70.
   degrees of, 268.

CONSERVATORS, 139-147.
1. When a conservator may be appointed, 139.
2. Summons to be issued, 139.
3. Conservator to give bond, 140.
4. Bonds may be put in suit, 140.
5. Duties of conservator, generally, 140.
6. To take charge of the estate of his ward, and return inventories, 140.
7. Requisites of an inventory, 140.
8. Conservator to settle his account at least annually, 140.
9. On final settlement to deliver estate and title papers, 141.
10. The final accounting, 141.
11. Conservator to settle all accounts of his ward, and sue in his own name, 141.
12. May with consent of court perform the personal contracts of his ward, 141.
13. To appear and represent his ward in all suits and proceedings, 141.
14. Contracts of a lunatic after finding of a jury, void as to the lunatic, 141.
15. Contracts made before such finding, when may be avoided, 142.
16. Trading, bartering or gaming with a lunatic, etc., prohibited, 142.
17. Conservator to frugally manage the estate, 142.
18. Investments to be made, 142.
19. Conservator may lease his ward's estate, 142.
20. He may by leave of the county court mortgage the same, 142.
21. Petition for leave to be filed, 142.
22. Strict foreclosure prohibited and redemption prescribed, 142, 143.
23. Sale of real estate may on petition of the conservator be ordered by the county court, 143.
24. The petition, 143.
25. Notice of application, 143.
26. Procedure as in chancery, 143.
27. Notice of sale, 143.
28. Report of sale and deed, 143.
29. Account of proceeds, 144.
30. Sureties of the conservator to be looked after and kept sufficient, 144.
31. Conservator may be required to give counter security, 144.
32. Conservator may be removed, 144.
33. To be first summoned, 144.
34. He may in a proper case resign, 144.
35. Another conservator may be appointed, 144, 145.
36. Fees and compensation of the conservator to be reasonable and just, 145.
37. Conservator may be discharged and the property restored to the owner on his restoration to reason or reformation, 145.
38. Notice of application to be given to the conservator, 145.
39. Procedure on the application, 145.

CONSERVATORS — *Continued.*
    40. Appeals, 145, 146.
    41. Conservator, guardian, curator, or committee of any non-resident idiot, lunatic, insane or distracted person, spendthrift or drunkard, may collect debts and recover property of ward in this state, 146.
    42. Application for sale of such ward's estate to be made to the circuit court, 146.
    43. Notice of application, 147.
    44. Bond may be required, 147.
    45. Bond for costs may be given, 147.
    46. Repeal of former laws, 147.

CONSTRUCTION,
    of the statute of administration, 276.

CONSTRUCTIVE SERVICE, 126–132.

CONTEMPT,
    attachment for; when the remedy to compel distribution, 87, 88.

CONTEST OF ISSUE OF VALIDITY OF A WILL,
    may be in probate, on appeal and in chancery, 41.

CONTEST OF THE PROBATE,
    may be had in the county court, on appeal or in chancery, 30.

CONTRACT,
    parol with the intestate, how enforced, 89, 275.

CONTRACTS,
    defined and specified, 160–167.
    of infants considered, 102.
    of the decedent, 275.
        See *Specific Performance.*

CONVERSION OF REAL PROPERTY, 158, 159, 186–214.

CONVEYANCES,
    by infants, voidable only, 103.
        See *Forms.*

CONVICTED CRIMINAL,
    not to be executor, 54.

COPY,
    of will to accompany the letters testamentary, 49, 298.

CORPORATE PROPERTY, 189.

CORPSES AND THEIR BURIALS, 190.

COSTS,
    when recoverable by the creditor, 90.
    claimants, after expiration of two years, to pay, 275.
        See *Costs and Fees.*

COSTS AND FEES, 294-300.
    1. The statute of costs and fees applies in probate matters, 294.
    2. In case of appeal in such matters, costs discretionary, 294.
    3. Actions and proceedings by non-residents and on office bonds; security in the first instance must be given, or suit on motion must be dismissed, 295.
    4. Form of preliminary security, 295.
    5. The motion to dismiss must however be made in apt time, 295.
    6. Security after suit brought, 295, 296.
    7. Affidavits of parties, 296.
    8. Form of security to be given, when required after suit brought, 296.
    9. Non-residents cannot be executors or administrators, guardians or conservators; foreign executors or administrators, guardians or conservators, however, may be empowered, but must always, before instituting proceedings, file security for costs, 296.
    10. Non-resident creditors of an estate in probate must file preliminary security, *quære*, 296, 297.
    11. Appraisers' fees $2 *per diem*, 297.
    12. Fees of the officers of court, 297, 298.
    13. Compensation of executors, etc., 299.
    14. Allowances to, for costs and disbursements, 299.
    15. After expiration of two years, claimants to pay costs in certain cases, 299.
    16. The applicant to be discharged on resignation as executor or administrator must pay the costs of the application, 299.
    17. Suits on bonds; the party for whose use suit is brought must give preliminary security, and is liable to pay costs on failure to maintain his suit, 299.
    18. Delinquent executors and administrators cited or attached, must pay costs, 299, 300.
    19. In probate, as in chancery, costs are usually discretionary, 300.
    20. Witness fees, 309.
    21. Commissioner's fees, etc., 300.
        sheriff's fees, 274.

COUNTY,
    the proper, or the venue, 76, 339.

COURT,
    power of, to compel obedience to orders, 274.
    of its own motion may institute proceedings to compel the production of a will, 16.
    must be the proper one in which to proceed, 39.
        See *Jurisdiction; Practice*, 274.

COVENANTS,
    doctrine of, when made by the administrator, 85.

CREDIBILITY,
    of witnesses to a will, 40, 45, 47.
        See *Witnesses*.

CREDITOR,
    attesting rendered competent, 46.
    laches of, what may be, 90, 91.
    lien of the, paramount to the rights of heirs, legatees and devisees, 64.

CREDITORS,
    unauthorized preference to, ground for removal, 100.
    rights, how enforced, 228, 229.
        See *Claims*.

CREDITS, RIGHTS AND, 83.
        See *Personal Estate*.

CRIMINAL,
    convicted, not to be an executor, 54.

CROPS,
    when real and when personal estate, 189.

D.

DEATH,
    the common lot of all, 62.
    at, the probate jurisdiction begins, 63.
    suit for negligence causing, 344.
        See *Appendix*.
    proof of, essential to jurisdiction, 67.

DEBT,
    as a legal relation arising out of a contract, 164.
    by specialty, 164.
    by record, 164.

DEBTS,
    must exist in order to warrant a sale of real property, 193

DECEASED PERSONS,
    either testates or intestates, 1, 8.

DECEDENT,
    one who has died, 1.
    there must be a, to give probate jurisdiction, 39.

DECREE,
    the hearing and, on the probate of a will, need not be formal, to be valid, 47.

DEDIMUS,
    for the examination of witnesses, 33, 34.
    short form of, with certificates of the execution thereof, 38, 39.
    must be annexed to the will, 37.
    and instructions, 33–37.
    to whom it may issue, 37.

DE FACTO, ADMINISTRATOR, 76.

DEFENSES,
    against claims and against applications to sell real estate to pay debts, 88.

DEFINITION,
    of a will, 10, 161.
    of administrator, 65.
    of executor, 28.
    of contract, 160.
    of distribution, 264.
    of descent, 251.

DEGREES OF CONSANGUINITY, 268.

DEMANDS, 215–237.
    See *Claims*.

DEPOSITIONS, 300.
    See *Dedimus*.

DESCENT, 251–270.
1. Estates both real and personal of intestates, after paying all just debts and claims, descend and are to be distributed, 252, 253.
    1. To the children and their descendants, in equal parts; descendants of a deceased child taking the share of their parents in equal parts among them, 252, 253.
    2. If there be no children, nor descendant of children, and no widow or surviving husband, then to the parents, brothers and sisters of the deceased, and their descendants, in equal parts, each parent taking a child's part, or to surviving parent, if one only be living, a double portion; and if no parent be living, then to the brothers and sisters of the intestate, and their descendants, 253.
    3. If there be a widow or surviving husband, and no child or children, or descendants of a child or children of the intestate, then one-half of the real and the whole of the personal estate shall descend to the surviving consort in fee, 253.
    4. If there be a widow or surviving husband, and a child or children, or descendants of a child or children of the intestate, to the surviving consort one-third of all the personal estate, 253.
    5. If there be no child or descendant of such child, no parent, brother or sister, or descendant of them, and no surviving consort, then to the next of kin to the intestate in equal degree, computing by the rules of the civil law; no representation among collaterals except with the descendants of brothers and sisters of the intestate, and no distinction between kindred of the whole or half blood, 253.

DESCENT — *Continued.*
    6. If there be a surviving consort and no kindred, then the estate descends to the survivor, 253.
    7. If there be no surviving consort or kindred, then the estate escheats to the State, 253.
  2. Illegitimate issue to inherit on the mother's side; rules for specified cases, 252, 253.
  3. Illegitimate issue may be legitimatized by subsequent marriage and acknowledgment by the father, 254.
  4–9. Advancement and rules relating thereto, 254, 255.
  10. Posthumous heirs placed on an equal footing with the other heirs, 255.
  11. Issue of deceased devisee or legatee to inherit, and how, 255.
  12. Undevised and unbequeathed real and personal property of any testator to be deemed and distributed as intestate; administrator *cum testamento annexo* preferred in administration, 255, 256.
  13. Repealed laws enumerated; saving clause, 256.
  14. Computation of the civil law adopted, 256, 268.
  15. Proof of heirship, 256.
  16. After accruing rent, an hereditament, 256.
  17. Husband and wife in no case next of kin to each other, 256.
  18. If the intestate die without issue, leaving only a mother, the estate goes to her, 256.
  19. The interest of a posthumous child not affected by a decree and sale to satisfy debts of relatives, *e. g.*, his mother and uncle, 256, 257.
  20. A posthumous child takes directly from the parent, 257.
  21. Distribution of personal estate not known to the common law except under the rules of the civil law, 257.
  22. Common-law rules as to the descent of real property, discussed in the light of the authorities, 257, 258.
  23. The word *heir* taken in a double sense; 1. Designating the person to take the estate; 2. Limiting the estate transmitted or conveyed; title by descent or purchase, 258, 259.
  24. The custom of gavel-kind, 259–261.
  25. The rule in Shelley's case, 261–263.
  26. Common-law rules prevail unless the provisions of an act of the assembly embrace the very case in controversy, 263.
  27. Heir at common law and statutory heir, 263.
  28. Distribution, 264.
  29. Proof of heirship before distribution, 264.
  30. Decisions in Illinois collated, 264–271.

DESTRUCTION OF A WILL,
  or secretion thereof, tantamount to larceny, 16.

DEVASTAVIT,
  evidence of, etc., 89.

DISTINCTION,
> between personal and real property, 150.
> See *Descent.*

DISPOSING MIND AND MEMORY, 40, 41, 47.

DISTRIBUTION, 264.
> See *Descent.*
> attachment for contempt, when the process to compel, 87, 88.

DIVISION OF A COUNTY,
> venue in case of, 339.

DOMICILE,
> the law of, governs in the distribution of personalty, 160.
> or home of decedent, as fixing the venue for probate procedure, 14.

DOWER,
> See *Hill's Chan. Pr.;* 1 *Gross.* 230; *Jones' Forms;* also, see *Forms; Wills, infra.*

DRUNKARD,
> guardian may be appointed for the habitual, 134.

DUE COURSE OF ADMINISTRATION, 161, 273.
> See *Bond.*

DUTIES,
> the importance of a faithful discharge of, by executors, etc., 2.
> preliminary by the executor, 28.
> the principal, of the executor, 55.
> the principal, of the administrator, 56.
> of the administrator to interpose defenses to claims, 86.

E.

EMINENT DOMAIN,
> when the place of burial is taken by right of, for public use, next of kin to claim indemnity, 190.

ENGLISH STATUTES,
> 1 Jac. II, ch. 17, 22 and 23. Car. II, ch. 10, etc., 68.
> See *Statutes.*

ENTRY,
> order and, on presentation of a petition for process to compel the production of a will, 15, 16.
> See *Forms.*

ESTATES, TESTATE AND INTESTATE, 1.

ESTATES, TESTATE, 10–16.
> See *Wills; Testate Estates; Executors; Intestate Estates; Administrators; Estates of Infants or Minors; Infants; Guardians; Estates of the Incapacitated; Idiots; Insane; Conservators; Personal Estate; Real Estate,* etc.

ESTATES, INTESTATE, 61–101.

ESTATES OF THE INCAPACITATED, 107–156.

ESTATES OF MINORS, 102–134.

ESTOPPEL,
 infants not effected by, 103.

EVIDENCE,
 by proper certificate of a foreign will, 42.
 letters testamentary as, 49, 50.
  See *Witnesses; Death; Intestacy.*

EXAMINATION,
 of witnesses *ore tenus* and by *dedimus*, 32, 33.
 of the witnesses in probating a will, 33.

EXCHANGE, BILL OF, 164.

EXCHANGE, SALE OR, 161.

EXECUTOR,
 renunciation by, 16, 17.
 preliminary duties of the, 28
 the principal duties of, 55.
 instruction to the, 28.
 his bond, 30.
 his oath, 29.
 criminal not to be, 54.
 de son tort, 85.
 power of, 85.

EXECUTORS, 53–60.
  I. Competency and appointment, 53, 54.
  II. Powers and duties, 54–57.
  III. Renunciation, resignation and removal, 57–61.

   I. COMPETENCY AND APPOINTMENT, 53, 54.

1. Who may be executors, 53.
2. Appointment of a debtor as executor, 54.
3. A *femme couverte* may be, 54.
4. A corporation, 54.

   II. POWERS AND DUTIES, 54–57.

1. The authority, 54, 55.
2. How appointed, 55.
3. Executor *de son tort*, 55.
4. Their principal duties, 55, 56.
5. Distinction between their duties and those of administrators, 56, 57.

EXECUTORS — *Continued.*

III. RENUNCIATION, RESIGNATION, AND REMOVAL, 57-60.

1. Renunciation, 57.
2. Form of, 57, 58.
3. Record of, 58.
4. Resignation, 58.
5. Removal, 58, 59.
6. Superseding, petition for, 59.
7. Revocation of letters testamentary, 60.

EXECUTRIX,
the acts of an, bind the estate, 84.

EXPENSES, ALLOWANCES, CLAIMS AND LEGACIES, 215-237.

I. Demands classified, the widow's award, funeral expenses, and expenses of last illness, 215-222.
II. Claims against estates, 222-232.
III. Legacies, 233-237.

I. DEMANDS CLASSIFIED, WIDOW'S AWARD, AND EXPENSES, 215-237.

1. Demands classified, 215, 216.
2. To be classed in order as prescribed, and paid class by class, when insufficient, demands paid *pro rata*, 216.
3. Demand of executor or administrator to be filed and defended against; how, 216.
4. Demands to be entered and classed, papers to be filed and preserved, 216, 217.
5. Award to the widow and children, or the "widow's award," 217, 218.
6. Duty of appraisers in making the award, 218.
7. Renouncing or failing to renounce under the will by the widow, not to affect her award, 218.
8. Award to be to the children, if there be no widow when decedent was a householder, 218, 219.
9. The widow or surviving husband may renounce in writing all benefit under the will, and receive property as if the decedent had died intestate, 219.
10. Legacies and bequests, if diminished by renunciation, to be equalized, 219, 220.
11. Widow, when liable for waste, 220.
12. Relinquishment of specified articles and further selection by the widow, 220.
13. Statement thereof to the court, 221.
14. Estimate of specific property, 221, 222.
15. Expenses attending the last illness, 222.
    See *Claims and Legacies.*

F.

FAILURE OF CONSIDERATION,
 a warranty made by an administrator if basis of negotiable paper may be set up as, 89.

FEES,
 the sheriff to have the same as if in the circuit court, 274.
 See *Costs and Fees.*

FERGUSON v. HUNTER,
 the case discussed, 47.

FIDUCIARY RELATION, THE, 303, 304.

FIXTURES, 189, 190.

FOREIGN ADMINISTRATORS,
 empowered to sue, 87.

FOREIGN EXECUTORS OR ADMINISTRATORS,
 may act, when and how, 82.

FOREIGN GUARDIAN,
 when may sue and act, 286, 287.

FOREIGN WILL,
 how evidenced, 42.
 may be probated, evidence of, 52.

FORM,
 and effect of judgment against personal representatives, 91, 92.

FORMS OR PRECEDENTS,
 adjudicate, citation to, 332.
 acceptance of appointment of guardian and guardian *ad litem*, 117.
 acceptance of resignation as executor or administrator, 98.
 acceptance of resignation of a guardian, 124.
 account, administrator's, 240–242.
 account of personal estate and debts, preliminary to sale of real estate, 202.
 absence, affidavit of, 130.
 administration, petition for letters of, 77.
 administrator, oath of, 79.
 administrator with the will annexed, oath of, 80.
 administrator's account, 240, 242.
 administrator's notice of settlement of claims, 225, 230.
 administrator's sale of personal estate, 181.
 administrator's notice of sale of real estate, 324.
 administrator's deed, 322.
 administration, entry of grant of, 310.
 administration, letters of, 79.

FORMS OR PRECEDENTS — *Continued.*

    administration, petition for revocation of letters of, 99, 100.
    administration, decree revoking letters of, 101.
    advertisement, certificate of, 51.
    advertisement, notice to guardian, 131.
    affidavit of death and intestacy, 77.
    affidavit of infancy, 117.
    affidavit of absence, 130.
    affidavit of concealment, 139.
    affidavit of non-residence, 129.
    affidavit of a claim against an estate of a decedent, 331.
    affidavit of posting notices, 182.
    affidavit for a *dedimus*, 37.
    allowance to the widow and children, 221.
    appointment of guardian *ad litem*, 117.
    appointment of appraiser to fill vacancy, 311.
    appraisers, order appointing, 310.
    appraisement, warrant for, 171.
    appraisement bill, 173.
    appraisement, citation to return inventory and, 331.
    apprentice, indenture of, 319, 320.
    apprenticeship, indentures of, 332, 334.
    assent to resignation of executor or administrator, 99.
    attachment to compel the production of a will, 16.
    attachment to compel the attendance of witnesses, 32.
    award, widow's, 221.
    bond of administrator, 78.
    bond of administrator, with the will annexed, 80.
    bond of executor, 30.
    bond of guardian, 113.
    bond by legatee or distributee, 334.
    bill, the appraisement, 173.
    bill of sale, 183.
    certificate to appraisement bill, 173.
    certificate of publication, printer's, 51, 290.
    certificate of the clerk to letters testamentary, 50.
    certificates of proof under a *dedimus*, 38.
    certificate of insanity, 156.
    citation to a minor, 112.
    citation, notice and proof of a nuncupative will, 51.
    citation to adjudicate, 331.
    citation to return inventory and appraisement, 331.
    citations, common forms for, 318, 319.
    claims, notice of settlement of, 225.
    claims, entry on the adjustment of, 314.
    codicil, 12.

FORMS OR PRECEDENTS — *Continued.*

concealment, affidavit of, 130.
conservator, petition for, 154.
conservator's inventory, 185.
commission to take deposition, 33, 34, 321.
　See *Dedimus.*
costs, execution for, 320.
death, affidavit of, 77.
debts, desperate, 176-179.
decree for removal of guardian, 133.
decree removing an executor or administrator, 101.
dedimus, 33, 34, 321.
dedimus (short form), 38.
dedimus, affidavit for, 37.
deed, administrator's, 322.
deed, executor's, 325.
deposition, commission to take, 33, 34, 321.
desperate debts, suggestion of, 177.
desperate debts, application to sell and compound, 177.
distributee, bond by, 234.
dower, claim for, 319.
　waiver of, 319.
entry of grant of administration, 310.
entry of adjustment of claims, 314.
entry of an order to compel the production of a will, 15.
executor's bond, 30.
executor's oath, 29.
executor, petition to remove an, 59.
executor's deed, 325.
executorship, renunciation of, 16.
execution for costs, 320.
guardian's bond, 113, 334.
guardian's inventory, 185.
guardian, petition of, for permission to resign, 123, 124.
guardian, petition for a removal of a, 124, 125.
guardian, summons to a, 125.
guardian, decree of removal of, 133.
　See *Constructive Service.*
guardian *ad litem*, order appointing, 117.
guardianship, petition for, 111.
guardianship, letters of, 116, 320.
guardian's sale, report of, 330.
indentures of apprentice, 319, 320, 332, 333.
infancy, affidavit of, 117.
inquisition as to insanity, 155.
insane, record of proceeding in case of the, 156.

FORMS OR PRECEDENTS— *Continued.*
    insanity, inquisition as to, 155.
    insanity, statement of (petition), 154.
    instruction for taking a deposition, 34, 35.
    intestacy, affidavit of, 77.
    inventory of the estates of the deceased, 170.
    inventory by the guardian and conservator, 185.
    inventory, citation to return, 331.
    legatee, bond by, 234.
    letters of administration, 79.
    letters of administration, petition for, 77.
    letters of guardianship, 116, 320.
    letters testamentary, petition for, 29.
    letters testamentary, 49, 50.
    letters testamentary and letters of administration, petition for revocation of, 99, 100.
    lunatico de inquirendo, writ of, 155.
    minor, citation to a, 112.
    non-residence, affidavit of, 129.
    notice and citation to heirs, etc., of probate of nuncupative will, 51.
    notice, publication, to guardian, 131.
    notice, administrator's sale of desperate claims, 176, 177, 329.
    notice of administrator's sale of personal estate, 181.
    notice, affidavit of posting, 182.
    notice, administrator's, of the settlement of claims, 225.
    notice of petition to sell real estate, 206.
    notice of application by guardian to sell real estate, 327.
    notices of sale of real estate by administrator, 315, 316, 324.
    notices of sale of real estate by guardian, 329.
    nuncupative will, 13.
    oath of executor, 29.
    oath of administrator, 79.
    oath of administrator with the will annexed, 80.
    oaths, 291, 294.
    order on granting a petition to compel the production of a will, 15.
    order appointing appraisers, 310.
    order on the return of the appraisement bill, 313.
    order on return of the inventory, 311.
    order for citation to compel an inventory, 311.
    order to file an inventory, 311.
    order for the sale of real estate, 315.
    order to compel sale of real estate, 314, 315.
    order appointing a guardian, 316.
    order of confirmation of sale of real estate, 316.
    order revoking letters, 312.
    order appointing administrator *de bonis non,* 312.

FORMS OR PRECEDENTS — *Continued.*
    pendency of suit to sell real estate, 206.
    petition for guardianship, 111.
    order appointing a guardian *ad litem*, 117.
    petition for a guardian by minors, 112, 113.
    petition for a guardian by a third party, 114, 115.
    petition of guardian for permission to resign, 123, 124.
    petition for the removal of a guardian, 124, 125.
    petition for process to compel the production of a will, 15.
    petition for letters of administration, 77.
    petition for letters testamentary, 29.
    petition to supersede the appointment of an executor, 59.
    petition for revocation of letters testamentary or of administration, 99, 100.
    petition for conservator of an insane person, 154.
    petition for the sale of real estate, 204.
    petition for sale of real estate by the guardian, 327.
    petition for restoration of a probate record, 334, 337
    placita, 308, 309.
    posting, affidavit of, 182.
    preamble and recital, 309.
    printer's certificate, 51.
    production of a will, petition for process to compel, 15.
    production of a will, order of entry, 15.
    production of a will, attachment, 16.
    proof of death of a testator, 317.
    proof of will (common form), 46.
    proof of execution of a will with the record, 48, 49.
    publication of notice to guardian, 131.
    publication, printer's certificate of, 51.
    publisher's certificate, 51.
    real estate, notice of application to sell, 206.
    real estate, sale of, petition for, 204, 205.
    real estate, account preliminary to sale, 202.
    recital, preamble and, 309.
    relinquishment of specific articles by the widow or children, 220.
    removal of guardian, decree for, 133.
    renunciation of executorship, 16.
    renunciation, forms of, 324.
    report of administrator's sale of real estate, 323.
    report of guardian's sale, 330.
    representation of a party to procure appointment of a guardian, 327.
    resignation, acceptance of a guardian's, 124.
    resignation of executor or administrator, 97, 98.
    resignation of executor or administrator, notice of, 97.
    resignation of executor or administrator, acceptance of, 98.

FORMS OR PRECEDENTS — *Continued.*
    resignation of executor or administrator, assent to, 99.
    residence unknown, affidavit of, 130.
    restoration of a burnt record, the petition for, 334, 337.
    return of *cepi corpus* on an attachment, 32.
    revocation of letters testamentary, etc., 101.
    sale, administrator's, of personal estate, 181.
    sale, bill of, 183.
    sale of desperate debts, 176, 179.
    sale of real estate, preliminary account, 202.
    sale of real estate, petition for, 204, 205.
    sale, report of guardian's, 330.
    service of a subpœna, proof of, 32.
    statement of insanity, 154.
    subpœna for subscribing witnesses to a will, 31, 32, 317.
    summons to a guardian, 125.
    testamentary, petition for letters, 29.
    testamentary, letters, 49, 50.
    testamentary, petition for revocation of letters, 99, 100.
    testamentary letters, decree of revocation of, 101.
    unknown residence, affidavit of, 130.
    venire for a jury on a writ *de lunatico inquirendo*, 156.
    waiver of dower, 319.
    waiver of provisions in a will, and assertion of claim of dower, 319.
    warrant for appraisement, 171.
    widow's award, 221.
    widow's relinquishment of specific articles, 220.
    will, 11, 12.
    will, nuncupative, 13.
    will, petition to compel the production of a, 15.
    will, proof of (common form), 46.
    witnesses, subpœna for, 31, 32.

FORUM,
    creditors may sue in the circuit court in the first instance, 88.
        See *Jurisdiction; Practice.*

FRAUD,
    vitiates every contract which it pervades, 120, 162.
    presumptive and constructive trust, 96.

FRAUDS AND TORTS OF INFANTS, 103.

G.

GOODS AND CHATTELS,
    defined, 83, 159, 160, 161.
    See *Assets.*

GRANT OF ADMINISTRATION,
the regular, 68, 69.
to be preceded by proof of death and intestacy, 67, 68.
See *Administrators.*

GRIGNON *v.* ASTOR,
2 *How.* 319, discussed, 6, 61, 63.

GUARDIAN *AD LITEM,*
appointment, powers and duties of, 133.

GUARDIAN, FOREIGN, 286, 287.

GUARDIANS, 107–117.

I.— COMPETENCY AND APPOINTMENT OF, 107–117.

1. Guardians, jurisdiction of the county courts to appoint, 107, 108.
2. Construction of the statute, 109, 110.
3. The court of chancery in cases of divorce, etc., 110.
4. When a minor may nominate, and when and how guardians may be appointed by the county courts, 110.
5. The application for appointment, 110, 111.
6. Petition to be appointed, 111, 112.
7. Citation to minors, 112.
8. Petition of minors for a guardian, 112, 113.
9. The bond, 113, 114.
10. Suits on bonds, 114.
11. Appointment of a guardian of a minor's estate when the father is living; petition, 114, 115.
12. Other cases, 115.
13. Letters of guardianship, 116.
14. Guardian *ad litem* for a minor in a justice's court, 117.
15. Guardian *ad litem* in a common-law cause, in the county or circuit court, or in chancery, 117.

II.— THE POWERS AND DUTIES OF, 118–122.

1. Generally, 118.
2. A guardian cannot appoint an attorney in fact to execute a deed; under decree or order of court of chancery he may make compromises; the power to mortgage the ward's land is limited, 118, 119.
3. He may, under a decree, sell real estate, 119.
4. Guardians are not allowed to make gain to themselves, 119, 303, 304.
5. Supervision of the trust, 119.
6. The husband of a guardian cannot act without express authority from the guardian, 119, 120.
7. Fraudulent proceedings instituted by a mother are open to attack, and how, 120.
8. A third person, generally, cannot question the power and acts of the guardian. A guardian has no power to sell the real estate of his

GUARDIANS—*Continued.*
    ward, unless authorized by a court of competent jurisdiction, or by legislative enactment. The power must be strictly pursued, it is a naked power, 120.
  9. Fraud; *caveat emptor*, how applied, 120.
 10. To act for the ward generally, 120.
 11. Guardian *ad litem*, 117, 120.
 12. Custody of child may be willed, 121.
 13. Removal from another State, and charge therefor, 121.
 14. Custody may be to one and guardianship to another, 121.
 15. Testamentary guardian, 121.
 16. Must be commissioned, 121.
 17. Frugally to manage the ward's estate, 121, 122.
 18. And educate the ward, 122.
 19. If the guardian neglects to educate, the court may interfere, 122.
 20. To invest funds, or be chargeable with interest for neglect, 122.

              III. RESIGNATION AND REMOVAL OF, 122.

  1. The court may permit a faithful guardian to resign, 123.
  2. Petition for permission to resign, 123.
  3. Settlement of accounts, surrender of estate, and acceptance of the resignation, 124.
  4. Guardians may be removed for cause, 125.
  5. Petition for removal; its form; petition to be verified and filed, 124, 125.
  6. The summons; *alias, pluries*, 125, 126.
  7. Constructive service, 126–132.
      1. Non-resident guardian, 129.
      2. Absent guardian, 130.
      3. Concealed guardian, 130.
      4. Residence of guardian unknown, 130, 131.
  8. The notice, 131.
  9. The publication, 132.
 10. Jurisdiction to appoint another guardian, and to enforce orders in such matters, 132.
 11. The marriage of a female ward discharges her guardian as to custody and education, but not as to property, 133.
 12. The hearing, 133.
 13. The decree revoking letters of guardianship, 133.

GUARANTY, 163.

H.

HEARING,
    and decree in the probate of a will, 47.
    in examination in probate of a will, 35.

HEIR AND HEIRS,
  distinguished, 258, 259.
  not liable, except for debts, etc., 96.

HEIRS,
  should proceed by bill in chancery, if dissatisfied with the settlement of the administrator, 88.
  appearance by, to contest claims, to be in the name of the administrator, 88.

HEIRSHIP,
  to be proved before distribution, 264.

HEREDITAMENT,
  accruing rent is a, 92, 93.

HEREDITAMENTS,
  chattels real as, 197.

HIRING AND BORROWING, 164.

HONEST,
  and prudent administration, if it result in loss, not to prejudice the personal representative, 85.

HOTCHPOT, 103.

HUSBAND,
  may administer on his wife's estate, 75.

I.

IDIOTS,
  lunatics and other incapacitated persons and their estates, 135–156.
    I. The insane, etc.; decisions, 135–137.
    II. Appointment of conservators, 138.
    III. Their powers and duties, 139–156.
    IV. Restoration and removal, 144.
  See *Conservators.*

INCUMBRANCE,
  administrator cannot sue to remove an, 88.

INDORSEMENT,
  of judge on a deposition, 48.
  by executor, 85.

INFANTS OR MINORS,
  persons and estates of, 102.
    I. Infants or minors, 102–107.
    II. Competency and appointment of guardians, 107–117.
    III. Their powers and duties, 118–122.
    IV. Resignation and removal of guardians, 122.
  See *Guardians.*

INFANTS OR MINORS — *Continued.*
- I.—INFANTS OR MINORS, 102–107.
  1. Females under eighteen years of age and males under the age of twenty-one in this State are minors, 102.
  2. Validity or invalidity of their acts generally, 102, 103.
  3. Ratification of a sale of land, right to hold property, etc., 104.
  4. Estoppel and laches, not applicable to infants generally, 104.
  5. Of their property, 104, 105.
  6. Actions by and against, 105–107.
    See *Guardians.*

INSANE, THE,
  1. Evidence as to insanity, and presumptions as to sanity, *onus probandi*, 135.
  2. Lucid intervals, contracts, etc., 135, 136.
  3. Questions relative to sanity and insanity, proper issues for a jury, 136.
  4. Facts indicating a disposing mind and *eo converso*, 136.
  5. Mere mental weakness insufficient to authorize equity to interfere in matters of contract, 136.
  6. Drunkenness producing inability or insanity, however, is sufficient, 136.
  7. Idiots and lunatics; conservators; their appointment and discharge 137.
  8. Insanity as a defense against a criminal charge, 137, 138.
    See *Conservators; Lunatics.*

INSOLVENT ESTATES, 275.

INSTRUCTIONS,
  to accompany the *dedimus*, 34, 37.
  to administrators, 76, 77, 238.

INSURANCE POLICY, 166.

INTEREST,
  qualified, of the testator, 83.
  when an administrator is liable to pay, 86.
  when guardian must pay, 86.

INTENTION,
  to revoke a will, how to be manifested, 13.

INTERMENT AND RE-INTERMENT, 190.

INTERPRETER'S OATH, 291.

INTESTACY,
  proof of death to be made prior to grant of administration, 67.

INTESTATE ESTATES, 61–102.
  I. Introduction, 61–64.
  II. Appointment of administrators, 64–82.

INTESTATE ESTATES — *Continued.*
    III. Their powers and duties generally, 82–96.
    IV. Resignation and removal, 96–102.
  introduction, 61–64.
    1. Estates generally, 61.
    2. Priority of the rights of creditors, 61.
    3. Testate estates and intestate estates distinguished, 61, 62.
    4. Administration of estates, 62, 64.
       See *Administrators.*

ISSUE,
  of a void marriage, have no right to administer, when, 76.

ISSUE IN CHANCERY,
  relative to wills, 43, 44, 47.
  question for the jury, new and original, 43.

J.

JUDGE,
  county, when the, is a witness, procedure to be in the circuit court, 45.

JUDGMENT,
  against the administrator, form and effect of, 91, 92.
  against the executor or administrator, to be against the goods and chattels in due course of administration, 85, 86.

JURISDICTION,
  in one country, not extended to estate in another country, 76.
  the proper county, 76.
  as between the counties, 76.
  and practice, the importance of a well-settled, in probate, 39, 40.
  should appear in the petition, 16.
  the court must have, points essential to, 39.
  the chancery, specific performance, etc., 94, 95.
  of probate, pertains to the estates of decedents, 1.

JURISDICTION AND PRACTICE IN PROBATE GENERALLY, 1–9.
    I. Introduction, 1–3.
    II. County courts — in probate, 3–9.

I.— INTRODUCTION, 1–3.

1. Testate and intestate estates, 1.
2. The probate of wills and execution of trusts thereby created, administration of intestate estates, guardians, conservators, etc., 1.
3. Subdivision and scope of the subject, 1.
4. The high character of the trusts involved, 2.
5. Care requisite in the development of the subject, 3.

JURISDICTION AND PRACTICE IN PROBATE, ETC.— *Continued.*

II. COUNTY COURTS — IN PROBATE, 3–9.

1. They are courts of record, 4.
2. They have general jurisdiction in probate, 4.
3. Their judgments, final and conclusive, unless reversed, 4.
4. Constitutional and statutory provisions, 4.
5. Constitution of 1818, 4.
    1. Courts of probate created in 1821, 4.
    2. Probate court in 1845, 4.
6. Constitution of 1848; county courts from 1849, 4, 5.
7. Constitution of 1870; original jurisdiction given to the county courts, in probate, 5.
8. This jurisdiction involves sacred trusts, 5.
9. Chapter 85, R. S. 1845, and amendments, 5.
10. Terms for probate business on the third Monday of every month, 5. See *Act* 1873, *Laws* 1873, *p.* 87.
11. County clerk, 5.
12. The judgments, orders and decrees in probate, not to be collaterally attacked; the rule in the United States supreme court, 6.
13. Decisions in Illinois, 6–9.
    1. Incidental powers; no discretion in prescribed cases; exclusive jurisdiction over personalty; none over realty; but, see *Act of February* 12, 1849, § 13, 6, 7.
    2. Rules of practice, 7.
14. Equitable jurisdiction over claims against intestate estate, 7.
15. Statutory provisions, 7.
16. Scope of the subject, 8.
17. Deceased persons, either testates or intestates; testate estates; intestate estates, 8.
18. Incapacitated persons — infants and other persons not *sui juris*, etc., 8.
19. Executors, administrators, guardians, conservators, all officers of the court, 8.
20. The law of descent, 9 (see chap. X), 252.
21. Appeals, 9.
22. Method characteristic of the subject, 9.

JURORS' OATHS, 284.

JURY,
   trial by, the question of the sanity of a testator may be submitted to, 43–47.

JUS DISPONENDI, THE, 10.

JUS REPRESENTATIONIS, THE, 69.
   waiver of, 31.

K.

KINDS,
of administrators, specified, 66.

KIN, NEXT OF,
who are, 75.
personal property of a minor vests immediately in, 75.
See *Appendix*.

L.

LACHES,
not attributable to minors, 103–107.
of a creditor, 90, 91.
the lapse of seven years usually a bar to the grant of administration, 76.

LAW, CIVIL,
degrees of consanguinity according to the, 268.

LAWFUL AGE,
males at 21, females at 18 years, are of, 102.
See *Jus Disponendi*.

LEASEHOLD INTERESTS,
pass to the personal representative, 191.

LEGACIES, 233–237.
1. Refunding bond to be given, 233.
2. Duty of legatee to refund; refusal on citation and demand, deemed a breach of the bond, 233.
3. Payment of legacies, 233, 234.
4. The bond, 234, 235.
5. Decisions, 235, 237.

LEGAL REPRESENTATIVES,
who are, 83.
See *Appendix*.

LETTERS TESTAMENTARY, 49, 50.
petition for, 29.
revocation of, 279, 280.
See *Forms*.

LIABILITY,
of heirs to ancestor's debts, stated, 163.

LICENSE,
to sell real estate must be obtained on notice, 187.

LIEN, 163.
of creditors, paramount to the rights of heirs, legatees and devisees, 64.
of bailees, 163.

LIMITATION,
lapse of seven years usually a bar to the grant of administration, 76.

LIMITATIONS,
 the statute of, applicable to minors and their acts, 103.
 the statute of, against claims, 90.

LOSS OF A PAPER,
 oath of, 293.

LOST WILL,
 how and where proved, 53.

LUNATICS, COMMITMENT AND DETENTION OF, 147–156.
 1. Jurisdiction of the county court may be invoked by petition, 148.
 2. Petition to be filed, process to issue, and be served and returned, 148.
 3. Subpœnas may issue, 148.
 4. Jury trial, continuance, 148, 149.
 5. Verdict, its form, 149.
 6. Verdict to be recorded, order of commitment entered, and application for admission of respondent to superintendent of a state hospital for the insane to be made by the clerk, 149.
 7. When commitment may be had, 149.
 8. Communication to be had between the clerk and superintendent relative to the reception of the respondent, 150.
 9. Mittimus may, if necessary, be issued by the clerk; its form, 150.
 10. Receipt to be given by the superintendent; its form, 150.
 11. Diseased persons and idiots not to be received, 150.
 12. Respondent may by order of court, pending proceedings, be restrained of his liberty, 150.
 13. Costs of the proceedings where respondent is not a pauper, 151.
 14. Costs where he is a pauper, 151.
 15. Bond to be given where he is not a pauper, 151.
 16. Clothing to be furnished each patient, 152.
 17. Clothing to be furnished where patient is a pauper by the county, 152.
 18. Patient to be removed when ordered to be discharged by the trustees, 152.
 19. Non-resident patient may be received, 152.
 20. Whenever reason is restored the patient may leave, 153.
 21. Insane pauper may be committed to a county hospital, 153.
 22. No one to be committed without a trial by jury, 153.
 23. Penalty for receiving or detaining any person not duly committed, 153.
 24. Forms, 154–156.

M.

MANURE,
 sometimes realty, sometimes personalty, 190.

MARRIAGE,
> issue of a void, have no right to administer on the estate of a deceased father, 76.
> formerly worked a revocation of a prior will in certain cases, 42.

MARRIED WOMEN,
> may make wills, 14.
> husband may administer on his wife's estate, 75.
> can a wife administer without her husband's consent? 75.

MEMORY,
> disposing mind and, 40, 41–47.

MERCANTILE TRANSACTIONS, 158.

MISCELLANEOUS MATTERS, 275–293.
> 1. The executor or administrator, or his security, not chargeable beyond the assets of the testator or intestate, 275.
> 2. Specific performance of the contracts made by decedent may be ordered, 275.
> 3. The books of account of the decedent to be subject to the inspection of all concerned, 275.
> 4. Estate, if found insolvent after two years from the grant of administration, to be so entered, 275.
> 5. The executor or administrator may be coerced to apply for an order to sell real estate, 275, 276.
> 6. County courts to have power to enforce due observance of its process, judgment, orders and decrees, the same as the circuit courts, 276.
> 7. The sheriff to serve and execute all process papers, 276.
> 8. Executors and administrators to receive compensation not to exceed six per centum on amount of personal estate, nor more than three per centum on amount of proceeds of the real estate sold, with allowances for costs and charges in collecting the estate and defending claims, 276.
> 9. Construction of the act relating to administration to be liberal, and to apply equally to executors and administrators, etc., 276.
> 10. Repeal of former laws with saving clause, 276, 277.

MISCELLANEOUS PROVISIONS OF THE ACT OF APRIL 1, 1872.
> 1. Power of administrator to collect, 278.
> 2. When his appointment shall cease.
> 3. General provisions as to bonds of executors and administrators, 279.
> 4. Causes for revocation of letters testamentary and of administration, 279, 280.
> 5. Causes for removal, 280, 281.
> 6. Surety on bond may apply to be released, 281, 282.
> 7. New appointment to be made if executor or administrator fail to give new bond, 282.
> 8. Letters *cum testamento annexo*, 282.

MISCELLANEOUS PROVISIONS OF THE ACT, ETC. — *Continued.*
- 9. Co-executor or co-administrator may be appointed, 282.
- 10. Liability of administrator, who has been discharged, to his successor in trust, 282, 283.

MISCELLANEOUS STATUTES AND DECISIONS, 283, 293.
- 1. Specific performance of contract in case of vendor's death, how enforced, 283-285.
- 2. Executor or administrator may of record discharge a mortgage or trust deed, 285.
- 3. Deposit of funds on final settlement belonging to unknown heirs or claimants and non-residents, 285, 286.
- 4. Foreclosure or *sci. fa.* necessary in case of death of mortgagee or debtor requisite, 286.
- 5. When surety is released in case of death of the maker of a joint note, 286.
- 6. Foreign guardian may receive the estate of his ward; procedure prescribed, 286, 287.
- 7. Competency of parties as witnesses, 287, 288.
- 8. Repealing clause of act of April 10, 1872 (guardian and ward), 288, 289.
- 9. Miscellaneous decisions, 290, 291.
- 10. Proclamations by the sheriff in opening and closing court, and at adjournment, 291.
- 11. Oaths, witnesses, jurors, etc., 291-293.

MIND,
disposing, and memory, 40, 41-47.

MINISTERIAL,
act of taking proof of a will, *quære*, 42, 47.

MINOR,
personal property of, vests immediately in the next of kin, 75.

MISTAKE,
the administrator has no authority to apply for the correctio: of, in a deed to his intestate, 94, 95.

MONEY,
may indeed partake of the character of realty, 191.

N.

NECESSITY OF ADMINISTRATION,
there is not always, 75, 76.

NEGLIGENCE,
of another causing death, action 344.
See *Appendix.*

NEGOTIABLE PAPER,
power of executors and administrators over, 85.

NEW PROMISE,
    by infant, action should be upon, 102.

NEXT OF KIN,
    who are, 75.
    are they included in the term Personal Representative ? 344.
        See *Appendix*.
    action on behalf of, in name of personal representative, for negligence causing death, 344.
        See *Appendix*.
    their rights as to corpses and sepulture, 190.
    to have indemnity in case of disturbance, 190.

NEWSPAPERS,
    dates of first and last publication to be given, 51.

NON-RESIDENT EXECUTORS, ADMINISTRATORS AND GUARDIANS,
    to give security for costs, 273.

NON-RESIDENT GUARDIANS, 328, 329.

NON-RESIDENTS,
    cannot legally be appointed administrators, 100, 101.

NOTE,
    the promissory, 166.
    of hand, 166.
    assignment of a, by executors, etc., 85.

NOTICE,
    the propriety of, of the hearing before probating a will, 31.
    and citation to heirs and legal representatives, 51.
    proof of, by publication, 51.
    claim to be presented on notice, 87.
    to the heirs, of application to sell real estate, essential to jurisdiction, 187.
    See *Service*.

NUNCUPATIVE WILL, 50–53.
    form of, 13.
        See *Forms*.

NUDUM PACTUM, 160.

O.

OATH,
    the solemnity of an, 305.
    to executor, 29.
        See *Forms*.

OATHS,
    of witnesses, jurors, etc., 291.
        See *Forms*.

ONUS PROBANDI,
    on a trial in chancery relative to a will, 43.

ORDER,
    on presentation of a petition for process to compel the production of a will, 15, 16.
    admitting will to probate, 48.
    approving bond of executor, 49.
    for letters testamentary to issue, 49.
    appointing appraisers, 49.
        See *Forms.*

ORDERS,
    the usual entries of, in probate of will, 48, 49.
        See *Forms; Probate Record.*

P.

PAPER, NEGOTIABLE,
    power of personal representatives over, 85.

PAPERS, NEWS,
    date of first and last, in which a notice has been published must appear, 51.

PAROL CONTRACT,
    with the intestate, how enforced, 89.

PARTIES,
    one of two administrators loaning money of the estate has the right of action to recover it, 87.
    heir a necessary party, in Illinois, to the disposition of real property, 6, 187.
    as witnesses, 287, 288.
        See *Notice.*

PARTNER,
    surviving not entitled to administer, 76.

PARTNERSHIP, 93.

PARTNERSHIP ESTATE, 166, 178.
    duty of surviving partner, 166.

PERJURY,
    the crime of, 306.

PERSONAL ESTATE IN ADMINISTRATION, 157–185.
        I. Collection and disposition of by the executor or administrator, 157–183.
        II. In the hands of guardians or conservators, 183–185.

PERSONAL ESTATE IN ADMINISTRATION — *Continued.*

I. — COLLECTION AND DISPOSITION OF, BY THE EXECUTOR OR ADMINISTRATOR, 157–183.
1. The retrospect, 159, 160.
2. Personal property in due course of administration, governed by the *lex domicilis*, 160, 161.
3. The title of the personal representative of a decedent to the personal estate, 161.
4. His trust, 162.
5. The *cestuis que trust*, the widow, the children, the creditors, legatees, devisees and distributees, of heirs, their relation to the proceedings in administration, 163, 164.
6. Special proceedings requisite to divest the title of the devisees or heirs to the real property, 165.
7. Scope of this chapter, 165, 166.
8. The inventory to be made and returned within three months from the date of letters testamentary or of administration; how made; failure to make, subjects the delinquent to citation to make inventory and account, 167–169.
9. Citation to exhibit inventory and account, 169, 170.
10. Form of inventory, 170, 171.
11. The appraisement, the warrant, the oath, 171, 172.
12. The bill of appraisement, 173.
13. Inventories and exemplifications thereof to be *prima facie* evidence, 173.
14. Additional appraisement, 173, 174.
15. Care and diligence required of executors and administrators in getting in the estates of their testates and intestates, 174.
16. Appraisers' fees two dollars per day each, 174.
17. Proceedings in case the assets do not exceed the amount of the widow's allowance, 174.
18. Collection and disposition of assets, 174–180.
19. Sale of personal property, 180–183.

II. — IN THE HANDS OF GUARDIANS OR CONSERVATORS, 184, 185.
1. The guardian to return an inventory within sixty days after his appointment, and additional inventory, 184.
2. Contents of inventory, 184.
3. Form of inventory, 185.
4. Conservators are required to do the like, 185.

PERSONAL PROPERTY,
of a minor vests immediately in the next of kin, 75.

PERSONAL REPRESENTATIVES,
who are, 83.
See *Appendix.*

PERSONAM, IN,
    sale of real estate partly, and partly *in rem*, 62.

PETITION,
    the usual form of application or representation to the court, 15.
    should show jurisdiction, 16.
    requisites of, 286, 287.
    for process to compel the production of a will, 15.
    for letters testamentary, 29.
    surety may file, to be released, 281.
        See *Forms*.

PEWS,
    in churches, sometimes real estate, and sometimes personal estate, 190.

PLEADING, 287.

POINTS,
    to be proved to probate a will, 39.

POLICIES OF INSURANCE, 166.

POWER,
    of executor before probate, 56.
    over realty, may be given by a will, it is not conferred by appointment or as administrator, etc., 186, 187.
    administrator takes only a power over real estate, 92.
    of administrator over the real estate, discussed, 94.

PRACTICE,
    for the executor on death of the testator, 28, 48.
    for the court in probating a will, 39, 48.
    how to be appointed administrator, 76, 77.
    the petition, 77.
    how to be appointed guardian, 111.
    to obtain a dedimus, 37.
        See *Jurisdiction; Jurisdiction and Practice generally; Wills; Executors; Wills; Testate Estates; Administrators; Intestate Estates; Estates of Infants or Minors; Guardians; Infants; Insane; Conservators; Estates of the Incapacitated; Drunkard; Probate of Wills; Personal Estate; Real Estate*, etc.

PRECEDENTS, FORMS OR,
    See *Forms; Probate Record; Wills*.

PREFRENCE,
    where an unauthorized is given by an administrator, it is ground for his removal, 100.

PRESENCE,
    of the witnesses at the time of the signature not essential, if the testator acknowledges the will, etc., 41.

PRINTER'S
  certificate, its office as evidence of notice, 51.

PRIORITY
  of judgments over claims of distributees, 88.

PRIVITY,
  there is none between the administrator and the heir, when, 193.

PROBATE,
  jurisdiction defined, 1–3.
  of wills, 27–53.
  1. Definition, 27.
  2. The probate record, 27.
  3. Preliminary duties of the executor, 28.
      1. Before probate, 28.
      2. Before entering upon his duties, 28.
  4. Practice, 28.
  5. Petition for letters testamentary, 29.
  6. Oath of executor, 29.
  7. His bond, 30.
  8. The hearing or examination, 30–39.
      1. Subpœna *ad testificandum* to subscribing witnesses, 31, 32.
      2. *Capias* or attachment to compel attendance, 32, 33.
      3. *Dedimus potestatum*, 33, 34.
      4. Instructions as to its execution and return, 34–39.
      5. Proof of wills, 39–48.
          1. The decisions, 39–44.
          2. The statute of 1872 (act March 20), 44–48.
  9. Clerk's entries and forms of certificate of proof, 48, 49.
  10. The letters testamentary, 49, 50.
  11. Noncupative will, 50, 52.
      1. Citation to persons interested, 51.
      2. Notice by advertisement to residents of other counties, 51.
  12. Foreign will, 52.
  13. Lost will, 33.
  record, 27, 301–337.
  record of a will, 48.

PRODUCTION OF THE WILL, 14–17.

PROMISSORY NOTE, 166.

PROOF,
  certificate of, of a will, 46.
  of wills, evidence, the law of relating to, 40–47.
  of death and intestacy to be made prior to grant of administration, 67.
    See *Evidence; Witnesses.*

PROFITS,
> when an administrator is to account for, if made by the use of the trust fund, 86, 87.
> See *Fraud*.

PROPERTY,
> of infants; sale of their realty, etc., 103, 104.
> personal, defined, 158.
> See *Assets; Real Estate*.

PUBLIC,
> sale of personal estate to be, 86.
> public administrator, 70-72.

PUBLICATION, 51.
> See *Constructive Service; Advertisement*.

Q.

QUALIFICATIONS,
> requisite for an administrator, 73, 74.

QUALIFIED INTEREST,
> of the administrator and absolute title to the personal estate, 83.
> See *Personal Estate*.

R.

RATIFICATION,
> of contracts, what essential to, by infants, 103.
> See *Infants or Minors*.

REAL CHATTELS,
> as hereditaments go to the personal representatives, 191.

REAL ESTATE,
> defined, 187.

REAL ESTATE IN ADMINISTRATION, 186.
> I. Through the executor, 186-192.
> II. Through the administrator, 192-207.
> III. Through the guardian, 207-213.
> IV. Through the conservator, 142, 146.

>> I.— ADMINISTRATION OVER REAL ESTATE THROUGH THE EXECUTOR, 186-192.
>>> 1. Power of executor to sell land valid, if given in the will, 186, 187.
>>> 2. Implied power of sale, 187, 188.
>>> 3. Power vests in those who qualify, where several are appointed and part refuse, 189.
>>> 4. Conveyance to a person as executor, his heirs, etc., conveys a fee, 189.
>>> 5. Co-executor may call a co-executor to account in chancery, 190.

REAL ESTATE IN ADMINISTRATION— *Continued.*

 6. Mortgages and leases by executors, on petition to the county court, 191, 192.

 7. Foreclosure of such mortgages confined to the county court having jurisdiction over the property, *i. e.*, in the county where it, or a greater part of it, is situated, 192.

 8. Decree of strict foreclosure in such case prohibited, and redemption as upon judgments at law prescribed, 192.

 9. Actions which survive, specified, 192.

 10. General directions; practice indicated; suggestions, 192.

II.— ADMINISTRATION OVER REAL ESTATE THROUGH THE ADMINISTRATOR, 192.

 1. After making a just and true account of the personal estate and the debts to the court, and it is ascertained that the personal estate of the decedent is insufficient to pay the just claims against his estate, enough of the real estate, if there be any held either by legal or equitable title, to pay the debts and expenses of administration, may be sold, 193.

 2. Proceedings to be commenced by petition; parties, 194.

 3. Requisites of the petition, 194.

 4. Cause to be docketed and prosecuted according to the practice in cases in chancery, 195.

  See *Hill's Chan. Pr.*

 5. Summons to issue, requisites of, 195.

 6. Service of summons, 196.

 7. Cases for constructive service; affidavit of non-residence, etc., 196, 197.

 8. Publication notice, 197.

 9. Guardian *ad litem*, 197, 198.

 10. The hearing, order and decree of sale, 198.

 11. The sale to divest title of defendants, 199.

 12. Preliminaries and regulations for making sale, the notice, penalties, etc., 200.

 13. Proceeds of sale to become assets in the hands of the administrator, for payment of debts, 201.

 14. Equitable estates; how sold or made legal estates and sold, 201.

 15. The practice indicated, 201, 202.

 16. Forms for pleadings, affidavits, process, orders, decrees, etc., etc, 202–207.

  See *Appendix; Forms.*

III.— ADMINISTRATION OVER REAL ESTATE THROUGH THE GUARDIAN, 207–213.

 1. The guardian may lease the ward's real estate with the approval of the court, 208.

REAL ESTATE IN ADMINISTRATION — *Continued.*

    2. He may by leave of court mortgage the same, 208.
    3. Petition for order must be filed, however, 208.
    4. Foreclosure of such mortgages only to be made by petition to the court in which letters of guardianship were granted, 208.
    5. Decree of strict foreclosure not to be entered, and redemption as in case of judgments prescribed, 208.
    6. Proceedings prescribed for the sale of the ward's real estate; petition, etc., etc., 208.
    7. The petition; its requisites to be verified and filed, 209.
    8. Notice to be published and served, 209.
    9. Cause to be docketed, and proceed as if a case in chancery, 209. See *Hill's Chan. Pr.*
    10. The sale, notice of the time and place to be given; sale may be on credit; credit, how given, securities required, 209.
    11. Report of sale to be forthwith made and approved and recorded, and to vest in the purchasers the title of the property, 209.
    12. Guardian to account for proceeds of sales of real estate on oath, 209.
    13. Duty of court to keep the securities of the guardian good, 209, 210.
    14. Guardian, if insolvent or in doubtful circumstances, may be required to give to his securities counter-securities, 210.
    15. The practice indicated, 210.
    16. Forms for pleadings, affidavits, process, orders, decrees, etc., etc., 210.
    17. Foreign guardians may sell when, 210.
    18. And under like process and procedure, 210, 211.
    19. Sales to invest purchasers with the title, 211.
    20. Foreign guardians must give security for costs before commencing any proceeding, 211.

IV.—ADMINISTRATION OVER REAL ESTATE THROUGH THE CONSERVATOR, 142, 146.

        Cases where an application will lie to sell the real estate of an idiot, lunatic or distracted person, specified, 143, 146.
        The petition, its requisities; parties, 143.
        Notice to be issued and served, as in cases in chancery, 143.
        Guardian *ad litem*, 143.
        The hearing and the decree or order of sale, 143.
        Orders of sale, requisites of, 143.
        Foreign conservator may apply, 146.
        Proceedings in case of, 146.
        Practice indicated, 146.
        Forms for petition, affidavits, process, etc., etc., 146, 147.

    sale of, in administration, a proceeding partly *in rem* and partly *in personam*, 62.

    only reached by a special proceeding partly *in rem* and partly *in personam*, 186, 187.

RECEIPT,
>   for rents by minor, not a ratification, 102.

RECORD,
>   the probate, 27, 293-329.
>   form of record of the proof of a will, 48, 49.
>   >   See *Forms*.

REJECTED,
>   case where a will was, 47.

RELATION,
>   . of the administrator's title back to the death of the intestate, 162.
>   of the appointment of administrator back to the death of the intestate, 83.

REM, IN,
>   a sale of real estate in administration, a proceeding partly, and partly *in personam*, 62.

REMOVAL,
>   of public administrator, 71.
>   >   See *Executors; Administrators; Guardians; Conservators; Resignation; Renunciation.*

RENUNCIATION,
>   by an executor; he is not to intermeddle before, with the goods, 16.
>   form of, 16, 17.

RENT,
>   accruing, a hereditament, 92, 93.
>   >   See *Chattels, Real; Real Estate.*

REPRESENTATION,
>   of facts usually made by petition, 15, 16, 301.
>   >   See *Petition; Forms; Practice; Jurisdiction, etc.*

REPRESENTATIVE,
>   administrator the *legal* or *personal* of the intestate, 84.
>   >   See *Appendix*, 344, 345.

REPUBLICATION, 344, 345.
>   not necessary to involve subsequently acquired lands, 42.

REQUEST,
>   and waiver of the *jus representationis*, 31
>   >   See *Renunciation*.

RETURN,
>   on a writ of attachment for a delinquent witness, 32.

RESIGNATION,
>   and removal of executors and administrators. 96-102.
>   >   1. The statute of 1872, 96.
>   >   2. Petition, 96, 97.
>   >   3. Order, 97.
>   >   4. Notice. 97.

RESIGNATION — *Continued.*
    5. Resignation, 98.
    6. Record, 98.
    7. Notice to security, 98.
    8. Assent, 99.
    9. Removal and revocation, grounds of, 99.
    10. Petition, 90, 100–102.
       ·See *Guardians; Conservators; Practice,* etc.

REVIVAL, ABATEMENT AND, 87.
    administrator of a deceased party, now brought in, 87.
      See *Abatement;* also 2 *Hill's C. L.* 209.

REVOCATION,
    of a will, 13.

REVOCATION OF A WILL,
    by a subsequent marriage, 41, 42.
      See *Resignation; Renunciation.*

RIGHT, THE,
    of the administrator over the personal estate, 86.

RIGHTS AND CREDITS, 83.
    See *Personal Estate.*

·S.

SALE OR EXCHANGE, 151.

SALE OF PERSONAL PROPERTY, 180–183.

SALE,
    bill of, 183.
    to be public, 86.

SALE OF REAL ESTATE,
    in administration, a proceeding partly *in rem* and partly *in personam,* 62.

SALES,
    of personal property by executor, administrator of guardian, if *bona fide* to be *upheld,* 84.

SAMPLE,
    buying and selling by, 162.

SCIRE FACIAS,
    will not lie against the heir upon a judgment against an administrator, 92.

SEPULTURE,
    the right of, the property of the next of kin, 190.

SERVICE,
    of a subpœna, proof of, 32.
    constructive, 126–132.
      See *Sheriff; Process.*

SEVEN YEARS,
    the lapse of, usually a bar to the grant of administration, 76.

SHARES,
　incorporations, 190.

SHELLEY'S CASE,
　the rule in, 261-263.

SHERIFF,
　See *Process; Statutes*, 132, 178.

SPECIAL PROCEEDING,
　necessary to divest the title of realty, which descends, 187

STATUTE OF LIMITATIONS, 70.
　See *Laches*.

STATUTE OF FRAUDS, THE, 163.

STATUTES,
　the English (1 *Jac.* II, ch. 17, 22, 23; *Car.* II, ch. 10), 68.
　the statute of wills, etc., 7.
　an act to provide for the appointment of guardians of habitual drunkards, and prescribing the duties of such guardians, February 10, 1872.
　Summary of act of March 20, 1872 (R. S. 1874, pp. 1101-1105).
　　absence of a witness by death or removal, 30, 39.
　　appeals, 274.
　　attesting creditor competent, 46.
　　circuit court, if the county judge be disqualified, procedure to be in the, 45, 46.
　　custodian, to produce the will, 14, 16.
　　county judge, if a witness, procedure to be had in the circuit court, 45, 46.
　　death, or a removal of a witness, 30, 39.
　　debtor as executor, 54.
　　execution of wills out of the State, 52.
　　　See *Requisites of a Will*, 11, 44, 46, 47.
　　interested witnesses excluded, 38, 42.
　　　See *Evidence*.
　　judge, county, if a witness, 45, 46.
　　nuncupative wills, 15, 16.
　　　probate of, 50, 51.
　　persons competent to dispose of property by will enumerated, 11, 44.
　　probate of wills, 16, 43, 50.
　　　See *Probate*.
　　record and preservation of wills, 17.
　　repeal of former laws, 7, 336.
　　　See *Statutes*.
　　requisites of a will, 11, 44, 46, 47.
　　revocation of wills, 11.
　　subscribing witnesses, their duty to appear and testify, 38, 39.

STATUTES — *Continued.*

    testimony of subscribing witnesses, 38, 39.
      if they be non-residents, 36, 37.
      See *Dedimus.*
    venue or proper county in which to prove the will, 14.
    witnesses, the subscribing, 30, 36, 37, 38, 39, 42.
      See *Dedimus; Evidence; Certificate; Record; Appendix.*

ACT APRIL 1, 1872 (ADMINISTRATION), CHAP. 3, R. S. 1874, pp. 103–127.

    SUMMARY, ACT APRIL 1, 1872 (ADMINISTRATION).
      account, books of, § 128; 274.
      accounts, §§ 112–115; 239, 240.
      actions which survive, § 123; 83, 192.
        See *Claims.*
      additional appraisement to be made if other property be discovered, and within three months after discovery, § 57; 173, 174.
      additional bonds, executors or administrators, etc., may be required to give, § 38; 282.
      additional inventory is to be returned whenever any other real or personal property becomes known to the administrator, § 52; 171.
      administrator, bond of, form, to be made applicable to all cases, *mutatis mutandis,* § 23; 79, 80.
      administrator *de bonis non,* may be appointed, § 37; 282.
      administrator's oath, form of, to be made and filed, § 22; 79.
      administrator, *de bonis non,* if no executor be named in the will, if the executor named therein die, refuse to act or become incapacitated or disqualified, may be appointed as if for an intestate estate, § 1; 49, 53, 54.
      administrator to collect, § 11; 67, 72.
        letters to, § 12; 72.
        bond of, § 13; 77.
        oath of, § 14; 73.
        power of, §§ 15, 16; 278.
        revocation of, § 17; 279.
      affidavit of applicant for letters, must first be filed showing names of heirs, and widow or widower, and probable amount of personal estate, § 20; 64, 75.
      allowance to executors and administrators may be made for costs and charges in collecting and enforcing claims, § 133; 276.
      allowance to widow, when assets do not exceed property to be transferred to her and administration closed, § 59; 174.
      appeal, §§ 124, 125; 272.

STATUTES — *Continued.*

   SUMMARY, ACT APRIL 1, 1872 (ADMINISTRATION).

      applicant for letters must file an affidavit, showing date of death and probable amount of personal estate, and the names of heirs, and widow or widower, if known, § 20; 64, 75.

      appraisers, to be three disinterested persons, their warrant to issue with the letters, their powers and duties, form of warrant, vacancy in number may be filled, § 53; 172.

      appraisers to take and subscribe an oath to be indorsed upon or annexed to the warrant; form of oath, § 54; 172.

      appraiser's fees, fixed at two dollars per day for necessary attendance, to be allowed by the court, § 59; 174.

      assets, collection of, §§ 81–96; 174–182.

        See *Personal Estate.*

          if, after appraisement, the assets do not exceed the widow's allowance, the executor or administrator is to report, and the court, if it find the facts true, is to order the same to be transferred to her and close the administration, § 59; 174.

          neither executor, administrator nor security shall be chargeable beyond the assets of the testate or intestate for omission, misfeasance, or malfeasance in pleading, § 126; 275.

      attachment, citation, and on failure of executor or administrator to report deficiency of assets, etc., for widow's allowance, § 59; 174.

      attachment, summons, subpœnas, citations, notices and other process to be served and returned by the sheriff or his deputies, § 132; 276,

      award, widows', §§ 74–77; 217, 218.

      bill of appraisement, to be certified by the appraisers under their hands and seals to the executor or administrator, and by him to be returned within three months after grant of letters, § 55; 172.

      bond of administrator, form of, § 23; 79, 80.

        to be changed and applied to all cases of administration *mutatis mutandis*, § 23; 79, 80.

      bond in case of estate more than enough to pay debts, testator may direct that no security be required, but the court may, in its discretion, even then require security, § 8; 56.

      bond of executor, form of, must be filed and recorded, §§ 6, 24; 28, 29, 80.

      bond of public administrator to be required as in other cases, failure to give for sixty days, a *vacatur* of his office, and upon certificate of the fact from the county judge, the governor is to fill the vacancy, § 47; 71.

      bond, suits on, may be instituted, and how, § 25; 278.

STATUTES—*Continued.*

SUMMARY, ACT APRIL 1, 1872 (ADMINISTRATION).

books of account of decedent, § 128; 274.

cancellation of a will in due course of law to revoke the letters testamentary thereon, § 29; 99, 280.

care, custody and management of the estate of intestates committed to the public administrator, § 49; 71.

claims, §§ 60–73, 215, 216, 222, 223, 224.

commission and expenses earned and incurred by a public administrator are not affected by a re-grant of administration to those entitled, § 47; 71.

construction of the statute, executor to mean administrator, and administrator to mean executor, his to mean her, and one to mean two or more, etc., whenever the sense requires it in applying the law, liberally construed, § 134; 276.

contracts of decedent may be performed by the executor or administrator, under the direction of the county court, § 127; 275.

costs and charges in collecting and enforcing claims as may be reasonable, may be allowed, § 133; 276.

costs and fees, appraisers', $2 *per diem*, § 59; 174.

costs to be paid by party obtaining letters fraudulently, and on their revocation, § 27; 280.

See *Costs and Fees.*

death, proof of, must be made before administration can be granted, §§ 18, 20; 64, 67, 77.

decrees, orders, etc., may be enforced; county courts shall have power to enforce due observance of all orders, decisions, judgments and decrees made by them in matters of administration by process for contempt, and may fine and imprison offenders as fully as the circuit court may do in similar cases, § 131; 276.

diligence; executors and administrators chargeable with due and proper diligence in getting in the estate, § 58; 174.

discovery of new assets; in such cases administration may be granted *de novo*, § 59; 174.

division of a county, on, if letters have been granted to proceed, notwithstanding, or on removal of executor or administrator to another county, § 9; 339.

disqualification of county judge, as a material or necessary witness, or a party interested, transfers the case to the circuit court of the county, case to be certified to circuit court, § 69; 224, 225.

duty of public administrator to protect estates generally, until administration, § 50; 71.

STATUTES — *Continued.*
   Summary, Act April 1, 1872 (Administration).
      executors and administrators chargeable for all estate which may or might after due and proper diligence be received, § 58, 174.
      executor's bond, form of, § 7; 28, 30.
        must be filed and recorded, § 7; 28, 30.
      executor, if not named in the will, if he die, refuse to act or is otherwise disqualified, administration *cum testamento annexo*, to take place as if testate had died intestate, § 1; 49, 53, 54.
      expenses incurred and commissions earned by a public administrator not to be affected by the revocation of his letters, on re-grant of same to those entitled, § 47; 71.
      fees of executors and administrators to be not exceeding six per centum on proceeds of real estate, and three per centum on proceeds of personal estate, with reasonable allowances for collecting and enforcing claims, § 133; 276.
      fees of sheriff to be the same as for similar services in the circuit court, § 132; 276.
        See *Costs and Fees.*
      foreclosure, §§ 120–122; 191, 192.
      foreign administrator's or executor's suit to insure a benefit of domestic executor or administrator, if one be appointed *pendente lite*, § 43; 82.
      foreign executor or administrator may file duly authenticated copy of his letters in court in the State, and enforce claims and sell land to pay debts, § 42; 82.
        if there be no executor or administrator in this State, § 43; 82.
      former administrator shall be liable for *devastavit*, etc., § 39; 282, 283.
      form of oath of executor or administrator *cum testamento annexo*, § 6; 28, 29, 80.
        oath to be attached to, and form a part of the record, § 6; 28, 29, 80.
      fraudulent pretenses in obtaining letters to work revocation at the cost of the administrator, § 27; 280.
      insolvent estates, after the expiration of two years from grant of administration, to be so reported and entered of record, persons entitled to be paid *pro rata*, costs then to be paid by party suing, § 129.
      intestacy, proof of, must be made before granting administration, §§ 18, 20; 274.
      intestates leaving no relatives or creditors, personal or real estate, the same is to be, on the application of any person interested therein, committed to the public administrator, § 47; 71.

STATUTES — *Continued.*

SUMMARY, ACT APRIL 1, 1872 (ADMINISTRATION).

inventories and appraisement bills and authenticated copies thereof, *prima facie* evidence only of their several contents respectively, §§ 51, 56; 167, 173.

inventory to be returned within three months after letters are granted containing, 1. Description of quantity, situation, and title of the real estate. 2. Specifying the nature and amount of all annuities, rents, goods, chattels, rights and credits, and money on hand, and whether the credits are good, doubtful or desperate, § 51; 174.

legacies, §§ 116–119; 190, 233.

letters of administration, to collect, §§ 11, 12; 67, 72.
    bond, under, § 13; 77.
    oath, under, § 14; 73.
    power, under, §§ 15, 16; 278.
    revocation, § 17; 279.

letters of administration, form of, § 21; 79.
    to be changed and applied *mutatis mutandis* to all cases of administration, § 21; 79.

letters of administration to widow or widower, next of kin, or in discretion; widow or next of kin must apply within sixty days after death of decedent; creditors within the next fifteen days, then the court may exercise its discretion, §§ 18, 19, 20; 64, 67, 75, 77.

letters testamentary, form of, § 10; 49.
    may issue on probate of will, accepting the trust and giving bonds, § 1; 49, 53, 54.

method of making appraisement, § 54; 172.
    to set down each article with the value thereof in dollars and cents in columns as prescribed, § 54; 172.

mortgage and foreclosure, §§ 120–122; 191, 192.

nonfeasance, misfeasance or malfeasance of executor or administrator not to create liability in certain cases, beyond assets of testate or intestate, § 126; 275.

oath of administrator, § 22; 79.
    form of, § 22; 79.
    to be made and filed, § 22; 79.

oath of executor or administrator, *cum testamento annexo*, § 6; 28, 39, 80.

order to sell real estate may be compelled, § 130; 276.
    form of, 314.

process, notices, etc., to be served and returned by the sheriff or his deputy, § 132; 276.

STATUTES — *Continued.*
  SUMMARY, ACT APRIL 1, 1872 (ADMINISTRATION).
    proofs of death and intestacy must be made to obtain administration, §§ 18, 20; 64, 67, 75, 77.
    public administrators are to be appointed by the governor, by and with the consent of the senate, one for each county whenever vacancy may occur, who must take the oath prescribed, § 44; 71.
    public administrator entitled, if the widow, next of kin and creditors are all non-residents, § 18; 64, 67, 77.
    real estate, sale of, etc., § 47; 111, 186, 201.
    relinquishment; administration not to be granted within seventy-five days after death of decedent, unless relinquishment be made by all those entitled; after seventy-five days court may act at its discretion, § 19; 64, 75.
    removal of executor or administrator not to affect the jurisdiction or power of the court first taking probate of the will, § 9; 339.
      generally, §§ 31–36; 80, 81, 279, 281, 282.
    repealed acts enumerated, § 135; 7, 276, 277, 343.
    resignation may be made by either executor or administrator in the discretion of the court, in full settlement of accounts and surrendering estate, §§ 40, 41; 96.
    revocation, discovery of will and probate thereof to work, § 28; 280.
    revocation of letters testamentary by cancellation of the will in due course of law, § 29; 99, 280.
    revoking letters. If letters be obtained upon false or fraudulent representations or pretense, the court must revoke them, § 26; 179, 280.
    saving clause of repealing act, suits pending and rights accrued, not affected by the repeal, § 135; 7, 276, 277, 343.
    sheriff or deputies to enforce order, serve process and execute writs, etc.; fees of, to be the same as in similar cases in circuit court, § 132; 276.
    suits on bonds may be had in the name of The People of the State of Illinois for the use and at the cost of whom it may concern, § 25; 279.
    testamentary letters, form of, § 10; 49.
    two or more appointed executors, if one or more die, refuse to act or become disqualified, the survivor or survivors may take the trust, § 5; 28.
      See *Wills.*
    wills, §§ 2, 3; 28, 53, 54.
    widow, her award, §§ 74–77; 217–219.
      may renounce, §§ 78–80; 219, 220.

STATUTORY REQUIREMENTS,
: to the validity of a will, recapitulated, 45.

SUBJECT-MATTER,
: of probate jurisdiction and of this treatise stated, 1.
: See *Preface; Estates.*

SUBPŒNA,
: for the subscribing witnesses to a will, 31.
: service of, 32.
: See *Sheriff; Process.*

SUBSCRIBING WITNESSES,
: to a will to appear, subpœna for, etc., 31.

SUITS,
: for negligence causing death, 86.
: See *Appendix.*

SURETIES,
: extent of liabilities of, 94.
: may petition to be relieved, 281.

SURVIVING PARTNER,
: of a deceased person not to be appointed to administer, 76.

T.

TESTATE ESTATES, 10–60.
: I. Wills, 10–27.
: II. Probate of wills, 27–53.
: III. Executors, 53–60.

TESTATE AND INTESTATE ESTATES, 1.
: See *Estates; Jurisdiction; Descent.*

TESTAMENTARY,
: petition for letters, 29.

TESTAMENTARY CAPACITY,
: must be shown, 40, 44, 45, 47.

TESTAMENTARY LETTERS, 49, 50.
: See *Practice; Executors; Wills.*

TESTATOR,
: one who makes a will, 1.
: must be of lawful age, of sound mind and memory, 40, 47.

TESTS,
: of an instrument, as a will, 40–47.

TITLE,
: of administrator to personal estate absolute; interest, however, qualified, 83, 84.
: and right of the administrator to personal estate, 159.

TITLE — *Continued.*
    to real property not conferred by appointment as executor, administrator, guardian or conservator, 187.
        See *Descent.*
TORTS,
    the right of action for, how far transmitted to the administrator, 83, 84.
TORTS, FRAUDS AND,
    of infants, 103.
        See *Actions (which survive).*
TREES,
    when personal estate, and when real estate, 189.
TRUST RELATION, THE,
    of the administrator, 162.
TRUSTS,
    the due execution of, the peculiar province of the probate jurisdiction, 1.
    the high character of those involved in probate, 3, 4.

V.

VENDOR AND VENDEE, 345.
VENUE,
    or proper county, 14, 76, 339.
    on division of a county, 339.

W.

WARRANTY, 162.
    by administrator not good, failure of consideration, 88, 89.
WILL,
    defined, 161.
    must be reduced to writing, 40, 47.
    must be attested, 40, 47.
    nuncupative, form of, 13.
    nuncupative, 50–53.
    lost, how and where probated, 53.
    foreign, evidence of, 42.
    revocation of, 13.
    production of the, 14.
    attachment to compel the production of a, 15, 16.
    copies of the, to go with the letters testamentary, 49.
WILLS,
    foreign, may be probated, 52.
    evidence of, 52.
    married women may make, 14.
        See *Married Women.*

WILLS — *Continued.*
  generally, 10–27.
    1. Definition, 10, 151.
    2. Who may make a will, 10, 11.
    3. Requisites of a will, 11.
    4. Nuncupative will, 11.
    5. Codicils, 11.
    6. Forms, 11.
      1. Of a will, 11.
      2. Of a codicil, 12.
      3. Of a nuncupative will, 13.
    7. Revocation, 13, 14.
    8. Production of the will, 14–17.
      1. Venue, 14.
      2. Proceedings, 14, 15.
      3. Petition for process to compel the same, 15.
      4. Order for process and the entry, 15.
      5. Attachment to compel the production of a will, 16.
      6. Jurisdiction, facts essential to, must appear, 16.
      7. The withholding the will, 16.
      8. Destruction or secretion, a felony, 16.
      9. Compulsory process, 16.
      10. Renunciation, how made and recorded, 16, 17.
      11. Administrator with the will annexed, 17.
    9. Construction of wills, 17–27.
  absolute prohibition of marriage until 21 years of age, in a will, good, 26.
  annuity, homestead election of widow, 17, 18.
  application to sell lands by executor when necessary, 18.
  bequest to a creditor, and his claim in view of it, 20.
  children, their existence does not affect the widow's right to one-third of the personal estate, 18.
  claim of the widow to the personal estate, 17.
  courts give effect, if possible, to every clause in a will, 17.
  creditor as a legatee, 20.
  devise "during her widowhood" does not pass an estate of inheritance, 18.
  devise and bequest to "heirs at law," 19.
  devise to "G. S." good in the heirs of G. S., 20.
  devise for life, with the *jus disponendi*, 20, 21.
  devise of lands to be sold and proceeds distributed, 21.
  disherison, words of, 20.
  dower act, construed, 17.
  fee simple estate devised, 22.
  fee simple estate subjected to a trust and liable to execution, 22.
  election by widow, annuity, homestead, 17, 18.

WILLS — *Continued.*
  execution, a life estate under a will is subject to, 19.
  executor, power limited, application to sell lands then necessary, 18.
  homestead, annuity, election by the widow, 17, 18.
  lands out of the State, when included, 22.
  life estate under a will, held subject to execution, 19.
  limited interest in realty, question of intention, as to a devise of, 21, 22
  limited and absolute estates, 22, 23, 24, 25, 26.
  limited estate, only created by the term "during her widowhood," 18.
  marriage may be prohibited in a will, when, 26.
  married woman may elect to take land or money under a will, 21.
  personal estate, qualified interest in, bequeathed, 19, 20.
  personal estate, claim of the widow to the, 17.
  perpetuity, a bequest not void for, in a certain case, 26.
  power to sell lands by executor, limitation of, to certain lands, 18.
  qualified estate in personalty under a will, 19, 20.
  real estate, power of executor limited to sale of certain lands, 18.
  real estate liable as a secondary fund to testator's debts and funeral expenses, 21.
  renunciation of will by the widow, 17.
  renunciation by widow of the provisions of a will, case of, 18.
  terms in a will, when interpreted according to their strict legal import, 18.
  "widowhood, during her," a term of limitation, 18.
  widow's allowance, in case of renunciation of a will, 17.
    See *Descent; Jurisdiction; Probate; Shelley's Case, etc.*

WITHHOLDING,
  the will subjects the custodian to a penalty of $20 per month, 16.

WITNESS,
  credible, 40, 45, 47.
  when the county judge is, proceedings to be had at the circuit, 45, 46.
  attachment for, 32.
  service of subpœna on, 32.

WITNESSES,
  the subscribing, to a will, 31.
  examination of the, in probating the will, 33.
  effect of certificate of, as evidence, 43.
  parties as, 287.

WOMEN, MARRIED,
  may make wills, 14.
    See *Husband.*

WRITING,
  a will must be in, 40–47, 263.
    See *Forms; Process.*

WRIT OF ERROR.
    See *Appendix; Appeals.*

WRONGS,
    of decedent, actions for, how far transmitted to the administrator, 83.
    See *Actions (which survive)*, § 123, *Act April* 1, 1872.

www.ingramcontent.com/pod-product-compliance
Lightning Source LLC
Chambersburg PA
CBHW051739300426
44115CB00007B/629